THE COMPLETE GUIDE TO
BEING YOUR OWN REMODELING CONTRACTOR

BEING YOUR OWN REMODELING CONTRACTOR

KENT LESTER

BETTERWAY BOOKS
CINCINNATI, OHIO

98 97 96 95 94   5 4 3 2 1

Library of Congress Cataloging in Publication Data

Lester, Kent.
   The complete guide to being your own remodeling contractor / Kent Lester. — 1st ed.
         p.   cm.
   Includes index.
   ISBN 0-55870-337-3
   1. Dwellings—Remodeling. 2. Contracting out. I. Title.
TH4816.L448   1994
643'.7—dc20   94-15295
                                                   CIP

Edited by Adam Blake
Cover photo by D. Altman Fleischer

METRIC CONVERSION CHART

TO CONVERT	TO	MULTIPLY BY
Inches	Centimeters	2.54
Centimeters	Inches	0.4
Feet	Centimeters	30.5
Centimeters	Feet	0.03
Yards	Meters	0.9
Meters	Yards	1.1
Sq. Inches	Sq. Centimeters	6.45
Sq. Centimeters	Sq. Inches	0.16
Sq. Feet	Sq. Meters	0.09
Sq. Meters	Sq. Feet	10.8
Sq. Yards	Sq. Meters	0.8
Sq. Meters	Sq. Yards	1.2
Pounds	Kilograms	0.45
Kilograms	Pounds	2.2
Ounces	Grams	28.4
Grams	Ounces	0.04

This book is dedicated to my family
for their constant support and encouragement
during the long hours of researching and
writing this book.

ACKNOWLEDGMENTS

I wish to thank the following organizations for their assistance:
United States Department of Housing and Urban Development
National Kitchen and Bath Association
National Association of the Remodeling Industry
Remodeling magazine
The Home Rebuilders in Atlanta, Georgia

INTRODUCTION

Remodeling a home for fun or profit is a rewarding experience that leaves you with a sense of pride and accomplishment. It can also save you substantial sums of money.

The purpose of this book is simple—to help you complete or manage an efficient remodeling project and save money through productive remodeling. Whether you are remodeling your existing home or a new purchase, this book will arm you with the essential information necessary to make maximum use of your remodeling dollar. Most people underestimate the knowledge and commitment in time necessary to achieve remodeling results of which you can be proud. This book will instruct you on all the techniques necessary to become a master remodeler, for fun or for profit.

YOU CAN REMODEL PROJECTS OF ANY SIZE

Whether your remodeling project is large or small, an existing house or new purchase, a single room or a historical restoration, this book covers your needs. An inspection checklist will help you evaluate the size and scope of your remodeling project. Chapters on evaluating the entire house will help you safely purchase a fixer-upper.

Remodeling projects that affect the entire structure are listed in Section II—Remodeling the Structure. This section covers projects such as new siding, electrical rewiring, painting, etc. Section III—Remodeling the Rooms covers the complete renovation of specific areas of the house such as the kitchen, bathroom, attic, and so on.

WHAT THIS BOOK WILL DO FOR YOU

This book is more than just a how to book. Many do-it-yourself manuals attempt to show readers how to complete each project themselves. But what if you can't or don't want to do all the work yourself? Many projects are too time consuming and difficult for many people to tackle. In fact, most large remodeling projects require the services of several professional contractors and are seldom completed entirely by the owner.

The Complete Guide to Being Your Own Remodeling Con-

tractor provides you with the information and skills to *manage* and *execute* a successful project whether you do the work yourself or whether you hire professional help. Your ultimate success depends much more on your project management skills than on your personal skills as a do-it-yourselfer. Some of these skills are listed below.

How to Act Like a Professional Contractor

To command the respect of contractors and suppliers, you need to know how to look and act like a person who knows remodeling. If you are not prepared, your lack of knowledge will alert suppliers and contractors who may take advantage of your inexperience when negotiating prices. Chapters on dealing with subcontractors and material suppliers give you the inside knowledge to negotiate like a pro.

How to Recognize Remodeling Problems and Correct them Before It's Too Late

Many remodeling problems are hidden from view and require great skill to pinpoint until *after* the project is started. This manual provides inspection checklists for each remodeling project to help in finding problems.

How to Be a Good Administrator and Project Manager

Many forms are included to help you keep a tab on expenses, material requisition, estimating, contract specifications, plan design, and project scheduling. These forms can be copied and used on your project.

How to Recognize and Prevent Poor Workmanship

Even if you plan to hire contractors to complete most of the work, you need to know enough about each project to judge the quality of work performed. Each project provides a checklist and punch list of critical workmanship hints to help you evaluate the job. Like an armchair quarterback, you do not need to be skilled at every remodeling project to recognize good work.

How to Find the Best Remodeling Projects

This book will help you find remodeling projects worth tackling. You'll learn how to improve your house without overshadowing the other houses in the neighborhood. You will learn what projects provide the most bang for the buck and what projects to avoid.

How to Evaluate the Structure

Not all remodeling challenges were meant to be conquered! Evaluating the potential of a remodeling project requires the skills of a keen detective. Many construction flaws are hidden and require close examination to uncover. You will learn how to spot the danger signals *before* the project begins.

How to Proceed Step-by-Step

This book provides the detailed instructions needed to accomplish any remodeling task. If you have the work done by professionals, these instructions will provide you with the knowledge to evaluate the work of others. Step-by-step instructions provide a checklist to follow so that you don't paint yourself into corners.

How to Avoid Common Pitfalls

Talk to several people who have tackled remodeling projects and you will discover a treasure trove of disaster stories, most of which result from poor management and planning. Many projects are started by well-meaning owners only to be interrupted by unseen problems and expenses. Below is a list of the main reasons for remodeling failures:

- Costs are underestimated. The remodeler's checking account is nickel and dimed to death through poor shopping, negotiating, estimating and theft management.
- Hidden problems are not discovered until well into the project, requiring more expenditures, time and labor.
- Subcontractors take advantage of unsuspecting remodelers or fail to complete the job as promised.
- Daily living is interrupted by poorly planned projects that seem to drag on forever, creating marital or family strife.
- Projects are not completed properly because workers were paid completely before the work was inspected.

THE TEACHING APPROACH OF THIS BOOK IS UNIQUE

This book is not a do-it-yourself book. There are many such books on the market that provide excellent how-to information for doing home repairs yourself. If you plan to do most projects yourself, these other books will be a helpful addition to your library. *The Complete Guide to Being Your Own Remodeling Contractor* goes much further—providing you with the step-by-step instructions for *managing* the project and overseeing the work. Renovations that are good candidates for do-it-yourself projects are covered in more detail. Projects that are best left to pros are covered from a project management standpoint. This book starts at the beginning and takes you through the project one step at a time. Once you start your project, this book prevents you from overlooking critical steps. Remember, "The devil is in the details."

This book is not a design book. Many books simply provide design and decorating suggestions. The popular remodeling magazines such a *Better Homes and Gardens* highlight decorating ideas and have the advantage of being up-to-date on the latest trends in home fashion. This book does not attempt to provide fashion suggestions, for it would be out of date a month after printing. Look in these magazines for your creative ideas. *The Complete Guide to Being Your Own Remodeling Contractor* is the essential companion to these magazines. It teaches you the management skill to turn your creative dreams into reality!

HOW TO USE THIS BOOK

This book is designed to be easy to use and straightforward. It has been carefully sequenced to provide you with the right information at the right time. This book contains three main sections:

Planning. The section on planning covers remodeling concepts, such as inspection, financial and legal issues, and dealing with members of the construction industry. These topics are important in the planning stages of your remodeling project. They will provide you with the management skills needed to keep your project on time and on budget.

Remodeling the Structure. Each part of the house structure requires different skills and contractors—flooring, plumbing, electrical, painting, and all other major trades. This section covers each trade one at a time so you can focus on the particular skills needed for your remodeling project.

Remodeling the Rooms. Every room in your house is like a miniature remodeling project, complete with its own special problems and procedures. This section takes each major room in the house, such as the kitchen, bath or attic, and walks you through the entire sequence of events step-by-step, using the skills covered in the structural section.

Each chapter includes several sections to help organize and control the projects:

- General discussion of the project.
- Step-by-step instructions for completing the remodeling.
- Sample specifications that can be included in your agreements with contractors.
- Inspection checklists to help you recognize and control the quality of work done.
- Sample material lists to help in estimating the cost of the project.

During Your Project

- Use the sample material lists in conjunction with the estimating section to calculate the total cost of the project before it begins.
- Refer to the sample specifications for ideas on what to include in your agreements with contractors. These are primarily intended to remind you of items easily overlooked and to illustrate the level of detail you should follow.
- Follow the steps outlined. Certain steps may not pertain to your project, so you may skip them. Interpreting the execution of many steps will naturally vary from project to project. *Do not start your project until you are familiar with the steps covered in this book.*
- Remodeling each room in the house encompasses

many of the same structural trades. Refer back to the structural chapters for additional information on each trade as you go along.

- Refer to the inspection checklists for ideas on how and what to inspect to help insure that you are getting good workmanship as your project progresses. It may take ten years to learn how to lay bricks properly, but only ten minutes to check the work for quality craftsmanship.
- Use the forms provided when applicable. Most of these forms are included in the Appendix:
  1. Inspection checklist
  2. Lien waivers
  3. Home remodeling contract
  4. Material and labor estimate sheets
  5. Purchase orders
  6. Sub-contractor specification form
  7. Change order

LET'S GET STARTED

If you are ready, remodeling can be a profitable and rewarding endeavor. It is hard to beat the satisfaction gained by restoring a piece of history to its former grandeur. Homes hold a powerful grasp over a person's feeling of well-being and accomplishment. There is an excitement in watching an older home flourish through your personal efforts. This book will take you through all the steps necessary to evaluate and renovate your next home. Let's begin!

SECTION ONE
PLANNING

CHAPTER ONE

Remodeling Your Own Home

If you are a novice remodeler, your first project usually will be your own home. This is good because it allows you to get a feel for the effort involved. You will have ample time to make mistakes, correct them and learn from them. Don't fool yourself—you will make mistakes! You, however, will make a more forgiving subject than a new tenant in an investment property.

BENEFITS OF REMODELING OVER NEW CONSTRUCTION

Increases in the cost of new home construction have renewed interest in renovating existing homes and investment properties. The financial return from remodeling is much greater than new construction because you can save the cost of labor and management that is built into new construction. In addition, recent tax laws have made remodeling even more attractive to the investor by limiting the tax write-offs allowed on new investment property. Remodeling, on the other hand, adds equity and therefore capital gains that can be deferred until the property is sold.

If you are remodeling for yourself, you are probably more interested in a homey and comfortable home than its investment potential. You should weigh carefully the advantages and disadvantages of remodeling over building a new home. This decision is a highly personal one and depends quite often on your tastes in housing. Remodeling an older home may require you to give up some modern conveniences and design flexibility associated with new construction; however, an older house can provide the warmth and charm not easily attained in new construction.

In addition, rehabilitation of your own home has other advantages:

■ Upgrading your present home eliminates the need to relocate to a new neighborhood. You can stay in famil-iar surroundings while the work is being done. If you just purchased the house, you can usually occupy it immediately, even while the remodeling is taking place.

■ Remodeling can save moving expenses. Moving to a new house has several hidden costs, since you are likely to spend money to redecorate the new house to fit your tastes, such as adding new carpeting, draperies and so on.

■ Remodeling can save the legal, real estate and closing cost expenses involved in purchasing a new home.

■ Some older houses provide more amenities than are available in new homes of comparable price.

■ Rehabilitation can usually be done as finances become available, which reduces your immediate financial burden.

■ Low interest rate mortgages can sometimes be assumed on older homes. Owner financing is often available on older homes because sellers are eager to sell their older homes. Owner financing is extremely valuable because it does not require the stringent qualifications of government-regulated loans. For investors with several properties, sometimes this can be the only way to obtain new properties.

■ There is a high potential for finding good bargains.

■ Tax laws provide many incentives for remodeling, especially in areas designated as historic districts.

■ Money can be saved by doing much of the work yourself.

■ Older neighborhoods are generally located closer to metropolitan areas.

■ Remodeling offers a higher return on investment. The value you add to the house by remodeling will be greater than the retail value, especially if you do much of the work yourself. As equity increases, you can obtain nontaxable equity loans on the additional value.

Fig. 1-1. The period styles of many older buildings are not always available in new construction.

Build Equity Rapidly by Remodeling

Remodeling is probably the country's most popular cottage industry. It allows you to rehabilitate your home while still holding down a full-time job. You will realize a tremendous increase in equity quickly by providing most of the labor—saving the costs of remodeling contractors and skilled laborers. These markups can add up to 75 percent to the cost of the remodeling project.

The remodeling you provide will add to the value of your home, but at the retail price of the remodeling contractor, not at your cost. You will be paying yourself as the remodeler in tax-free dollars that are added to the equity of the house. These dollars are essentially tax free until the house is sold. If the additional profit is applied toward your next house purchase, it may *never* be taxed. The IRS allows you to defer profits on principal residences if the purchase price of your new home meets or exceeds the price of the house sold.

Use Sweat Equity as a Source of Funds

The equity you build in your home through the sweat of your brow can be a source of additional tax-free investment funds. As your property appreciates, second mortgages or home equity loans based on the increase in equity will provide you with a source of money that is not taxable. A loan is not considered taxable income, but the interest on home mortgages and home equity loans is still deductible. By obtaining a second mortgage, you can use the equity in your home as a source of income that is tax free. New changes in the tax law have reduced the source of other tax shelters, making your home investment even more valuable.

Buying and Remodeling Investment Properties

Soon after realizing the monetary gains of your first remodeling project, you will be tempted to renovate investment properties. This can increase your net worth and provide a constant source of income. With that goal in mind, let's look at the reasons why remodeling will accelerate this process, providing you with net worth at an astounding rate.

REMODELING IS NOT EASY

Make sure you are aware of the work involved before forging ahead. Prepare yourself mentally for the frustrations that will be encountered. Rest assured, problems will occur. Be ready for them

■ Many subcontractors ("subs") are hesitant to do remodeling because of the hassles involved. Good remodeling contractors are hard to find. Many require payment by the hour.

■ The true cost of remodeling may be hard to calculate before the project begins because of hidden factors (rotten wood, air infiltration, foundation flaws, poor wiring, poor plumbing, and the like).

■ The improvements on the house may upgrade it to a value above the surrounding neighborhood, holding down the resale value of your home and making it diffi-

cult to realize a return on your investment. Consider though, that these same factors can work in your favor if you buy the least expensive home in the area.

■ Appraisers have a hard time determining the final remodeled value of a home before the work is complete.

■ Utility costs in older homes are usually higher due to less or poorer quality insulation. Sometimes this factor can be difficult or impossible to overcome.

LIVING WITH THE REMODELING PROJECT

Regardless of whether you do the work yourself or hire a professional, remodeling an occupied home can be challenging and dangerous. Be prepared for dirt, sawdust, interruptions of electrical and water service, noise and general inconvenience. Don't underestimate the psychological toll this will take on your personal life. Use the following techniques to ease the burden:

■ Keep children and pets away from workers during the project. Encourage children to sleep over with their friends during the most intense part of the job. Isolate pets in a secure area such as a fenced yard or basement. Barking dogs will make subcontractors nervous and cranky.

■ Cover all exposed furniture fully, using bedspreads or preferably plastic sheeting.

■ Seal off other parts of the house from any construction area with plastic. This will prevent construction dust from entering the rest of the house. Gypsum dust created when sanding drywall is extremely fine and will work its way into everything in the house, including clothes in closets, stereo equipment, and computers.

■ Provide a protected alley for construction foot traffic. Put up signs to direct the subcontractors. Cover the floor with strips of vinyl carpet protector.

■ Arrange with friends or neighbors to use their facilities if water or electrical services must be turned off. Projects never go as smoothly as expected—plan for delays.

■ Rent a temporary apartment if the renovation requires major changes to the structure of the house or restricts the use of the bathroom or kitchen. This will expedite the project and make life much more bearable. A rented or borrowed camper also can serve as temporary quarters.

CHAPTER TWO

Contracting Yourself Versus Using Professionals

Once you have decided to move forward with a remodeling project, decide how much of the work you plan to do yourself. The more work you do, the more you will save. However, in many cases, hiring the right professionals at the right time can be more cost effective than trying to do all the work yourself. Mistakes caused by inexperience can be costly and time consuming.

Your level of participation in the project and the money you save can fall into several categories. The following list shows the level of participation for you. Each subsequent level will save less money but it will also require less investment of your time:

- Providing the labor and materials yourself.
- Serving as the contractor and providing materials.
- Serving as the contractor and project manager only.
- Hiring a remodeling contractor.

When Should You Use a Professional?

To answer that question, you must first examine your available time, trade skills, and ability to manage a construction project. If you are new to remodeling, you should start with a few small projects to build experience and confidence. See how well these projects turn out before you decide to jump into a large renovation project. Look at the following factors to determine your degree of involvement in the project.

The Size of the Job

This may seem like an obvious factor to consider, but attempting an oversize project is the most common mistake made by aspiring do-it-yourselfers. Small jobs such as decks, repainting, or new flooring make the best starter projects. They can be completed quickly and will not cause too much interference with daily living. Since time is not critical, you can move carefully and deliberately to guarantee a quality job.

Larger projects like a kitchen renovation or room addition require many more skills to complete properly. You must be able to schedule the work efficiently and manage several subcontractors such as plumbers and electricians. The longer duration of the project will also put a strain on daily living.

Your Experience

Certain remodeling projects require only patience and care to complete properly. Other projects require a great deal of skill and craftsmanship that takes years to develop. For instance, achieving a smooth finish when taping drywall joints requires a certain artisan's technique that is difficult to master no matter how slowly or carefully you do it. A talented drywall sub can finish a job in one-fifth the time required by a rookie—and do it better. Let the professional do this job. Your time will be more effectively spent elsewhere.

Cost of Your Labor Versus Others'

Most people forget that their time is worth money. You may make much more money per hour at work than the subcontractors you hire. If you lose time at work to complete a construction project, you may actually lose money in the process. If you plan to complete much of the work yourself, choose the jobs with the highest per hour cost savings. This will maximize your return on investment (your time).

WHEN YOU ARE THE SUBCONTRACTOR

If you have the time to tackle several projects, you can save a lot of money. By doing the work yourself, you can eliminate the total cost of labor and the markup added by the subcontractor and the remodeling contractor. The amount saved will depend upon your degree of involvement and the job you choose to complete. Here are some of the savings you can expect.

SAVINGS	PERCENT
Contracting fees	15–30
Labor costs	20–30
Material markup	5–15
Total	40–75

Additional savings on materials can be made by shopping for bargains and by coordinating your project efficiently. A remodeling contractor will seldom take this time since he is passing the costs on to you, the consumer. A common misconception is that professionals will always get the best price for materials. This is not always true. Professionals usually get a wholesale discount, but only if they develop an ongoing relationship with the supplier. Professional contractors usually purchase several items at a time at the regular price minus the professional discount.

As a part-time remodeler, you have a distinct advantage. You can look for and purchase close-outs and special sales that come only in quantities of one. Markdowns on close-outs, demonstration models, and factory seconds are much greater than any professional discount. These savings can be very significant on high-ticket items such as kitchen appliances, cabinets, plumbing fixtures and HVAC systems. Even if you don't plan to do the work yourself, take the time to shop for bargains and provide the materials your subcontractor will need.

How Much Labor Should You Attempt?

It's true that you can save money by providing the labor to complete the job. This can be fun, if you have the time and energy. But be honest with yourself. Do you have the time it takes to do the work? Is your time worth more than the money you would save?

If you have another full-time job, you will be remodeling after hours. If you do remodeling work yourself, make sure that you are saving more than the cost to hire a subcontractor. There are two main reasons why you shouldn't get carried away with doing too much of the work yourself.

First, there are many jobs you shouldn't even consider doing. Where special skills are needed, professional contractors can save you from injury, expensive mistakes, frustration and wasted time. Certain jobs may only appear easy. You can ruin your health sanding hardwood floors or drywall. You can ruin a den trying to put up raised paneling and crown molding.

Second, work can distract you from the most important job—overseeing the work of others. Your most valuable skill is that of project manager—scheduler, inspector, coordinator and referee. Saving $50 performing a small chore could cost you even more in terms of problems caused by an oversight elsewhere. Doing the work yourself invariably extends your project timetable. It will typically take you from two to three times longer to do the work than a seasoned professional.

Jobs to Consider Doing Yourself
- Painting and sanding
- Hanging wallpaper
- Installing light fixtures
- Cabinetry
- Plumbing
- Light landscaping
- Cleaning up

Jobs Better Left to Pros
- Framing
- Drywall
- Structural changes
- Installing doors and trim work
- Masonry
- Electrical
- HVAC
- Roofing
- All others not listed

BEING YOUR OWN CONTRACTOR

Contracting your own remodeling project will provide significant savings and can be done even while working full time. The contractor can be thought of as the *project manager*, making sure that subcontractors and materials show up at the site when needed. By scheduling other subcontractors to perform the work, you will depend on their expertise to complete the project properly. This will maximize your time and allow you to concentrate on other things such as design and purchasing. If your own remodeling experience is limited, rely on these professionals on the first few jobs.

An effective project manager must have good management and people skills. This book will help you develop them. You must be able to:

- Get people to do what you want and when you want.
- Bargain with suppliers and subcontractors for the best prices and service.
- Estimate the time and costs of remodeling accurately.
- Reduce costs in creative ways.
- Insure the quality of work done by you and others.

Becoming an Experienced Contractor

Before you embark on a major remodeling project, you must become educated. This book is designed to help you learn the skills necessary to handle all the details, people, surprises, insanity and periodic frustration associated with remodeling. Suppliers and subcontractors will determine quickly if you are an amateur and may take advantage of that fact when negotiating prices and schedules.

This book will not necessarily make remodeling a bed of roses for you. Remodeling requires hard work, perseverance, guts, the ability to horse trade, common sense, and anything else you can muster to get the job done. To get yourself on the right path to being a contractor, get your mind set for doing three things right from the beginning:

- Act professionally.
- Keep good records.
- Develop a tough skin.

Act Professionally

Get comfortable using building terms and present yourself in a self-confident and professional manner. Trade-specific terms are covered in the glossary. The respect of your subs and suppliers is essential to your effectiveness as a contractor. The better you relate to those you work with, the easier your job will be. Much of a contractor's job is human relations, so increasing your professional knowledge will help you to get along with others involved in your project. Order a set of business cards. It is amazing how many doors a simple business card will open.

Keep Good Records

If this book accomplishes anything, it should be to emphasize the need for keeping track of costs and expenses. Some of the primary records are:

Cost Estimate

The single most important tool you can use to save money on your project is the cost estimate. It will tell you approximately what your project will cost before starting. It also gives you that checklist of materials necessary to make sure that all essential materials are ordered at the proper time. The cost estimate has a further advantage of giving you a budget to strive for when purchasing materials. When bargaining with materials suppliers don't hesitate to point out "I've got to stay within my budget."

Purchase Orders

Make sure to use purchase orders when ordering materials. This will eliminate possible future confusion over what items were ordered and from whom.

Invoices

Most of the checks you write will be initiated by invoices. It is your responsibility to make sure they are accurate and that you pay them on time, especially if discounts apply. Match your original purchase orders to the resulting invoices to control payments.

Receipts and Canceled Checks

Lots of money is going to flow out on invoices. Keep them in a book. You'll need to compare them against purchase orders to avoid paying for things you didn't order and paying for things twice. Compare what was delivered with the invoice. Keep all proofs of payments together in an organized manner. Try to get a receipt — not just a canceled check. Your canceled check may take a month to get back to you as proof of payment.

Contracts

Make sure you have a sound, written contract with each subcontractor. When a dispute arises, refer back to the contract. Without a written contract, each person will interpret and remember events differently. Contracts and their related specifications can almost never be too detailed. You can specify anything you want; but if you don't specify it, don't count on it being done.

Worker's Compensation Records

You must keep track of which subs have their own worker's compensation policy. Worker's compensation is insurance that protects workers from injuries on the job. If your subcontractor doesn't have insurance for himself or his workers, you should obtain coverage or look elsewhere. If you provide insurance, retain approximately 6 percent of the total bid to cover the cost. Without worker's compensation coverage you may become liable for any injuries that occur at your home. Check with your insurance agent to see what your homeowner's policy will cover. For subs with their own worker's compensation, you should make note of their policy number and its expiration date.

Develop a Tough Skin

No matter how well you plan the project, unexpected events and delays will occur. If you allow every unforeseen event to cause frustration, you will quickly become a nervous wreck and your subcontractors will notice it. Remember the old saying, "Never let them see you sweat." Subcontractors will test your experience and resolve. If you appear frustrated or unsure of yourself, subcontractors may take advantage of the situation by putting off critical work or adding additional charges to bids. With limited time to work in each week, subcontractors are going to finish projects for demanding contractors first and then finish up other jobs when they can get around to it. This can cause delays, liens, poor workmanship, additional costs due to carelessness, and lots of frustration and headaches.

Try to develop a friendly but firm approach to the people you work with. Respect their abilities and opinions, but let them know clearly that you expect them to follow through with their obligations—on time and on budget. Here are some important attitudes you'll need to cultivate:

Persevere. Don't let anything get you down. When problems arise; tackle them immediately. Keep the project moving forward as close to the original schedule as possible. Realize that time is money and that you are responsible.

Be firm. When you have a dispute with a sub over sloppy work or a high bid, stick to your guns. Don't let anyone talk you up against a wall. Remember the "golden" rule: "He who has the gold makes the rules."

Don't be a perfectionist. You want the work done on your home to be of high quality, but don't be upset every time you see a bent nail (provided you don't see too many of them). Chances are, the flaws you see in your home will not be noticeable by others when completed.

Be frugal. Always look for new and creative ways to save money on anything pertaining to the project. Small savings can really add up on a large project.

Be thorough. Think your ideas through and be meticulous. Pay attention to detail. Keep detailed records organized and up to date.

Don't insult others. Avoid chiding your subs on the job as this will reduce their desire to cooperate with you.

Don't worry too much. Instead of worrying, do something about the problem.

The Contractor's Responsibilities

The laborers and subcontractors on your project are responsible for performing quality work and providing materials as specified and when specified by written contracts. That is their single most important responsibility. As the contractor, your responsibilities include the following:

- Provide clear, detailed specifications for those who work for you.
- Pay laborers and subcontractors promptly.
- Schedule material to arrive when or just before needed.
- Schedule labor and subs to work when needed.
- Schedule inspections ahead of time.
- Minimize costs while maximizing quality.
- Provide a safe site for yourself and others.
- Maintain control of the project and the subs.
- Inspect work as it proceeds and is completed.
- Maintain accurate, up-to-date records.

Do You Need a License?

Some states require builders and remodelers to be licensed. Many states have no licensing requirements for builders or remodelers. If you are remodeling your own home, you probably won't need a contractor's license, but you will need a building permit. Most municipalities require the permit so they can inspect your work to insure that it meets building code requirements. Check with your county building inspection department for a copy of the local building code and information on licensing.

Remodeling Part-Time

How can you finish a renovation project with limited time? One option is to look for an assistant who can serve as the project supervisor. Check the want ads for retired carpenters or contractors who would like some light remodeling work. These part-time workers are usually very flexible and make excellent assistants if you plan to do a lot of the work yourself. Arrangements can probably be made on an hourly, daily or even monthly basis. The part-timer can serve as a supervisor to be present when supplies are delivered or other subcontractors are present. Keep in mind that you may be trusting this person with access to your home. A thorough background check on this person is essential. The right individual can play an important part in your remodeling project.

Most subs can do work unsupervised when not being paid by the hour. Your supervisor only needs to confirm that the subs are doing the proper work, answer questions, and assist in inspecting the work. He's there to keep the job rolling along and to answer questions that would otherwise bring work to a halt.

DEALING WITH PROBLEMS

Being a contractor means handling problems. Every project is different and has its peculiar quirks, but there are several problems that occur to some degree on just about all remodeling projects. Although you may not be able to avoid these problems altogether, it may be helpful for you to anticipate them so that you take precautions to minimize their impact. Here is a list of the most common problems and proposed solutions.

Subs Who Show Up Late
- Let subs tell you when they'll be there.
- Include the completion date in your contract.
- Call subs the day before they are scheduled to arrive at the site.
- Meet the sub at the site at a certain time.

Subs Who Don't Show At All
- Let them know up front that you expect prompt attendance and that you will spread the word around if they cancel with no warning.
- Have other subs as backups.

Subs Who Proceed Slowly
- Give subs a bonus for finishing work on or before schedule. A cash bonus makes a great incentive.

- Require a performance clause in your contract that reduces the fee if work is not completed on time.

Incorrect or Poor Quality Work
- Ask the sub to repeat instructions back to you.
- Have detailed specifications and drawings where needed.
- Don't let too much work get done without checking on it. Visit the site daily.
- Discuss detailed drawings with subcontractors and make sure they understand them.
- Have a pager or cellular phone so that the sub can call you when questions arise.

Disputes Over Payments and Changes
- Put the payment amount and payment schedule in writing and have it signed by both parties.
- All changes to the original plans should be written on a change order form and signed by both parties.
- Use lien waivers to control your liability. A lien waiver guarantees that subcontractors or their suppliers will not attach a lien on your property to cover unpaid bills. (See legal section.)
- Pay with checks to insure proper records.

Materials Unavailable When Needed
- Order custom pieces early to insure that they are on site when needed.
- Confirm delivery dates with suppliers and have them notify you of delays several days in advance.
- Determine which suppliers deliver after hours and on weekends.
- Get friendly with the delivery men and schedulers at your supply houses.

Wrong Type or Quantity of Material
- Use detailed descriptions or part numbers on all purchase order items.
- Print legibly.
- Don't order over the phone unless absolutely necessary.
- Have materials delivered early so they can be exchanged or corrected before they are actually needed.
- Have your subs help you determine actual quantities and materials.
- Get to know salespeople and work with the same person every time.

Bad Weather

- Don't begin the project during or just before the rainy season.
- Cover any open roof with plastic or complete roofing as soon as possible.
- Make the most of good weather.
- Pour a drive area of gravel or wood chips around any construction site to avoid muddy areas.
- Get a roll of poly (plastic sheet) to cover materials.

Theft and Vandalism

- Store valuable supplies inside whenever possible.
- Call the local police department and have your site put on surveillance.
- Don't keep too much material on site. This is especially true for windows, doors, millwork, good plywood, and expensive tubs and appliances.
- Get risk and theft insurance with a low deductible.
- Check quantities of supplies right before and after subcontractors visit the job.

Cost Overruns

- Put subcontractors' bids in writing and have them include the cost of materials in the bid. This will avoid surprises on material costs later.
- Complete a thorough cost estimate and order materials from the estimate. Use purchase orders to track costs. Make sure all materials are available locally before the project starts. Ordering special items at the last minute will drive up costs.
- Use your estimate as a bargaining tool when getting bids.

Unscrupulous Contractors

- Make sure you know your stuff before negotiating with a subcontractor. Be firm and confident. Let the subcontractor know that you won't tolerate theft or shoddy work.
- Ask for a list of references and call them.
- Always keep 10 to 20 percent retainage until the job is complete and inspected. Retainage is payment retained until the job is satisfactorily completed.
- Always have someone present at the site whenever a worker is there. Discreetly check the worker's truck at the end of the day to insure that your materials don't mysteriously disappear. Caution: Make sure you are not noticed doing this. Nothing

will irritate an honest worker more than lack of trust and respect.

RULES FOR SUCCESSFUL PROJECT MANAGEMENT

- Put everything in writing. "A man's memory is only as good as the paper it's written on."
- Be prepared before starting and don't get behind.
- Keep a project binder current with all project details.
- Be fair with money. Pay subs what was agreed, when agreed.
- Always get references and check out three on each major sub. You must see their work.
- Don't try to do too much of the actual physical work yourself. Your time and skills are often better used managing the job.
- Shop carefully for the best material and labor prices. Don't hesitate to insist on contractor discounts.
- Use cash to your maximum advantage.
- Rely on your contractors for advice in their field. But above all, use common sense.
- Don't assume anything. Material is not on site unless you see it. Subs are not on site unless you see them there. Don't expect subs to know what you want unless it's in writing.
- Use as few subs as possible without sacrificing cost or quality.
- Use the best materials you can afford.
- Keep changes to a minimum and budget funds for them carefully.
- Estimate on the high side and have a contingency fund.
- Keep money under control and track progress versus your original budget.
- Rely on your local building code as a primary reference for specifications, inspection criteria, material guidelines and settling of disputes.
- Stay at least a week or two ahead of the game. Staying ahead will allow you time to compensate for material delays or time needed to replace unreliable or unsatisfactory subs.
- Let your fingers do the walking. If it looks like rain, call the roofer. If something can't be delivered, advise your subs.

USING AN ARCHITECT

If you plan to do all or part of the work yourself, you may need an architect or draftsman to provide the initial design and scaled drawings. Structural changes such as adding a second story to a ranch or expanding the existing floor plan require the expertise of a structural engineer to ensure that the changes are made according to code. An architect is trained to provide structural advice. The money invested in a good renovation is usually well worth it. The architect is also skilled at providing design suggestions to improve appearance and traffic flow. Architects can be very expensive. Many of them do not like to work on small remodeling projects. Look for architects that specialize in remodeling. Many large cities have a local chapter of the American Institute of Architects. Call them for a listing of local architects.

USING A REMODELING PROFESSIONAL

Now that we have described the talents and dedication needed for contracting, you can see why professionals charge a premium price for their work. This book is designed to teach you the professional secrets to manage your product like a pro. However, you might decide that you don't have the time or the energy to tackle a large remodeling project on your own. You might want to consider hiring a professional remodeler, especially if your project is complicated or if you are new to remodeling. Even if you hire a professional, the information in this book will help you to:

- Pick the best possible professionals to work with.
- Know what level of quality to expect from these professionals.
- Feel comfortable that you know enough about the remodeling process to guarantee a quality job.
- Move you one step closer to becoming a qualified remodeling expert.

If you hire a professional remodeler, you will be paying for the security and convenience of having someone else responsible for the successful remodeling of your house. The remodeling professional will either do the work or function as the general contractor for the project. A competent contractor can complete the job faster than you can and with a minimum of frustration. The disadvantage of this convenience is cost. Many full-service remodeling contractors will mark up costs as much as 40 to 100 percent depending on the job, because they are incurring significant risk. This risk is high because of the difficulty in estimating the exact cost of the project. Many problems may be hidden from view until the project has begun. The high prices you pay for a project may be to provide "insurance" in case the remodeler incurs hidden costs. Many remodeling contractors include contingency clauses in their contracts to protect against unseen problems.

There are two ways to price a remodeling job: (1) fixed price and (2) cost-plus. Fixed price means just that. Remodelers will give you a fixed price for the job. Their markup will reflect the degree of risk they experience in completing your project. Because of the hidden risk factor, a cost-plus price may be much lower. You and the remodeler will agree on a markup (usually between 15 to 25 percent) that represents the remodeler's profit. The remodeler will then charge you the actual cost for materials and labor and add a percentage to it. In this way, you will know the exact cost of the project and you can take advantage of savings by providing your own materials. This approach can save you money, but you will then be taking the risks of unseen problems. The moral? *Inspect your home thoroughly before you meet with professionals.* Know your project completely.

The quality of these professionals varies considerably, so shop carefully. Remodeling contractors are found easily in the yellow pages, in the classifieds, or posted at local home improvement centers. If you are starting your first remodeling project and are worried about having limited personal time to put into the project, the remodeling professional may be the best alternative. Watch the professionals in action and learn their secrets. You will be much better prepared for the next project.

TYPES OF REMODELING CONTRACTORS

If you choose to work with a remodeling contractor, you will have several levels of skill, professionalism, and cost from which to choose. Remodeling contractors fall into three major categories:

The Weekend Remodeler — Subcontractor

The weekend remodeler is often a subcontractor or other tradesman who moonlights on evenings or weekends to supplement income from another job. You will most often find these individuals in classified newspaper ads or on bulletin boards at building supply stores. They are always the least expensive to hire and will usually make concessions to get the job. The money you save, however, may not be worth the risk. Part-timers seldom have good references and may walk off the job or provide substandard work. If they were really talented remodelers, they would probably be doing it full-time.

If you use a part-timer, make sure you are on site during the job and *never* pay for the job until it is finished satisfactorily. Ask for several references and *call them*. Did the contractor finish the job on time and on budget? These references are essential. If the part-timer cannot provide them, keep looking.

A part-timer can be an excellent source of help if you plan to do most of the work yourself. In this case you will always be on hand to supervise the work and insure that the job is done right. Make sure the part-timer is willing to work along with you and follow your instructions. Make sure the individual knows who is in charge of the project.

The Professional Remodeler

A professional remodeler usually will be a builder or contractor with an established office, employees, and a client list. These contractors usually specialize in mid-size remodeling projects such as kitchen renovation or siding replacement. Most contractors advertise in the yellow pages and newspaper. They also act as the contractor and project manager.

The professional remodeler will usually work from the plans and specifications you provide, managing and scheduling the skilled trades needed to finish the project. You will still need to provide the design specifications of the project and scale drawings, if the job includes structural changes or additions. Remodelers are skilled tradespeople and they concentrate on completing the mechanical tasks you specify. They seldom have the design skills necessary to make decorative recommendations. You may need an architect or design consultant to provide the initial design specifications and drawings. If your project isn't too complicated, drawings may not be necessary.

The Design-Build Contractor

Design-build contractors represent a new breed of remodeling contractor. They are usually builders or commercial contractors who have expanded or changed to the remodeling field. They usually can provide a complete one-stop design and remodeling service. The term "design-build" originates from the fact that they usually employ a draftsman, designer, or architect on staff to develop the initial design. They may also develop close relationships with independent architects. They are accustomed to managing the job from start to finish.

You may think that their markup would be the highest, but this is not always the case. Since the design and completion of the project is controlled by one company, the design-build contractor keeps costs under control and ensures that the project is completed quickly and efficiently. Their resident architect is qualified to handle extensive structural changes to the house if needed. If you plan a complete overhaul of your house with structural changes and additions, the design-build contractor may be your best choice.

Bill Bartlett owns Home Rebuilders, a design-build remodeling company in Atlanta, Georgia. When asked about the advantages of hiring a design-build company, Bill had this to say:

Many do-it-yourselfers think they can save tons of money by doing it themselves. In reality, they sometimes pay more. We have taken over many failed remodeling attempts by owners who were unprepared for the task at hand. When the project was done, they had spent more money than we would have charged to do the job from scratch.

When do-it-yourselfers get bids from subcontractors, the subs will bid high on the project because it is a one-time job. The subcontractor will often offer a lower bid to a professional company because he knows the professional will schedule the project right and will be ready for him when he starts. The subcontractor also knows that if he lands the first project, he may obtain additional work from the professional later. Subcontractors are more likely to take advantage of a do-it-yourselfer's lack of experience by overcharging. Professional remodelers have had years of experience negotiating and dealing with subcontractors. Many homeowners have been ripped off by subcontractors.

The professional remodeler can also maintain better subcontractor control. If he schedules the sub for Friday and the sub fails to show, the remodeler won't use him again; the sub knows that. The sub knows that he must show up on time for the professional. As a result, one-time jobs for do-it-yourselfers will always become the expendable project if the sub must make choices. He will fit in the homeowner's job when he can. This can create a domino effect that pushes the project further and further behind schedule. A professional can finish in 3 weeks what it takes the owner 6 months to complete.

Use Professionals for the Tough Jobs

Use the professionals if you are unsure about your abilities or the complexity of the job. It is much easier to learn from the mistakes of others the first time around. Some examples of remodeling projects that would benefit from the professional are:

- Adding rooms to an existing structure.
- Converting a ranch into a two story house.
- Adding new bathrooms.
- Changing the floor layout.

In these examples, the design-build firm's in-house draftsman or architect can provide an overall plan that will accommodate the changes while upgrading the appearance and livability of the house. Since the architect obtains feedback from the contractor, the two can work as a team to keep costs under control while achieving the homeowner's original vision.

CHAPTER THREE

Inspecting the House

Do not skip this chapter. It covers the steps necessary to inspect your remodeling project.

If you are remodeling your existing home, this inspection will alert you to potential problems that may be hidden. Your remodeling plans may be affected by these discoveries. If your foundation is crumbling (hopefully not) you may decide to forgo your plans to finish off the attic and add a new kitchen. In a less catastrophic example, you may find rotting timbers under the bathroom that must be fixed before you can upgrade it. A thorough inspection of the house is *essential* if you want to accurately predict the cost of your remodeling project.

If you are buying a fixer-upper, unseen problems lurking behind walls and under floors can emerge after the sale to spoil your remodeling dreams and turn a remodeling bargain into a remodeling nightmare. No home is a good bargain if it harbors undetected problems that will surface after the sale.

A well-built house that is properly maintained should last for over 100 years. Tests conducted by the Forest Products Laboratory show that wood does not deteriorate in strength or stiffness for periods of 100 years or more. *If properly maintained*, an older wood frame house can be in excellent structural condition.

If poorly maintained, the timbers of older houses may be slowly destroyed by decay, insects, rodents and the elements. Many older houses have deteriorated to the point where rehabilitation would be impractical. Don't fall in love with a house in this condition. This chapter will insure that you spot the danger signals before it's too late.

Plan your own walk-through in advance, so you know what to look for. Use the complete inspection checklist in this chapter to remind you of key items to check. Use this form on your own house before estimating your remodeling project. With careful evaluation, you can

guarantee that your dream house can be restored to a sound condition, without unpleasant surprises. Start with the foundation and work your way through the house.

FOUNDATIONS

The most important structural component of a house is the foundation. Structural problems here will be difficult and expensive to repair. Look for general deterioration—this may suggest that moisture or water has entered the basement. It is expensive to repair this damage and difficult to prevent from becoming a recurring problem. Check for uneven settlement, which can distort or even pull apart the house frame. Uneven settling may have caused your windows and door frames to be pulled out of square, or it may have loosened the interior finish and siding, creating cracks that can cause drafts and heat loss.

A minor settling problem can be corrected by releveling beams or floor joists. Widespread uneven settlement, however, may require a new foundation or, more critically, may make the house unsuitable for renovation. Be sure to check the joint between the foundation and the wood frame construction. If you find gaps of an inch or more, this may be an indication of significant settling—a danger signal that more severe problems exist. Further investigation is needed to determine how much remodeling may be necessary.

Masonry Walls and Piers

If the house has a stone or brick foundation supported on masonry piers, check for cracks and crumbling mortar. This common defect can usually be repaired, depending on its extent. Cracked or chipped mortar between bricks or stone can be removed and the joint repointed, but large cracks may still be visible after repair. Extensive cracking may indicate complete separation of the stone or brick from the mortar. This will require extensive repair or replacement.

If the house has a crawl space, it probably has a foundation wall or piers supporting the floor joists. Check these supports for cracks and settlement, just as you have checked the perimeter foundation.

Basements

Damp or leaky basement walls may require major repair, especially if you wish to convert the basement space into a living space. Dampness and water encroachment can ruin a renovation project, creating costly delays and constant repairs. Dampness can be caused by clogged drain tiles, clogged or broken downspouts, cracks in walls, incorrect sloping of the finished grade away from the house foundation, or a high water table. Be sure to figure out the cause of your problem before proceeding. Some causes may be easily remedied—others may be too costly or too extensive to undertake.

Check for dampness by examining the basement a few hours after a heavy rain. Look for cracks in the foundation or signs of leakage in the basement that seem to emanate from one location. Examine the walls for signs of dampness. Deposits of white flaky material on the surface of the wall indicate minerals leeching out of the concrete. This less localized seepage requires extensive waterproofing measures. Well-localized leaks, however, can sometimes be patched with waterproofing compound.

The most common source of dampness is surface water from downspouts discharging directly at the foundation wall or from surface drainage flowing directly against the foundation wall. The cardinal rule is to keep water away from the foundation—this is best accomplished by proper grading.

A high water table is a more serious problem. There is little possibility of achieving a dry basement if the water table is high, even if only periodically. Heavy foundation waterproofing or footing drains may help; but this will require excavating the ground around the entire perimeter of the foundation—an expensive proposition.

Chimneys and Fireplaces

Look for cracks in the masonry or loose mortar in your chimney. Such cracks usually result from the foundation settling or from attaching a television antenna that puts undue stress on the chimney. Cracks are a particular hazard if the flue does not have a fireproof lining.

If the chimney is masonry, it should be supported on its own footing. (Prefabricated fireplaces do not require footings, because of their light weight.) Check the attic to see if either the ceiling or roof framing is closer than 2 inches from the chimney. Either problem is a fire hazard and should be corrected immediately.

Does the fireplace have a damper? If not, add one to prevent heat loss up the flue when the fireplace is not in use. A fireplace that looks like it has been used a lot probably draws well; however, make sure by lighting a few sheets of newspaper in the fireplace and observing the flow of smoke. A good fireplace will draw immediately; a usable one will draw after about a minute.

Frame Construction

Examine the building frame carefully for distortion from foundation failure or improper/inadequate framing. Look for evidence of termites, decay or sagging.

Floor Supports

If your house has a basement, its interior support is probably provided by wood or steel girders supported on wood or steel posts. Wood posts should be supported on pedestals and should not be embedded in the concrete floor, where they may collect moisture and decay. Steel posts are normally supported on metal plates. Always examine the base of wood posts for decay even if they are set above the floor slab. Check wood girders for sag and for decay around the perimeter of the wall. Some sag is common in permanently loaded wood beams and is not a problem unless parts of the house have obviously distorted. Some deflection—about ⅜-

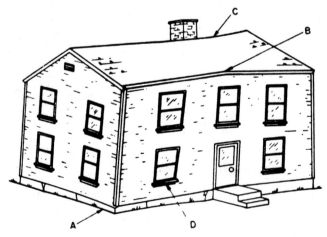

Fig. 3-1. Uneven foundation settlement (A) may result in a house badly out of square. Evidence may include (B) eaveline distortion; (C) sagging roof ridge; or (D) loose-fitting frames or even binding windows and doors.

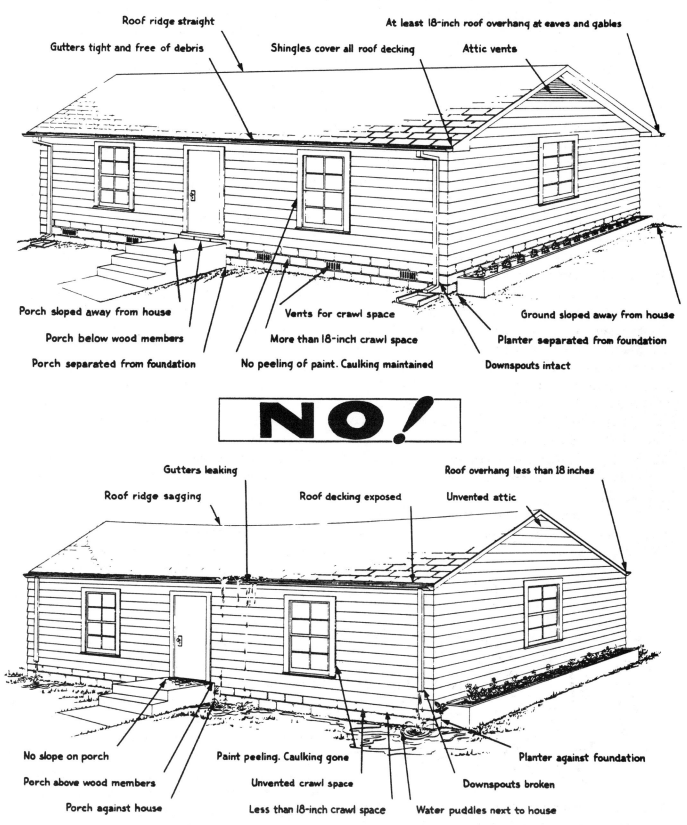

Fig. 3-2. House inspection.

inch deflection in a 10-foot span girder—is acceptable in design. Excessive sagging can usually be corrected with permanent floor jacks that will raise the floor back to its original level. This can be an inexpensive solution to a potentially major problem.

Floor Framing

The sill plates, or joists and headers if sill plates are not used, rest on top of the foundation. So, they are exposed to moisture and therefore vulnerable to decay or insect attack. Carefully examine these members and the entire floor framing system for decay and insect damage, particularly if the basement or crawl space is very damp.

Joists, like girders, should be examined for sagging. Here, too, some sagging can be expected and is not necessarily a sign of structural damage. Sagging is not usually a serious problem unless the foundation system has settled unevenly, causing certain parts of the floor to sag more than others. Look for areas where a load-bearing wall runs parallel to the floor joists and check for sagging with a long builder's level. The sagging might be considered excessive if you can easily spot it visually. If the floor seems springy or unstable when walking across it, check the condition of the floor joists. If they are in good condition, plan to add extra floor joists or girders to increase the floor stiffness. Replace any rotten joists.

Some builders estimate that 50 percent of the houses built have inadequate framing around stairs. So, check the framing of the floor joists around all stair openings. Check the floors around these openings for levelness. Where floors are sagging, the framing will have to be carefully leveled and reinforced.

Wall Framing

The common stud wall is designed to have more than adequate strength to support the weight bearing on it from above. It may still be distorted and require adjustment for reasons already covered. Open and close all doors and windows, observing their fit. Minor adjustments can be fixed easily, but large distortions will require new framing. Also check for sagging of the headers over wide window openings or in the wide openings between rooms. Where sagging is noticeable, new headers will be required.

Roof Framing

Examine the roof for sagging of the ridge, rafters and sheathing. Simple visual observation is all that is

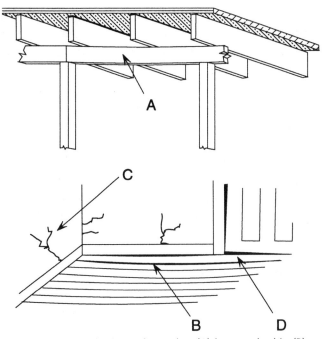

Fig. 3-3. Sagging horizontal member (A) has resulted in (B) uneven floor; (C) cracked plaster; and (D) poorly fitting door.

needed. The ridge will sag due to improper support, inadequate ties at the plate level, or from sagging of the rafters. If the ridge line is not straight or the roof does not appear to be in a uniform plane, some repair may be necessary. Rafters will sag due to inadequate stiffness or because they were not well seasoned when installed. Sheathing sag may suggest too wide a spacing between rafters and strip sheathing or plywood that is too thin or has delaminated.

EXTERIOR

Exterior problems should be easy to spot. Walk around the entire house and scan from the foundation to the roof. Exterior wood on a house will last many years if it is kept free of moisture and is given reasonable care.

Siding and Trim

The main problems encountered with siding and trim occur from excessive moisture, which can enter from either inside or outside your home. One of the main contributors to the problem is the lack of a proper amount of roof overhang, allowing rain to run down the face of the wall. Another source of excessive moisture may come from inside the house because of the lack of a vapor barrier, causing condensation within the wall. Bubbling of the paint indicates a moisture problem from within.

Look for excessive space between horizontal siding boards by standing very close to the wall and sighting it. Minor cracks can be caulked, but extensive cracks and gaps will require new siding. If the boards are not badly warped, simple renailing may solve the problem. Always remember to check siding for decay. Examine the areas where two boards are butted end to end, all corners, and around window and door frames.

Your shingle siding, if in good condition, should appear as a perfect mosaic. Worn shingles will have a ragged appearance and may be broken, warped, and upturned. New siding will be required if the shingles are badly weathered or worn.

Masonry Veneers

Uneven settling of the foundation will cause cracks in brick or stone veneer. Cracks can be grouted and joints repointed, but large or numerous cracks will be unsightly even after they are patched. The mortar also may be weak and crumbling, with joints that are incompletely filled or poorly finished. If these faults are limited to a small area, regrouting or repointing may be feasible. For improved appearance, the veneer can be cleaned with water or chemicals.

It is important to prevent water from entering the masonry wall or from flowing over the face of the wall. Examine the flashing or caulking at all projecting trim, copings, sills, and intersections of roof and walls. Plan to repair any places where flashing or caulking is not provided or where repair is needed. Clear water repellent should be applied with caution on brick or stone because it can trap moisture within the material.

Windows

Old windows are one of the more prevalent and difficult-to-repair problems of old frame houses. If they are loose fitting and not weatherstripped, they will be a major source of both uncomfortable drafts and considerable heat loss. Examine the sash and sill for decay. Also check the operation of the window. Casement windows should be checked for warping at top and bottom. The fit should be tight.

When you plan to replace the windows, check the window dimensions. If the window is not a standard size, the opening will have to be reframed or a new sash may have to be constructed.

In cold climates the windows should be double glazed or have storm windows installed. Both will reduce heat loss and avoid condensation. To learn if your windows have double panes, open the window and press your fingers against both sides of the window. A gap between your fingers of more than a quarter inch indicates double glazing. Don't expect to find double glazing on houses built before about 1980 that still have the original windows. Heat retention can be improved with storm windows or interior acrylic glazing products. However, storm windows are expensive for windows that are not a standard size.

Doors

Exterior doors should fit well without sticking. Weather stripping will help to avoid air infiltration. If you have difficulties in latching a door this can usually be attributed to warping or settling of the frame. Adjusting the door latch will solve most of these problems, but badly warped doors should be replaced.

Storm doors are necessary in cold climates for heat efficiency and comfort. They also reduce moisture condensation and protect the door from severe weather.

If the door frame is out of square due to foundation settling or other warping of the house frame, the opening will probably have to be reframed. Look for an even gap between the door and frame. The lower parts of exterior doors and storm doors are particularly susceptible to decay and should be carefully checked. Also observe the condition of the threshold, which may be worn, weathered, or decayed, requiring replacement.

Porches

The porch is very vulnerable to decay and insect attack. Since it is open to the weather, wind-blown rain or snow can easily raise the moisture content of the wood. This leads to conditions that promote the growth of wood-destroying organisms, such as termites or fungus. Also, steps to the porch are often placed in contact with soil; this is always a poor practice with untreated wood. If wooden steps touch the ground, dig down around the step and check for decay.

Check all wood members for decay and insect damage. Give particular attention to the base of posts or joints between two wood members where water can collect. Decay often occurs where posts are not raised above the porch floor to allow air to dry out the base of the post. It may be worthwhile to replace only a few members; however, the porch with a lot of decay should be completely rebuilt or removed.

Finishes

Exterior finish failures result most commonly from excessive moisture in the wood. This may result either from direct rain or from moisture vapor condensing in the walls. Finish failures may also be caused by poor paints, improper application of good paints, poor surface preparation or incompatible successive coatings. Many types of paint are incompatible with each other. New coatings can peel if applied over old paint without knowledge of the previous finishes. So, be sure to record the composition of all paints used on each surface. Refer to this information when repainting the house in successive years. Excessive peeling or blistering of paint may require complete stripping of the old finish and repainting.

Roof

If the roof is leaking, it should be obvious from water damage inside the house. Look for water stains on the ceiling around the perimeter of the house and at wall junctions in each room. Extensive water damage will cause the ceiling tile or drywall to sag.

A look in the attic may also reveal water stains on the rafters and along cracks in the roof sheathing, indicating small leaks that will eventually cause damage. These stains are usually black with white spots of fungus. Damage inside the house can also be caused by faulty flashing or condensation problems.

Asphalt Shingles

Asphalt shingles are the most common roof covering and are made in a wide range of weights and thicknesses. The most obvious deterioration of asphalt shingles is loss of the surface granules. The shingles may also become brittle. This wear may extend completely through to the roof boards without being apparent from a casual visual inspection. A good asphalt shingle should last 18 to 20 years.

Wood Shingles

Wood shingles are also common and are usually made of durable woods such as cedar in No. 1 or No. 2 grades. A good wood shingle roof should have a uniform appearance, but a roof with worn shingles will show splitting and a ragged appearance. Individual shingles on the worn roof will be broken, warped and upturned. The roof with this worn appearance should be completely replaced even if there is no evidence of leaking. Excessive shade may cause fungus growth and early shingle

deterioration. A good wood shingle roof will last up to 30 years under favorable conditions.

In recent years, several types of fake (composite) wood and concrete shingles have reached the market. These shingles have the appearance of wood shingles, but are much more durable.

Built-Up Roof

Built-up roofing, popular in the fifties on flat or low-sloped roofs, should be examined by looking for bare spots in the surfacing and for separation and breaks in the felt. Bubbles, blisters or soft spots also suggest that the roof needs major repairs; however, an alligator texture alone may not be a failure of the roof. The life of a built-up roof varies from 15 to 30 years, depending on the number of layers of felt and quality of application.

Flashing

Flashing should be evident where the roof intersects walls, chimneys or vents and where two roofs intersect to form a valley. Check for corroded flashing and replace it to prevent future problems. Likewise, check for corroded gutters and downspouts. They should be replaced or repaired.

Overhang

If the house was built with no roof overhang, the addition of an overhang should be considered in the remodeling plan. It will greatly reduce your maintenance on siding and window trim, not to mention improving the appearance of your house.

INTERIOR

Interior surfaces deteriorate due to wear, distortion of the structure, and the presence of moisture. Sometimes problems occur because of cheap or improper materials, improper application of paint, or excessive layers of wallpaper.

Wood Floors

When examining wood floors, look for buckling or cupping of boards that can result from high moisture content or wetting of the floor. Also notice if the boards are separated due to shrinkage. This shrinkage is more probable if the flooring boards are wide. If the floor is generally smooth with no large gaps between boards, refinishing may put it in good condition. However, be sure there is enough thickness left in the flooring to permit sanding. Most flooring cannot be sanded more than two or three times. If it is softwood flooring without a subfloor, even one sanding might weaken the floor too much. Similarly, sanding of plywood block floors should also be quite limited. If your floors have wide cracks or are too thin to sand, some type of new flooring will have to be added.

Resilient Tile

Floors with resilient tile should be examined for loose tile, cracks between tile, broken corners, and chipped edges. Look to see if any ridges or uneven areas in the underlayment are showing through. Replacing any one tile may require replacing the entire floor since tiles change color with age. New tiles will not match the old ones.

Interior Wall Covering

The interior wall covering in old houses is usually plaster, but it may be drywall in more recently built or remodeled homes. Wood paneling may also be found, but it is usually limited to one room, a single wall, or an accent area.

Plaster usually has some hairline cracks, even when it is in good condition. Minor cracks and holes can be patched, but a new wall covering should be applied if there are many large cracks and holes or if the plaster is loose in spots. The same general rule applies to ceilings.

If walls are wallpapered, check the thickness of the paper. If more than two or three layers of paper are present, they should be removed before applying new paper. Remove all wallpaper before painting.

Painted Surfaces

The paint on interior surfaces may have built up to excessive thickness as the result of repeated painting. It may be chipped due to mechanical damage, incompatibility between successive layers, or improper surface preparation prior to repainting. If the paint is so thick that the entire surface is starting to crack, then it will need to be stripped and repainted.

Trim, Cabinets and Doors

Trim should have tight joints and fit closely to walls. If the finish is worn but the surface is smooth, refinishing may be feasible. If the finish is badly chipped or checked, removing it will be tedious regardless of whether the new finish is clear sealer or paint. Trim or cabinetry with smooth surfaces will be easier to refinish

than ornately carved designs. If any trim, doors, or windows must be replaced, modern trim may not match existing trim. Many older trim styles are not manufactured any longer. Small sections of special trim might be custom made, but the cost should be compared with complete replacement of the original trim. Check with your building supply dealer to see if the particular trim is still being produced. Also check some older cabinet shops to see if they have shaper knives of this trim design.

Problems with interior doors are the same as for exterior doors, except that there are seldom any decay or threshold problems.

WOOD DECAY

Look for decay in any part of the house that is subject to prolonged moisture. Decay thrives in a mild temperature and in wood with a high moisture content. Decayed wood usually has an abnormal color and a loss of sheen. In the early stages of decay, the abnormal color will be a deeper shade than normal. In its advanced stages, the wood will crack and collapse. The wood may also be lighter in color, eventually progressing to a bleached appearance. Fine black lines within the bleached appearance may also appear. Fungal growths, appearing as strand-like or cottony masses on the surface of wood, indicate excessive exposure to water and consequently the presence of decay.

Just seeing the evidence of decay does not necessarily reveal the extent of it. The two strength properties severely reduced by decay are hardness and toughness. To test hardness, prod the wood with a sharp tool and observe its resistance to marring. Compare this resistance with that of a sound piece of wood. To determine loss of toughness, use a pointed tool to jab the wood and pry out a sliver. If toughness has been greatly reduced by decay, the wood breaks squarely across the grain with little splintering and lifts out with little resistance. Sound wood tends to lift out as one or two long slivers, and breaks are splintery. Decay may exist in any part of the house, but some areas are particularly vulnerable. Check the following areas carefully.

Foundations and Floors

Decay often starts in framing members near the foundation. It may be detected by paper-like, fan-like growths that are initially white with a yellow tinge and turn brown or black with age. Look for these growths between the subfloor and finish floor and between the joists and subfloor. They may become exposed by shrinkage of flooring during dry weather. These growths may also exist under carpets, in cupboards, or in other protected areas that tend to stay damp.

Siding and Exterior Trim

Where siding is close to the ground, look for discoloration, checking or softening. Also check for signs of decay where siding ends butt against each other or against trim.

Roof System

Observe wood shingles for cracking, softening and breaking of the exposed ends. Asphalt shingles have deteriorated if they can be easily pulled apart or if they are split at the channels. Edges of roofs are particularly vulnerable if not properly flashed. If the roofing is deteriorating, check the underside of the roof sheathing for evidence of condensation or decay.

Porches

Give particular attention to step treads or deck surfaces that are so cracked or worn that they trap water. Also, check joints in railings or posts. Enclosed porches may have condensation occurring on the underside of the deck and framing. Check the crawl space for signs of dampness and look for the origin of the moisture.

Windows and Doors

Look for brown or black discoloration near joints and blistering or cracking of nearby paint. Both are signs of possible decay. Also check the inside for water stains on the sash and sill resulting from condensation running down the glass. Wherever these stains exist, check for softening and molding.

Insect Problems

The three major kinds of wood-attacking insects that cause problems in frame houses are termites, powder post beetles, and carpenter ants. Where there is any indication of one of these insects, probe the wood with a sharp tool to determine the extent of damage.

Termites

There are two main classifications of termites:
1. Subterranean termites, which require access to the ground or other water source, and

2. Nonsubterranean termites, which do not require direct access to water.

Examine all areas near the ground for subterranean termites. Earthen tubes built over the surface of foundation walls indicate termite activity. They provide runways from the soil to the wood above. Termites may also enter through cracks or voids in the foundation or concrete floors. They do not require runways to the soil if there is a source of water in the house such as a plumbing leak or condensation.

Another sign of termites is the swarming of winged adults early in the spring or fall. Termites resemble ants, but the termites have much longer wings and do not have the thin waist of an ant. Look for hollow tubes in the wood that follow the grain. This is a sure sign of termite damage.

Nonsubterranean termites live in damp or dry wood without outside moisture or contact with the ground. These termites leave sand-like excretory pellets that are discarded outside the wood. They cut freely across the grain of the wood instead of following the grain as the subterranean termites do. To combat termites, contract a certified professional exterminator. This is one job you don't want to leave to chance.

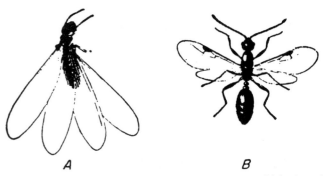

Fig. 3-4. Differences between (A) winged termite and (B) winged ant

Powder Post Beetles

Powder post beetles are most easily recognized by their borings, which are about the consistency of flour. Many borings remain inside the wood. The adults leave the wood through a hole about the diameter of a pencil lead, giving the wood the appearance of having been hit by birdshot. Such holes may be just the result of a previous infestation; so, check for fresh, clean sawdust as a sign of current activity. Activity may also be recognized by the rasping sound the beetles make while tun-

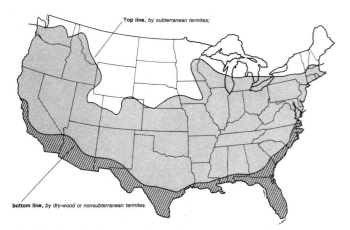

Fig. 3-5. Relative hazard of termite attack in the United States.

neling. Consider purchasing a doctor's stethoscope to help in locating these sounds.

Look for powder post beetles in humid locations, such as near the ground. Sometimes the homeowner may destroy them with an approved insecticide, but in severe cases, fumigation by a professional exterminator is required.

Carpenter Ants

The presence of carpenter ants is often discovered by their chewed wood, which resembles coarse sawdust and is placed in piles outside the wood. They do not eat the wood, but only nest in it. Working ants may be as much as half an inch long. They make a rustling noise in walls, floors or woodwork. Look for signs of carpenter ants in softwood in high-humidity locations.

Fig. 3-6. Black carpenter ant.

INSULATION AND CONTROL OF MOISTURE

Good insulation cuts heating costs and adds to comfort by making the temperature in the house more uniform. Humidifying the air in the winter increases comfort and saves fuel by reducing the temperature level required

for comfort. Although both humidification and insulation are desirable, their addition to older homes without vapor barriers in walls and ceilings may create moisture condensation problems. If large differences exist between indoor and outdoor temperatures, pressure forces water vapor out through the walls.

In the uninsulated house, this vapor usually moves to the outside without any problem. If the wall is insulated, condensation often occurs within the insulation, causing wet insulation and siding. This can lead to problems such as fungus growth, rotting and blistering paint. If the indoor relative humidity is low and the outside covering material allows moisture in the walls to escape readily, then no moisture problems will occur. However, excess humidity from cooking, bathing and respiration amplifies moisture problems and may ruin the insulation. Vapor barriers in walls and ceilings reduce the rate of moisture movement into these areas. This helps control the moisture problems otherwise created by adding new insulation.

Ceiling Insulation

Look in the attic to determine the amount of ceiling insulation. The ceiling represents the greatest source of heat loss on cool days and the greatest source of heat gain in warm days. At least 3 inches of insulation should be provided for homes in mild climates, and 4 to 6 inches for those in cold climates. To find out if the walls are insulated, remove a piece of siding and sheathing or interior covering. Check the utility bills for the past year. Unusually high utilities probably indicate poor or nonexistent insulation.

Insulation in walls should be included in any house renovation in cold climates and in warm climates where summer cooling is essential. Insulation should also be installed under the floors of crawl space houses in cold climates.

Vapor Barriers

Vapor barriers should be provided on the warm side of all insulation. Most houses built before the mid 1930s do not have vapor barriers. If the ceiling insulation is in blanket form with a covering around it, the covering material may resist the passage of moisture. If the ceiling insulation is loose fill, however, look under it for a separate vapor barrier of coated or laminated paper, aluminum foil, or plastic film.

The same thing is true of insulated walls. The vapor barriers should be on the inside of the walls. After turn-

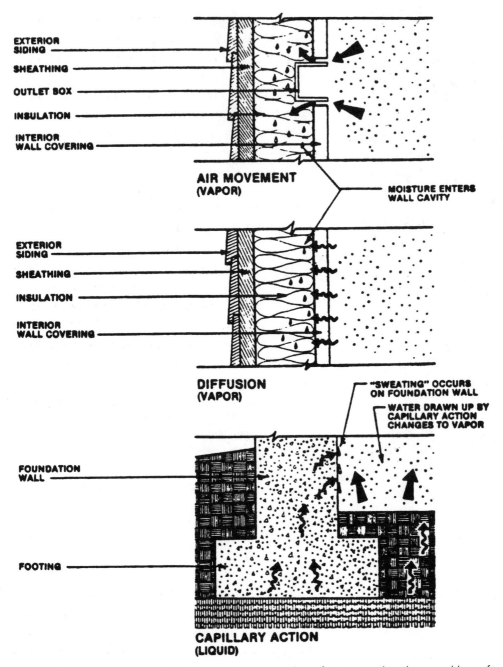

EXTERIOR SIDING
SHEATHING
OUTLET BOX
INSULATION
INTERIOR WALL COVERING

AIR MOVEMENT (VAPOR)

MOISTURE ENTERS WALL CAVITY

EXTERIOR SIDING
SHEATHING
INSULATION
INTERIOR WALL COVERING

DIFFUSION (VAPOR)

"SWEATING" OCCURS ON FOUNDATION WALL

WATER DRAWN UP BY CAPILLARY ACTION CHANGES TO VAPOR

FOUNDATION WALL

FOOTING

CAPILLARY ACTION (LIQUID)

Fig. 3-7. Moisture may enter the insulation cavity in a number of ways, causing decay and loss of insulation value.

ing off the power to the outlet, remove the covering of an electrical outlet or switch and look around the switch box for insulation, paper vapor coverings, or pieces of plastic sheeting. Check in crawl spaces for a vapor barrier laid on top of the soil. If there is none and the crawl space seems quite damp, a vapor barrier should be added.

There is no convenient way to determine if there are vapor barriers under floor slabs. If the floor seems damp most of the time, there probably are none. To have a dry finish floor, a new barrier or sealant would have to

be added on top of the slab, with a new finish floor applied over it.

Ventilation

The two major areas where good ventilation is required are the attic and the crawl space. Moist air passes into the attic from the house and condenses as it cools or where it contacts the cold roof members. Both inlet and outlet vents must be located properly for good circulation of air through the entire attic area. These vents not only help keep the attic dry in winter, but also keep

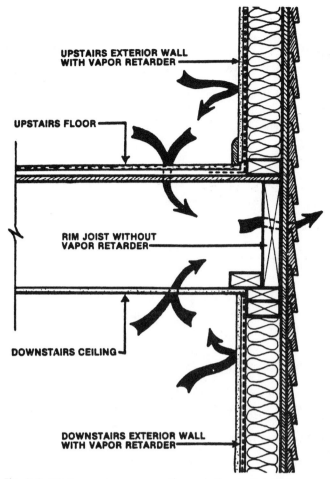

UPSTAIRS EXTERIOR WALL
WITH VAPOR RETARDER

UPSTAIRS FLOOR

RIM JOIST WITHOUT
VAPOR RETARDER

DOWNSTAIRS CEILING

DOWNSTAIRS EXTERIOR WALL
WITH VAPOR RETARDER

Fig. 3-8. Water vapor can move through the rim joist when a vapor retardant is not installed.

hot air moving out from the attic during summer, helping to keep the house cool.

Observe the size and location of crawl space vents. There should be at least four vents located near building corners for optimum cross ventilation and minimum dead air space.

MECHANICAL SYSTEMS

Because most plumbing, heating and wiring systems in a house are concealed, it may be difficult to examine them. For the same reason, it is difficult to make major changes without considerable cutting of wall surfaces and, in some situations, even structural members.

In a very old house the mechanical systems may have to be replaced. This is a major cost item. However, newer, energy-efficient systems can pay for themselves quickly through reduced energy costs and improved comfort levels. One extra bonus can be a dramatic improvement in the appearance of the basement when an

old "octopus" gravity warm-air heating system is replaced by a modern forced-air system.

Before contemplating any major heating and air changes, consult your local building and HVAC codes. Certain limitations such as clearances, duct sizes and heating loads may prevent you from making the change you desire. Consider hiring a professional contractor to examine the existing system.

PLUMBING

Water Supply System

Water pressure is important. Check several faucets to see if the flow is adequate. Low pressure can result from various causes. The pipe size may be too small or it may be reduced in diameter due to lime or mineral deposits. A ¾-inch inside diameter service is usually adequate.

The main distribution pipes should have a ¾-inch inside diameter, but branch lines may have only a ½-inch inside diameter. Below is a listing of the most common sizes of pipe. Measure first the outside diameter of your pipe. Then refer to the table to determine its inside diameter.

Pipe Diameter, inches

	INSIDE	OUTSIDE
Copper	½	⅝
	¾	⅞
Galvanized	½	⅞
	¾	1⅛

Check the flow of water from the sink and tub. If the flow seems low, the water supply pressure may be inadequate. If the house has its own water system, check the gauge on the pressure tank. This should read a minimum of 20, and preferably 40 to 50, pounds. Anything less indicates that the pump is not operating properly or the pressure setting is too low.

Check shutoff valves at the service entrance and at various points in the system to see if they have become frozen with age or lack of use. Check on your property for leaks in the water supply system. White or greenish crusting around pipes or joints may indicate leaks.

Water hammer may also be a problem. This results when the water flow in the pipe is abruptly stopped by closing a faucet. A loud thumping sound occurs. Air chambers placed on the supply lines at the fixtures usually absorb the shock and prevent water hammer. If you have water hammer, the air chambers may be clogged or filled with water. Simply clearing or draining these chambers should alleviate the problem. If you have no air chambers, they should be added.

Plumbing Drainage System

The drainage system consists of the sewer lateral, the under-floor drains, the drainage pipes above the floor, and the vent stacks. Pipes may have become clogged or broken or they may be of inadequate size. Venting, in particular, may be inadequate and far below code requirements. Flush the fixtures to see if your drains are sluggish. If so, check the following:

■ Old sewer laterals are commonly of vitreous bell tile. These may have been poorly installed or may have broken, allowing tree roots to enter at the breaks or through the joints. Roots can be removed mechanically, but this may have to be repeated every few years.

■ The under-floor drains may be of tile or even of steel and could be broken or rusted out. They may have become clogged. Simple cleaning should resolve the problem.

■ Vents may be inadequate or may have become clogged. In extreme cases they may cause the water in the traps to siphon out, allowing sewer gas to enter the house. Note any excessive suction when a toilet is flushed. Check for odors that may indicate leaks in the sewer pipes.

Required Plumbing Additions

Additional supply and drain lines may be desirable in modernizing a house. New lines may be required for automatic washers, added baths, adequate sill cocks or reorganizing the layout. If you plan to add any of these amenities, make sure that present plumbing lines are accessible. Beware of plumbing lines cast in concrete slabs. The slab may have to be torn up to reach present drainage lines.

Water Heater

Check for an adequate hot water heating system. Older homes may have water-heating coils in the hot-air furnace; however, the hot water produced is seldom adequate. During summer months, when hot-air heating is not needed, a separate system is required to provide hot water.

Most houses are fitted with a gas or electric water heater. A gas heater should have at least a 30-gallon capacity. An electric water heater should have a capacity of at least 50 gallons, especially if it is an older slow-recovery type. Look for the capacity rating on a plate affixed to the side of the tank.

Plumbing Fixtures

Plumbing fixtures that are quite old may be rust stained and may require replacement. It may be desirable to replace them just for appearance sake alone. Washers and other parts may also be hard to find. Many old fixtures have separate spigots for hot and cold water, making it impossible to adjust the water temperature without filling the basin with water.

HEATING

Heating system advances and current comfort standards make most old heating systems obsolete. Central heating, with heat piped to all rooms, is considered a necessity in all but very small houses.

The only way to satisfactorily check the adequacy of the heating system is to use it. If the system seems adequate, check the general condition of the furnace or boiler.

Gravity Warm-Air Heating

Gravity warm-air systems are common in older homes. Some gravity warm-air furnaces may provide adequate heat, but a forced-air circulation system is far superior.

If a warm-air system is exceptionally dirty, there may be soot marks above the registers. This will require some repair work. If the furnace is old, it may need to be replaced. In any event, rusty ducts may need replacement.

Steam Heating

One-pipe gravity steam-heating systems are common in older homes. The system is similar in appearance to hot water heaters. This is an extremely simple system and, if properly installed, it will provide adequate heat, but with no great speed or control. It can be modernized by replacing standing radiators with baseboard heaters.

A one-pipe gravity steam system can be upgraded by converting it to a two-pipe system. This requires adding traps and return lines.

A two-pipe steam system can in turn be converted to a circulating hot water system. Circulating pumps must be added, but this results in greater speed of heat distribution and excellent control. In most cases, steam systems should be replaced. Most homeowners today want central air conditioning that requires installing a forced-air ducted system. You should upgrade the heating system to forced air at the same time, since the new ducts can be used for both systems.

Radiant Heating

Radiant heat from hot water flowing through coils embedded in concrete floors or plastered ceilings is less common, but may provide excellent heating. Such systems may become air-locked and require professional repair. Breaks in ceiling coils can be repaired easily, but repairing breaks in floors is extremely difficult. If breaks in the floor are extensive, the system will probably need to be replaced.

Electric Panel Heating

Electric heating panels have no moving parts to wear out and should be in good condition unless a heating element has burned out. They are not very efficient, however, and they provide no ducting for central air conditioning.

ELECTRICAL

So many new electrical appliances have come into common use in recent years that old houses may not have adequate wiring to accommodate them, particularly if air conditioning is installed. The service level of your electrical system should be at least 100 amperes for the average three-bedroom house. If the house is large or if air conditioning is added, the service should be at least 200 amps. If the main distribution panel has room, additional circuits can be added to supply additional circuits. Otherwise, another distribution panel may have to be added. Check the existing service panel. It should have a power rating printed on it.

Examine electrical wiring wherever possible. Some wiring is usually exposed in the attic or basement. Wiring should also be checked at several wall receptacles or fixtures. If any armored cable or conduit is badly rusted, or if wiring or cable insulation is deteriorating, damaged, brittle, or crumbly, the house wiring should be replaced. Many local electrical codes will require old wiring to be upgraded if additional circuits are added to the house.

Check the location and number of electrical outlets in every room. At least one electrical outlet on each wall of a room, and two or more on long walls, is desirable. Ceiling lights should have a wall switch. Rooms without a ceiling light should have a wall switch, preferably near the door, which controls at least one outlet.

FINAL EVALUATION

If you evaluate your existing house by these guidelines and discover some danger signals in the structure, don't get too upset! The sooner you find them, the easier they will be to repair. After you have examined the house completely and listed all repair requirements, list all the pros and cons of each renovation project on paper for evaluation. Consider each problem and decide whether it is cost effective to repair. You must consider the age and overall condition of the house and the potential return on investment of repairing major problems. Some problems must be fixed and others may best be left alone. For example, moisture problems may eliminate the basement as a renovation candidate. In the end only you can weigh the pros and cons accurately.

If you are evaluating a potential purchase, you have the luxury of passing on the property, so be much more rigorous in accepting potential problems. Some general guidelines for accepting or rejecting the purchase are presented here. Judgment will be required to draw conclusions from these guides.

Major Reasons for Rejection

Some major reasons to reject a house are:

■ The foundation may be completely irreparable. Houses are occasionally moved onto new foundations, but this is generally not economical unless the house is otherwise in extremely good condition.

■ If the entire frame of the house is badly out of square, or if the framing is decayed or termite infested, do not consider purchasing.

■ If there are many replacements, or major repairs and replacements combined, renovation may not be cost effective.

Final Decision Factors

If the foundation and frame are in reasonable condition, and the repair and replacement items do not appear excessive, base a final decision on the following factors.

Cost

If the cost of rehabilitating the house does not exceed the fair market value of houses in the area, it is a sound investment. A general rule of thumb is that the rehabilitation cost should not exceed two-thirds of the cost of a comparable new house. The cost can be determined in two ways:

1. If the work is to be done by a remodeling contractor, the fixed-price bid will give you a definite dollar amount to consider. This figure should be increased by 10 percent for unforeseen extras. Use the retail value of the renovations, not your cost.

2. If you plan to do most of the work yourself and are concerned with the economics of the project, get bids on all items that will be done by others. Then, figure the cost of all materials for the work you plan to do yourself. Finally, estimate your labor time and establish costs using a fair hourly rate. If you are not experienced in building construction, increase your labor estimate by at least 50 percent. You will waste much time starting and stopping projects, reading instructions and correcting mistakes. You will probably underestimate your time and available resources.

Location

A good location is justification for spending more. An undesirable location greatly lowers the value.

Sentimental Value

Sentimental attachments are subjective, so only you can value the rehabilitated house. Remember, however, that neither the finance company nor a prospective buyer will add anything to the value of the house for your sentimental attachments.

Cautions

Projects will proceed slowly when you work only in your spare time. If you plan to occupy the house immediately, complete the essential repairs at once and then work on the rest of the projects one at a time with a breather space between them. Nobody wants to live in a mess continually and nobody can work continuously without having the project go sour. Be as realistic as possible. It will increase the enjoyment of doing the work and the satisfaction of your finished home. Finally, don't be too rigid. Realize at the start that your ideas may change as your remodeling progresses and the final product begins to emerge. At the end of each phase, stop and evaluate the results of your efforts. Consult your plans to ensure that the remaining projects are still consistent with your image of the final project.

CHAPTER FOUR

Planning the Remodeling Project

Once you have thoroughly inspected the house, make a list of items you want to change or improve. This chapter will help you to analyze your options for improvements and decide which projects to pursue.

Our approach here is to discuss rehabilitation in a way that is applicable to a broad range of individual interests and capabilities. Some people may be able to do the entire job themselves; others may want to learn only enough to design an intelligent plan, contract the necessary labor, and supervise the project effectively. And those in between may perform substantial amounts of the work themselves, calling in consultants/experts as needed.

Don't be afraid to call in expert guidance from architects, engineers, contractors, decorators or carpenters. This is especially true when making major structural changes. Likewise, other licensed contractors may be required for electrical, plumbing or heating work. By delegating the most difficult projects to experts, you can optimize your time and effort. This will result in a smoother and more professional job.

UPGRADING THE LAYOUT

Most older homes will need changes to improve the layout, provide more space, add modern conveniences and improve the appearance. If your house requires no changes and needs only restoration to its original condition, you are indeed fortunate—and in the minority. Usually, some structural changes will be necessary to improve the layout. Over the years, changes in living patterns, conveniences and standards of comfort have changed the typical floor plans of most houses. Be creative and use your imagination to design a modern layout with a minimum of expense. Take your time. The improved layout will influence the rest of your remodeling requirements. The result will be a great improvement in convenience and livability.

The general layout of your home should provide separate zones for various family functions and good traffic circulation. Most modern floor plans now emphasize open living plans with a lot of interaction and light. This usually means that walls will need to be removed. The structural effect of these changes must be considered.

Remember, after formulating your plan and before commencing your project, check with your local building department to obtain a building permit, if required.

Zoned Living

The layout of your house should be zoned to provide three major family functional areas—one each for relaxation, working and privacy.

1. The relaxation zone will include recreation, entertaining and dining areas. In a small house all three functions may occur in one room, but larger homes may have separate living rooms, dining rooms, family rooms, dens, studies and recreation rooms.
2. The working zone includes the kitchen, laundry room, and utility room. It may also include an office or workshop.
3. The privacy zone consists of bedrooms and baths. The master bedroom and bath is often located

away from the rest of the bedrooms, sometimes on a different level.

The relaxation zone should be located for good visibility and accessibility to the outdoors. If the backyard is the primary outdoor area used, the living room should be near the back of the house. The working zone should have good access to the garage, dining room and outdoor work areas. The main entrance to the house should have good access to the driveway or usual guest parking area, which may be located in front of, in back of, or on either side of the house.

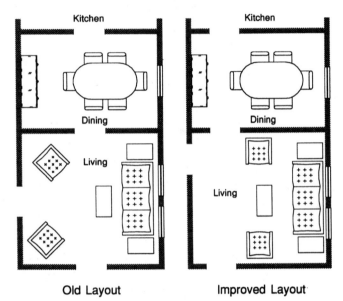

Fig. 4-1. Relocation of doors to direct traffic to one side of rooms.

Traffic Circulation

One of the most important, yet most overlooked, items in layout design is traffic circulation. Ideally, foot traffic should not have to pass through one room to reach another. This is difficult to accomplish in living and work areas. A more feasible plan is to prevent traffic from cutting through the middle of the room. Many older homes have doors centered in the wall of a room. This not only directs traffic through the middle of the room, but also cuts the wall space in half, making furniture arrangement difficult. Study the plan and determine if the door could be moved from the middle of a wall space to the corner of the room. You may be able to remove the door completely. Moving doors and partitions is expensive and should be limited to moderately priced remodeling projects. Fig. 4-2 shows examples of layout improvements by relocating doors.

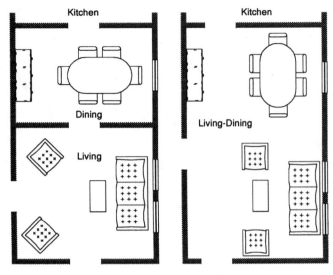

Fig. 4-2. Removal of partition for better space utilization.

Changing Partitions

Often room partitions must be moved to achieve rooms of the desired size. This is not difficult if the partition is nonload-bearing and plumbing, electrical or heating services are not concealed within it. Load-bearing walls help to support the house and cannot be moved without special structural changes. It is possible to move load-bearing partitions by replacing the wall with a beam to support the ceiling.

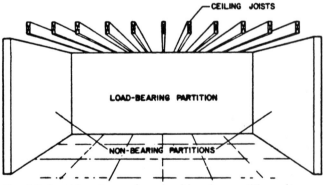

Fig. 4-3. Load-bearing and nonload-bearing partitions. (A second-floor load may place a load on any partition.)

To determine whether a partition is load-bearing or not, check the span direction of ceiling joists. If joists are parallel to the partition, the partition is usually nonload-bearing. It may be supporting a second floor; so remember to check this as well. In most structures where the second floor joists are perpendicular to the partition, they require support and are load-bearing. An exception occurs when the roof or floor is framed with trusses. Truss framing is engineered to span greater distances than conventional framing. If trusses span the width of the building, the partitions are probably non-load-bearing. Although removal of a nonload-bearing partition will not require a structural modification, the wall, ceiling and floor will require repairs where the partition intersected them.

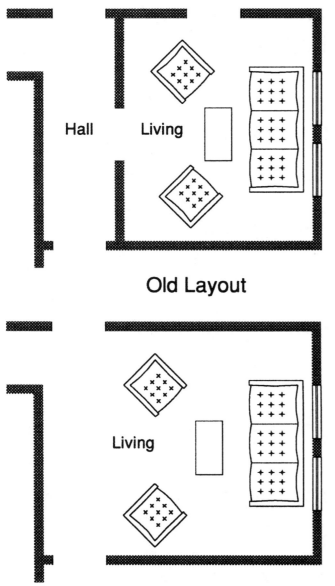

Fig. 4-4. Removal of partition for more spacious feeling.

If rooms are small, you may want to remove partitions to gain a more open, spacious feeling. A partition between living and dining rooms can be removed to make both seem larger and to gain a dual purpose space. Sometimes, unneeded bedrooms can be converted into additional living area. Removing a partition between a hallway and a room will give it a more spacious feeling, even though the traffic flow continues through the hall area.

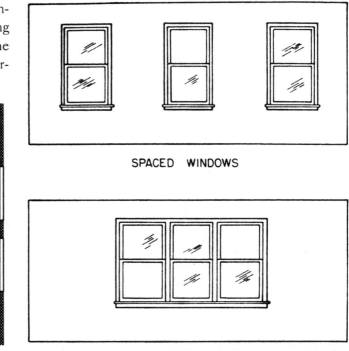

Fig. 4-5. Improved window placement through grouping.

Window Placement

Windows influence the general arrangement of both your layout and your furniture; so, consider them carefully when planning your remodeling project. Although the moving of windows is costly—involving changes in studs, headers, interior and exterior finishes and trim—properly placed windows can enhance the livability of a house, to say nothing of its visual appeal. Where possible, avoid small windows scattered over a wall. They cut up the wall space and make it unusable. Attempt to group windows into one or two large areas, leaving more wall space available for furniture placement.

The best location for new windows is facing south, especially in cold climates. Winter sun shines into the room, heating the house. In summer, the sun is at a higher angle, so even a small roof overhang will shade the window and keep out excess heat. In extremely warm climates, northern windows may be preferable for avoiding heat gain in the summer. Western windows should be avoided as much as possible because the late afternoon sun is so low that there is no way of properly shading the window. Eastern windows are usually preferred for breakfast nooks and other areas used primarily in the morning. The morning sun, while bright and cheery, does not produce the heat of a noonday or setting sun.

Windows provide three major functions. They admit

daylight and sunlight, allow ventilation of the house and provide a view. Some general practices to ensure adequate light are:

1. Provide glass areas equal to at least 10 percent of the room area.
2. Place principal window areas toward the south, except in warm climates.
3. Group window openings in the wall to eliminate undesirable contrasts in brightness.
4. Screen only those parts of the window that open for ventilation.
5. Mount draperies, curtains, shades and other window hangings above the head of the window and to the side of the window frame so that the entire glass area is revealed when the window coverings are drawn back.

To insure good ventilation:
1. Provide ventilation area equal to at least 5 percent of the room area.
2. Locate the ventilation openings to take full advantage of prevailing breezes.
3. Locate windows for the greatest flow of air across the room and within the level where occupants sit or stand. Ventilation openings should be located in the lower part of the wall unless the window swings inward, directing airflow downward.

To provide a good view:
1. Minimize obstructions in the line of sight of those sitting or standing in the room.
2. Set sill heights of openings based on room use and furniture arrangement.

Closets

An item sometimes overlooked in planning your layout is closet space. Most older houses have few, if any, closets. Plan for a coat closet near both the front and rear entrances. There should be a cleaning closet in the work area, and a linen closet in the bedroom area. Each bedroom also requires a closet. If bedrooms are large, it will be a simple matter to build a closet across one end of the room. The small house will be a greater challenge. Look for wasted space, such as the end of a hallway or a wall offset. If the front door opens directly into the living room, a coat closet can sometimes be built beside or in front of the door to form an entry. In the story-and-a-half house, closets can be built in the attic space where headroom is too limited for living space.

Closets used for hanging clothes should ideally be at least 24 inches deep, but shallower closets are also practical. Other closets can vary in depth depending on their use, but a depth greater than 24 inches in any

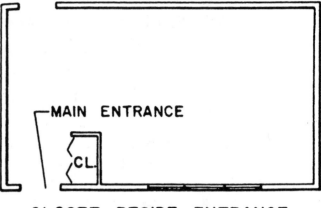

CLOSET BESIDE ENTRANCE

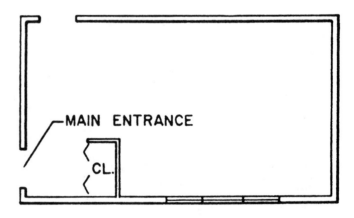

CLOSET IN FRONT OF ENTRANCE

Fig. 4-6. Entry formed by coat closet.

closet other than a walk-in is usually impractical. To make the best use of closet space, plan for a full-front opening.

In many remodeling situations, plywood wardrobes may be more practical than conventional closets that require studs, drywall, casing and doors. These closets can be fitted into tight spaces. More elaborate closets can be built by dividing the wardrobe into separate storage zones and installing doors and/or drawers.

Porches

Porches on older houses are often very narrow, with sloping floors. They do not lend themselves well to the type of outdoor living, such as dining and entertaining, usually desired today; however, these porches are very difficult to enlarge. It is often found preferable to tear off the old porch and completely rebuild a new one.

ADDING SPACE TO THE EXISTING HOUSE

Regardless of the size of the house, there is always a need for more space. Most homes never seem to have enough storage space. Work space for a shop or other hobbies, recreational and informal living spaces, and family rooms are seldom found in older houses. Rooms may be small or additional bedrooms may be needed. Many older houses have only one bathroom, so bathroom additions are very popular renovation projects. Many houses provide opportunities for expansion—existing unfinished space such as the attic, basement or garage. Converting these areas provides the most cost-effective way to add space without major construction costs.

If your space needs are greater than the available space, then new construction is the only alternative. Use the new addition for your most critically needed space. It will be the most expensive construction, so it should become the centerpiece of the renovation. The important thing to remember when adding on to your home is to preserve the original architectural style. Roof-lines, siding and windows should all match the original structure as closely as possible.

One of the most difficult problems encountered in building additions to your home is connecting the addition to the original structure effectively. In some house designs it might be best to use the satellite concept. With this approach, the addition is built as a separate building. It is then connected to the original house by a narrow section that serves as an entryway or mudroom. One disadvantage of this approach is the resulting large exterior wall, with its corresponding heat loss and exterior maintenance.

Additions as Complete Construction Projects

If you plan to add additional rooms or floors to an existing house, you will be managing what is in essence a new construction project. This will require building permits, excavation, and new foundations. New construction is beyond the scope of this book. There are, however, several excellent books on the market that cover new con-

struction. I, of course, like to recommend *The Complete Guide to Contracting Your Home* by Dave McGuerty and Kent Lester. Like this remodeling book, *The Complete Guide to Contracting Your Home* takes you through the entire construction project, with complete lists of forms, steps, specifications and checklists. If you like this book, the other one is a natural addition to your library.

Matching the Existing House Style

Make sure that any additions to the house match or blend in with the existing structure. Consider using the same stylistic elements and siding to help the new addition blend in. The main item peculiar to additions is achieving a seamless connection between the addition and the existing structure.

When the addition is added by extending the length of building, the structure, siding and roofing must match the existing portion. To accomplish this, you may need to reshingle the entire roof. If you can match the existing shingles, remove some shingles near the end and overlap the existing saturated felt with new material. The new shingles are then worked into the existing shingle pattern. Remove short pieces of lap siding so that the new siding can be blended into the existing siding with the end joints offset. A new paint job will then hide the new material. If the addition is perpendicular or offset from the existing house, the siding can either match or contrast with the existing siding.

An Additional Floor

If you need additional space and the existing roof needs replacing, consider adding an additional floor to the original structure. This is accomplished by completely removing the existing roof and building an additional floor and new roof on top of the existing floor. This is a difficult procedure and should not be undertaken without the help of a trained carpenter. You must make sure that the existing walls can support the weight of the new floor. If the existing walls meet modern construction standards and are in good condition, this option is feasible.

Adding a Cantilever or Room Extension

A new addition is so expensive because the addition must have all the components of new construction—a foundation, floor, walls, and roof. The foundation is one of the most expensive items. If only a small amount of space is needed—for instance, to add a new bath or

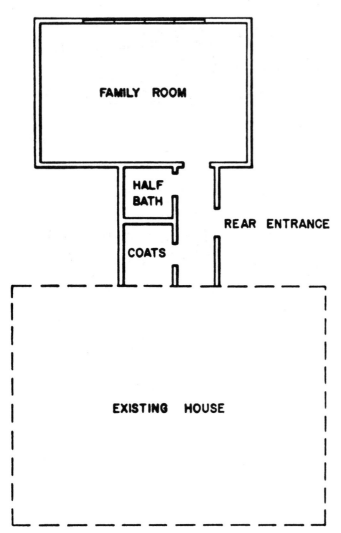

Fig. 4-7. Addition using the satellite concept.

Appearance

Many older houses possess traditional design features that should be retained during renovation. Many new house designs copy styles of the past to capture the dignity of the two-story colonial, the quaintness of the Victorian house, the charm of the old English cottage, the look of solid comfort of the midwestern farmhouse, or the rustic informality of the ranch house. To retain the character of the house, choose the materials for all additions, new windows and doors carefully. Make sure they reinforce the stylistic elements of the existing architecture.

Fig. 4-8. Preserve traditional styling of house to provide uniformity of design.

If you want to give your home a completely new look and break from the past, plan all changes in appearance carefully. The two key considerations are unity and simplicity. To achieve unity and simplicity, make rooflines continuous. Use the same style and type of windows and use only one or two different siding materials. Avoid trim that appears stuck on the house without serving any purpose. Remove such trim where it does exist. The result is not only simplicity, but also a reduction in maintenance costs. An exception to this treatment of trim is the gingerbread style found in some older homes. Gingerbread trim is considered a "period" style of architecture that is usually integral to the style of the house. Keep the trim if you are restoring the home to its original appearance. This trim, if restored, requires added maintenance on an ongoing basis to ensure its preservation. In two-story houses, windows are generally lined up and placed over each other on the first and second floors. Relocation of a window on either floor could destroy the unity and simplicity of the home's traditional lines.

enlarge a breakfast room—a "punch out" or cantilever can be installed. This consists of an extension of the existing floor framing that hangs out past the foundation without the need for its own support. This construction method is quite common in new construction to add bay windows without the need to provide a foundation extension. Chapter twenty-five shows some examples of this technique.

Extensions should extend no more than 4 feet from the structure. However, this may be enough to add a new window seat or squeeze in a new bathroom in a tight floor plan. The resulting construction cost will be much lower than building a new structure on a foundation. The tricky part will be tying the new floor framing into the existing floor joists. The existing floor must be temporarily supported and floor joists cut to make room for the new floor framing members. Although inexpensive to implement, this construction should be done only by a qualified professional framer.

One of the biggest improvements you can make to the style of an old house is to add roof overhang. There should be a roof overhang of at least 1 to 2 feet all around the house. Not only does roof overhang improve the appearance of a house, it also performs a vital function — the protection of your siding and windows. It will pay for itself in reduced maintenance.

For an exceptionally plain house, add interest in the main entrance. This is the natural focal point of your home. An attractive door, a raised planter or interesting steps will enhance the area seen most often by guests. Keep the entrance in scale and in character with the rest of the house.

The house that looks too tall can often be improved by adding strong horizontal lines, such as the addition of a porch or strong carport rooflines. Painting the first and second story different colors can also produce a lower appearance. A light color makes a house appear large whereas a dark color will make it appear much smaller.

The interior appearance should also be considered before finish materials are selected. The most convenient materials to apply are not always the most attractive. Ceiling tile that is attractive in a recreation room may not be suitable in a living room.

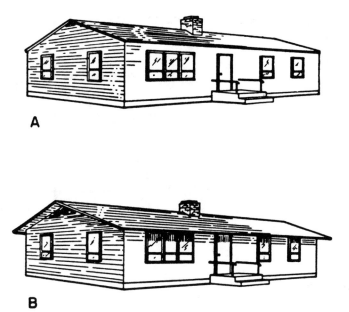

Fig. 4-9. Improved appearance by adding roof overhang: (A) without overhang or (B) with overhang.

CHAPTER FIVE

Stretching the Remodeling Dollar

Once you have decided to remodel your home, sit down and plan the complete scope of the remodeling task at hand. The size and type of remodeling project will depend heavily on your future plans for the home. Is the home your final residence—your "palace"—or are you planning the remodeling as an investment?

If you plan to live in the home permanently, you will obviously improve those areas that appeal to your needs. If you are buying the home for an investment or to build equity, then you must be very concerned about the monetary value of every improvement. It is so easy to become excited about the potential of your home that you fall into the trap of overimproving the property. If you overdo your improvements, you may not realize a return on your investment when you sell. Even if you choose to stay in the home indefinitely, wanton overimprovements may catch up with you. How often have you had a career change or other incident that has forced you to move? Trying to sell an overbuilt home can take time and cost you money.

Once you have selected the improvements you plan to make, prioritize the projects that bring the greatest return for the least investment. Do these projects first. Remodeling projects tend to take longer to complete than planned. If you must sell ahead of schedule, your most productive improvements will have been done first.

The following list shows remodeling projects ranked from the most productive project to the least productive project:

1. Cosmetic improvements
2. Solving minor functional problems
3. Basement finishing
4. Attic conversion
5. Addition of a deck
6. Kitchen remodeling
7. Bath remodeling
8. Garage addition
9. Fireplace addition
10. Energy upgrade
11. Sunspace addition
12. Room addition
13. New siding
14. New roof
15. Solving major functional problems
16. New windows and doors
17. Swimming pool

THE IMPORTANCE OF COSMETIC IMPROVEMENTS

Nothing will increase the value of a home more than a cosmetic face-lift. These include interior and exterior painting, new trim, new flooring, cleaning up of unsightly areas, landscaping, and other items that damage the appearance of the home. Most people's impressions of a home are made in the first 5 minutes, and are always related to how the home looks and feels. Cosmetic face-lifts are also primary do-it-yourself projects, which will increase their return on investment.

Colors—Painting Inside and Out

Consumer marketing experts have long known the power of color and texture to influence the moods and perceptions of the buying public. That's why so many plain products are sold in fancy packaging. The proper use of paint can accomplish several goals:

- Make the home appear clean and fresh
- Eliminate "old house" odors
- Cover patches and imperfections in walls
- Make a room appear larger and brighter
- Set the mood of the room

Try to choose exterior colors that complement the neighborhood and the period flavor of the house. Avoid interior colors that are too wild or bright. Allow accent pieces in the house to provide the bright colors.

Landscaping

No true exterior face-lift can be successful without an attractive yard. Many older houses are overgrown with large ragged foliage that obscures the house and may provide a dark and dreary atmosphere. Trim back large plants to expose the house. Adding small accent plants around the yard can make the yard appear more groomed. If your lawn suffers from poor upkeep or bare spots, consider rock or foliage gardens to cover the affected areas.

Don't overspend on your landscaping. A few landscaping dollars can go a long way. Excessive landscaping will not increase the home value significantly. In fact, it can reduce home value if the buyer perceives hours spent in the yard grooming, cutting and pruning.

Flooring and Trim

Like painting, the floor and trim are the most visible clues to a home's upkeep. Carpets can hold "old house" odors that are hard to eliminate. If the carpet is in good shape, steam cleaning may suffice. Older period flooring such as linoleum is best replaced when worn. There is no way to improve its appearance.

If you want to retain the period atmosphere of the home, examine the flooring carefully. Most older homes have solid wood floors under carpeting. You can refinish wood floors for a fraction of the cost of new carpeting.

OVERCOMING MINOR FUNCTIONAL PROBLEMS

The second most profitable improvement is the elimination of design or physical limitations of the home. These limitations fall into two categories

1. Physical problems with the structure
2. Functional obsolescence

Physical Problems

Physical repairs to the property can sometimes provide tremendous returns on your remodeling dollar. Obviously, any physical problems with the house, such as a leaking roof or basement or a sagging floor, demand immediate attention. Fixing these problems will return the house to its former potential. Make sure when buying a fixer-upper, that you know all the hidden costs of repair or you may find yourself inheriting someone else's albatross.

Get these repairs out of the way first. Most physical repairs will require tearing up or removing existing material. You will want cosmetic changes to occur only after the structure is sound.

Dealing with Functional Obsolescence

Functional obsolescence refers to design problems in the house that may make it obsolete by today's living standards. These design flaws may make the home undesirable for modern homeowners. Examples of functional obsolescence include:

- A home with an outhouse
- One bathroom
- Small kitchen
- Little or no insulation
- Insufficient electrical rating or outlets
- No garage
- Poor floor plan
- A house with a dirt floor

Traffic Flow

Many old houses were designed around the fireplaces or heaters. Each bedroom had a space heater or fireplace, with other rooms acting as heat buffer zones. This design made for some unusual traffic patterns—traveling through a bedroom to get to the bathroom, for instance.

Examine your prospective house carefully to decide if you can solve these design problems. If you cannot, look for another house to buy. No matter how quaint a house may be, if the design is not practical for modern living, avoid it.

BASEMENT CONVERSION

Basement conversions provide an excellent opportunity to add space and amenities to the house for a minimum of cost and trouble. This space can solve many other problems in functional design by providing space for additional bedrooms, bathrooms and recreational areas. Basements are one of the lowest cost spaces in a home. They offer a high return on your remodeling dollars.

Examine a basement carefully to determine its remodeling potential. Older basements are notorious for moisture and leakage problems. Sewage connections may not be available without the use of a flush-up toilet. New developments in waterproofing materials have made this job easier. Many parts of the country have partially enclosed basements built on sloping lots. These walk-in basements are particularly suited for bedroom and bath conversions and will bring a high return. Basements completely below ground will bring a much lower return due to lack of suitable lighting.

ATTIC CONVERSION

Attics are another source of low-cost conversion space and may enhance a house's value more than a basement conversion. This is because attics are free from the moisture and sewage problems inherent in basement conversions. As with the basement, attics already have the structural walls and ceiling present, making the job easier to complete. Make sure that structural roof members do not obstruct the location of walls. If the conversion is to be used for additional bedroom or recreational space, make sure to include a bathroom. This will ensure the greatest return on your remodeling investment.

If the roofline is too shallow for a conversion, you might consider removing the entire roof and adding another story to the structure. This is a good option if the lot is small or the roof already needs extensive repair. The underlying structure must be structurally sound enough to bear the weight of the new floor.

DECKS

Decks have become increasingly popular in all parts of the country. They are easy to install and can greatly enlarge the entertainment area of the house. This addition has a greater return in the southern states where weather permits ample use of the deck. This is another good do-it-yourself project.

Many owners like to add additional amenities to their decks such as trellises, privacy walls and hot tubs. These devices make attractive selling devices, but may not return their full investment at selling time. This may be a minor point, since they add to your own enjoyment of the house.

KITCHENS

The kitchen has become one of the most popular renovation projects. Almost all kitchens in older homes are small and ill equipped for modern lifestyles.

Minor kitchen remodeling can be quite cost efficient and may entail as little as new floor coverings and painting of the cabinets. Many manufacturers now offer refinishing kits that replace only the face and doors of the cabinets, leaving the old shelving intact. Minor facelifts can brighten up a kitchen, but will do little to solve major space or functional problems.

Typically, a major kitchen overhaul will bring a greater return on investment than a minor face-lift. A major overhaul will allow you to add new and more spacious cabinets, solve traffic flow problems and lighten up the kitchen with windows. A full face-lift is expensive and may not return the full value of the investment, so try to do as much of the work yourself as is possible. If your existing kitchen is out of date, consider the remodeling project a necessity.

BATHROOMS

Recent trends are toward lavish and spacious baths. The two-bath house has become a standard. Adding a second bath to a home may not return its full value, but it eliminates a major obstacle in selling the home. This is true because buyers will be comparing your bath features to the ones present in new construction. Because of the high cost of tearing out old fixtures and installing new ones, consider doing much of the work yourself. Tasteful decorating and a wise choice of fixtures will also add to your home's value without costing a fortune. Whenever possible, consider adding a bathroom to the master bedroom.

GARAGE

If your home does not have a garage or carport, consider adding a two-car garage. It will provide extra storage and a workshop area. When combined with a room addition, a garage will return all of its investment and more. Make sure you don't overbuild for your neighborhood.

FIREPLACE

The fireplace adds charm to any home and fits in nicely with most older structures. Adding a masonry fireplace would be costly and would require major structural adjustments, so consider installing a prefabricated one. They are less expensive, more energy efficient, and much easier to install.

ENERGY UPGRADE

Energy efficiency improvements are more likely to save you money over the long run than bring you a high return on your investment. However, they may help you to get a better price for your home upon resale. Like most unseen benefits, energy efficiency will seldom return its cost when selling the house. Therefore, your decision to improve energy efficiency will largely depend upon your personal use of the property.

Minor energy improvements, which are inexpensive, can help to sell the property. These improvements include weather stripping around doors, plastic films for windows, and caulking. If insulation is poor, consider adding additional insulation to the attic first. It is the easiest to apply, costs the least, and produces the greatest efficiency gains. These improvements also have the benefit of being more visible to prospective purchasers.

SUNSPACE ADDITION

Sunspaces are becoming more popular and can serve several functions, depending on their location in relation to the other rooms in the house. A sunspace off the kitchen, for example, can serve as an airy and attractive breakfast area, saving that space within the house for other uses. Sunspace additions, however, will not produce great returns on investment unless done along with other improvements. The cost of glass windows is an unavoidable expense even if you do the work yourself. The space is not usable year-round in most locales. A good compromise is to cut down on the exposed glass so that the heat gain/loss will decrease. Then the space is usable as regular living space year-round.

ROOM ADDITION

The value of a room addition will vary, depending on its use and the need for the space. Look closely at the utility an addition can provide. If the addition adds a much-needed bathroom or bedroom, it can add significantly to the value of the house. Just make sure that you are not overbuilding for the neighborhood. Your addition may make your home the largest in the neighborhood. Sometimes a better choice is to open up the existing space by knocking out walls. Consult with a knowledgeable framing contractor before attempting this conversion, because many walls are load-bearing and cannot be easily removed.

NEW SIDING

New siding is usually a poor investment. However, if the existing siding on the house is run down or cannot be refinished, then new siding can add significantly to the house's value. Refinishing the existing siding is a much lower cost alternative and will add the same value to the house if done properly. This is especially true if the original siding preserves the original flavor of the house. If you must install new siding, consider doing it together with an energy upgrade. Since you will be removing the old siding, the installation cost of new wall insulation will be minimal.

NEW ROOF

Nothing will scare a prospective buyer away faster than an unattractive, leaking roof. If the roof is in poor condition, you may have no choice but to replace it. But don't expect it to add much value to the house. The roof is one of those must do maintenance items. A stained or unattractive roof can sometimes be improved with a steam cleaning.

NEW WINDOWS AND DOORS

Replacing windows and doors is not a good short-term investment unless the existing ones are beyond repair. However, if you plan to stay in the house for a long time, replacement can save later maintenance headaches. Consider double-pane, vinyl-clad windows for replacement. If you do the work yourself, the addition of patio or French doors can provide attractive, improved access to the outside at a reasonable cost.

SWIMMING POOL

A pool is one popular home improvement that seldom returns its investment. Obviously, people are installing pools for reasons other than investment return. Don't consider the addition of a swimming pool unless your home is in a high-price bracket or you plan to be around for a while.

CHAPTER SIX

Estimating Remodeling Costs

Jumping into your first remodeling project without a realistic estimate of the costs involved could spell financial disaster. The single biggest cause of failed remodeling projects is poor or nonexistent estimating. Many do-it-yourselfers (and professionals for that matter) fail to complete even a rudimentary estimate of the costs associated with their project. Why? Partly because estimating is time consuming and requires a good knowledge of construction and accounting. Another reason is bad habits.

Remodeling usually starts with a small project. The remodeler can calculate all the materials in his head, and if he's off a little bit, who cares? On a large remodeling project, an accurate estimate is *essential*. The nickels and dimes will start to run away with the entire budget until the overall project is hopelessly deadlocked, and several projects will have to be canceled for lack of money. This is especially true in remodeling, since many costs are hidden and can't be calculated accurately until the project is started. Therefore, make sure that the rest of your estimate is totally accurate and that you add in extra for the unseen costs.

This chapter will help you to complete an estimate accurately and quickly by showing you some calculating shortcuts used by professionals. The most critical task is to include everything in the estimate—every nail, screw, tax, discount, and cost of extra trips to the supplier. This book provides sample material lists to help serve as a checklist. Since every remodeling project is different, the material list will serve as a starting point. You will need to complete your own takeoff, the term used by contractors for a material estimate. Sample takeoff forms are included in this chapter and in the appendix. When starting a takeoff, assemble the sample lists from each section that apply to your specific project and list them on the calculation forms. Refer to this chapter to estimate each item. Once the estimate is complete, you can use the purchase orders in the appendix to requisition and track the items.

Estimating a remodeling project can be a real challenge, since many necessary repairs may be hidden behind walls and floor coverings. Inspect your project rigorously using the checklist supplied in the inspection chapter. If you are remodeling a room such as the bath, you will need to make a checklist of each item you intend to replace. If you are building a room addition, you will actually be estimating a small construction project that has all the expenses associated with a full-scale construction project.

The first thing you will want to do is sketch out the addition in detail. If you are building a structure from the ground up, you should get a draftsman or architect to draw up full-scale blueprints. You can use these scaled blueprints to calculate your construction costs.

If you are not confident of your ability to estimate, ask other experts for help. One important source of information will come from the subcontractors you plan to use. These subs are familiar with the type of construction in your area and can be very knowledgeable in calculating the amounts of materials needed. Most of your subcontractors will offer to calculate the amount of materials needed for you. This can be very valuable, especially for framing, because of the sheer number of different materials used.

Don't rely solely on your subcontractor's estimate. Make sure to run your own figures for comparison, because subs tend to overestimate just to be on the safe side. If your estimate comes close to the subcontractor's, consider it a good starting point. Just make sure that you add at least a 5 to 10 percent waste factor to each estimate. Another good source of estimating information is your local materials supplier. Suppliers used to do quite a bit of estimating for their customers.

If you can find suppliers who still do, they are worth their weight in gold.

If you are working with a remodeling contractor, that person will complete a takeoff before bidding the job. Contractors usually include a hidden costs clause in their contracts to insure them against unexpected problems that may be invisible until the project is started. This is especially true when a sub is bidding a fixed price for the job. Examine this clause carefully to make sure that it can't be used to tack on additional bonuses. Your contract should describe the remodeling project in detail. Ask that the contractor's estimate be attached to the contract with the costs removed. This will help to define the project. If the contractor is working on a cost plus basis, *demand* that the estimate be included.

ESTIMATING NEW CONSTRUCTION

When your project includes additions to the house, the cost estimate will include all the items normally associated with new construction. This chapter covers all facets of construction, including renovation and new construction.

Excavation

Excavation is usually charged by the hour of operating time. Larger loaders rent for higher fees. Excavating a basement for waterproofing will require a loader with a shovel on an extended arm. This type of loader is often used for digging footings and plumbing trenches. Approximate times for loader work appear in the table. Remember, these are only approximations. Every lot is different and may pose unique problems. Your grader may supply chain saw labor to cut up large trees.

Excavation Labor Approximation Table
For Half-Acre Lot, In Hours

TASK	SMALL LOADER	LARGE LOADER
Clear trees/shrubs	2-5	1-4
Excavate basement	3-5	3-5
Dig foundation	2-3	1-3
Grade building site	1-5	1-3

Larger loaders can be an advantage and can be cheaper in the long run, especially if the lot is heavily wooded or has steep topography. The larger loader can clear a large area quickly and efficiently. A smaller loader is more appropriate when clearing around a base-

ment or when working in tight spaces with many obstructions.

Concrete

When calculating concrete, it is best to create a formula or conversion factor that will simplify calculations and avoid having to calculate everything in cubic inches and cubic yards. For instance, when pouring a 4-inch slab, a cubic yard of concrete will cover 81 square feet of area. This is calculated as follows:

1 cubic yard = 27 cubic feet = 46,656 cubic inches

1 square foot of 4-inch-thick concrete = 576 cubic inches ($12'' \times 12'' \times 4''$)

46,656 cubic inches / 576 cubic inches = 81 square feet of coverage

By doing this equation only once, you now have a simple formula for calculating 4-inch slabs that you can use for driveways, basement floors and slab floors. For instance, to determine the concrete needed for a slab 1,200 feet square simply divide by 81.

1,200 square feet / 81 = 14.8 cubic yards of concrete

Note: Always add a 5 to 10 percent waste factor to all calculations.

Use this same principle of creating simple formulas for footings, calculating blocks, pouring concrete walls, and so forth. Just remember to calculate your own set of formulas based on the building codes in your area. For your convenience, refer to the concrete tables to determine the conversion factors for your project.

Footings

Footing contractors will be hired to dig the footings and to supervise pouring of the footings. Footing subs generally charge for labor only and charge by the lineal foot of footing poured. Pier holes are extra. You must provide the concrete. These subs may charge more if they provide the forms. If you use a full-service foundation company, it will charge you for a turnkey job for footing, wall and concrete. This makes estimating easy.

Footings generally must be twice as wide as the wall they support and the height of the footing will be the same as the thickness of the wall. The footing contractor will know the code requirements for your area. Ask him for the dimensions of the footing and then figure an amount of concrete per lineal foot of footing. (See the equations on calculating concrete.) Here is a typical calculation for supporting an 8-inch block wall:

Footing dimension: 8″ high × 16″ wide
8″ × 16″ × 12″ (1 foot of footing) = 1,536 cubic inches
46,656 cubic inches / 1,536 cubic inches = 30.38 lineal feet of footing per cubic yard

With this size footing, figure 1 cubic yard of concrete for every 31 lineal feet of footing. Make sure to include 4 extra feet of footing for every pier hole. Add 10 percent for waste. Refer to the footing table for concrete factors.

CU. YDS. CONCRETE NEEDED PER LINEAL FOOT OF FOOTING							
Depth Ins.	Width of Footing in Inches						
	4″	6″	8″	10″	12″	14″	16″
4″	0.004	0.006	0.008	0.010	0.012	0.014	0.016
6″	0.006	0.009	0.012	0.015	0.019	0.022	0.025
8″	0.008	0.012	0.016	0.021	0.025	0.029	0.033
10″	0.010	0.015	0.021	0.026	0.031	0.036	0.041
12″	0.012	0.019	0.025	0.031	0.037	0.043	0.049
14″	0.014	0.022	0.029	0.036	0.043	0.050	0.058
16″	0.016	0.025	0.033	0.041	0.049	0.058	0.066

Concrete Floors or Slabs

Use the conversion factor of 81 square feet for 4-inch slabs or basement floors. If your slabs must be more or less than 4 inches make sure to calculate a new conversion factor or refer to the table.

Monolithic Slabs

Break a one-piece slab into two components—the slab and the footing sections; then figure the items separately using the tables.

SQUARE FOOTAGE OF SLAB THAT 1 CU. YD. OF CONCRETE WILL FILL			
Slab	S.F.	Slab	S.F.
1″	324	7″	46
1½″	216	7½″	43
2″	162	8″	41
2½″	130	8½″	38
3″	108	9″	36
3½″	93	9½″	34
4″	81	10″	32
4½″	72	10½″	31
5″	65	11″	29
5½″	59	11½″	28
6″	54	12″	27

Block Foundations and Crawl Spaces

Concrete blocks come in many shapes and sizes, the most common being 8″ × 8″ × 16″. Blocks that are 12 inches thick are used for tall block walls with backfill to provide extra stability. Blocks 8 inches deep and 12 inches deep cover the same wall area: .888 square ft.

To calculate the amount of block needed, measure the height of the wall in inches and divide by 8 inches to find the height of the wall in numbers of blocks. The height of the wall will always be in even numbers of blocks plus a 4-inch cap block or 8-inch half block (for pouring slabs). Cap blocks are solid concrete 4″ × 8″ × 16″ blocks used to provide a smooth surface to build on. If you are figuring a basement wall, multiply the perimeter of the foundation by .75 (three blocks for every 4 feet); then multiply the result by the number of rows of block. To calculate the row of cap block multiply the perimeter of the foundation by .75. Always figure 5 to 10 percent waste when ordering block.

If your foundation is a crawl space, your footing is likely to have one or more step-downs, or bulkheads, as they are called. Step-downs are areas where the footing is dropped or raised the height of one block. This allows the footing to follow the contour of the land. As a result, sections of the block wall will vary in height, requiring more or fewer rows of block. Take each step-down section separately and figure three blocks for every 4 feet of wall. Multiply the total number of blocks by the total number of rows and then add all sections together for the total number of blocks needed.

Poured Concrete Walls

Your poured-wall subcontractor will charge by the lineal foot for setting forms. Usually, the price quoted for pouring includes the cost of concrete; but if not, you must calculate the amount of concrete needed. Determine the thickness of the wall from your poured-wall

CU. YDS. CONCRETE NEEDED PER LINEAR FOOT OF WALL							
Height of Wall	Width of Wall in Inches						
	4″	6″	8″	10″	12″	14″	16″
4′	0.049	0.074	0.099	0.123	0.148	0.173	0.198
5′	0.062	0.093	0.123	0.154	0.185	0.216	0.247
6′	0.074	0.111	0.148	0.185	0.222	0.259	0.296
7′	0.086	0.130	0.173	0.216	0.259	0.302	0.346
8′	0.099	0.148	0.198	0.247	0.296	0.346	0.395
9′	0.111	0.167	0.222	0.278	0.333	0.389	0.444
10′	0.123	0.185	0.247	0.309	0.370	0.432	0.494
11′	0.136	0.204	0.272	0.340	0.407	0.475	0.543
12′	0.148	0.222	0.296	0.370	0.444	0.519	0.593
13′	0.160	0.241	0.321	0.401	0.481	0.562	0.642
14′	0.173	0.259	0.346	0.432	0.519	0.605	0.691
15′	0.185	0.278	0.370	0.463	0.556	0.648	0.741
16′	0.198	0.296	0.395	0.494	0.593	0.691	0.790
17′	0.210	0.315	0.420	0.525	0.630	0.735	0.840
18′	0.222	0.333	0.444	0.556	0.667	0.778	0.889

sub and find the square foot conversion factor for the number of square feet coverage per cubic yard. Divide this factor into the total square footage of the wall. Example:

8″-thick poured concrete wall $\times$ 12″ $\times$ 12″ =
1,152 cubic inches per square foot of wall
46,656 cubic inches / 1,152 cubic inches = 40.5
square feet per cubic yard of concrete

Refer to the concrete wall table on page 44 to quickly calculate the concrete needed.

Brick

To figure the amount of brick needed, figure the square footage of the walls to be bricked and multiply by 6.75. (There are approximately 675 bricks per 100 square feet of wall.) Add 5 to 10 percent for waste.

Mortar

Mortar comes premixed in bags of masonry cement, which consist of roughly one part portland cement and one part lime. Each bag requires about 20 shovels of sand when mixing. To calculate the amount of mortar needed for brick, figure one bag of cement for every 125 bricks. For block, figure one bag of cement for every 28 blocks. Make sure to use a good grade of washed sand for a good bonding mortar. Most foundations will require at least 10 cubic yards of sand.

Framing

Estimating your framing lumber requirements will be the most difficult estimating task and will require studying the layout and the structural design of your house carefully. If you have a scaled blueprint of the project, use it to measure the length of walls and framing members. Before you begin, consult with a framing contractor or architect for advice on size and grade of lumber used in your area.

This is the time you will want to pull out your books on construction techniques and study them to familiarize yourself with the components of your particular house. Local building code manuals will include span tables for determining the maximum spans you are allowed for supporting beams. An architectural rendering of the project should list the sizes of any new framing members and should include construction detail drawings, which will list the size and type of lumber needed for framing. If load-bearing walls are being removed, this architectural plan can be invaluable. Architects are trained to properly calculate and insure that a load-bearing alteration is completed according to code requirements. Detailed drawings will illustrate precisely how the new framing supports should be installed.

Floor Framing

For new construction, determine the size and length of floor joists by noting the position of piers or beams and by consulting with your framing contractor. Floor joists are usually spaced 16 inches on center (O.C.). Joists spaced 12 inches O.C. are used for extra sturdy floors. If floor trusses are used, figure 24-inch O.C. spacing. Calculate the perimeter of the foundation walls to determine the amount of sill and box sill framing.

Add in extra floor joists for headers if a stair opening is to be included. Attic conversions usually require doubling the number of ceiling joists (which are now floor joists) to strengthen the new floor. Simply count the number of existing joists and add extras for framing around stair openings.

When replacing a load-bearing wall with a beam, measure the length of the wall to be replaced. Add any extra length needed to extend the beam over any supporting walls. Make sure to calculate beam lengths accurately. Custom fabricated beams such as glue-lam beams are difficult to cut on-site. They should be delivered at the proper length. If the beam is to be installed in or above the ceiling, make sure to include the proper number of joist hangers or hanger straps.

If you are adding or upgrading a basement or crawl space, you will probably be using a steel or wood beam to support the floor members. If floor trusses are used, this item may not be needed since floor trusses can span much greater distances. Consult with your local truss manufacturer.

Calculate the square footage of the floor and divide by 32 (square footage in a 4′ $\times$ 8′ sheet of plywood) to determine the amount of subflooring plywood needed. Use the same quantity for underlayment. If the APA Sturdifloor design is used, order ¾-inch or ⅝-inch tongue-and-grooved exterior plywood.

Bridging between floor joists is used to reduce twisting and warping of floor members and to tie the floor together structurally. Bridging is calculated by taking the total number of floor joists and multiplying by 3. This gives the lineal feet of bridging needed for one course of bridging. Most floors will require at least two courses of bridging, so double this figure.

Wall Framing

When calculating wall framing lumber, add together the lineal feet of all interior and exterior walls. Since there is a plate at the bottom of the wall, and a double plate at the top, multiply wall length by 3 to get the lineal feet of wall plate needed. Add 10 percent for waste. For precut wall studs, make sure to get the proper length; they come in many sizes. Allow one precut stud for every lineal foot of wall and two studs for every corner. Count all door and window openings as solid wall. This will allow enough for waste and bracing.

Headers are placed over all openings in load-bearing walls for structural support and are doubled. Add together the total width of all doors and windows and multiply by 2. Check with a framing sub or architect for the proper size header.

Roof Framing

If roof trusses are to be used, figure one truss for every 2 feet of building length, plus one truss. If the roof is a hip roof or has two rooflines that meet at right angles, extra framing for bridging must be added.

The roof truss manufacturer should calculate the actual size and quantity of roof trusses at the site or from blueprints to ensure the proper fit. Request a bid and material list during the estimating process.

CONVERSION FACTORS FOR ROOFS			
Pitch (slope)	Conversion Factor	Pitch (slope)	Conversion Factor
1"	1.01	9"	1.26
2"	1.02	10"	1.31
3"	1.04	11"	1.36
4"	1.06	12"	1.42
5"	1.09	13"	1.48
6"	1.12	14"	1.54
7"	1.16	15"	1.61
8"	1.21	16"	1.67

Stick building a roof is much harder to calculate and requires some knowledge of geometry to figure all the lumber needed. A stick built roof is one that is built completely on-site. The following techniques can also be used to calculate rafters for dormers. The simplest way of finding the length of ceiling joists and rafters is to measure them from scaled blueprints. Always round to the nearest greater even length, since all lumber is sold in even-numbered lengths.

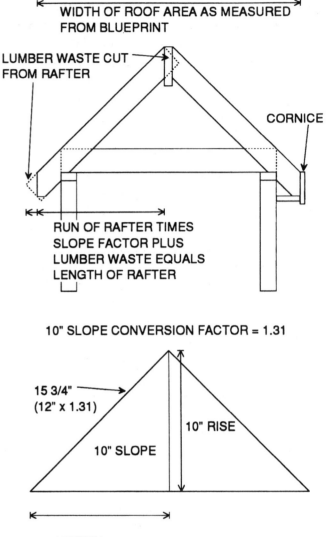

Fig. 6-1. Length of rafter and area of roof calculated by using conversion factor for a 10-inch slope roof.

If you can't measure the length of the rafter from your plans, you can calculate rafter length and roof area using a conversion factor similar to the one used for concrete. Think of a roof as two identical triangles back-to-back. If you know the length of the triangle base, you can calculate the length of the long side of the triangle (the rafter) by using trigonometry. I have spared you this headache by providing a conversion factor for each roof slope (rise/run). See the accompanying table for this multiplication factor. A 10-inch slope roof means that the roof rises 10 inches for every foot of run (distance). This term is sometimes mistakenly referred to as pitch slope.

To use this table, measure the total width of the house (including roof overhang) from the peak of the roof to the cornice edge. Multiply this number by the conversion factor to obtain the rafter length. Don't forget to add in waste for lumber cut from the ends of each rafter (see Fig. 6-1). This same conversion factor can also be used to calculate roof area for shingles and tar paper. Calculate the total area of the ceiling plus overhang and multiply by the conversion factor to obtain the total roof area. By the way, a 10-inch slope roof is very steep.

When calculating ceiling joists, draw a joist layout with opposing joists always meeting and overlapping above a load-bearing wall. Figure one ceiling joist for every 16 inches plus 10 percent extra for waste.

Rafters are also spaced 16 inches on center. The length of the rafters can be determined by measuring from blueprints, making sure to allow for cornice overhang. Where two rooflines meet, a valley or hip rafter is necessary. Multiply the length of a normal rafter by 1.5 to get the approximate length of this rafter.

Gable studs will be necessary to frame in the gable ends. The length of the stud should be equal to the height of the roof ridge. Figure one stud per foot of gable width plus 10 percent waste. This will be enough to do two gable ends since scrap pieces can be used in the short areas of the gable.

Decking for the roof usually consists of ½-inch CDX exterior plywood. Multiply the length of the rafter times the length of the roof to determine the square footage of one side of the roof. Double this figure to obtain total square footage area of the roof. Divide this figure by the square footage of a sheet of plywood (32). Add 10 percent waste. This is the number of sheets of plywood needed. Remember the square footage of the roof for figuring shingles.

Roofing Shingles

Roofing shingles are sold in *squares* or the number of shingles necessary to cover 100 square feet of roof. First, find the square footage of the roof, adding 1½ square feet for every lineal foot of eaves, ridge, hip and valley. Divide the total square footage by 100 to find the number of squares. Shingles come packaged in one-third square packages, so multiply the number of squares by three to arrive at the total number of packages needed.

Roofing felt is applied under the roof shingles as an underlayment and comes in 500-square-foot rolls. Divide the total square footage of the roof by 500 and add 20 percent for overlap and waste to determine the number of rolls needed.

Flashing is required around any chimney or area

where two roof-lines of different height meet and comes in 50-foot rolls. Measure the length of the ridge if installing roof ridge vents.

Siding and Sheathing

Multiply the perimeter of the outside walls by the height to obtain the total square footage of outside walls. If gables are to be covered with siding, multiply the width of the gable by the height (this figure is sufficient for both gable ends) and add this to the square footage of the outside walls. This figure is the total square footage of area to be sided.

Different types of siding are sold using different unit quantities. Sheathing and plywood siding are sold in $4' \times 8'$ sheets (32 square feet). Divide this figure into the total square footage to determine the number of sheets needed. Add 10 percent for waste. Lap siding, on the other hand, is sold by squares or 1,000s. Make sure to ask if siding is sold by actual square footage or by coverage area (the amount of area actually covered by the siding when applied). Add 10 percent for waste or 15 percent if lap siding is applied diagonally.

Corner trim boards are generally cut from 1×2 lumber. Figure two pieces for every inside and outside corner; the length is the height of the wall being sided.

Cornice Material

To estimate cornice material, first determine the type or style of cornice and the trim materials to be used. Consult blueprints for any construction detail drawings of the cornice. The following materials are generally used in most cornices:

- Fascia boards — $1'' \times 6''$ or $1'' \times 8''$
- Drip mold (between fascia and shingles) — $1'' \times 4''$
- Soffit — $\frac{3}{8}''$ exterior plywood
- Bed mold — $1'' \times 2''$
- Frieze mold — $1'' \times 8''$

Calculate the total lineal feet of cornice, including the gables, to find the total lineal feet of each trim material needed. Calculate the square footage of the soffit by multiplying the lineal feet of cornice by the depth of the cornice. Divide this by the square footage of a plywood sheet to determine the number of sheets needed.

Insulation

Calculating the amount of wall insulation is easy. Batts of insulation are sold by square footage coverage. Simply multiply the perimeter of the exterior walls to be insulated by the wall height to determine the total square footage to be insulated. To calculate the amount of blown-in insulation needed, first determine the type of insulation to be used. Each type of insulation — mineral wool, fiberglass, and cellulose — has its own R-value per inch. This must be known to determine the thickness of fill. Then multiply the depth in feet (or fraction thereof) by the square footage of the ceiling area to arrive at the cubic foot volume. Blown-in insulation is sold by the cubic foot. If batt insulation is used in the ceiling, it can be figured in the same manner as the wall insulation.

Most insulation contractors will give you an estimate that includes materials and labor when installing insulation. Ask the contractor to itemize the amount of insulation used, for comparison with your figures.

Drywall

Gypsum drywall is sold by the sheet (4×8, 4×10, 4×12, and so on) but is estimated by square footage. To find the total amount needed for walls, multiply the total lineal feet of inside and outside walls by the wall height. Make sure to count each interior wall twice, since both sides of the wall will be covered. Count all openings as solid wall and add 10 percent for waste. Some subs will charge by the square foot for material and labor, then add extras for special work.

For the ceiling, simply take the finished square footage of the house. Add 10 percent for waste and then add this to the wall amount for the total amount of drywall needed. If the house has any vaulted or tray ceilings, extra drywall and labor must be figured in. Joint finishing compound comes premixed in 5-gallon cans and joint tape in 250-foot rolls. For every 1,000 square feet of drywall, figure one roll of joint tape and 30 gallons of joint compound.

Trim Work

Base molding comes in many styles, with clamshell and colonial the most common, and is installed along the bottom of the wall in every room. Therefore, the lineal feet of walls used to calculate wallboard is equal to the lineal feet of baseboard trim needed. Add 10 percent for waste.

Make sure to measure the perimeter of any room that requires shoe molding or crown molding. Shoe mold (quarter round) is usually installed in any room with vinyl or wood flooring to cover the crack between the floor and wall. Crown molding around the ceiling may be used in any room, but is most common in formal areas such as foyers and living and dining areas. Add 10 percent for waste.

When ordering interior doors, you may want to purchase prehung doors with preassembled jambs. These doors are exceptionally easy to install and already have the jamb and trimwork attached. Study the blueprints carefully to be sure that the doors ordered open in the right direction and don't block light switches. (There are right-hand and left-hand doors.) To determine which door to order, imagine standing in front of the door and walking in. If you must use your right hand to open the door, it is a right-hand door. Most blueprints will have the size and type of each door marked in the opening.

Flooring

Because of the complexity of laying flooring materials — carpet, hardwood floors, vinyl or ceramic tile — it is essential to get a flooring contractor to estimate the flooring quantities. An approximate figure would be equal to the square footage of the area covered plus 10 percent for waste. Carpet and vinyl are sold by the square yard, so divide the total square footage by 9 to determine square yardage (there are 9 square feet to a square yard). Keep in mind, however, that carpet and vinyl are sold in 12-foot wide rolls. This dimension may affect the amount of waste in the estimate.

Miscellaneous Coverings

Other coverings include ceramic tile for bathrooms or floors, hardwood floors, parquet floors, slate for foyers or fireplaces, and fieldstone for steps or fireplaces. Virtually all these materials are sold by the square footage area covered. Subcontractors who install these items also charge by the square foot, sometimes with material included and sometimes without. Grouts and mortars used in installing these items (with the exception of rock) are premixed and the container indicates the coverage expected.

Paint

When hiring a painting contractor, the cost of paint should be included in the cost of the estimate unless you specify otherwise. If you decide to do the painting yourself, you will need to figure the amount of paint needed. The coverage of different paints varies considerably, but most paints state the area covered on the container. Calculate the square footage of the area to be covered and add at least 15 percent for waste and touch up. Divide this amount by the square foot coverage of the paint you are purchasing to determine the number of cans needed. Follow the same procedure for calculating the primer needed. Write the color code on each paint can with permanent marker. If colors are custom mixed, make sure that you have enough paint to finish the job. It is sometimes difficult to get an exact match of a custom color if mixed again at a later date.

Cabinets

Most kitchen designers and supply houses offer kitchen blueprints with cabinet layouts when bidding on a job. In this case, the kitchen cost will be calculated in their bid. If you are working from an architect's kitchen layout you can use it to calculate the type and quantity of cabinets. Be sure that painting, staining and installation are included in the price. Some cabinetmakers may even do a kitchen design for free.

Wallpaper

One roll of wallpaper will safely cover 30 square feet of wall area including waste and matching of patterns. The longer the repeat pattern the more waste. Some European wallpapers vary in coverage. Be sure to check coverage area with the wallpaper supplier. When figuring the square footage of a room, do not delete anything for openings. Treat openings as a solid wall. Also check to see if you are buying a single or double roll of wallpaper. Most wallpaper is sold in a roll that actually contains two true rolls of wallpaper, or 60 square feet of coverage. Always buy enough paper to finish the job. Buying additional rolls at a later time can cause matching problems if some of the rolls are from a different dye lot. Look for the same lot numbers (runs) on all rolls purchased to assure a perfect match. Use only vinyl wallpaper in baths and kitchen areas for water resistance and cleanup. Look for prepasted wallpaper to reduce the labor needed for installation. This paper has the glue already applied to the paper backing.

Millwork and Miscellaneous

The ordering of windows, lights, hardware and other specialty items will not be covered here as they are fairly straightforward to calculate. Other estimates such as heating and air, plumbing, electrical and electrical fixtures must be obtained from the contractors themselves since they provide the materials and labor.

SUBCONTRACTORS

This subsection outlines the work done by various subcontractors and how most of them charge for their services. Some subs may or may not include the cost of materials in their estimates. Make sure you know your particular sub's policy.

Block. Lays block. Charges by the block. Extras: stucco block.

Brickwork. Lays brick. Charges by the skid (1,000 bricks).

Cabinetry. Builds or installs prefab cabinets and vanities and applies Formica tops. Charges by the lineal foot for base cabinets, wall cabinets and vanities. Standard price includes Formica countertops. Extras: tile or marble tops, curved tops, pull-out shelves, lazy Susans, kitchen design. Kitchen designers serve as brokers—designing, estimating and ordering prefab cabinets. Will charge a set fee for design and cabinet installation.

Ceramic tile. Installs all ceramic tile. Charges by the square foot. Extras include fancy bathtub surrounds and tile countertops.

Concrete finishing. Pours concrete, sets forms, spreads gravel and finishes concrete. Charges by the square foot of area poured. Extras: monolithic slab, digging footing.

Cornice. Usually done by the siding subcontractor. Applies soffit and fascia board. Charges by the lineal foot of cornice. Extras: fancy cornice work, dentil mold. Sometimes sets windows and exterior doors.

Drywall. Hangs drywall, tapes and finishes, stipples. Charges by the square foot of drywall. Materials are extra. Extras: smooth ceilings, curved walls, tray and vaulted ceilings and open foyers.

Electrical. Installs all switches and receptacles; hooks up A/C compressor. Will install light fixtures. Charges by the receptacle. Extras: connecting dishwasher, disposal, flood-lights, doorbells.

Fireplace. Supplies and installs prefab fireplace and flue liner. Extras: gas log lighter, fresh air vent, ash dump.

Flooring. Installs all carpet, vinyl, linoleum and prefinished flooring. Charges by the square yard. Extras: contrast borders and thicker underlayments.

Footings. Digs footings, pours and levels concrete, builds bulkheads (for step downs). Charges by the lineal foot of footings. Extras: pier holes.

Framing. Installs framing, applies sheathing, and sets windows and exterior doors. Charges by the square foot of framed structure (including any unheated space such as garage). Extras include bay windows, chimney chase, stairs, dormers and anything else unusual. Charges extra for demolition and alteration of existing framing, such as when adding a dormer to the attic or removing a partition. Estimates can vary considerably, so obtain several bids.

Garage door. Installs garage doors. Fixed fee. Extras: garage door openers.

Grading. Does rough grading and clearing. Charges by the hour of bulldozer time. Extras: chain saw work, hauling away of refuse, travel time to and from site (drag time).

Gutters. Installs gutters and downspouts. Charges by lineal foot plus extra for fittings. Extras: half-round gutters, collectors, special water channeling, and gutters that cannot be installed from the roof.

Hardwood floor. Installs and finishes real hardwood floors. Charges by square foot. Extras: beveled plank, random plank, herringbone.

HVAC. Installs furnace, air conditioner, all ductwork and gas lines. Charges by the tonnage of A/C or on bid price. Extras: vent fans in bath, roof fans, attic fans, dryer vents, high-efficiency furnaces and compressors.

Insulation. Installs all fiberglass batts in walls, ceilings, floors. Charges by square foot for batts, by the cubic foot for blown-in.

Landscaping. Levels with tractor, puts down seeds, fertilizer and straw. Charges fixed fee. Extras: trees, transplanted shrubs, pine straw, bark chips.

Painting and stain. Paints and stains interior and exterior. Charges by square foot of finished house. Extras: high ceilings, stained ceilings, painted ceilings.

Pest control. Chemically treats the ground around the foundation to protect against termites. Charges a flat fee.

Plumbing. Installs all sewer lines, water lines, drains, tubs, fixtures and water appliances. Charges per fixture installed or by bid. (For instance, a toilet, sink and tub would be three fixtures.) Installs medium-grade fixtures. Extras: any special decorator fixtures.

Poured foundation. Digs and pours footings, sets forms, and pours walls. Charges by the lineal foot of wall. Extras: bulkheads, more than four corners, openings for windows, doors and pipes.

Roofing. Installs shingles and waterproofs around vents. Charges a set fee per "square" plus slope of roof. Example: $1 per square over slope on a 6/12 slope roof = $7 per square. Extras: some flashing, ridge vents, and special cutouts for skylights.

Septic tank. Installs septic tank. Charges fixed fee plus extra for field lines.

Siding. Applies exterior siding. Charges by the square of applied siding. Extras: diagonal siding, decks, porches, and very high walls requiring scaffolding.

Stonework. Lays stone. Charges by the square foot or by bid.

Trim. Installs all interior trim and closet fixtures and sets interior doors. Charges a set fee by the opening or by lineal feet of trim. Openings include doors and windows. Extras: stairs, rails, crown mold, mantels, book cases, chair rail, wainscoting and picture molding.

Wallpaper. Hangs wallpaper. Owner provides wallpaper. Charges by the roll. Extras: high ceilings, wallpaper on ceilings, grass cloth.

USING THE INCLUDED FORMS

Each chapter in Sections II (remodeling structure) and III (remodeling rooms) includes sample material lists to help in assembling a comprehensive takeoff. These lists contain many of the items used in most remodeling projects. Obviously, your project will be different, but you can use these lists as starting points for creating your own estimate. The Item Estimate Worksheet at the end of this chapter can also be used as a calculation sheet. By combining these two forms together you can complete a total material estimate for your project in record time.

BIDS BEAT ESTIMATES EVERY TIME

Now that you know how detailed an estimate can be, look at the other side of the coin. You can spend a day calculating how many cubic yards of concrete you will need and approximately how many hours of labor it will take; or you can call up a full-service foundation company and get a bid. The moral here is to use bids whenever possible in completing your takeoff. The bottom line is what counts; if your estimate comes out to be $600 to tile a floor and your lowest bid is $750, you've obviously missed the boat—and wasted a little time.

KITCHEN MATERIAL ESTIMATE

DESCRIPTION	QTY.	UNIT	PRICE	COST	TAX	TOTAL COST	VENDOR
Cabinets							
Wall Cabinets 12" deep *Heritage Oak*	18	L.F.	72.50	1305.00	62.25	1370.25	Best
Base Cabinets 24"deep "	18	L.F.	86.50	1557.00	77.85	1634.85	"
Blocking- 2x4 for wall cabinets	40	L.F.	.43	17.20	.86	18.06	"
Island Cabinet	1	ea.	519.60	519.60	25.98	545.58	"
Corner lazy susan							
Valance boards	1	ea.	54.00	54.00	2.70	56.70	"
Mounting screws *1 5/8" Phillips*	1	Box	1.71	1.71	.09	1.80	ACME
Cornice trim							
Floor							
Plywood underlay. -4x8x1/2" *A/c Plywood*	5	Shts.	24.75	123.75	6.19	129.94	ACME
Flooring *Vinyl Roll 12' - Sandstone*	16	S.Y.	10.50	168.00	8.40	176.40	"
Floor felt - *Roll #15*	1	Roll	7.60	7.60	.38	7.98	"
Flooring Adhesive *Vinyl floor adhesive*	1	Gal.	13.95	13.95	.70	14.65	"
Flooring nails *1 1/4" Ring Shank Underlayment*	1	Box	1.07	1.07	.05	1.12	"
Quarter round trim *Paint Grade*	36	L.F.	.35	12.60	.63	13.23	"
Finishing nails *6d*	1	Box	.84	.84	.04	.88	"
Counter top							
Sub-base -4x8x3/4" *Particle Board*	3	Shts.	13.50	40.50	2.03	42.53	Best
Plastic laminate *4x8 Pebblestone*	3	Shts.	32.00	96.00	4.80	100.80	Best
Laminate contact adhesive	2	Qts.	6.53	13.06	.65	13.71	Best
Wood counter trim *Oak-for Island*	20	L.F.	1.49	29.80	1.49	31.29	ACME
Lights & electrical							
Track lights *Halogen Strips*	3	ea.	89.50	268.50	13.43	281.93	ACE
Can lights - Sink	2	ea.	18.50	37.00	1.85	38.85	"
Fluorescent fixture - ceiling *Oak Trim MOD153*	1	ea.	189.00	189.00	9.45	200.30	"
Ground Fault Interrupters *-Almond*	4	ea.	7.25	29.00	1.45	30.45	"

Fig. 6-2. Sample material estimate.

DESCRIPTION	QTY.	UNIT	PRICE	COST	TAX	TOTAL COST	VENDOR
Fixtures							
Cooking Range - built-in _ACME Model RA165-Almond_	1	ea.	599.00	599.00	29.95	628.95	ACME
Range Hood _ACME R4111- Almond_	1	ea.	75.00	75.00	3.75	78.75	"
Stovetop _ACME ST317-Almond_	1	ea.	189.00	189.00	9.45	198.45	"
Microwave _ACME MW309 - Almond_	1	ea.	399.00	399.00	19.95	418.95	"
Trash Compactor							
Refrigerator _ACME RE007-Almond s×s._	1	ea.	1150.00	1150.00	57.50	1207.50	"
Garbage Disposal _ACME GD7416_	1	ea.	139.99	139.99	7.00	146.99	"
Dishwasher _ACME Deluxe DW171_	1	ea.	359.99	359.99	18.00	372.99	"
Plumbing							
Kitchen sink _Stainless 2 bowl_	1	ea.	117.00	117.00	5.85	122.85	George
Faucet set _Eurostyle w/sprayer_	1	ea.	129.00	129.00	6.45	135.45	"
Finish							
Paint - primer - wall _Latex White_	1	Gal.	9.97	9.97	.50	10.47	ACME
Paint - trim _Latex Almond Semigloss_	2	Qts.	5.47	10.94	.55	11.49	"
Paint - base coat _Latex Cream Semigloss_	1	Gal.	12.97	12.97	.65	13.62	"
Labor							
Kitchen design _Best Cabinets_				250.00	0	250.00	Best
Cabinet install _Best Cabinets_				250.00	0	250.00	Best
Electrical _ACE Electric_				500.00	0	500.00	ACE
Plumbing _George's Plumbing_				500.00	0	500.00	George
Flooring _Self Install_				NC			
Carpentry - misc. _Self_				NC			
Removal of old kitchen _Self_				NC			

	COST	TAX	TOTAL COST
TOTALS	9,177.04	381.27	9,558.31

MATERIAL ESTIMATE

DESCRIPTION	QTY.	UNIT	COST	TAX	TOTAL COST	COST TYPE	VENDOR
					TOTAL		

Fig. 6-3. Blank material estimate.

ITEM ESTIMATE WORKSHEET

VENDOR NAME	DESCRIPTION	MEASURING		CONVERSION FACTOR	ORDERING		PRICE EACH	COST	TAX	TOTAL COST	COST TYPE
		QTY.	UNIT		QTY.	UNIT					

EXPENSE CATEGORY	MATERIAL COST	LABOR COST	SUBCONTRACTOR COST	TOTAL COST

CHAPTER SEVEN

Financing

Unless you are one of the few who remodel with cash, financing is a necessity. When remodeling, you must be bookkeeper, financier and salesperson. The lender will want evidence that you know what you are doing and that you can finish your project within budget.

THE HOME IMPROVEMENT LOAN

The home improvement loan is an unsecured loan, meaning that its security is not attached to the property. Most banks limit the amount of home improvement loans to under $10,000, with a maximum 5-year term. It is typical for interest on a home improvement loan to be several points higher than permanent financing. This gives you further incentive to finish the project as quickly as possible to cut your finance costs. Remember, changes and upgrades can be expensive and should not be considered once the project is in progress unless you are willing to pay for them out of pocket.

THE SECOND MORTGAGE

Like the first mortgage on a property, the second mortgage is a secured loan attached to the value of the property itself. This is the most common loan for major renovation projects and can be obtained from banks or savings and loan companies. The interest on second mortgages is usually two points above the market rate for first mortgages. Most lenders restrict the total principal of the first and subsequent mortgages to 70 to 90 percent of the total appraised value of the property. You may be required to obtain a certified appraisal if the property has appreciated significantly since the first mortgage.

THE HOME EQUITY LOAN

A recent development in the home loan business, the home equity loan provides the homeowner with a line of credit that is secured by the home or other property. In this way, the home equity loan is like a second mortgage, except that you as borrower have a line of credit — you can borrow the funds at will, up to the limit of the loan. This is a very flexible loan that can be used for any number of reasons. Since the money can be borrowed and paid back at any time, the interest expenses can be reduced somewhat by borrowing the money at the last minute and paying it back as soon as possible. Home equity loans are also tax deductible.

APPLYING FOR YOUR LOAN

Make sure that your financial package is complete before visiting the lender. The package should be neat, informative and well organized and should comply with all of the lender's requirements. Your lender will want to be sure that you can keep good records. Your financial package should include the following:

1. A personal financial statement that includes all your assets and liabilities. Make sure to include everything of value that you own, including personal property. Many people tend to underestimate the value of items like furniture and clothing. Your liabilities should include any loans, charge accounts and credit balances. Ask your lender for one of their own standard forms.

2. A resume designed to sell yourself to the lender. Start with a standard job resume, but be sure to emphasize any construction interests or experience.

3. A cost estimate, which is very important because your remodeling loan will be based on it. Make sure to include a 7 to 10 percent cost overrun factor in your estimates as a cushion for unexpected expenses. Many lenders can provide you with a standard cost sheet form.

If not, use the one included in this book.

4. A description of materials form that will aid the lender's appraiser in estimating the appraised value of your property. Many lenders use the standard FHA form for this purpose, but check to see if your lender uses a different format.

5. A set of blueprints, complete with all intended changes, should be submitted.

CREATIVE FINANCING TECHNIQUES

If you are about to purchase a fixer-upper, you will need financing for the renovations. For instance, you want to purchase an older house for $60,000 with a down payment of 10 percent or $6,000. You want to do $20,000 worth of renovations that will make the property worth $100,000. You go to the local bank for a new mortgage. The lender will loan only up to the home's *current value*. The bank will not lend you enough money for the renovations, because it has no guarantee that your $20,000 expenditure will increase the home's value to the claimed $100,000. In essence, the bank will not lend you the money until you don't need it—after the project is complete.

Don't despair. Creative individuals have found many innovative solutions to this cart before the horse problem. You are limited only by your imagination in finding financing options. That's why it's called creative financing. One word of caution: Make sure you are *absolutely certain* of your remodeling ability before starting a high-risk remodeling project. If you are pushing the limits and fail, you can lose everything and damage your credit rating for years. Let's look at a few ways to generate financing.

Solution 1. The most obvious solution is to get a *first mortgage* on the original value of the home *and ask for an unsecured home improvement loan* for the renovation. If you have good credit, most banks will lend you a healthy sum on your credit standing alone. If you can obtain financing from several banks, you can accumulate quite a bit of unsecured funds. Most banks are very strict about disclosure of all other loans you possess, so make sure to list all preapproved loans. It is not necessary to list loans for which you have applied, but have not received approval.

Solution 2. *Credit cards* are a great source of quick cash. Because of their high interest rates, banks are eager to provide you with sizable credit limits. Most card services have cash withdrawal options; if not, simply live off the card while using your regular cash for remodeling. If you submit applications for five or six cards at a time, you may be approved for at least half. Even though the interest rates are high, credit cards function like a line of credit—you may pay them back any time. Simply finance the renovation with the credit card and then apply for a second mortgage after the renovation is complete. *Just make sure you pay off the cards when you are done!* The house will now be valued at its appreciated rate of $100,000, allowing a second mortgage of $24,000. The $56,000 original mortgage + $24,000 = $80,000, exactly 80 percent of the $100,000 value. *Use this money to pay off the credit cards.*

Solution 3. Another source of credit is the *regular unsecured line of credit*. This source of money must be the result of carefully thought out strategy on your part. You should immediately start to cultivate credit relationships with as many banks as possible. Open checking accounts with several banks and ask for small loans at first and build up to larger ones. Make sure to pay back each loan slightly ahead of time. As time goes by, you will be surprised how much unsecured credit you can accumulate.

Solution 4. Use a *combination* of all the above.

Solution 5. *Owner financing* is by far the best source of money. The seller is eager for you to purchase the property and is often willing to extend credit with much more lenient requirements than banks. This is especially true when the seller is a "don't wanter." This owner financing will be used to reduce or eliminate the down payment on the property. By avoiding a large down payment, you can save your cash reserve for the renovation. Let's look at one possible strategy.

Lease with Option to Buy

This technique may be the only way to effectively finance an extensive remodeling project. Let's look at an example. You have found a quaint one-story, two-bedroom house with one bathroom in an up-and-coming neighborhood. Upon examination, you realize that the roof pitch is steep enough to allow the attic to be finished off as living space. Three cute dormers on the front will turn this small cottage into a three-bedroom, two-bath 1½-story home. The seller wants $65,000 cash and is not willing to finance the down payment.

The current loan is not assumable, so you will have to obtain new financing. You estimate that the improvements will add $25,000 to the value of the house, but the renovations will cost you approximately $12,000, which you now have in cash. If you get a new loan and put 10 percent down ($6,500), you will not have enough cash to complete the renovation. The bank cannot give you a mortgage for the new value of the house until the renovation is complete. You are trapped in the cart before the horse dilemma. What do you do?

Ask the seller to lease the property to you for a monthly rent equal to his mortgage payment. The lease will include an option for you to buy the property within the first year. Explain that you are a professional remodeler and plan to renovate the property. If you do not choose to buy the property, the seller will inherit the improvements you have made at no cost. If you choose to buy, you will pay the full asking price minus your monthly payments.

The seller is happy because he will be receiving tax write-offs on his new "rental property" that can offset the profits made when the property is sold. When you have finished the renovation, you exercise your option to buy and apply for a new mortgage for $81,000 (90 percent of the home's new appraised value of $90,000). The result? You just paid $12,000 for the renovation and $65,000 to the seller—a total of $77,000. But note that these payments are fully paid by the new $81,000 mortgage! You could walk away with $4,000 cash and a new house worth $90,000. However, discuss this situation with your banker ahead of time. Many lending institutions will not provide mortgages for more than the amount of money you have invested in the property ($77,000). Even so, you should still be able to obtain a loan for $77,000 and complete the deal.

The point of these examples? There is no limit to the type of financial bargains you can devise. All it takes is a willing seller and creativity. Once you know the needs and circumstances of the seller, you are ready to use your creativity to put together an innovative deal where both parties will benefit.

CHAPTER EIGHT

Legal Issues

Depending upon the size of your project, you may need legal counsel. To avoid unpleasant surprises, consult the appropriate professionals — attorneys, insurance agents and financial lenders — whenever faced with key legal issues such as:

- Easements
- Covenants
- Zoning
- Variances
- Liens
- Subcontractor contracts
- Builder's risk insurance
- Building permits
- Worker's compensation

EASEMENTS

Easements can affect where and what additions you may make to the house. Easements give rights of traverse to local governments (sidewalk easements), utility companies (sewer or power line easements), or to individuals for various reasons. Consult your survey or conduct a title search to reveal any easements presently affecting your property. Make sure any additions you make to the structure do not violate existing easements.

COVENANTS

Covenants are building restrictions, such as minimum square footage or the type and style of construction materials. These restrictions are usually placed on houses in a subdivision by the developer to protect the value of the homes in the subdivision. Ask your lawyer to check for any building restrictions in the public record before purchasing the property. The renovation project you planned may not be allowed by covenant restrictions.

ZONING RESTRICTIONS

Zoning restrictions, like covenants, control the use of, and the type of structures that can be built on, the property. These restrictions are placed by the local government planning board in order to protect land values in the area. Check with your local planning office, which can tell you the zoning or provide you with a zoning map of the county for a nominal fee.

Zoning laws also define the actual area that the structure can occupy upon the lot, that is, the minimum setback, which is the minimum distance the home must be from neighboring homes. There also may be restrictions on the minimum size of your backyard and side yard. Make sure that any planned additions to the house do not encroach on these side yard and backyard setback limits. In many planned subdivisions, these boundaries are strictly enforced to make the homes appear consistent, orderly and planned. To avoid hefty fines and possible reconstruction, it is imperative to acquaint yourself with the baselines and zoning restrictions prior to commencing your remodeling project.

VARIANCES

Variances, when granted, allow you to deviate from standard state and local zoning ordinances within prescribed approved limits. For example, if you want to extend your home to within 30 feet of the front curb, but the local zoning ordinance requires a 40-foot setback, you must apply for a 10-foot setback variance. Unless your request adversely affects neighborhood appearance or safety, your variance usually will be approved.

To obtain a variance, you must apply at the zoning office, paying an application fee. Then, a hearing will be set at which you must appear to describe or illustrate your intentions and the reasons for them. Usually a notice of your variance request will be posted on your lot so that the public is aware of your intention to request a variance and of the date on which the hearing will be held. Anyone has the right to appear at the variance hearing to either support or oppose your request.

LIENS

Liens, because of their potential effect on the remodeling project, are extremely important to a remodeler. A lien is a claim to a portion of the property. For example, if the plumbing contractor does not feel that he was fully paid for his work, he may file a lien against the property. When filed, the lien becomes a matter of public record. It will prevent the sale or mortgaging of the property until the dispute is settled and the lien is released. It is important to note that many states do not require the owner be notified of the lien, so be sure your title search is done carefully to avoid nasty surprises.

If you are contracting the remodeling, you can protect yourself from liens by requiring your suppliers and subcontractors to sign a subcontractor's affidavit. This agreement states that all bills have been paid and that the subcontractor has no legal claim against your property. This will prevent the sub from filing any liens on the property. So, for your protection have all subcontractors with whom you deal sign a subcontractor's affidavit.

SUBCONTRACTOR CONTRACTS

Subcontractor contracts, like affidavits, protect you from surprises. All arrangements must be in writing, no matter how good anyone's memory, reputation or integrity. Subs often develop contract amnesia if a problem arises. Your contract should include job specifications, time frame for completion and a payment schedule. To avoid having to pay for rushed, below standard work, it is wise to include a statement such as "Final payment will be made when work is satisfactorily completed."

BUILDER'S RISK INSURANCE

Builder's risk insurance is another ounce of prevention necessary before starting your project. This insurance will protect you should someone be injured on the building site.

BUILDING PERMITS

Building Permits must be obtained from your city or county building inspector's office before construction can begin. They usually cost a certain amount per $1,000 of construction value or per square foot. Obviously, construction value is somewhat intangible, so you may be forced to accept the authority's estimate of construction value. The permit is usually required even if the remodeling project is only on the interior of the building. Once a permit is issued, the building inspector will schedule the required inspections before, during and after the remodeling project. This permit must be displayed in a prominent location at the site.

WORKER'S COMPENSATION

Worker's compensation is required in every state to provide workers with hospitalization insurance for job-related injuries. This accident insurance must be taken out by any person or company who has employees. Each building trade is assessed an insurance rate depending on the relative risk involved in the work. For instance, roofers are charged a higher rate than trim carpenters. If your remodeling subcontractors do not carry the proper insurance, you may be liable for injuries occurring on your property. So, make sure your subcontractors are properly insured. If any subcontractors carry a policy for their own workers, obtain the policy number and expiration date and call the carrier to verify coverage. Contact your local insurance agent for more information about worker's compensation in your state.

Don't underestimate the importance of this policy. You are liable for any work-related injuries that occur on your property. Without this policy, a negligence lawsuit could deplete your life savings. Look for any situations around the project that could nullify worker's compensation coverage. For example, in some states, drywall subcontractors who use drywall stilts are not covered.

CHAPTER NINE

Purchasing a Fixer-Upper

If you are planning to renovate your existing home, you must work with its existing problems to find the right remodeling solutions. If you are at the purchasing stage, you have the perfect opportunity to find the best possible remodeling potential by using this book as a shopping guide. Use chapter three to carefully examine potential purchases for major remodeling problems. Study your choices carefully. Don't feel that you must jump at the first opportunity. Many good remodeling possibilities exist in most areas.

This chapter covers some of the other factors to consider before purchasing a fixer-upper. The items that make a home desirable all add up to its total value or sale price. These are:

- Land value
- Location of home (proximity to schools, shopping centers and work)
- Status and trend of the neighborhood
- Condition of the site
- Condition of the home
- Suitability for remodeling
- The flavor or romance of the structure
- The functionality of the structure

Many would-be remodelers get caught up in the dream of remodeling and the potential of the structure and fail to pay enough attention to the other livability factors. Make sure your potential purchase meets the following criteria before you even begin to analyze the structure itself.

THE LOT

Study the lot carefully. Make sure to check with the local county zoning officials to determine the lot setbacks and future zoning plans for the neighborhood. Does the yard have enough room for possible expansion of the house? Is there room for a carport or garage on the side or back? Will you be able to socialize in the backyard in relative privacy?

Many old houses have mature trees and bushes that contribute to that "lived in" look. This shrubbery can be very valuable as a buffer zone between your house and the next. Check the condition of these plants to determine if they are in good health. Many older plants encroach on neighboring yards or hang precariously close to the house. They may need to be removed or trimmed. Many older shrubs have reached the age that pruning the plant back to a proper size will risk killing it. If the plants are in healthy condition, they can add significantly to the atmosphere, energy efficiency, and desirability of the lot.

Drainage is also very important. Look for washed out areas around the foundation or driveway. These can become chronic problems that are difficult to repair. Bad drainage can also restrict the location of new construction or cause difficulties during construction. Drainage trenches or washed out areas running across your lot are sure signs of runoff from neighboring yards or, worse, runoff from your yard to neighboring properties. If you find evidence of these, talk with neighbors to get a history of the neighborhood and their reactions to the drainage. You may find that the homeowner's reason for selling is to avoid litigation from neighbors.

If the area has no public sewer, make sure to investigate the condition of the septic tank. Older septic systems are notorious for problems. Ask the seller and neighbors if any drainage problems exist. If you find problems and you are serious about purchasing, consider having the septic tank inspected and a percolation test done. This test determines the capacity of the soil to drain properly and can be administered by local surveyors or city sewage engineers.

LOCATION OF THE PROPERTY

Real estate agents like to say that the three most important factors in choosing a home are "location, location and location." In our increasingly mobile society, the location of your home has become even more important as a buying factor. This can work to your advantage, since older homes tend to be located nearer to metropolitan developments. The most important considerations are the home's proximity to shopping, schools and work. Take a city map and draw a circle around the house you are evaluating at intervals of 1, 5 and 10 miles. If all three activities are located within the 1-mile circle, consider the location to be excellent. If all three activities are located within 5 miles, the location is still good. Activities more than 10 miles away may spell trouble.

The condition of the neighborhood is another vitally important issue. The best location in the city can be ruined if your house is in a run-down or crime-ridden area. Drive around the neighborhood at all times of the day and night. Take notes on the condition of the neighbors' houses. Are they run down or ill kept? Ideally, the neighborhood should be in a condition of improvement, not degradation.

Many older neighborhoods follow a definite aging cycle. During the first few years of development, the neighborhood is at its peak. Age begins to take its toll by the tenth year, and the neighborhood starts downhill as the homes age and become out of style. At some point, however, these homes will begin to rise in value for several reasons. First, when homes reach their lowest level, they have nowhere to go but up. Second, the homes reach an age where they are considered antiques — their out-of-date qualities become quaint reminders of a bygone time. At this stage, usually 30 to 50 years after development, these houses become assets to the community because of their central location. Of course, not all areas experience a rebirth. Some neighborhoods continue the spiral downward until commercial development or condemnation reclaims the land. Judging the direction of the neighborhood takes a keen eye for social trends and attitudes.

Good signs of an area on the rise are:
1. The granting of historical district status to the area or surrounding areas
2. Other remodeled houses or renovation projects in the vicinity
3. A renewed sense of pride in the area, characterized by clean-up projects or other public service projects
4. New shopping developments or school renovations in the surrounding area
5. Resistance of the area to encroachment by commercial or multifamily projects
6. New home or condominium construction on reclaimed property in the area

Look for these signs in your drive-by survey and by research at the local zoning office. These officials know the trends in the local community and are usually happy to share their knowledge.

Danger signals for an area include:
1. Commercial or industrial development nearby.
2. The closing of local schools.
3. The migration of local retail stores to other areas.
4. The proliferation of low income or multifamily developments in and around the area.
5. Excessive parking on the street. Drive by the area at night and on weekends to see if overflow parking occurs from local bars or stadiums.
6. An abnormally large number of for sale signs in the area — evidence that something is scaring away the residents. Many "don't wanter" sales occur because the seller is aware of something that will reduce the value of his property. He or she will do anything to sell the property. Make absolutely sure before purchasing that you know the future of the neighborhood

If a neighborhood has just started its upward trend, you should consider purchasing only if you plan to retain the property long enough for the local property values to escalate. This increase in value will happen slowly. Your safest investment is a run-down property in a neighborhood that is well on its way to recovery. Don't try to be the pioneer who is going to turn the neighborhood around. Remember, pioneers are the ones with the arrows in their backs.

INTERIOR LAYOUT

The pleasure of living in your new home will be greatly affected by its interior layout and appearance. Examine carefully the relationship and convenience of areas to each other, traffic circulation, privacy and room size. Many houses will not lend themselves to an ideal arrangement without excessive cost and restructuring.

The restrictions imposed by load-bearing walls may make it impossible to achieve suitable living conditions without some sacrifice in arrangement.

Traffic Patterns

Observe the circulation and traffic patterns of each room. A floor plan with good circulation should direct traffic flow to one side of the room rather than through its center. Some circulation problems can be improved simply by moving doors to the corners of rooms or by placing furniture to direct traffic where desired.

Kitchen Area

The location of the kitchen in relation to other areas of the house is critical. It should have direct access to the dining area and should be accessible to the garage or driveway for ease in unloading groceries. Being near the utility room is also convenient if you plan to have work in progress in the kitchen and utility room simultaneously. Traffic should not pass through the kitchen work area.

Kitchen size is important. There was a time when small kitchens were thought to be convenient, but with the advent of modern appliances, kitchens now require more space. So, if the kitchen is too small, a major addition or alteration may be necessary.

Private Areas

To ensure privacy, the bedroom and bathroom area should be separated visually and acoustically from the living and work areas of the house. Make sure you can reach the bathrooms without going through any other room and that at least one bathroom is accessible to the work and relaxation areas. One of the basic rules of privacy is to avoid traffic through one bedroom to another. Check the size of the bedrooms. They should have a minimum floor area of 125 square feet for a double bed and 150 square feet for twin beds.

Living Areas

The living areas include the dining room, living room and den. In most older homes, these areas are broken into individual rooms. The den area is usually located at the front of the house, but rooms at the side or rear may be desirable, particularly if they provide a view into a landscaped yard. If the house has adjacent but separate living and dining rooms, see if partitions can be removed for a more spacious feeling. The main entrance is usually at or near the living room. Check for a coat closet near this entrance and a passage into the work area without passing though the living room.

The Effect of Load-bearing Walls

When evaluating the floor plan layout, pay careful attention to the location of load-bearing walls. They are usually located near the center of the structure and support floor or ceiling joists. These walls are difficult and expensive to move, restricting floor plan changes.

APPEARANCE

Taste is so subjective that only basic guidelines can be given. The quaint feel of older houses may be hidden by years of painting and redesigning. Historical homes are in a special category, and professional advice should be obtained for their appraisal.

Look for simplicity and unity of design. Observe the main lines of the house. The house should have simple, classic lines or have a definite historical style. Some variety adds interest, but several rooflines at a variety of slopes create a busy, confused appearance. Strong horizontal lines are usually desirable in a conventional residence to give the appearance of being tied to the ground. Strong vertical lines tend to make a house look tall and unstable.

Unity is as important as simplicity. The house should appear as a unit, not as a cluster of unrelated components. Windows and trim should be in keeping with the house style. Shutters should be half the width of the window so that, if closed, they would cover the window. Porches and garages should blend with the house rather than appear as haphazard, last-minute add-ons. If the dwelling looks unattractive, consider how paint and landscaping may affect it. Even an attractive house can look ugly if improperly painted or landscaped.

APPRAISAL

You should confirm that the appraised value of the property matches the selling price. Houses in older neighborhoods are notoriously hard to price because of the many variables created by their age. What is a fair price? Often, the fair price is one that satisfies to a reasonable degree both the needs of the buyer and the needs of the seller. You, as the buyer or the seller, will want to bring to the bargaining table as much cost information as possible. Although subjective, a reasonable and fair price can be calculated by a professional appraisal.

The Appraisal Professional

Calculating the appraisal value of older properties can be tedious and difficult. Professional appraisers do this for a living and have access to comparable pricing information that makes their work potentially more accurate than that of an amateur. Professional appraisals cost anywhere from $100 to $500, but they can prove invaluable when you are seriously negotiating with a seller. If possible, ask the seller to pay for the appraisal by making the sales contract contingent on a stated value from an appraiser. If you are confident that the appraisal will show a lower value than the asking price, consider bringing the appraisal to the bargaining table as a negotiating tool. Most sellers of older homes find it hard to argue with a professional appraisal. Make sure to hire an appraiser who is a member of a professional appraisal society, such as the American Institute of Real Estate Appraisers or the Society of Real Estate Appraisers. The highest level of designation is the MAI appraiser (Member of the Appraisal Institute).

FLOOR PLAN CHECKLIST

- ☐ There should be unobstructed access to the kitchen from the garage.
- ☐ All bathrooms should be accessible without traveling through another living area (bedroom).
- ☐ The kitchen should be convenient to the living and dining areas for entertaining.

AMENITIES CHECKLIST

- ☐ There should be a location for a garage or carport.
- ☐ There should be two bathrooms or the capability of adding one easily.
- ☐ The house should have central air and heat or the ability to add them.
- ☐ Kitchens and baths should be of modern design and have modern appliances or be conducive to being remodeled.

LOCATION EVALUATION CHECKLIST

Accessibility
- ☐ Distance to nearest school
- ☐ Distance to nearest shopping
- ☐ Distance to metro area or office complex

Strengths
- ☐ Lot is on sewer line. Sewer is in good repair.
- ☐ Landscaping is in good repair. Trees and shrubs are healthy and not too close to home or adjoining lots. Pruning of trees or shrubs is possible without permanent damage.
- ☐ Safe, quiet atmosphere.
- ☐ Clean, well-kept neighboring houses.
- ☐ Higher priced and recently renovated houses nearby.
- ☐ Good drainage from lot and around house.
- ☐ Situated in improving/growth area.
- ☐ Area is zoned exclusively for single family.
- ☐ Underground utilities. Phone, electrical, cable TV.
- ☐ Recreational areas nearby.
- ☐ Sufficient lot clearance for room additions or garage.
- ☐ Adjoining neighbors are friendly and have no complaints about seller.

Weaknesses
- ☐ Sandy or unstable soil base with washouts or signs of erosion. Evidence of recent flooding. Signs of drainage across neighbor's lots from your lot.
- ☐ Property in flood plain. (Check with local authorities for verification.)
- ☐ Area on septic tank. (Ask seller and neighbors if any septic tank problems exist.)
- ☐ On or near major thoroughfare. Future road development nearby.
- ☐ Near airport, railroad tracks, landfill, exposed electric power facilities, industrial areas, or swampy areas (mosquitoes).
- ☐ Steeply sloped lot. Lot slopes toward house. Difficult to mow. Difficult access by car if iced over.
- ☐ Located in or near declining neighborhood
- ☐ Isolated from services/amenities such as shopping, schools, parks.
- ☐ Apartment, commercial, or industrial development prevalent in area.
- ☐ Unfriendly or untidy neighbors
- ☐ Narrow or crowded street. Parking on street.
- ☐ Zoning or deed restrictions prevent improvements to the property.

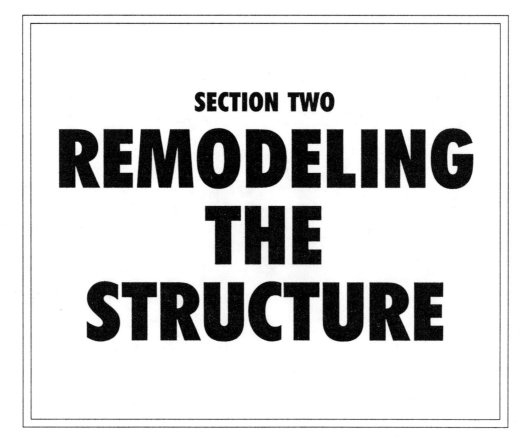

SECTION TWO

REMODELING THE STRUCTURE

CHAPTER TEN

Working With Contractors

The contractors you use are in business for themselves and withhold their own taxes. Your contractors may consist of workers who supply labor only (such as framers and masons) or businesses that provide materials and labor (such as heating and air contractors or remodeling contractors). Use contractors whenever possible to avoid the paperwork headaches that go along with payroll accounting. The IRS may require you to file a 1099 form on your subs. This form shows how much you have paid your subs so that the IRS can be sure that they are paying their share of taxes. Check with the IRS or your accountant to obtain the necessary forms.

REMODELING CONTRACTORS

The remodeling contractor falls into the category of a general contractor. The general contractor serves as the project manager and hires (and pays) all the other subcontractors used on the job. If you decide to hire and control the subcontractors on your own remodeling project, *you become the remodeling contractor*.

If you decide to hire a remodeling contractor for most of your remodeling, you will avoid many hassles of working with subcontractors, controlling records, purchasing and so on. This can be the main reason to use a professional. You may be more than happy to incur the extra expense of a remodeling contractor if you do not have the time or the motivation to manage the project effectively.

On the other hand, if you decide to do the work yourself, your financial rewards will be much greater. You will also need to learn the skills possessed by the remodeling contractor. Look at your present job and what your time is worth. Do you have the extra time and energy to learn new skills, work overtime at night and weekends to finish the job, and schedule subcon-

tractors? If you do, then embarking on the adventure of becoming skilled at a trade can provide a tremendous amount of self satisfaction and financial reward.

One other factor to consider is the complexity of the remodeling project. If you are adding rooms, making massive structural changes, or framing stairways to finished attics, the expertise of the remodeling contractor might be a blessing. A compromise financial arrangement might be to allow the remodeling contractor to take care of the major structural changes while you look after the smaller remodeling projects.

SUBCONTRACTORS

Finding good subs and labor is an art. The following is a surefire list of sources for locating subs and for helping you determine the best combination of skill, honesty and price:

- *Job Sites*. Job sites are an excellent source because you can see their work.
- *The Yellow Pages*. Look under specific titles. Most major remodeling subs advertise here. Expect to be charged a bit more for these subcontractors.
- *Classified Ads*. Many advertisers in the classifieds are part timers or moonlighters. Their rates can be very competitive.
- *On the Road*. Look for phone numbers on trucks. Busy subs are normally good subs.
- *Material Supply Houses*. Many supply houses keep a bulletin board on which subs can leave their business cards.
- *References* from builders and other subcontractors.

References

References are essential in the remodeling business. Nobody can earn a good reputation without showing good work and satisfied customers. Insist on at least three references, one of which should be their last job. If their last reference is 4 months old, it may be their last good reference.

Some people feel that companies that use a person's name as the title, such as "A. J. Smith's roofing," will tend to be a "safe" choice as compared to "XYZ Roofing." The premise is that a person's name follows his or her reputation, but this obviously cannot be taken at face value. Contact references and inspect the work. You may even wish to ask customers what they paid for the job, although sometimes this may be awkward.

Acquiring reference information should be a rule. It is not a bad idea to have your candidate subcontractors fill out a brief form in order for you to find out a little about them. By asking the right questions, you can get a good idea about their character.

Accessibility

It is important to be able to reach your subs. Try not to hire subs that live too far away. If they need to make a quick visit to fix something, if may not be worth their time. Your subs must have a home phone where they can be reached.

Paying Subcontractors

When you have your checkbook out to pay your subs, remember Lester's Law — "The quality of a man's work is directly proportional to the size of his investment." If you want your subs to defy human nature and do the best job possible, then give them motivation. *Do not pay any subcontractor until you are completely satisfied with the work and materials.* Once you have paid, you have killed all incentive for the sub to perform for you. Do not expect to see the sub again. Subs make money by getting lots of jobs done, not by taking lots of time on one job. Always *retain* 10 to 20 percent of the payment due until job completion and inspection. This is called retainage and motivates the subcontractor to return and finish the job. Below is a suggested schedule for payment:

1. 45 percent after rough-in.
2. 45 percent after finish work complete and inspected.
3. 10 percent retainage held for about two weeks after finish work.

This is to protect yourself if something is detected a bit later. Set the terms of payment in writing before you seal the deal.

Paying Cash

Paying with cash gets results. Telling a sub that you will pay in cash upon satisfactory completion of the job should be ample incentive to get the job done. It may motivate the subcontractor to do a good job to boot. Make sure when obtaining cash to pay for any work done that you keep documentation for the IRS. Write a check in the sub's name and have him or her co-sign it. Then, cash the check. In this way you will have an audit trail to prove that you paid the sub for work done.

Be fair with money. Pay the amount you promised. However, be discretionary in your payment schedule. Pay your subs and any contract labor as work is completed. Not everyone can go a week or two without money. It is customary to pay major subs (such as plumbers, HVAC subs and electricians) 40 percent after rough-in and the remaining 60 percent after final inspection and approval. This keeps the pot sweet. If you pay subs too much too early, their incentive to return to complete the work satisfactorily may diminish. If they don't return, you'll have to pay another sub a healthy sum to come in and finish the job. Some subs may not even guarantee work they didn't do completely. The moral of the story is clear: Never pay subs for more than the work that has already been done. Give them a reason to come back.

Specifications

Remember — not written, not said. Don't count on getting anything you don't ask for in writing. A list of detailed specifications reduces confusion between you and your sub and will reduce call-backs and extra costs. Different subs have different ways of doing things. You are paying; so, make sure they do it *your* way.

Paperwork

Many subs live from week to week and despise paperwork. You will have difficulty getting some subs to present bids or to sign affidavits. Many are stubborn and believe that their word is their bond. You must use discretion in requiring these items. Generally, your more skilled trades such as HVAC, electrical and plumbing subcontractors will be more businesslike and will cooperate more fully with your accounting procedures. These trades are the most important from which to get affidavits because they purchase goods from other suppliers that become a permanent part of your house. Labor-only subs need not sign affidavits, if you make sure that they provide you with an invoice for work done and marked "paid in full." This practice will save you many headaches later.

Licenses

Depending upon who does your work, you may want them to furnish a business license. If required, make sure that plumbers, electricians, HVAC subs and other major subs are licensed to work in your county. If they have not obtained the required license, have them do so, or get another sub who is licensed.

Arrangements for Materials

Material arrangements must be agreed upon in a signed, written job order. All arrangements must be spelled out in detail whether your sub is providing all or some materials. If subs are supposed to supply materials, make sure they aren't billing the materials to your account, expecting you to pay for them later. If you are to supply the materials, make sure they are at the site ahead of time and that there is enough material to do the job. This will be appreciated by the subs and will encourage additional cooperation in the future, not to mention a savings to you because less wasted time will result.

Keep Your Options Open

Don't count on any one subcontractor for any task. Have at least one or two backup subs who can fill in when the primary one doesn't show up. It is best to be up front with your primary subcontractors. Let them know that you plan to count on them and expect them to live up to their word. If they can't be there to do the work, skip to your second-string subs without delay.

Be Flexible With Time

Because of variables in weather, subs, and their work, expect some variation in work schedule. Chances are they are doing four or five other jobs simultaneously. Expect some problems in getting the right guy at exactly the right time.

Equipment

Your work specifications should specify that subs are to provide their own tools including extension cords, ladders, scaffolding, power tools, saw horses, and so on. Before hiring, make sure the sub has all the tools. Don't plan on furnishing them. Defective tools that you supply can make you liable for injuries incurred when using them. If you don't have sawhorses available for your framing crew, count on them spending their first 10 minutes cutting up your best lumber to make a few.

Worker's Compensation

Make sure your sub's worker's compensation policy is up to date before the job is started. Get a copy of the insurance binder. Call the carrier to make sure the coverage is still in effect. If the sub doesn't have worker's compensation, make it clear that you intend to withhold a portion of payment to cover the expense. This can be a sore spot later if you forget to arrange this in advance.

The Bidding Process

The steps below apply to the process of reaching final written agreements with your subs.

- Review your project scrapbook and locate potential subcontractors.
- Finalize all design and material requirements affecting each subcontractor.
- Prepare standard specifications for each remodeling job.
- Contact the subcontractor and discuss plans. Mention any forms to be completed and specify the deadline.
- Select the best three bids, based on price and your personal assessment of the sub.
- Compare the bids against your budget.
- Negotiate with prospective subs. Ask them what their best cash price is. When you can't get the price any lower, ask for more services for the same amount of cash.
- Select the subs you plan to use. Make it clear to them that now that they have been selected, they must commit to a specific time frame for completion of your job. Explain that you will be fair with payments but that you expect timely, quality work according to the written agreement.
- Contact subs well in advance of their job and tell them when you expect them at the site. Follow them closely or you will lose them. If your building schedule changes, let the subs know as soon as possible so that they can make other plans. This courtesy will be appreciated and will be returned when you or the subs have last-minute changes.

WORKING WITH MATERIAL SUPPLIERS

Saving Money on Materials

Remodeling provides you with the opportunity to shop around for material bargains. Since most remodeling projects can be planned ahead of time, you will have ample opportunity to accumulate your materials as bargains present themselves. Make sure that all items you choose will work properly together and will provide a uniform and planned look. Remodeling is a huge industry; materials can be purchased from a host of different sources.

Retail Chains

Most large retail chains carry a diverse inventory of remodeling supplies. Many of these supplies are called professional supplies. Unfortunately, they seldom perform up to the consumer's expectations. If you want true professional quality, purchase from suppliers who service the professional community.

Large Building Material Suppliers

These include consumer-oriented and trade-oriented stores. These stores increasingly cater to a mixed clientele of professionals and amateurs. Because of this, good material bargains can be found at these outlets. Dealing with large companies offers the advantage of greater savings because of their ability to purchase material in volume. Large companies may also offer wider selections than their smaller counterparts.

Product Manufacturers

Deal directly with manufacturers when possible. Companies that specialize in windows, doors, carpet, bricks or other items may provide you with merchandise at close to wholesale prices. Be prepared to pick many of these purchases up yourself since delivery may be costly or unavailable.

Use a Limited Number of Suppliers

To reduce confusion and accounting, limit the number of vendors with whom you deal. This will help you get volume discounts because you will be purchasing large quantities.

Set Up Contractor Accounts

Open contractor accounts at your suppliers. Most suppliers offer special discounts for remodelers and professional contractors. You are now a remodeling contractor, so ask for these discounts. Most large material supply houses have special contract sales personnel in the back of the store.

Use "float" techniques as much as possible. Contractor accounts often allow special payment schedules. For example, payment of the open balance may not be due until the first of each month. In this case it would be to your advantage to purchase materials early in the month and gain a full month's use of them before paying for them. The time value of money is on your side. Paying accounts within a specified period is a surefire way to earn early payment discounts. Many suppliers give a percentage discount if full payment is made by the end of the month, the beginning of the month, or within 30 days of purchase. Make sure you take advantage of these discounts; they can really add up. They're money in your pocket.

Shop Carefully

Get several bids on all expensive items or whenever you feel you could do better. The old saying, "Only one thing has one price—a postage stamp," is alive and well in the building material business. Shop around and chances are you'll find a better price. Check with the local builders or remodelers in your area and ask them where they buy their materials.

Sources of Bargains

If you plan to remodel on a regular basis, keep a constant eye out for close-out sales, yard sales, and scratch and dent sales. Many surplus shops buy discontinued items direct from the manufacturers. Often, these items are still in new condition and can be purchased at tremendous savings if picked carefully.

Place an ad in the classifieds for any items you need for a project. Many renovations of older homes require unusual or discontinued items. Quite often, the only way to find these items will be to find other individuals who have collected them.

Drive by projects where older buildings are being demolished. Many older styles of trim, hardwood and antique brick can be salvaged at little or no cost.

Handling Material

Inspect material as it arrives on site and determine what is returnable. If something is damaged or just doesn't look right, insist on having it returned for exchange or credit. This is normal and expected. You're paying good money and should expect quality material in return. Indicate returned items on the bill of lading as proof of return to prevent having to pay for them later.

In the normal course of construction, you will probably order too many of certain items accidentally (or on purpose to avoid delays due to shortages). Find out what overages can be returned to suppliers. For your protection, ask for written return policies. Certain cardboard cartons, seals, wrapping or steel bands may have to be intact for an item to be returnable. There may be minimum returnable quantities; for example, bricks may have to be returned in full skids (1,000 units). Restocking charges may also be incurred when returning materials.

Use Purchase Orders

Manage your purchases with purchase orders. Explain to your suppliers up front that you plan to control purchases this way and that you will not pay any invoice without a purchase order number on it. Purchase orders ensure that you receive and pay for exactly what you ordered, but no more than you ordered. Make sure to use forms with carbon copies. This makes it impossible for someone to create or alter a form. Prenumbered, multipart purchase orders are available at most local office supply stores.

Minimize Inventory

Schedule your material deliveries carefully, to avoid excess materials on site. This is easier said than done. Minimizing the materials on site minimizes your investment and exposure to theft or damage. Most material suppliers will be glad to store purchased items for you and deliver them when you are ready for them. Fragile materials such as doors and windows should not be left lying around too long. These are easily damaged and are the prime targets of theft. Make sure to lock up all movable items in a storeroom or basement.

Have materials dropped close to where they will be used to save time and effort. Bricks, loads of sand and gravel are good examples. Require delivery men to move plywood, drywall and other heavy items up to the second floor if that is where they will be used. Again, make sure to write your delivery instructions and directions to the site on the purchase order.

Keep materials protected from weather by covering them with plastic or keeping them inside whenever possible. Lumber, especially plywood, is susceptible to water damage. Lumber should be covered with heavy-duty plastic and should be ordered shortly before it will be used. Rocks, brick or scrap wood should be used to hold down the plastic on windy days.

CHAPTER ELEVEN

Foundation

Since a sound, repairable foundation is a crucial prerequisite for rehabilitation, massive repairs or replacement should not be necessary. If major repairs are needed, you will almost certainly need professional help. Deciding to make major foundation repairs is a major undertaking, one that may require drastic measures such as jacking up the entire house and installing a completely new foundation. Hopefully this will not be necessary in your case. This chapter concentrates on medium to minor repairs that can be accomplished within the existing structure.

DETERMINE THE EXTENT OF THE DAMAGE

First, you need to inspect the house for any signs of foundation damage. These may include termite infestation, settling or cracking, drainage problems, or water in the basement. Refer to chapter three for more information on sleuthing out these problems. If you find any damage, develop a game plan for fixing it and estimate the time and money involved in repairing it. The additional expense may make your other remodeling plans impractical. Do not continue an extensive remodeling project on an unsound foundation. Your hard-earned efforts can be quickly ruined by additional settling, termite damage, and so on.

Soil Poisoning Around Foundation

Subterranean termites are the only wood-destroying insects that may require preventive measures that go beyond just sound construction techniques. Most new houses have the soil around the foundation treated with a termite poison during the construction of the foundation. On an existing home with a termite problem you may need to treat the soil again to gain additional protection. You will also need to repair any existing damage to the structure.

Studies made by the U.S. Department of Agriculture show that certain chemicals added to the topsoil under buildings or around foundations will prevent or control termite infestation for many years. Specific chemicals to be used for control should be those registered by the Environmental Protection Agency. Every precaution should be taken when using chemicals. You do not want to risk the good health of your family and friends by indiscriminately or improperly applying chemicals to the soil around your home. Be sure to use chemicals exactly in the manner and in the strengths indicated on the container. When you can, it is advisable to have these chemicals applied by a professional exterminator.

Chemicals for termite control are poisonous to people and animals. Be sure to use them properly and safely. Some basic safety rules are (1) Carefully read all labels and follow directions, (2) store insecticides in labeled containers out of reach of children and animals, (3) dispose of empty containers, and (4) wash contaminated parts of your body with warm, soapy water immediately after exposure.

Slab construction. The treatment of soil under slab-on-ground construction is difficult. One method of treatment is to drill holes about a foot apart through the concrete slab next to all cracks and expansion joints and to inject a chemical into the soil beneath the slab. Another method is to drill through the perimeter foundation walls from the outside and force the chemical just beneath the slab along the inside of the foundation and along all cracks and expansion joints.

Houses with crawl space. To treat buildings having crawl spaces, dig trenches adjacent to and around all piers and pipes and along the sides of foundation walls. Around solid concrete foundations the trenches should be 6 to 8 inches in depth and width. The chemical is poured into the trench and as the excavated soil is put back into the trench it is also treated. The soil is tamped and the trench filled to a level above the surrounding soil to provide good drainage away from the foundation.

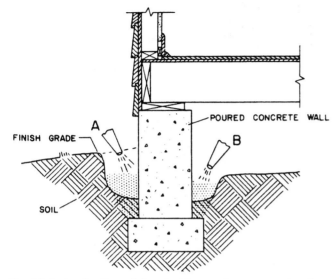

Fig. 11-1. Application of chemical to crawl space construction soil treatment: (A) along outside wall and (B) inside foundation wall.

In brick, hollow-block or concrete foundations that have cracked, dig the trench to, but not below, the footing. Then, as the trench is refilled, treat the soil. Treat voids in hollow-block foundations by applying the chemical to the voids at or near the footing.

Houses with a basement. Application of soil poisoning for houses with basements is much the same as for slab-on-ground and crawl space construction. Treat the basement floor in the same way as a slab-on-ground house.

Cracks in Concrete Foundation

Minor hairline cracks frequently occur in concrete walls during its curing process and usually require no repair. Open cracks should be repaired, but the type of repair depends on whether the crack is active or dormant and whether waterproofing is necessary. One of the simplest methods of determining if the crack is active is to place a mark at each end of the crack and observe at future dates whether the crack extends beyond the marks.

If the crack is dormant, it can be repaired by routing and sealing. Routing is accomplished by following along the crack with a concrete saw or chipping with hand tools to enlarge the crack near the concrete surface. Chisel out the crack ¼ inch or more in width and depth, with the inside of the crack wider than the outside. Then, rinse the joint and allow it to dry. A joint sealer such as an epoxy-cement compound or hydraulic ce-

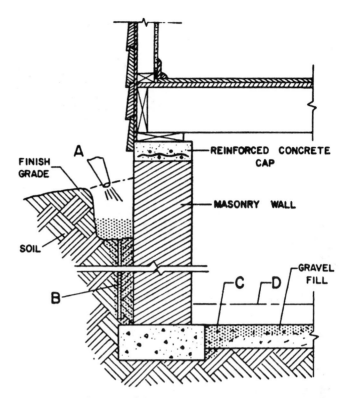

Fig.11-2. Application of chemical to the soil in and around a full basement: (A) soil treatment along outside of the foundation; (B) pipe and rod hole from bottom of trench to the top of the footing to aid distribution of the chemical; (C) drill holes for the treatment of fill or soil beneath a concrete floor in basement; and (D) position of concrete slab.

ment should then be applied according to the manufacturer's instructions. Cover the area with plastic for a few days to allow gradual curing.

Working cracks require an elastic sealant. Sealants vary greatly in elasticity, so a good quality sealant that will remain pliable should be used. The minimum depth and width of routing for these sealants is ¾ inch to 1 inch. The elastic material can then reform with movement of the crack. Strip sealants that can be applied to the surface are also available, but these protrude above the surface and may therefore be objectionable. When applying sealants, always remember to follow the manufacturer's instructions closely.

Crumbling Mortar

Where masonry foundations or piers have crumbling mortar joints, these should be repaired. First, chip out all loose mortar and brush the surface thoroughly to remove all dust and loose particles. Before applying new mortar, dampen the clean surface so that it will not absorb water from the mixture. Mortar can be purchased premixed. It should have about the consistency of putty and should be applied like a caulking material. For a good bond, force the mortar into the crack to contact all depressions. Then, smooth the surface with a trowel. Provide some protection from sun and wind for a few days to keep the mortar from drying out too fast.

Uneven Settlement

Uneven settlement in a concrete foundation may be caused by poor footings or no footings at all. If this type of settling occurs, the foundation is usually too damaged to be repaired. The only alternative in this case would be a complete replacement of the foundation, a very expensive proposition. In a pier foundation the individual pier or piers could be replaced or, if the pier has stopped settling, blocking could be added on top of the pier to level the house. In either situation, the girder or joists being supported must be jacked and held in a level position while the repairs are being made.

Basement Posts

Any type of basement post may have settled due to inadequate footings. Wood posts may have deteriorated due to decay or insect damage. To correct either problem, a well-supported jack must be used to raise the floor girder off the post in question. This releveling must be done slowly and carefully to avoid cracking the plaster in the house walls. Jacking up the house may

take several days to accomplish. Steel jack posts are convenient replacements for the post removed. If a wood post is used, a pedestal should be built to raise the base of the post slightly above the surface of the floor. This allows the end of the post to dry out if it becomes wet.

Excessive Moisture

If you are considering refinishing a basement, your first concern should be the existing moisture condition.

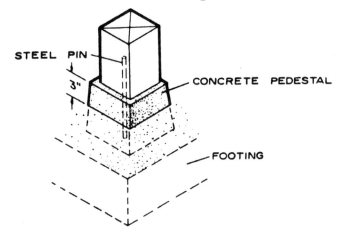

Fig. 11-3. Basement post on pedestal above the floor.

Standing water in the basement or excess dampness can lead to a finished basement that resembles a dungeon more than a living area. Refer to the basement chapter for more information on waterproofing options.

CHAPTER TWELVE

Floor System

The floor system is made up of two major components, the supporting structure of the floor and the floor covering itself. Before you decide to refinish or replace the floor covering, make sure to assess the condition of both components. Installing a new floor covering over warped, squeaky or damaged floor framing members will only create a disappointing job. Any repairs to the foundation will inevitably lead to the need for reinforcing the floor system, which is directly affected by foundation problems.

Check out the existing floor joists and subfloor and make corrections to them to fix sagging and to eliminate squeaks and creaks first. Only then will a new floor covering provide the effect you desire. The quality of your new finish floor will only be as good as the supporting subfloor. A subfloor that is rough, uneven or loose will transmit its problems to the new floor. Make sure to check for broken or rotting lumber and carefully replace it.

CHECKING THE FLOOR FOR SAGGING

A common problem in older houses is the settling and sagging of floor joists and girders. This is usually caused by a combination of settling foundations, inadequate floor joists, old or rotting lumber, or the additional weight being added to the structure (as in adding a new room or finishing an attic). Sagging usually occurs where walls cross floor joists that are unsupported underneath or in the middle of a long span, such as in the middle of the room (see chapter three for more information). Check the floor joists for rotten timbers or gaps between the joist and the subfloor. A sagging floor will be most noticeable on hardwood or tile floors. The hardwood planks will pull apart and separate from the subfloor. Grout between tiles will crack and tiles will delaminate from the mortar.

REPLACING FRAMING MEMBERS

If your examination of the floor framing reveals decay or insect damage in a limited number of framing members, the members affected will have to be replaced or the affected sections repaired. Hopefully, you will have detected any large-scale damage to the floor during the inspection process. If not, the house may not be worthy of rehabilitation. If the damage is the result of rotting or insect damage, replace the damaged members with pressure-treated wood. The chemicals in treated wood protect against rotting and termites. If the framing is just old and not damaged, you can reinforce the structure by attaching a second joist parallel to the existing joist. In either case, the floor must be supported temporarily by jacks while you put the new framing members in place.

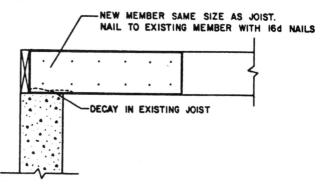

Fig. 12-1. Repair of joist with decay in end contacting the foundation.

Floor jacks can be rented for temporary tasks or can be purchased to provide permanent structural reinforcement. Permanent jacks usually have a telescoping center column that is adjusted to the proper height and held in place with a pin. Wood shims are used to complete the final adjustments. If these jacks are purchased, another jack must be used to actually lift the structure. More expensive jacks have an adjustable built-in screw mechanism that allows fine adjustment.

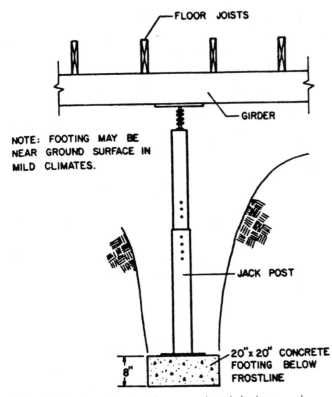

FLOOR JOISTS

NOTE: FOOTING MAY BE NEAR GROUND SURFACE IN MILD CLIMATES.

GIRDER

JACK POST

20" x 20" CONCRETE FOOTING BELOW FROSTLINE

8"

Fig. 12-2. Jack post supporting a sagging girder in a crawl space house.

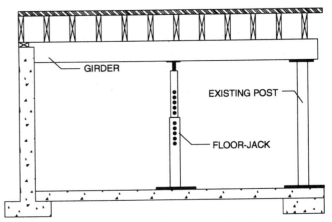

GIRDER

EXISTING POST

FLOOR-JACK

Fig. 12-3. Jack post used to level a sagging girder in a basement house.

When jack posts are used temporarily to carry light loads, they can be set directly on the concrete floor slab. When supporting heavy loads, place a steel plate or length of lumber underneath the jack to distribute the load over a larger area of the floor slab. The jack post should not be used for heavy lifting. Use a heavy-duty jack to carefully lift the load and then put the permanent jack post in place. A heavy girder of lumber or steel can be placed on top of the jack to support several floor joists at once. Where additional support is necessary, more jacks are required. Raise the floor carefully and slowly, just enough to take the weight off the member to be removed. Don't get impatient here. You want to raise the floor a maximum of ¼ inch to ½ inch per day to allow the structure to adjust to the movement. This will prevent further damage to the wall or floors. Excessive movement of the jack will pull the building frame out of square. If the damaged framing member is completely rotten, saw the damaged end off with a reciprocating saw. Attach new end pieces on both sides of the remaining floor member with 16d nails or 3-inch galvanized screws. Make sure to overlap the original framing member at least 4 to 6 feet. After the new or repaired member is in place, gradually take the weight off the jack and remove it.

Sometimes decay affects only a small part of a member. For example, the end of a floor joist supported on a concrete foundation wall could contain decay only where the wood contacts the concrete. After applying a brushed-on preservative to the decayed area, raise the existing joist and nail a short length of new material to the side of the joist. Since this repair occurred because of moist conditions, use pressure-treated wood for the new material.

LEVELING THE FLOOR

If any foundation repairs have been made, the support points for the floor should be level; however, the floor may still sag. A permanent set may have settled in and little can be done except to replace the floor joists. This may be more trouble to fix than it is worth. A slight sag can be repaired by nailing a new joist alongside alternate joists. If the new joists are slightly bowed, install them with the crown up. The floor will have to be raised just enough to allow the new joist to be inserted next to the older one. Once in place, the new joist should be nailed or bolted to the existing joist with lag screws. This dual joist treatment will stiffen springy floors or reinforce an area that must support more weight, such as the attic.

ELIMINATING SQUEAKS

Squeaks in flooring frequently are caused by movement of the tongue of one hardwood flooring strip in the groove of the adjacent strip. The simplest remedy is to apply a small amount of mineral oil to the joints.

Sagging floor joists often pull away from the subfloor and result in excessive deflection of the floor. In this case, the subfloor will actually slide up and down on the flooring nails. If this is the cause of squeaks, squeeze all-purpose construction adhesive into the open joints. An alternate remedy is to drive small wedges into the spaces between joists and subfloor. Drive them only far enough for a snug fit. You can also squeeze flooring adhesive around the wedges to hold them in place. Install flooring screws to pull the joist and subfloor back together. Whenever possible, predrill the screw holes to prevent splitting.

Undersized floor joists that deflect excessively are also a major cause of squeaks. The addition of girders to shorten the joist span is the best solution for that problem.

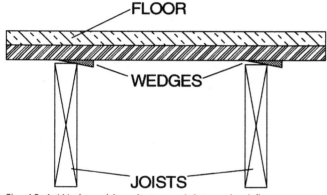

Fig. 12-4. Wedges driven between joists and subfloor to stop squeaks.

Strip flooring installed parallel to the joists may also deflect excessively. Solid blocking nailed between joists and fitted snugly against the subfloor will prevent this deflection if spaced close together.

The most common cause of squeaking is inadequate nailing. To correct this, drive a nail through the face of the flooring board near the tongue edge into the subfloor, preferably into a joist. Set the nail and fill the hole. You can hide the repair by working from underneath the floor and inserting screws through the subfloor into the finish floor. This method will also bring warped flooring into a flat position.

REPLACING OR ADDING A SUBFLOOR

A common problem in bathrooms and kitchens occurs when moisture collects in the area around fixtures and causes the floor to rot. This happens quite often in bathrooms. Condensation from the toilet's water tank or a faulty seal around the toilet will allow water to collect. When this happens, plan to tear up the existing floor and install a new subfloor. This is the only real solution for a rotting subfloor. Although this can be a major undertaking, it has a possible silver lining. If you plan to remodel the kitchen or bath, removing the subfloor gives you easier access to any structural, plumbing or electrical changes that need to be done.

To prevent future problems with rotting, make sure to use ½-inch exterior grade plywood or $\frac{7}{16}$-inch OSB board for the subfloor. OSB stands for oriented strand board and consists of long wood strands oriented in one direction and glued under pressure to create a strong material. The exterior grades of this material are very resistant to moisture and provide a strong, solid floor. Caution: Don't confuse this material with chipboard or particle board, the material used for underlayment. Chipboard does not have the water-resistant and strength properties of OSB and should not be used for subflooring.

UNDERLAYMENT

Before any floor can be installed, a smooth and level base must be prepared. Unless existing wood flooring is exceptionally smooth, it should receive a light sanding to remove irregularities before installing new floor covering. If there is no underlayment, wide joints between floor boards should be filled to prevent them from showing through on the less rigid types of finish floor. An underlayment of plywood or wood-base panel material is required when linoleum or resilient tile is used for the new finish floor.

Underlayment is broadly defined as a nonstructural covering over the subfloor but under the finish floor that provides a smooth surface for the flooring material. When installing a new finish floor, you may want to first install an underlayment over the existing floor or subfloor to provide a smooth surface for the new finish. The underlayment can deaden sound and stiffen the floor as well. The biggest problem with installing underlayment is in keeping the resulting finish floor height from extending above the bottom of doors and existing floors. If the new floor is not too high, you can work around this problem by installing thresholds along the seam between the two floor levels to provide a transition area. Install a layer of roofing felt between the subfloor and the underlayment. This will reduce squeaks and provide a vapor barrier.

Where underlayment is required, use 4 × 8-foot or larger sheets of untempered hardboard, luan, plywood, pressboard or particle board ¼ inch or ⅜ inch thick. Apply nails, staples or screws every 4 inches around the perimeter of the sheet and along floor joists. Some underlayments cannot be used with certain floor coverings, so be sure to check the manufacturer's recommendations before forging ahead with perhaps the wrong underlayment for the floor covering being installed. Ignoring this precaution could nullify the floor-covering warranty.

Underlayment-grade plywood has a sanded surface, with all knots plugged. It is available in interior types, exterior types, and interior types with exterior glue. The interior type is usually adequate, but install exterior grade plywood wherever there is possible exposure to moisture. Use an exterior grade underlayment in the kitchen and bath, especially if you are not replacing the subfloor. Underlayment should be laid with 1/32-inch edge and end spacing to allow for expansion. Nail the underlayment to the subfloor using the type of nail and spacing recommended by the underlayment manufacturer.

If the subfloor surface is especially difficult to get smooth, for instance, rough concrete or well-worn wood planks, you can use flooring concrete. This material is a lightweight gypsum-based concrete that flows evenly across the floor and will find its own level. It will level out a sagging floor and provide a very smooth and solid surface for almost any floor covering. You must make sure that your subfloor is very solid and rigid to use this method. A springy or loose floor will cause the surface to crack over time. This material will also raise the level of the floor substantially.

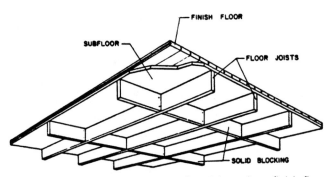

Fig. 12-5. Solid blocking between floor joists where finish floor is laid parallel to joists.

Wood flooring, sheet vinyl with resilient backing, seamless flooring and carpeting can all be installed directly over the old flooring after major voids are filled and the surface sanded smooth. These coverings can also be installed over old, firmly attached resilient tile.

NEW FLOOR COVERING

Floor covering is available in a variety of materials. The most widely used floorings include:

- Carpet
- Hardwood strips (finished and unfinished)
- Wood tiles (parquet)
- Vinyl floor covering
- Ceramic tile or stone
- Sheet vinyl
- Resilient tile

The material selected depends on existing conditions, the planned use of the floor, and your budget.

Wood Flooring

Hardwood flooring is measured by the board foot (oak or other plank flooring) or by the square yard (parquet). Oak is laid in tongue-and-groove strips nailed to the subfloor, stained and sealed. Parquet is normally installed as 6-inch squares with an asphalt adhesive. Parquet squares are available in stained and unstained styles. Avoid laying hardwood floors in humid weather because when the air dries out, gaps will appear between the boards. Buy the flooring a week or two before it is needed and store it in the rooms where it will be laid to let the moisture content stabilize.

After installation you may want to sand the floor for an extra smooth finish. Pine flooring normally isn't sanded after installation. On all other wood floors, sanding should be done only with the grain, or sanding marks will show up. Use a professional-sized drum sander. An edger should be used to sand the edges. If you lay hardwood floors on a concrete slab, you need to seal the concrete and use a concrete adhesive. A better method would be to lay down runner strips and nail the floor to the strips. Wood strip floor installers usually work as a pair. One nails strips in place while the other saws pieces to the proper length and sets them in place. If you can avoid it, do not lay wood floors on slabs.

Hardwood flooring is available in strip or block and is usually tongued, grooved and end matched, but it may be square-edged in thinner patterns. The most common pattern of hardwood strip flooring is 25/32 inch by 2¼ inches with a hollow back. Strips are random lengths varying from 2 to 16 feet. The face is slightly wider than the bottom so that tight joints result.

Softwood flooring is also available in strip or block. Strip flooring has tongue-and-grooved edges; some types are also end matched. Softwood flooring costs less than most hardwood species, but it is less wear resistant and shows surface abrasions more readily. It can, however, be used in light traffic areas.

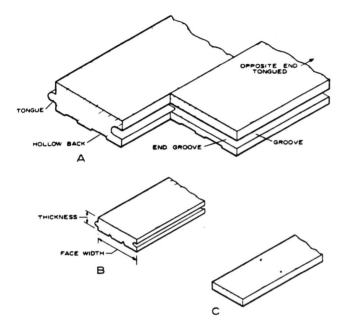

Fig. 12-6. Strip flooring: (A) side and end matched; (B) side matched; (C) square edged.

Square-edged strip flooring must be installed over a substantial subfloor and can only be face-nailed. The installation procedures concerning spacing at walls, spacing of joints and general attachment are the same as those for matched flooring.

Wood Tile – Parquet

Most wood or wood-base tile is applied with an adhesive to a smooth base such as underlayment or finished concrete with a properly installed vapor barrier. Wood tile may be made up of a number of narrow slats held together by a membrane, cleats or tape to form a square. It also may be plywood with tongue-and-grooved edges. To install wood tile, spread the adhesive on the concrete slab or underlayment with a notched trowel and lay the tile in it. Follow the manufacturer's recommendation for adhesive and method of application.

Wood block flooring usually has tongues on two edges and grooves on the other two. It is usually nailed through the tongue into a wood subfloor. It may be applied on concrete with the use of an adhesive or floated over the slab on wood strips called runners (see basement chapter). The effects of shrinkage and swelling are minimized by changing the grain direction of alternate blocks.

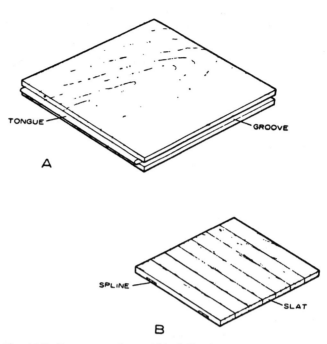

Fig. 12-7. Two types of wood block flooring.

Sheet Vinyl

Sheet vinyl with resilient backing smooths out minor surface imperfections and has become one of the most popular floor coverings in kitchens and baths. Most vinyl will lay flat, so a strong adhesive is not required. A stronger adhesive and a seam cement is used at joints and around the edge to keep the seam from coming loose. Vinyl rolls are wide enough so that entire rooms can be covered without seams. Most sheet vinyls are available in widths of 6, 9, 12 and 15 feet. This permits a fast, easy installation. The material is cut to room size using scissors or a knife.

Vinyl floor covering is measured by the square yard or roll length and comes in a variety of styles and types. Padded vinyl rolls have become very popular because of their ease of installation and maintenance. Installation procedures vary depending on the material and manufacturer, so take care to follow the manufacturer's recommendations when installing. Warranties can be voided if the material is not installed properly.

When installing vinyl floors, consider laying an underlayment over the area to be covered. This additional layer provides a smoother surface for the floor and brings the level of the floor up to the same level as any surrounding carpet.

Resilient Tile

Resilient tiles comes in several types of material, such as vinyl, vinyl-asbestos, rubber and cork, and are available in squares of 9 or 12 inches. Most resilient tile is applied with a floor adhesive, but some types come with a peel-and-stick adhesive back for quick and easy installation. Resilient tile requires a smooth surface—either an underlayment or a concrete slab. Square tiles make an attractive and durable floor covering. They are easy to install and make good do-it-yourself projects. Resilient tiles provide a great opportunity for imaginative floor designs by using several different color tiles to develop artistic patterns and shapes. Tiles may be alternated in a diagonal pattern or used to create a border effect around the edge of the room. This can increase the perceived size of the room. In a bathroom, the pattern could be used to match a pattern in the wall tile.

If you are installing square tiles in an out-of-square room, the straight lines will accentuate the out-of-square condition. One way to avoid this is to use a tile pattern that is diagonal to the walls. This will mask the out-of-square condition. Take care—laying out a good diagonal pattern is more difficult and requires careful planning. Make sure that the tile is installed so that its joints do not coincide with the joints of the underlayment. The manufacturer's directions usually include instructions on laying baselines near the center of the room and parallel to its length and width. The baselines are then used as a starting point in laying the tile.

Carpet

Carpeting is an excellent floor covering to use in remodeling. It can cover a multitude of sins. It is easily installed over almost any flooring that is level, relatively smooth, and free from major surface defects. Carpeting is now available for all rooms in the house, including the kitchen, where close weaves are used so that spills stay on the surface and are easily wiped up. The cost of carpeting may be two or three times that of a finished wood floor; its life, however, is much shorter. On the other hand, some advantages of carpeting include less maintenance, sound absorption and resistance to impact.

Carpet is measured, purchased and installed by the square yard and comes in rolls 12 feet wide. Do not try to install carpet yourself unless you have experience; it is not as easy as it appears. Carpet should be installed with a foam pad, which adds to the life of the carpet and makes the carpet feel more plush. A stretcher strip is nailed around the perimeter of the room and the carpet is stretched flush with the wall. Stretching the carpet prevents it from developing wrinkles. After two to three months, the carpet may need to be stretched again. Make sure your carpet company will agree to do this at no cost. When pricing carpet, always get the installed price with the cost of the foam pad included. A thicker foam pad will make your carpet feel more luxurious but may cost extra. Make sure that all bumps and trash have been cleaned from the floor before installation. Even the smallest bump will be noticeable through the carpet after installation.

Tile

Ceramic tile is a versatile and highly durable surface appropriate for floors, bathroom walls, and countertops. The application techniques are similar in all three cases. Tile for flooring usually comes in larger sizes than for wall installation and can consist of several types of material. True ceramic tiles come in glazed and unglazed types and can be made from porcelain, clays, quarry tile, and other clay-like substances. Soft rocks such as slate and granite can also be cut into tile-size squares and used in the same manner. Almost all types are installed using similar techniques. The stone-based tiles are usually more easily scratched than the harder ceramic-based products.

Countertop tiles are usually glazed porcelain and come in 1- to 6-inch squares. Tile is measured and sold by the square foot, although tile units can come in any size. Floor tile can be installed over a wood subfloor, although a special adhesive cement and latex grout must be used. Consider using a colored grout that can hide dirt. If you coat the tile grout with a protective coating, you may void the tile warranty.

Tile installation is a tedious procedure and requires special tools to cut and shape the tiles. Unless you are a patient do-it-yourselfer, consider using a tile sub for this job. Make sure your tile sub is experienced and quality conscious. Improper installation can result in buckling, cracking and delamination. To insure that tiles adhere properly, avoid installation in cold weather or make sure that the floor is heated for 24 hours after installation.

Colored grouts add a special touch without adding to costs. Don't bother with a colored grout unless the joint is at least 1/8-inch wide. You may wish to use a grout additive instead of water. This will strengthen the grout and bring out the color. To save time, also consider using a special protective coating applied to tile prior to grouting. This will allow you to wipe the grout film off the tile easily when the job is done.

If you plan to install tile in kitchens or other large areas, check the height of the installed floor (tile and mortar bed) to ensure that you aren't higher than the adjoining carpet or hardwood floors. This becomes even more critical if you are installing a new subfloor.

Remember that you have a half-inch fudge factor around floor perimeters if you use shoe molding. If you tile yourself, ask your supplier to loan or rent you a tile cutter with a new blade or buy a new blade. This will make a world of difference.

Tiling shower and bath stalls is trickier than tiling floors. You may want to do the floors, but hire a sub for the rest. Use spacers when tiling the floor to keep the tiles straight. If you insist on doing the work yourself, follow the directions carefully and be patient. Since you are the owner, and speed is not important, you have the potential to do a better tile installation than a subcontractor. New consumer-oriented tile products are now available to make the installation easier. These include 1-inch tiles bonded to a plastic net and tiles prebonded with a plastic grout in 1 foot squares. These make spacing and installation faster and easier

FLOOR FRAMING STEPS

1. Inspect floor framing and subfloor for rotting, termites, warping, squeaking and inadequate support.

2. Conduct standard bidding process for repair of any structural repairs to the floor framing. Make sure to include the cost of concrete if permanent jacks are installed. Since the jack is supporting the weight of the house, it must rest on a solid foundation below the frost line, just like the regular foundation.

3. Purchase and store new framing members, if any. Purchase concrete or steel plates for installation of permanent jacks.

4. Pour concrete piers for permanent floor jacks, if needed. Allow 2 to 5 days for curing. Make sure to locate piers below the frostline for your area. Since the concrete pier is not tied into the regular foundation, it must be stable and protected from settling. Make sure that any hole dug for the pier does not become a drainage site for water. This can cause the pier to wash out underneath and settle.

5. Rent or purchase floor jacks and steel I beams for support of floor. Jack up the structure slowly to prevent further warping or cracking.

6. Replace damaged floor joists and slowly lower the floor.

FLOORING STEPS

1. Select floor covering brands, styles, colors and coverage. This includes all carpet, padding, hardwood, vinyl, and so on. Keep different styles and colors to a minimum. This helps your buying power, minimizes scrap, and provides for easier resale.

2. Select tile brands, styles, colors and coverage, including tile for bath walls, bath floors, shower stalls, patios and kitchen countertops. Once your subfloor is in, borrow about a square yard of your favorite tile from your supplier. Lay it down where it will be used and see how it looks.

3. Conduct standard bidding process. For best prices on carpet, go to a carpet specialist or carpet mill. When possible, have the supplier bid for material and labor. If your supplier does not install, ask for installer references.

4. Order hardwood flooring. Hardwood flooring should remain in the room in which it will be installed for several weeks in order for it to expand and contract based on local humidity conditions. You may want to order a few extra bundles of shorter, cheaper lengths to do closets and other small areas.

5. Remove old flooring. Remove base trim and quarter-round trim. To remove sheet flooring, start in a corner and peel up the material. Disconnect carpet from the stretcher strips. Pull up the carpet strips unless you plan to re-cover the floor with carpet. To remove strip flooring, look for the side where the original flooring was nailed from the top and pry loose with a crowbar. This will allow you access to the blind nails. Pry off the rest of the strips. To remove a tile floor, crack a tile in the center of the room with a hammer and remove the pieces. Then you can work outward, prying up each tile from the grout. To remove resilient tile or linoleum, aim a blowtorch or heat stripper at the tile and work under it with a putty knife. Always remove as much of the adhesive as possible. Sand the remaining residue until smooth and level.

6. Replace damaged subfloor. Replacement of framing and subfloor may be done simultaneously to ease the installation of framing members and ensure a good fit. This is also a good time to run new electrical and plumbing fixtures.

7. Remove all trim, appliances and plumbing fixtures. If you are replacing only a small portion of the subfloor, cut out the damaged section with a reciprocating saw. Make sure the new plywood is the same thickness as the existing floor or plan to cover the lower area with a thin underlayment. Make sure the replacement piece meets the other subfloor material on the top of a floor joist. If this is not possible, install blocking between the joists at the seam to provide a solid surface for the subfloor edge. If you are replacing the entire subfloor, cut out the existing floor flush with the walls (with the trim removed). You can leave a small gap for expansion at the wall, since it will be covered by trim. Make sure to caulk the gap if the underlying area is crawl space.

8. Sand and clean the subfloor to remove any high spots. If necessary, rent a floor sander to smooth out uneven or cupped floor boards. Check the existing floor to make sure it is firmly attached to the framing. If not, reanchor the floor with ridged flooring nails or preferably flooring screws.

9. Install underlayment if needed. Use a waterproof underlayment in kitchen and bath areas. Start by covering the existing subfloor with strips of 15-pound roofing felt. Butt each strip up against its neighbor, gluing each strip down with flooring mastic. Make sure to work from the center and roll out any air bubbles.

Lay out the underlayment so that its seams fall between the seams of the subfloor to provide the smoothest surface. Nail along the center and edge of the underlayment every 4 inches with underlayment nails, staples or screws. Make sure to use fasteners long enough to pass through the subfloor and into the floor joist below. Fill any seams and nail holes with an approved flooring mastic to provide a smooth seamless surface. Do not use plaster since it will not hold up under heavy foot traffic.

HARDWOOD FLOOR FINISHING STEPS

1. Rent or purchase a floor sander, edge trimmer or random orbit sander if needed for finishing the hardwood floor.

2. Prepare the underlayment for hardwood flooring. Make sure that all dirt and drywall compound are thoroughly cleaned off the floor. The surface must be totally clean and level. If you are laying hardwood on a slab, you have two choices:

Seal the slab with a liquid sealer and install flooring with an adhesive.

Prepare a "sleeper" subfloor:

a. Sweep slab.

b. Apply $1'' \times 2''$ treated wood strips called bottom sleepers with adhesive and 1½-inch concrete nails, 24 inches apart, perpendicular to the oak strips.

c. Lay 6-mil poly vapor barrier over strips.

d. Lay a second layer of $1'' \times 2''$ wood strips over the vapor barrier.

e. Nail wood flooring strips to the sleeper strips.

3. Layout the hardwood flooring. Wait until all drywall and painting work is complete before installing hardwood. This will protect the finish. Hardwood strips are installed perpendicular to the floor joists. However, when installed over old strip flooring, they should be laid perpendicular to the existing flooring. Lay out all the strips loosely so that you can arrange the various lengths for the most pleasing effect. Stagger the ends of the planks so that they don't all line up in a row. Save the best planks for the center of the room and place less desirable planks along the walls where they will be covered by furniture.

4. Install the hardwood flooring. Begin installing matched flooring by placing the first strip ½ inch to ⅝ inch away from the wall to allow for expansion along with changes in moisture content. Nail straight down through the board near the grooved edge. The nail should be close enough to the wall to be covered by the base or shoe molding. It should be driven into a joist when the flooring is laid perpendicular to the joists. The remaining strips are blind nailed into the wood below by driving the nail into the tongue at an angle of 45 to 50 degrees. The nails are not driven completely flush, to prevent damaging the edge with the hammer head. Countersink the nail with the end of a large nail set. Contractors use nailing devices designed especially for flooring. Many flooring suppliers provide these tools for home installation. Nail sizes and types vary with the thickness of the flooring. For ²⁵/₃₂-inch flooring, use 8d flooring nails; use 6d flooring nails for ½-inch flooring, and use 4d casing nails for ⅜-inch flooring. Other nails,

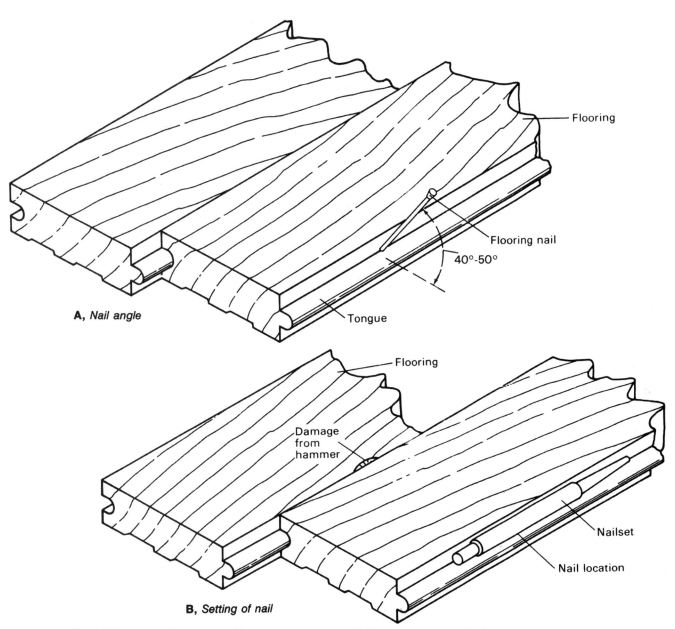

A, Nail angle

Flooring

Flooring nail

40°-50°

Tongue

B, Setting of nail

Flooring

Damage
from
hammer

Nailset

Nail location

Fig. 12-8. Nailing of flooring: (A) angle of nailing; (B) setting the nail without damage to the flooring.

such as the ring-shank and screw-shank types, can be used, but it is always wise to check the flooring manufacturer's recommendations. Flooring brads with blunted points that prevent splitting of the tongue are also available.

The last course of flooring should be left ½ inch to ⅝ inch from the wall, just like the first course. Face-nail it near the edge where the base or shoe will cover the nail. Crooked boards should be forced into alignment or cut off and used at the ends of a course or in closets. If you hire floor installers, ask them to leave some scraps. Store them for repair work or other use.

5. Sand the hardwood flooring. Although most floors are presanded, you may still need to have them sanded

for the smoothest possible finish. Sand only with the grain. Cross-grain sanding will show up as soon as stain is applied. Once floors are sanded, there should be no traffic until after the sealer is dry. Lay down vinyl walking strips or carpet strips if you must walk through the area.

6. Inspect the hardwood flooring. Refer to specifications and inspection guidelines.

7. Correct any problems with the hardwood flooring. Common problems are split strips, hammer dents in strip edges, uneven spacing, gaps, squeaks, nonstaggered joints, and last strip not parallel with wall. Make sure to watch the installation closely. It's almost impos-

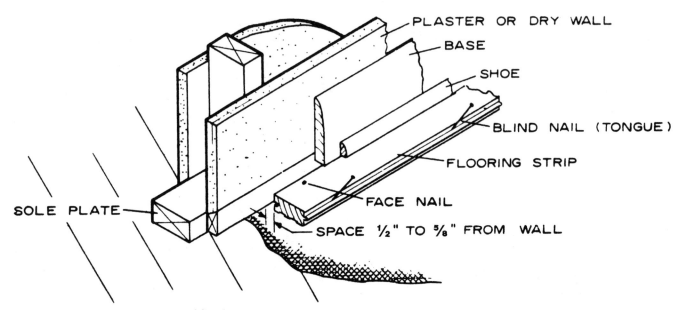

PLASTER OR DRY WALL
BASE
SHOE
BLIND NAIL (TONGUE)
FLOORING STRIP
FACE NAIL
SPACE ½" TO ⅝" FROM WALL
SOLE PLATE

Fig. 12-9. Installation of first strip of flooring.

sible to fix one tongue-and-groove plank in the middle of a room.

8. Stain the hardwood flooring. The floors must be swept completely clean before this step is performed. Close windows if it is dusty outside.

9. Seal the hardwood flooring. Polyurethane is the most popular sealant. You normally have an option of either gloss or satin finish. Place construction paper over dry floors to protect them from foot traffic.

10. Inspect the hardwood flooring again, this time primarily for finish work.

11. Pay the hardwood flooring sub, requiring a signed affidavit.

12. Pay the hardwood flooring sub retainage.

VINYL FLOOR INSTALLATION STEPS

1. Prepare the subfloor for vinyl floor covering. Sweep the floor clean and nail down any last squeaks with ringed nails. Plane down any high spots.

2. Purchase vinyl flooring. Make sure all the material comes from the same roll of vinyl. Sheets from two different rolls may not match exactly in color and texture.

3. Measure the floor for installation and determine the best fit for the vinyl. Try to use only one solid piece of material if possible. Graph the dimensions of the room to scale on a piece of graph paper and transfer the measurements to the back of the vinyl sheet. Draw

chalk lines along these measurements and cut the material, leaving an extra 2 inches around the lines outside of the lines. Snap a chalk line wherever a seam exists.

4. Lay out the vinyl in place. If you have a seam between two pieces, line up the seam on the chalk line, making sure that the two pieces overlap at least an inch. Note: If you have a pattern in the vinyl, try to position the seam along a straight line in the pattern so that the resulting seam will be less noticeable.

5. Trim the excess material where the vinyl meets walls and counters.

6. Install vinyl floor covering by rolling back each sheet and applying the factory-approved floor adhesive with an adhesive spreader. Roll the vinyl back out onto the adhesive carefully, smoothing out any wrinkles.

7. Cut any adjoining seam by overlapping both sheets of vinyl and cutting through both pieces simultaneously with a hog-nosed knife. This will insure that the two seams match exactly. Apply the special seam adhesive to the underside of the vinyl, about 3 inches on either side of the seam. This stronger adhesive insures that the seam will stay anchored to the floor. Carefully run a thin bead of seam cement between the gap between the two pieces of vinyl. This final adhesive bonds the edges of the vinyl together and creates a virtually seamless installation. Carefully wipe up any excess glue.

8. Install door and carpet thresholds. Ask installers to leave behind any large scraps of vinyl that can be used later for repair work.

9. Inspect the vinyl floor covering. Refer to specifications and inspection guidelines. Let the floor dry for a day or two before allowing foot traffic.

10. Correct any problems with the vinyl floor.

11. Pay the vinyl floor covering sub, requiring a signed affidavit.

12. Pay the vinyl floor covering sub retainage.

TILE INSTALLATION STEPS

1. Purchase tile and grout. If you do the job yourself, borrow or rent a tile cutter from the tile supplier or rental company. Look for good bargains on seconds—tile with slight imperfections—to use as cut pieces. Don't use sanded grout with marble tiles. The sand will scratch the marble surface. Make sure that all tile comes from the same batch. Tile colors can vary from batch to batch.

2. Prepare the area to be tiled. Sweep the floor clean and nail down all squeaky floor areas with ridged nails. If you have tile in the kitchen, do not tile under the floor cabinets or the island. Snap a chalk line down the middle of the room and another chalk line perpendicular to it across the room. The two lines should form a cross. Using these two lines, lay out a course of tiles in both directions using tile spacers to determine the layout and spacing of each tile. Measure the position of the first row of tiles against one wall and nail down a board to use as a backstop.

3. Apply tile adhesive and tiles. Use a trowel with grooves suitable for your tile and grout. Use large curved, sweeping motions and cover a small area at a time. Press the tile into the adhesive gently. Start in one corner and work down one wall and across the room. Make sure tubs are securely in place before placing tiles. Make sure to save a few extra tiles in case of subsequent damage to floor tiles. This will ensure a perfect color match if repairs are needed.

4. Install tile base in shower stalls. This normally involves applying concrete over a wire mesh on top of the shower pan. The tiles are usually set in a bed of mortar instead of using tile adhesive, partly because the floor of the shower must be sloped for proper drainage into the drain. The mortar is easy to shape into a sloped surface. It also provides a very strong base that will withstand a lot of use. Because of the skill needed for this job, consider using a tile subcontractor. Prior to tiling around a whirlpool tub, make sure the tub is secure and has been fully wired, grounded and plumbed.

5. Install wall and counter tile. Since wall tiles can settle, make sure to use removable tile spacers or tiles that have been preattached to a net backing. This assures accurate spacing.

6. Cut odd shaped tiles with tile cutter or tile snips. Snips will work for small counter tiles, but a tile cutter is recommended for larger floor tiles.

7. Install tile and marble thresholds.

8. Apply grout over tile. After the adhesive has dried for 24 hours, remove the spacers and apply the grout.

9. Apply silicone sealant between the tub and tile.

10. Inspect the tile. Refer to specifications and inspection criteria.

11. Correct any problems that need fixing.

12. Seal grout. This should be done only after grout has been in place for about 3 weeks. Use a penetrating sealer to protect the grout from stains.

13. Pay the tile sub, requiring a signed affidavit.

14. Pay tile sub retainage after floor has proven to be stable and well glued.

CARPET INSTALLATION STEPS

1. Prepare the subfloor for carpeting. Sweep the floor clean and nail or plane down any high spots. This is your last chance to fix squeaky floors easily and install hidden speaker wires. Carpet installation is a tricky operation best suited to professional installers. Carpet seams are difficult to cut and glue effectively. Consider using the carpet supplier's recommended installers for this job.

2. Install carpet stretcher strips.

3. Install carpet padding. Use an upgraded pad if you use a tongue-and-groove subfloor.

4. Install carpet using a carpet stretcher to get a professional job. The stretcher pulls the carpet tightly over the stretcher strips, which dig in and hold the carpet in place. Ask the installer to leave larger scraps for future repair work.

5. Inspect the carpet. Refer to specifications and inspection guidelines.

6. Correct any problems with carpeting installation. Most carpet will stretch more in the ensuing months. Get your carpet installer to agree to return in a few months at no charge to restretch the carpet.

7. Pay the carpet sub, requiring a signed affidavit.

8. Pay carpet retainage.

FLOORING SPECIFICATIONS

Carpet
- Full-size upgraded pad is to be provided and installed under all carpet.
- Stretcher strips are to be installed around carpet perimeters.
- All seams should be invisible. (This is critical to a good carpet job.) Seams should be located in inconspicuous and low-traffic areas.
- All major carpet and padding scraps should remain on site.
- All necessary thresholds should be installed.
- All work is to be performed in a professional manner.
- Installer agrees to restretch carpet in 2 months at no charge.
- Carpet is to be top-grade stain-resistant quality free of chemical irritants.

Oak Flooring
- Bid is to provide and install "select and better" grade flooring free from blemishes and knots.
- Best pieces are to be installed in most visible areas.
- Planks should be blind nailed and free from gaps and cracks.
- Oak strips should be single width, 3¼-inch strips.
- Two perpendicular layers of heavy gauge paper should be installed between subfloor and oak flooring.
- All oak strips should be nailed in place with flooring nails at a 45 degree angle. Nails should be installed only with a nailing machine to prevent hammerhead damage to floor.

- Shorter lengths should be used in closets.
- All oak strips should be staggered randomly so that no two adjacent joint ends are within 6 inches of each other.
- Oak flooring and oak staircase treads to be sanded to a smooth surface.
- Oak flooring and oak staircase treads should be swept, stained, sealed and coated with satin finish floor grade polyurethane.
- Stain should be a medium brown.
- Ridged or spiral flooring nails should be used exclusively.
- Only the first and last strip should be surface-nailed, concealable by shoe mold.

Parquet Flooring
- Bid is to provide and install parquet flooring in the following areas: (list rooms in which it is to be installed).
- Parquet flooring should be stained and waxed.
- Parquet should be installed with grain of adjacent tiles perpendicular.

Vinyl Floor Covering
- All seams should be invisible.
- All seams should be edge glued with factory approved seam adhesive.
- All major scraps should remain on site.
- All necessary thresholds should be installed.
- All seams should be pattern matched.
- All vinyl should come from the same factory roll.

Tile
- Master bath shower stall walls should include one course of curved base tile around perimeter. Tile should go all the way to ceiling.
- Master bath shower floor should be installed over approved shower pan with ¼ inch per foot slope toward drain.
- Kitchen floor should have tan grout sealed with grout sealer.
- Bath floor should have white grout sealed with grout sealer. There should be one course of base tile around perimeter.
- Grout colors should be as specified by owner.
- All necessary soap dishes, tissue holders, towel racks and toothbrush holders should be supplied and installed in white unless otherwise specified by owner in writing.

- Matching formed base and cap tiles should be used as needed to finish edging and corners.
- All necessary tub and shower drains should be installed.
- All grout should be sealed three weeks after grout is installed.
- Extra tile and grout should remain on site.

FLOORING INSPECTION

Carpet
- ☐ Proper carpet is installed.
- ☐ No visible seams.
- ☐ Carpet is stretched tightly and secured by carpet strips.
- ☐ Colors match as intended. Watch for color variations.
- ☐ Carpet installed on stairs fits tight on each riser.

Oak Flooring and Parquet
- ☐ Proper oak strips and/or parquet installed. (Make, color, etc.)
- ☐ No flooring shifts, creaks or squeaks under pressure.
- ☐ Even staining and smooth surface.
- ☐ No scratches, cracks or uneven surfaces. Scratches normally indicate sanding across the grain or using too coarse sandpaper for final pass.
- ☐ Smaller lengths used in closets to reduce scrap and waste.
- ☐ All necessary thresholds are installed and are parallel to floor joints.
- ☐ Only edge boards have visible nails. No other boards have visible nails.
- ☐ Edge boards are parallel to walls. Edge board nails covered by trim.
- ☐ No irregular or excessive spacing between boards.
- ☐ No floor registers covered up by flooring.

Vinyl Floor Covering
- ☐ Proper vinyl floor covering is installed. (Make, color, pattern, etc.)
- ☐ Vinyl floor covering has smooth adhesion to floor. No bubbles.

- ☐ No movement of flooring when placed under pressure.
- ☐ No visible or excessive seams.
- ☐ No scratches or irregularities. No dents or cuts from appliance installation.
- ☐ All necessary thresholds have been installed and are parallel to floor joints. Carpet threshold installed and tight against carpet.
- ☐ All necessary thresholds are of proper height for effective door operation. No more than ⅛-inch gap under interior doors.
- ☐ Pattern is parallel or perpendicular to walls as specified.

Tile
- ☐ Proper tiles and grouts are installed. (Make, style, dimensions, color, pattern, etc.)
- ☐ Tile joints are smooth, evenly spaced, parallel, and perpendicular to each other and walls where applicable.
- ☐ Tiles are secure and do not move when placed under pressure.
- ☐ No scratches, cracks, chips or other irregularities.
- ☐ Grout is sealed as specified.
- ☐ Grout lines parallel and perpendicular with walls.
- ☐ Tile pattern matches artistically.
- ☐ Cut tile pieces on opposite sides of the room are of the same size.
- ☐ All tile cuts are smooth and even around perimeter and floor register openings.
- ☐ Marble thresholds are installed level with no cracks or chips.
- ☐ Marble thresholds parallel with door when closed.
- ☐ Metal thresholds installed between tile and wood joints.
- ☐ Marble thresholds are at proper height.
- ☐ Matching formed tiles used at base of tile walls as specified.
- ☐ Cap tiles used at top of tile walls.
- ☐ Proper tile edging for tubs, sinks and shower stalls.
- ☐ No cracked or damaged tiles.
- ☐ Tile floor is level.
- ☐ Extra tile and grout available on site.

FLOORING MATERIAL ESTIMATE

DESCRIPTION	SPECIFICATION	QTY.	UNIT	COST	TAX	TOTAL COST	COST TYPE	VENDOR
Floor Framing								
Floor joists 16 inches O.C.								
Sill plates								
Nails								
Stove bolts — joists								
Joist hangers								
Steel I-beam girder								
Floor jacks — permanent								
Floor jacks — rental								
Foundation — concrete, bags								
Contract labor — floor repair								
Subfloor								
Sub floor sheathing ¾-inch 4′ × 8′ sheets								
Flooring nails — ring shank								
Flooring screws								
Underlayment — 4′ × 8′ sheets								
Underlayment mastic								
Felt paper — 15 pound								
Trim								
Trim base — ranch								
Trim quarter round								
Carpet								
Carpet, 24-ounce nylon								
Carpet pad								
Carpet stretcher strips								
Nails — strips								
Contract installation — carpet								

FLOORING MATERIAL ESTIMATE

DESCRIPTION	SPECIFICATION	QTY.	UNIT	COST	TAX	TOTAL COST	COST TYPE	VENDOR
Hardwood								
Hardwood oak plank— $^{25}\!/_{32}'' \times 2\frac{1}{4}''$								
Hardwood parquet tiles								
Flooring nails								
Flooring adhesive								
Floor grade polyurethane finish								
Wood threshold								
Blind nailer—rental								
Floor sander—rental								
Contract installation— hardwood								
Tile								
Ceramic tile thinset, $4\frac{1}{4}'' \times 4\frac{1}{4}''$								
Ceramic tile edge trim								
Porcelain flooring tile, $1'' \times 1''$								
Ceramic floor tile, $12'' \times 12''$								
Tile adhesive								
Tile spacers								
Tile mortar—shower								
Tile grout—color								
Tile threshold								
Tile cutter—rental								
Contract installation—tile								
Vinyl								
Sheet vinyl roll, 15′								
Vinyl floor mastic								
Floor adhesive								
Seam cement								
Rental—100-pound floor roller								
Contract installation—vinyl								

CHAPTER THIRTEEN

Insulation and Moisture Control

The importance of insulation depends on the climate in your area. Extra ceiling insulation is necessary in most climates, although not essential in extremely mild climates where there are neither hot nor cold extremes. Extra wall insulation is not as essential as ceiling insulation, but it is required for comfort in cold climates and will pay for itself in heat savings. Floor insulation is also necessary for comfort in crawl space houses in a cold climate.

When planning to upgrade your insulation, consider all major causes of heat loss. Heat loss per unit area through windows and exterior doors is much greater than through most wall materials. Another major source of heat loss is from air infiltration around doors and windows. Storm doors, storm windows, and newer energy efficient windows can reduce air infiltration and heat transfer by 50 percent or more. Weatherstripping around doors and windows will produce major heat savings.

Regardless of the type and location of insulation, vapor barriers are required on the warm side of the insulation. Vapor barriers prevent warm moist air from migrating into the insulation in the walls and condensing when it meets the colder outside air. Houses without vapor barriers can have trouble with rotting wood, termites and blistering paint.

CEILING INSULATION

Most houses have an accessible attic with exposed ceiling framing so that any type of insulation can easily be applied. If batt or blanket insulation is used, get the width that will conform to joist spacing, usually 16 or 24 inches. Loose-fill insulation can also be used by simply dumping it between joists and screeding it off to the desired thickness. In the northern states with severe winters, at least 6 inches of fill or batt insulation should be used. The same thickness is recommended in the central states. In the South, thickness of ceiling insulation could be reduced for heating requirements, but cooling requirements may dictate 6 inches or more.

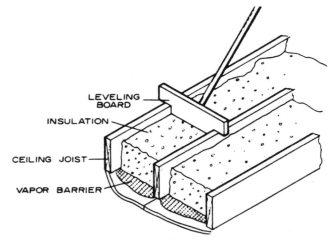

Fig. 13-1. Installation of loose-fill ceiling insulation.

WALL INSULATION

Wood-frame walls in existing houses are usually covered both inside and out; so, application of batt or blanket insulation is impractical. It is possible, however, to blow fill-type insulation into each of the stud spaces. This is done by a contractor equipped for such work. In houses having wood siding, the top strip just below the top plates and the strips below each window are removed. Then 2-inch-diameter holes are cut through the sheathing into each stud space. The depth of each stud space is determined by using a plumb bob, and additional holes are made below obstructions in the spaces. Insulation under slight pressure is forced through a hose and nozzle into the stud space until it is completely filled. Special care should be taken to insulate spaces around doors and windows and at intersections of partitions and outside walls.

Stucco, brick and stone veneer walls can be insulated in a similar manner. The same method can also be used in attic and roof spaces that have vaulted ceilings or finished areas where drywall is nailed directly to the roof rafters.

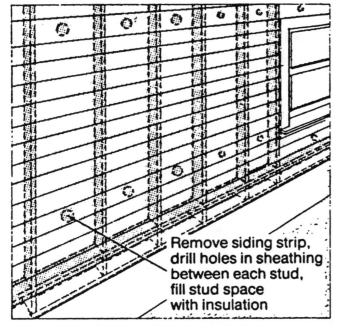

Remove siding strip, drill holes in sheathing between each stud, fill stud space with insulation

Fig. 13-2. Reinsulating a wall.

Solid masonry walls, such as brick, stone and concrete, can be insulated only by applying insulation to the interior surface. Remember that in doing this some space is being lost. One method of installing such insulation is to bond insulating board with adhesive directly to the interior surface. The insulating board can be plastered, left exposed or covered with any desired finish material. Thicker insulating board can be used for added insulation. Make sure that the concrete has been coated with a waterproofing compound first, so that moisture does not accumulate behind the insulating board.

Another method of installing insulation on the inside surface of masonry walls is by attaching 2" × 2" furring strips to the walls at 16-inch centers and installing 1-inch blanket insulation between strips. Thicker furring strips would allow use of thicker blanket insulation. The techniques used on masonry walls above grade can also be applied to basement walls.

FLOOR INSULATION

Older houses with basements usually did not have insulation under the floor because the heating unit, which was usually in the basement, warmed the basement. Houses with crawl spaces should have an insulated floor in severe climates. Insulated floors will add much to comfort even in moderate climates. Batt-type insulation is often used for floors, although blanket insulation can also be used. Friction batts fit tightly between joists and are secured to the bottom side of the subfloor with an adhesive. Insulation batts that are not friction type require some support in addition to the adhesive. This can be provided by wood strips cut slightly longer than the joist space so that they spring into place. They should be about $\frac{3}{16}'' \times \frac{3}{4}''$ and spaced 24 to 36 inches apart. Another method of supporting floor insulation is by nailing or stapling wire netting between joists. This method can be used for blanket and batt-type insulation.

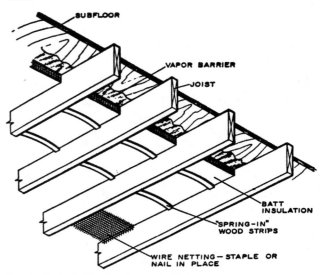

Fig. 13-3. Installing insulating batts in floor.

VAPOR BARRIERS

Vapor barriers are essential wherever insulation is used. They are always placed on the warm side of the surface. They must be continuous over the surface to be effective. Since insulation reduces heat flow, the surface of an exterior wall or roof is colder if insulation is used

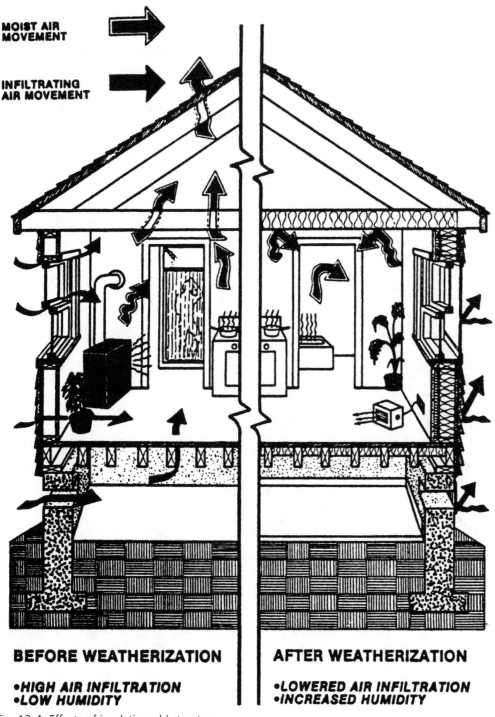

BEFORE WEATHERIZATION

•HIGH AIR INFILTRATION
•LOW HUMIDITY

AFTER WEATHERIZATION

•LOWERED AIR INFILTRATION
•INCREASED HUMIDITY

Fig. 13-4. Effects of insulating old structures.

than when the wall is not insulated. This colder surface is likely to be below the dew point of the air inside the house, so condensation occurs when moist air is allowed to travel through the wall.

The common functions of cooking, bathing, laundry and respiration contribute to moisture inside a house. Additional water vapor may be added by humidifiers operated during the winter. The high vapor pressure inside causes vapor to move out through every available crack and even through most building materials. In older homes the construction allowed a great deal of air flow through cracks in the walls. This circulation allowed most moist air to work its way out of the house. As houses become tighter and tighter, this excess moisture has nowhere to go but into the walls. This water vapor condenses in the wall at the point where the temperature is below the dew point of the inside atmosphere. The purpose of a vapor barrier is to slow the rate of vapor flowing into the wall so that it can exit into the outside atmosphere without building up.

Continuous Membrane

The most effective vapor barrier is a continuous membrane that is applied to the inside face of studs and joists in new construction. In renovations, such a membrane can be used only where new interior covering materials are to be applied.

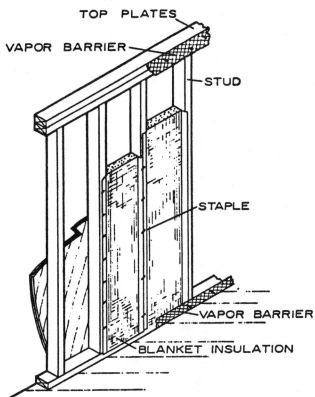

Fig. 13-5. Installation of blanket insulation with vapor barriers on one side.

The rate of vapor movement through a material is measured in perms. The lower the perm rating of a material, the more effective it is as a vapor barrier. Suitable materials for a membrane are polyethylene 2 mils or more in thickness, asphalt-impregnated and surface-coated kraft papers, and duplex or laminated paper consisting of two sheets of paper cemented together with asphalt.

These vapor barriers can be stapled to furring strips before applying new ceiling or drywall. If the old ceiling or wall finish is removed, staple the vapor barrier directly to the studs or joists. This type of barrier can also be laid on a subfloor directly under any finish floor or floor-covering material. Roofing felt serves this purpose when applied between the subfloor and underlayment. When installing the membrane, be sure to lap all joints

at least 2 inches, being careful not to puncture it. Naturally, driving nails to anchor the finished floor will puncture the barrier; however, this will not greatly affect its performance.

Blanket Insulation With Vapor Barrier

Most blanket insulation has a vapor barrier on one side. Place the insulation with the vapor barrier toward the warm surface. Tabs on the blanket must be stapled to the inside face of the stud or joist and adjacent tabs should lap each other. Tabs stapled to the side of studs or joists in the cavity will be ineffective because vapor will move out between the tabs and framing members. This type of vapor barrier can be used only when old interior plaster or drywall is completely removed or when furring strips are added on the inside. Insulation is installed between furring strips in the same manner as between studs.

Vapor-Resistant Coating

Where loose-fill insulation has been used in walls and ceilings and no new interior covering is planned, a vapor-resistant paint coating should be applied to the inside surface. Several types of vapor barrier primers are now available for this purpose. This does not offer as much resistance to vapor movement as a membrane, so it should be used only when there is no other alternative. If the exterior wall covering is permeable enough to allow moisture to escape from the wall, a vapor-resistant coating on the inside should be adequate.

One of the biggest mistakes made by many remodelers is to seal the outside of the house and not the inside. This happens when a new vapor-resistant material is used on the outside. For instance, if new siding is installed over Styrofoam insulation, the Styrofoam acts like a vapor barrier. Certain brands of vinyl siding with no ventilation will do the same thing. If this is done to an older house without an adequate vapor barrier on the inside, vapor will enter the walls and become trapped with nowhere to go. The result can be a very soggy, moldy house. If you are adding new siding to the house and want to avoid these problems while increasing energy efficiency, try this approach: Many companies now market products called "air barriers." These consist of long continuous rolls of olefin fiber (similar to the material that rip-proof mailing envelopes are made of). These rolls are meant to be wrapped around the outside of the house before siding is attached. They stop the flow of air in the insulation which robs heat, but they are very permeable to water vapor, letting it escape properly.

Soil Cover

Crawl spaces can be ventilated to remove most moisture, but a soil cover will keep a lot of moisture from ever entering the crawl space. Any of the continuous membranes just mentioned can be used. Lay the membrane so that it contacts the outside walls and has a lap of at least 2 inches at all joints. Use bricks or stones on top of the membrane to hold it down and to prevent curling. This will reduce the need for ventilation.

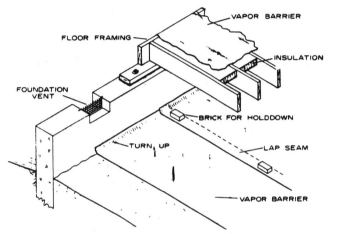

Fig. 13-6. Vapor barrier for crawl space (ground cover).

VENTILATION

Ventilation of attics and crawl spaces is essential in all houses located where the average January temperature is 35 degrees Fahrenheit or lower. Vapor barriers help to control moisture problems, but there are always places, such as around utility pipes, where some moisture escapes. In older houses that do not have proper vapor barriers, ventilation is especially important.

Attic and Roof

Moisture escaping from the house into the attic tends to collect in the coldest part of the attic. Impermeable roofing, such as asphalt shingles or a built-up roof, complicates the problem by preventing the moisture from escaping to the outside. The only way to get the moisture out is to ventilate the attic. Attic ventilation also helps keep a house cool during hot weather.

Where possible, inlet vents should be provided in the soffit area and outlet vents should be provided near the ridge. This results in natural circulation regardless of wind direction. The warm air in the attic rises to the peak and goes out the vents and fresh air enters through the inlet vents to replace the exhausted air. In some attics only gable vents can be used. Air movement is then dependent upon wind. The open area of such gable vents should be greater than when both inlet and outlet vents are provided.

Hip roofs cannot have gable vents near the peak, so some other type of outlet ventilator must be provided. This can be either a ventilator near the ridge or a special flue provided in the chimney with openings into the attic space. Both types require inlet vents in the soffit area. The hip roof can also be modified to provide a small gable for a conventional louvered vent. Flat roofs with no attic require some type of ventilation above the ceiling insulation. If this space is divided by joists, each joist space must be ventilated. This is often accomplished by a continuous vent strip in the soffit. Drill through all headers that impede passage of air to the opposite eaves.

Cathedral ceilings require the same type of ventilation as flat roofs. A continuous ridge vent is also desirable because, even with holes in the ridge rafter, air movement through the rafter space is very sluggish without a ridge vent. Houses with intersecting roofs or hip roofs create special problems. If you are planning to finish an attic, make sure to provide for some type of ventilation and make sure to use a heavy-duty vapor barrier such as 6-mil poly behind the drywall. This reduces the ventilation requirements.

Methods of ventilating gable roofs and the amount of ventilation for the many types vary. The size of the requisite vent opening varies with total ceiling area. The open area required should be completely unobstructed. Where 16-mesh screen is used to cover the opening, the vent area should be doubled.

Crawl Space

An enclosed crawl space under the house floor receives moisture from the soil below. This moisture produces both a decay and termite hazard. To keep the crawl space dry, vents are required with a total free area of not less than $\frac{1}{150}$ of the ground area. This vent area must be divided into four or more openings distributed around the foundation. If it is a partial basement, the crawl space can be vented to the basement instead of to the outside. Where a soil cover or a vapor barrier is laid over the entire area of the crawl space, the required ventilation area is reduced. A total free area of only $\frac{1}{1500}$ of the ground area is sufficient. These minimum areas are free areas and must be enlarged when screens or other obstructions are included with the vent.

Several types of foundation vents can be purchased commercially for easy installation in the appropriate size opening. Screen sizes vary, depending on whether they are insect-proof or rodent-proof.

Other Insulation Techniques

Unless you are planning to completely strip your house of walls and siding, many of these insulation techniques will be unavailable to you. However, there are many other weatherproofing techniques for improving the energy efficiency of your house without major structural changes. Heat and water vapor move through a house by three different actions: convection, diffusion and ventilation. Of these three, ventilation produces the lion's share of heat and moisture transfer. You can achieve an amazing amount of energy savings simply by plugging the leaks in your home. The steps in this chapter outline a whole-house retrofit to weatherize your home without major structural modifications. These seemingly minor changes can reduce your energy needs and air infiltration by as much as 40 percent.

WEATHERPROOFING STEPS

1. Examine the house thoroughly from the foundation to the attic and determine current insulation conditions and requirements. Your local energy company can help give you guidelines and suggestions.

2. Install plastic sheeting in the crawl space to reduce moisture and ventilation requirements. Anchor the plastic with rocks or bricks. Calculate the square footage of the exposed soil and divide by 1500. If your total vent area in the crawl space is greater than this, you can close some crawl space vents.

3. Seal concrete floors and walls in basement to reduce moisture problems.

4. Add insulation to the walls in the basement if you plan to finish it.

5. Install floor insulation. Floor insulation will be installed on crawl space and basement foundations. Metal wires cut to the length of joist spacing can be used to hold the insulation in place.

6. Wrap fiberglass batts around the hot water heater. If the water heater is gas, follow the manufacturer's instructions carefully when installing water heater blankets to avoid possible fire hazard.

7. Seal all spaces around plumbing, electrical wires, vents and HVAC vents with urethane foam to stop air infiltration. Do this in the attic and floor areas. Seal any gaps between HVAC ducts and floor vents where heated air could escape.

8. Apply fiberglass batts to HVAC vents where exposed to the outside air.

9. Caulk gaps between the siding and foundation.

10. Caulk gaps between the floor trim and drywall. Use caulk the same color as the paint.

11. Remove wall outlets, switch plates and ceiling fixtures and seal all gaps with urethane foam. This includes holes where wires enter the switch box.

12. Carefully remove trim around windows and stuff all gaps with fiberglass insulation or urethane foam. If using foam, make sure to nail the trim back on before the foam dries or the foam may bulge out, preventing the trim from being reinstalled flush to the wall.

13. Add storm windows and storm doors.

14. Install new weatherstripping kits around doors and windows.

15. Blow in additional wall insulation through holes in the wall.

16. Prime interior walls with vapor barrier primer.

17. Caulk gaps around siding and windows.

18. Install extra attic insulation, which normally consists of additional batts or blown-in insulation. This can also include reflective foil-backed paper to reduce radiant heat through the roof. Apply foil to roof rafters, not to the attic floor.

19. Check vents in attic and add vents if needed. Add an attic fan for cooling in the summer.

20. Plant hardwood trees around southern windows. These will provide shade in summer and drop leaves in winter to let in sunlight and heat.

21. Install water saver shower heads. Reduce temperature of water heater by 15 degrees. This will lower hot water consumption and reduce your water heating bill.

INSULATION MATERIAL ESTIMATE

DESCRIPTION	SPECIFICATION	QTY.	UNIT	COST	TAX	TOTAL COST	COST TYPE	VENDOR
Weatherizing material								
Urethane foam — cans								
Fiberglass batt insulation								
Cellulose blow-in insulation								
Weatherstripping kit — door								
Weatherstripping kit — window								
Storm doors								
Storm windows								
Hot water heater blanket								
Water saver shower heads								
6-mil poly								
Vapor barrier primer								
Concrete sealing paint								
Foil-backed attic insulation								
Soffit vents								
Ridge vent								
Gable vent								
Crawl space vent								
Attic fan								
Insulation — contract labor								
Hardwood trees								

CHAPTER FOURTEEN

Electrical

The most common need for electrical renovation occurs when adding new rooms or appliances to the existing service. An explosion of electric devices in the past twenty years has taxed the current capability of most houses. If you are adding new outlets, kitchen appliances, track lighting, or heating or cooling systems or running electrical service to a newly refinished attic, you will need to upgrade the electrical service.

All electrical service comes into the house through a service panel known commonly as the circuit breaker or fuse box. The service panel acts as the traffic cop, directing electricity through separate electrical circuits, each controlled by a circuit breaker or fuse. Most older homes had 100-amp service panels. Today's homes should have 100- to 200-amp service panels to handle the needs of modern appliances.

Electrical service is one of the building trades that is tightly controlled by local building inspectors and the national electrical code. You will definitely need the services of a licensed electrician if you plan any electrical changes more extensive than a new outlet or light dimmer. Many areas will not allow new electrical service to be added to the house without upgrading all the wiring in the house to meet new standards. If your house was built after about 1965, this shouldn't be a problem. Older houses will almost certainly need upgrading. Caution: Don't add new electric outlets or large appliances to the existing service without checking with an electrician first. If you add too much electrical load to a circuit you may be inviting a fire hazard.

The electrician can help to add new circuits to the existing service panel or install a new 200-amp service panel as well as run the electrical circuits to their new destination. All home wiring must meet certain minimum standards. For instance, the national code requires wall outlets spaced no more than 6 feet apart on any

wall 2 feet wide or wider. You may want to add more outlets than the minimum for convenience. Mark the locations of new outlets and switches so the electrician can place them where they are needed. Make sure you mark areas next to wall studs.

The electrician can perform all the necessary wiring for interior and exterior fixtures and appliances. Electricians usually charge a fixed price for providing and wiring each switch, outlet and fixture. Double switches will count as two switches and so on. There is an extra charge for running new wiring in existing walls. This can be very tedious work.

UPGRADING THE LIGHTING

If your budget requires that you stick with the existing electrical service, but you want to add new accent lights to certain rooms, consider lowering the electrical demand on the circuit to make room for the new lights. This can be done by substituting low wattage fluorescent lights for general indirect lighting and using low wattage halogen lights for the new accent lights. The added benefit can be substantial energy savings.

Consider multiple switches for a single light (such as at the top and bottom of stairs), floodlight switches in the master bedroom and photoelectric cells for driveway and porch lights. Low-voltage electrical lighting can be used outside for exterior lighting. The low-voltage wiring can be safely buried in the yard to provide lighting wherever needed.

Make sure to install ground fault interrupters (GFIs) in all bathroom outlets. GFIs are ultrasensitive circuit breakers that provide an extra margin of safety in areas where the risk of shock is high. Hobby shop and garage areas are also good sites for these devices. Key areas for additional outlets:

- Plugs in breakfast areas
- Along kitchen counters
- Switched outlets in attic
- Foyer area

Wire gauges used for circuits will vary. Electric stoves, ovens, refrigerators, washers, dryers and air compressors are each normally on a separate circuit and use heavier gauges of wire. Your local building code will describe load limits on each circuit and the appropriate wire types and gauges to use.

If you are adding new partition framing or replacing existing siding or drywall, make sure to call in the electrician before re-covering these walls. It is much easier to run new wiring in exposed framing than in existing walls. To run new wiring in existing areas, the electrician must find access to the wall through the crawl space or attic and snake the wiring through the wall using several unique techniques. In new construction, make sure to have the HVAC and plumbing subcontractors complete their rough-in before calling in the electrician. This will prevent any wiring from having to be cut or rerouted to make room for plumbing or ducting. It is much easier for the electrician to work around obstructions.

ADDITIONAL WIRING

While new electrical wiring is being installed, consider installing other necessary wiring for appliances such as phones, alarm systems, TV antennas, doorbells, intercoms and computers. This type of wiring makes an excellent do-it-yourself project if you are eager to get involved. Installing this wiring before drywall is installed is easy and saves considerable installation expense later. There are very few code restrictions on running phone wire and cable. Hiring someone to do this can be very expensive.

ELECTRICAL INSTALLATION STEPS

1. Determine electrical requirements. Check the amp rating of the existing service panel. Anything under a 100-amp service should be upgraded. Hire an electrician to give you a professional appraisal of the existing system. This may not need to be the electrician that you hire for actual wiring. Decide on the style and location of any new lights and make a list for the contractor so the electrician will know the additional load needed.

You may want to consider furniture placement while you are doing this.

2. Select electrical fixtures and appliances. Visit lighting distributor showrooms. Keep an eye out for attractive fluorescent lighting that will be a long-term energy saver (but cannot use a dimmer switch). Special orders should be placed now due to delivery times.

3. Determine if the phone company charges to wire the home for additional phones. Even if you plan wireless phones, install phone jacks in several locations.

4. Conduct the standard bidding process. Have subs give a price to install each outlet, switch and fixture. They will normally charge extra for wiring the service panel and special work. Use only a licensed electrician.

5. Schedule to have the phone company install modular phone wiring and jacks if applicable. If your phone company charges too much for this service, just have your electrician do the job or do it yourself.

6. Schedule any other appliance installation. This includes any new kitchen or bath appliances or new heating systems. These should be in place when the electrician arrives to save him another trip.

7. Perform rough-in electrical. This involves installing wiring in wall studs and above ceiling joists or snaking the wires through existing walls. All the wiring for light switches and outlets will be run to the location of the service panel. To insure that your outlets and switches are placed where you want them, mark their locations with chalk or a marker. Otherwise, they will be placed wherever the electrician desires. It is important to have lights, switches and outlets exactly where you plan to place furniture and fittings.

8. Install modular phone wiring and jacks and any other wiring desired. You may also wish to run speaker, cable TV, security and computer wiring throughout the house.

9. Schedule electrical inspection. The electrician will usually do this.

10. Perform finish electrical work. This includes terminating all wiring appropriately (switches, outlets and so on). Major electrical appliances such as refrigerators, washers, dryers, ovens, vent hoods, exhaust fans, garage door openers, doorbells and other appliances are installed at this time. Any new heating equipment will also be wired.

11. Inspect finish electrical. All switch plates and outlets should be in place. All lights and appliances should work as planned.

12. Correct electrical problems if any exist.

13. Pay the electrical sub, final, requiring a signed affidavit.

14. Pay electrical sub retainage after all switches and outlets are tested.

ELECTRICAL SPECIFICATIONS

- Bid should include all supplies except lighting fixtures and appliances. Bid to include installation of light fixtures.
- Bid may include wiring and installation of the following items:
  200-amp service panel with circuit breakers
  Light switches (one-way)
  Light switches (two-way)
  Furnace
  Dishwasher
  Garbage disposal
  Microwave (built-in)
  Door chime set
  Door chime button(s) with lighted buttons
  Bath vent fans
  Bath heat lamp with timer switch
  Jacuzzi pump motor with timer switch
  Light fixtures (all rooms and exterior areas)
  Three-prong (grounded) interior outlets
  Three-prong (grounded) waterproof exterior outlets
  Electric range
  Double lamp exterior flood lights
  Electric garage door openers with auto light switch
  Washer
  Dryer
  Central air conditioning compressor
  Climate control thermostats
  Electric hot water heater
  Hood fan
  Central vacuum system
  Intercom, radio units, speaker wires
  Coaxial cable TV lines and computer cables
  Sump pump
  Electronic security system with sensors
  Ceiling fans
  Whole house attic fan with timer switch
  Automatic closet switches
  Humidifier/dehumidifier
  Time-controlled heat lamps
  Thermostatic roof vents
  Phone lines in all rooms as shown
  Time-controlled sprinkler system
- All work and materials should meet or exceed all requirements of the national electrical code unless otherwise specified.
- Dimmer switches should be installed on fixtures as requested.
- Rheostat should be installed on ceiling fans.

ELECTRICAL INSPECTION

Rough-In

- ☐ Outlets and switch boxes are offset to allow for drywall and base molding.
- ☐ All outlets are placed at 12-inch height and switches placed at 42-inch height as indicated on plans. Outlets and switches are unobstructed by doors.
- ☐ All special outlets, switch boxes and fixtures are in place where intended. Refer to your specifications and drawings.
- ☐ Electrical boxes for chandeliers and ceiling fans are adequately braced to hold weight of fixture.
- ☐ All lines are grounded.
- ☐ All electrical splices have approved splice cap securely fastened and located in accessible electric box.
- ☐ Bath ventilator fans are installed.
- ☐ Attic power ventilators are installed.

Finish

- ☐ All outlets and fixture wires measure 117 V with circuit tester or voltmeter. Test between the ground and each socket.
- ☐ Dimmer switches are installed where specified (dining room, den, foyer and master bath).
- ☐ No scratches, dents or other damage to electrical appliances and fixtures.
- ☐ All appliances are connected and operational.
- ☐ Door chimes (all sets) are connected and operational.

- [ ] Phone outlets work at all locations.
- [ ] Service panel is installed properly with sufficient load-carrying capacity. Breakers are labeled properly.
- [ ] Exterior lighting fixtures are installed and operational.
- [ ] All recessed lighting, ceiling lighting, heat lamps and other lighting fixtures are connected as specified and operational.

- [ ] Jacuzzi pump motor is connected and operational. For safety reasons, switch should not be reachable from the tub.
- [ ] All kitchen and bath circuits start with ground fault interrupters. GFIs test out properly.
- [ ] All switch plate and outlet covers are installed as specified (in rooms to be wallpapered, these will be temporarily removed).
- [ ] Finish electrical inspection is approved and signed by local building inspector.

ELECTRICAL MATERIAL ESTIMATE

DESCRIPTION	SPECIFICATION	QTY.	UNIT	COST	TAX	TOTAL COST	COST TYPE	VENDOR
Electrical service								
200-amp service installation—contract								
200-amp panel with circuit breakers								
Cable—service entrance								
Ground cable								
Conduit—service entrance								
Weather cap								
Meter socket								
Master switch								
Electric outlets								
Wiring 12-3 gauge with ground								
Ground fault interrupters								
Standard grounded duplex outlet								
220 appliance receptacle								
Single pole switch								
Three-way switch								
Dimmer switch								
Wall plate—duplex outlet								
Wall plate—switch								
Wall plate—dimmer								
14-3 nonmetallic sheathed cable								
Wire nuts								
4-inch electric box—steel								
Duplex gem electric box—plastic								
Ceiling box—aluminum								

CHAPTER FIFTEEN

Heating and Air

Like electrical systems, heating and air-conditioning systems should be installed by licensed contractors. Their systems are complex and closely regulated. A mistake here could be very expensive. Older heating systems might need to be upgraded to handle the load of new additions to the structure. Old furnaces without integral air-conditioning systems can lower the value of your home, even after a renovation. Upgrading to a new energy efficient heating and air-conditioning system can increase comfort and save big on energy bills.

In modern systems heating and air-conditioning units share the same ventilation and ductwork. If you have a two-story home, a large split level or a long ranch, consider a zoned (split) system. This is particularly efficient if you have just added new rooms that might tax the current system. Zoned systems work on the premise that two smaller, dedicated systems operate more efficiently than one larger one. Heating is measured in BTU's (British thermal units) while cooling is normally measured in tons. Normally, it takes 30,000 BTU's of heat and 1 ton of A/C for each 800 square feet of area.

If you have added just one new room, installing a completely new heating and cooling system may be impractical. If so, use local systems such as electric baseboard heat and window air conditioning. This can often be the most cost-effective option if the existing heating system is sufficient for the rest of the house. A good example of this situation would be a remodeled attic that is isolated from the house heating system. A basement conversion might be more effective as an extension of the existing furnace, since the furnace is likely to be located in the basement already.

The efficiency of heating and cooling systems varies widely. Select your systems carefully with this in mind. Most heating systems now come with an EER (energy efficiency rating) that provides a point of comparison between systems. The higher the number, the more efficient the unit. Contact your local power and gas companies for information regarding energy efficiency ratings. When shopping for systems, check the efficiency rating and be prepared to pay more for more efficient systems. Your power and gas company may also conduct, free of charge, an energy audit of your home, and help suggest heating and cooling improvements. If you are upgrading your cooling and heating systems, talk to local builders and power companies about the most effective units for your area. Each system has unique properties.

HEATING SYSTEM TYPES

Heat Pumps and Air Conditioners

Heat pumps and air-conditioning units operate by transferring heat from the air inside your home to the outside via a fluid such as Freon. Heat pumps are just air conditioners that can work in reverse—cooling the outside air and heating the inside air in the winter, and switching to conventional cooling in the summer. Heat pumps are more efficient heaters than other systems because they move heat from one place to another instead of creating heat like conventional furnaces. Heat pumps can deliver more energy to the home than it consumes in electricity. They deliver a large volume of moderate temperature air for long periods, which makes them very quiet. The large volume of air also increases the distribution of heat, reducing hot and cold spots, resulting in a very comfortable environment. If you are retrofitting a home with existing forced-air ducts, a heat pump has the advantage of providing a new heater and an air conditioner in the same package.

There are some disadvantages to heat pumps, however. They are complicated and expensive to maintain and their efficiency drops off considerably when the outside temperature drops below 30 degrees Fahrenheit. They work better in more moderate climates where temperature swings are smaller. Some new systems provide underground pipes to withdraw heat from the surrounding soil instead of the air, since soil temperatures are much more stable year round than air temperature. These systems work well in extreme climates but are very expensive.

Gas and Oil Forced-Air Furnaces

Traditional gas furnaces come in a variety of types and efficiency levels. Some of the newer types have reached efficiencies of 95 percent and higher. These units are some of the most efficient available for areas with extreme weather and low gas prices. They deliver short blasts of hot air and can be noisy. The hot air is also harder to distribute throughout the house, leading to hot and cold spots. Older homes with small heating ducts will work well with the high-temperature air, however. Except for the ultra-high-efficiency models, gas furnaces are inexpensive and easy to maintain and operate. Oil furnaces operate much like gas systems and have many of the same advantages and disadvantages. Which type you choose will depend on the relative prices of oil and gas in your area. Since these are heaters only, you will need to add an air conditioner to the system for summer cooling.

Underfloor Heat

Underfloor heat systems come in a variety of types. They typically consist of a hot water heating system and underfloor pipes. The hot water distributes heat evenly through the floor into the room. Rooms with carpet will keep the heat from entering the room efficiently since the carpet acts as an insulator. However, underfloor heat works great under a tile or hardwood floor by keeping the floor toasty warm for bare feet. Underfloor heat is usually installed in new construction where the pipes can be cast into the floor slab or built into the subfloor. Frequently their installation in an existing house is impractical because of the necessity of installing the underfloor piping. Additional ducts must also be run to provide central air conditioning.

Steam

Once the most popular heating system in older homes, steam heat has almost disappeared. The systems were complicated and noisy and room had to be made for the (very hot) radiators. There are companies that can repair and retrofit steam systems; however, the results are rarely worth the effort. The challenge in replacing a steam system is finding the room to install new heating ducts for a forced-air system. Most ducting runs under the floor or in the attic. If you have access to these areas, you shouldn't have too many problems locating ducts.

Electric Baseboard

Electric baseboard heat is an excellent alternative for new room additions if the current heating system is inadequate or inaccessible. They are very inexpensive and easy to install. Although electric heat is not very energy efficient, total energy usage may be lower than adding additional ducting to an existing system. Long runs of ducting waste a certain amount of energy just getting the conditioned air to the room.

Window Air Conditioners

Like electric baseboard heat, window air conditioners may be the most effective solution for single-room upgrades. The newer models are very energy efficient and quiet. They probably use less energy to cool a room than an extension from a central air conditioner, since there is no energy loss from the ducting. Like baseboard heat, window air conditioners have the additional advantage of being user installable.

Gas Space Heaters

Gas or kerosene space heaters can be reasonable alternatives to electric baseboard heat and are usually more energy efficient. However, they create fumes and gaseous byproducts and create a greater fire hazard. Make sure your room has adequate ventilation if you choose this option. Gas heaters will require professional installation of the gas line by a licensed HVAC contractor.

CLIMATE CONTROL

At your option, your HVAC sub can also install other climate control devices. Electric air filters attach to your HVAC system air intake, eliminating up to 90 percent of airborne dust particles when cleaned regularly. Humidifiers, popular in dry areas, add moisture to the air. Special water supplies can be attached for automatic water dispensing. Dehumidifiers, popular in the Southeast and other humid areas, draw water out of the air. These units may be attached to a water drain for easy disposal of accumulated water.

HVAC SUBS

HVAC subs charge based on the size of your system (BTUs and tonnage). There is a tendency for subs to overestimate your heating and cooling requirements for three reasons:

- More cost, more profit.
- Nobody ever complains about having too much heating and cooling.
- Better safe than sorry.

Have your HVAC sub submit a separate bid for the ductwork. Your HVAC sub will also install your natural gas line (if you use natural gas) and hook it up to the gas main. The gas company will install your gas meter. Shop carefully for your HVAC sub. A wrong decision here can cost you increased utility bills in the future.

Ductwork

The ductwork circulates conditioned air to specific points in the home and is split between air supplies, which deliver conditioned air, and air returns, which recirculate the air back to the HVAC system. Ducts are usually constructed of sheet metal or insulated fiberglass cut and shaped to fit at the site. Fiberglass ducts are rapidly gaining in popularity due to their ease of fabrication at the site. The duct itself is made of insulated fiberglass and can be cut with a knife. This extra insulation makes for a more efficient and quieter air system. Sheet metal ducts are notorious for developing mysterious noises caused by expansion and air movement that may be difficult or impossible to eliminate. If your home has an existing duct system, stick with it. It will be much cheaper than retrofitting a new system.

Register Placement

Proper placement of new supplies and returns is critical to making your total HVAC system efficient and economical to run. Most registers are placed near doors or under windows. This type of placement puts the conditioned air near the sources of greatest heat loss and promotes more even distribution of air.

Supplies should be located primarily along the exterior walls of the home. This is known as a radial duct system. Where possible, hot air supplies should be positioned directly below windows and alongside exterior doors near the floor since heat rises. Cold air supplies should be located up high in rooms since cool air falls.

Returns for warm air should be located low since the cooled air drops. Cool air returns should be located high to remove the air as it warms up. It is a good idea to have two supplies (high and low) and two returns (high and low) in critical rooms to handle either season. Your HVAC sub can help you with the proper quantity and placement of your supplies and returns. As a general rule, you will need at least one supply per room and one return per three rooms.

Thermostats

Many elaborate thermostats are available on the market today. Many automatically shut heating systems down or set them at a low level during off-peak hours. In any event, do not put the thermostat within 6 feet of any air supply register or facing one on an opposite wall. Never place a thermostat in a room with a fireplace. Consider placing a thermostat in the hallway. New energy efficient thermostats can upgrade the efficiency of existing HVAC systems.

HVAC INSTALLATION STEPS

1. Conduct an energy audit of the home to determine HVAC and heat requirements. Your local gas and electric companies can be very helpful with this, sometimes providing computer printouts at little or no cost. Decide if local heating and cooling solutions are adequate, such as electric baseboard heat and window air conditioners. If so, you can do the work yourself.

2. Shop for the best combination of cost, size and efficiency in heating and cooling systems, if retrofitting. The higher the efficiency, the higher the price.

3. Conduct the bidding process on the complete HVAC job. Ask contractors for a separate bid for the ductwork.

4. Finalize the HVAC design. Have a representative from the local gas company or an inspector look over your plan to make sure you aren't doing anything that could be a problem.

5. Install heating and air-conditioning ducting and finish material. Any additional ducting, thermostat, and HVAC electrical work is hooked up and tied into the existing system. All registers are installed. Any new AC compressor is installed and charged with Freon. Discuss the placement of the A/C compressor location with the HVAC sub. He may supply the concrete pad if you do not have one.

6. Remove the old heating system. Ask the HVAC sub to remove the old system from the premises. Sometimes they will cooperate. If not, make sure to dispose of the old unit at an approved site.

7. Inspect heating and air conditioning final. This inspection should be conducted by your county inspector. Call him several days in advance so you can be present for the inspection. You may want your HVAC sub present, too. Make a note of any deficiencies. Be sure the electrician has run service to the unit and that it is functional.

8. Correct all deficiencies noted in the final inspection.

9. Call the gas company to hook up gas lines.

10. Pay the HVAC sub for finish work, requiring a signed affidavit.

11. Pay the HVAC sub retainage after the system is fully tested.

HVAC SPECIFICATIONS

- Bid is to install heating, ventilation and air-conditioning system (HVAC) as requested.
- Install two zoned forced-air gas-fired (FAG) heating units with five-year warranty, one in basement and one in attic.
- Install two A/C compressors.
- Install sloped PVC tubing for A/C drainage.
- All work and materials to meet or exceed requirements of the local building code.
- Provide and install all necessary air filters.
- Make the opening to the furnace large enough to permit removal and replacement.
- Charge all A/C lines with Freon.

HVAC INSPECTION

- ☐ All equipment UL-approved with warranties on file.
- ☐ Heating and air units installed in place and well anchored.
- ☐ Heating and air units are proper make, model and size.
- ☐ Zoned systems have proper units in proper locations.
- ☐ Air compressors are firmly anchored to footings.
- ☐ All ductwork is installed according to specifications.
- ☐ Proper number of returns and supplies have been installed.
- ☐ All ductwork meets local building codes.
- ☐ All ductwork joints are sealed tightly and smoothly with duct tape.
- ☐ There are no return ducts in baths or kitchen.
- ☐ All ductwork in walls is flush with walls, not to interfere with drywall.
- ☐ Attic furnace has a floor drain pan.
- ☐ All heat exhaust vents are isolated from wood or roofing by at least 1 inch.
- ☐ No exhaust vents are visible from the front of the home.
- ☐ All ductwork outlets are framed properly to allow installation of vent covers.
- ☐ HVAC inspection is approved and the required papers are signed by the local building inspectors.
- ☐ Gas line is connected to gas main.
- ☐ HVAC electrical hookup is completed.
- ☐ Thermostats operate properly and are installed near the center of the house. Thermostats are located away from heat sources (fireplaces and registers) and doors and windows to provide accurate operation.
- ☐ A/C condensate pipe drains properly. This will be difficult or impossible to test in cold weather. The pipe should at least have a slight downward slope to it. You cannot test A/C if the temperature is below 68 degrees.
- ☐ Fan noise is not excessive.
- ☐ Furnace, A/C and electronic air filters are installed.
- ☐ Water line to humidifier is installed and operating.
- ☐ Water line from dehumidifier is installed and operating.
- ☐ All vent covers on all duct openings are installed in the proper direction.
- ☐ All holes and openings to exterior are sealed with exterior grade caulk.
- ☐ All HVAC equipment papers are filed (such as warranty and maintenance).
- ☐ There is strong air flow out of all air supplies.
- ☐ Air returns function properly.

HVAC MATERIAL ESTIMATE

DESCRIPTION	SPECIFICATION	QTY.	UNIT	COST	TAX	TOTAL COST	COST TYPE	VENDOR
HVAC Furnace								
Gas-fired forced-air furnace								
Gas supply pipe								
A/C compressor								
A/C piping								
A/C – PVC condensation piping								
Thermostat – energy-saving								
Floor grille								
Return air grille								
Supply duct trunk – rigid fiberglass								
Supply duct register – 6-inch flexible								
Return duct								
Individual Space Heat								
6-foot Electric baseboard heater								
Electric thermostat								
Electric circuit breaker – contract labor								
Window air conditioner – energy efficient								

CHAPTER SIXTEEN

Plumbing

Most changes in the plumbing system will result from upgrading existing plumbing fixtures, moving plumbing lines because of remodeling, or adding plumbing for new additions. Replacing old plumbing fixtures is not difficult and makes a good do-it-yourself project. Moving existing plumbing around is more difficult and should be attempted only by experienced plumbers. Adding new plumbing and tying it into the existing system is definitely a job for professional plumbers. Plumbing regulations in most areas are very strict and must be followed exactly. Adding new lines to existing vents is tricky and can lead to some pretty bizarre problems if not installed by an experienced plumber.

The size and type of plumbing pipe coming into your home is regulated by the local plumbing code. If you are adding new plumbing to the house (such as a new bathroom), hire a plumber to inspect the current pipes and fixtures. He can tell you if your current water supply is sufficient. An alternative person to call is your local plumbing/building inspector.

Before starting to design your project, locate the existing plumbing components. A plumbing system is composed of three interrelated systems:

1. The water supply
2. The sewer system
3. The (wet) vent system

THE WATER SUPPLY

Unless your house has an individual water supply (such as a well), it will be attached to the public water supply. Water flow into the house is controlled by the size of the supply pipe and the water pressure. If your local water supply is 80 psi or greater, you probably have a pressure reduction valve at the main water service pipe. You might be able to make minor adjustments to the water pressure to achieve a higher flow rate. Note: Water pressure that is too high can and will take its toll on most pipes and fixtures in a short period.

Copper has been the material of choice of plumbers for many years, but new materials available today have many advantages over copper. CPVC pipe is a plastic used for hot and cold supplies. Its cousin, PVC, is rated only for cold water and sewer installations. CPVC offers several advantages over copper, including ease and speed of installation and some cost savings. CPVC can make an owner installation much easier. Some people complain of a slight aftertaste in the water for the first year or so.

Polybutylene is a new semiflexible material that has taken the plumbing world by storm in recent years. It offers many advantages over copper and CPVC. It is totally inert and imparts no taste to the water. Its flexible nature allows it to be installed with a minimum of joints, which are the most expensive material in water systems. Polybutylene is also virtually freezeproof, a characteristic that can be appreciated by anyone who has had pipes freeze in cold weather. It is very quiet in operation and reduces the effect of water hammer. Polybutylene joints are installed by one of two methods: crimping or grabber fittings. Crimp joints are the most cost effective, but the grabber joints are ridiculously easy to install. You simply insert the pipe into the fitting and push; that's it.

Polybutylene pipe is by far the least expensive method of installing plumbing, but you may have trouble finding plumbers willing to work with it. Plumbers are slow to accept innovations and may not pass the full savings of the installation to you. Many plumbers fail to realize the full cost savings available to them because they tend to install many more joints than are necessary. The flexibility of polybutylene allows it to be wrapped and molded around obstructions, eliminating the need for many joints. Check with your local plumbing inspector for plumbers familiar with this new material. It is well worth the research.

The Sewer System

The sewer system collects all used water and waste and disposes of it properly. Waste water systems are either connected to a septic tank or to the public sewer system. If you are adding a new bathroom, you should have the county health inspector examine the existing septic system to see if it will handle the additional waste water. If it is inadequate you must factor in the cost of additional septic lines in your estimate. A less costly solution is to install new water-saving toilets and shower heads in each bathroom. Sometimes this can reduce the load on the septic system enough to handle the new bathroom.

When designing the renovation, keep in mind that sewer systems are powered by gravity. Therefore, your lowest sink, toilet or drain must be higher than the sewer line. The sewer line must have at least ¼-inch drop per foot to operate properly.

With sewer pipe materials, technology has created a new problem. PVC pipe is now the most common material used because of its ease of installation; however, plastic pipes transmit the noise of flushing and water draining much more than the old cast iron pipes. Install cast iron sewer pipe if possible to reduce this noise. If you use PVC pipe, take care to position the pipes in walls that are isolated from bedrooms or you will hear water noises constantly.

The Wet Vent System

Also known as the vertical wet venting system, the (wet) vent system permits your plumbing system to breathe. This system protects against siphoning, back pressure and sewage gases. All drains are attached to one of several vents in a network. These vents are seen as pipes sticking out of the back side of your roof and are called soil stacks. You must know the locations of your main vents and determine a route for attaching new plumbing to them. This can be tricky, since there are very specific rules about placement of vent pipes. This is where the plumber will earn his fee.

Each fixture must have a drain with a trap, a curved pipe that retains water to prevent sewage gases from escaping into the house. The drain must slope downward ¼ inch for every foot of drain pipe. Beyond the trap, each drain must have a vent that either goes up through the roof or connects to another vent stack. These vent stacks must connect into the soil stack above any toilet drains. The vent allows gases to escape and equalizes pressure in the drain pipes. This keeps the water in the traps from siphoning out and allowing gases into the house.

These rules and many others make the task of designing and installing a proper vent system the domain of professionals. If you plan to tackle this job yourself, make sure to study the plumbing codes carefully. These can be obtained from the local building inspector.

PLUMBING SUBS

Plumbers normally bid and charge a fixed price per fixture to install all three systems described above. On remodeling projects, the plumber will add in extras for working with existing systems. You are likely to pay extra for jacuzzis, whirlpools and the like. The price of all fixtures (tubs, sinks, disposals) should be obtained from your sub. Fixtures above builder grade usually cost more. If you use many custom fixtures, or if your renovation positions plumbing close to existing plumbing, which conserves plumbing material, consider asking for a bid based on actual material and labor costs. Such a bid can save you a considerable amount of money. If you purchase fancy fixtures, have the plumber deduct the standard fixture charge for the ones you have purchased. After you have received the estimate, ask for the cash price. Ask your plumber how many hours it will take to do the job. You will pay the plumber 40 percent after passing the rough-in inspection and 60 percent after passing the final inspection.

PLUMBING INSTALLATION STEPS

Rough-In

1. Examine existing plumbing and determine plumbing upgrades to the supply or septic tank, if needed. This is best done with the help of a licensed plumber or county inspector.

2. Determine the type and quantity of new plumbing fixtures (styles and colors). This includes sinks, bathtubs, shower fixtures, toilets and toilet seats, water spigots, refrigerator ice maker, and any other plumbing-related appliance.

3. Conduct the standard bidding process. Shop prices carefully; subs who bid on your job may vary greatly on their bid price, depending on what materials they use and their method of calculating their fee. Now is when you must decide what kind of pipe to use.

4. Walk through the site with the plumber to discuss placement of plumbing and any special fixtures needed. For instance, can your plumber tie in to the existing vent stacks or will a new one need to be installed?

5. Order special plumbing fixtures. Do this well before installation because supply houses seldom stock large quantities of special fixtures. These will take time to get in.

6. Place all large plumbing fixtures such as large tubs, fiberglass shower stalls and hot tubs near the installation point. If you are reframing a bathroom or window opening, bring in shower fixtures before the wall framing or windows are installed. Many of these fixtures will not fit through normal stud or door openings. Make sure to check the dimensions of the shower enclosure before ordering it to make sure it will fit through available openings.

7. Mark locations of all plumbing fixtures including sinks, tubs, showers, toilets, outside spigots, wet bars, icemakers, utility tubs, washers and the water heater. Make sure the plumber knows whether you have a regular vanity or pedestal sink. Mark the end of tubs where the drain should be located. Mark areas in wall and ceiling where pipes must not be located, such as locations for recessed lights or medicine cabinets.

8. Install rough-in plumbing. This involves the laying of hot (left) and cold (right) water lines, sewer and vent pipe. Pipe running along studs should run within holes drilled (not notched) in the studs. All pipe supports should be in place. Your plumber should use metal FHA straps across studs to protect pipe from being pierced by drywall nails. FHA straps are metal plates designed to protect the pipe from nail punctures. The plumber will conduct a water pipe test using air pressure to insure against leaks.

9. Tie in sewer line.

10. Install the septic tank and line, if applicable.

11. Schedule the plumbing inspector.

12. Conduct the rough-in plumbing inspection. Note: This is a *very* important step. No plumbing should be covered until your county inspector has issued an in-

spection certificate. Plan to go through the inspection with the inspector so you will understand any problems and get a good interpretation of your sub's workmanship.

13. Correct any problems found during the inspection. Remember, you have the county's force behind you. You also have the specifications. Since your plumber has not been paid, you have plenty of leverage.

14. Pay the plumbing sub for rough-in, requiring a signed receipt or equivalent.

Finish

1. Install finish plumbing. This involves installation of all fixtures selected earlier. Sinks, faucets, toilets and shower heads are installed.

2. Turn on the water supply. Now is when your plumbing gets a real test. You will have to open all the faucets to allow air to bleed out of the system. The water will probably look dirty for a few minutes, but don't be alarmed. The system needs to be flushed of excess debris and solvents.

3. Conduct the finish plumbing inspection.

4. Correct any problems found during the final inspection.

5. Pay the plumbing sub for finish, requiring a signed affidavit.

6. Pay plumber retainage.

PLUMBING SPECIFICATIONS

- Bid is to include all material and labor including all fixtures specified.
- All materials and workmanship shall meet or exceed all requirements of the local plumbing code.
- No plumbing, draining and venting is to be covered, concealed or put into use until tested, inspected and approved by local inspectors.
- All necessary licenses and permits are to be obtained by plumber.
- Plumbing inspection is to be scheduled by plumber.
- All plumbing lines shall be supported so as to insure proper alignment and prevent sagging.
- Worker's compensation is to be provided by plumber.

- Floor drain pan is to be installed under washer if it is located upstairs or under a water heater in the attic.
- Install approved pressure reduction valve at water service pipe.
- Drain pans are to be installed in all tile shower bases.
- Plumb the water supply to completely eliminate water hammer.
- Water pipes are to be of adequate dimension to supply all necessary fixtures simultaneously.
- Cut-off valves are to be installed at all sinks and toilets and at water heater.

Sewer System

- Hook into public water system.
- Install approved, listed and adequately sized backwater valve.
- Horizontal drainage is to be uniformly sloped not less than 1 inch in 4 feet toward the point of disposal.
- Drainage pipes are to be adequate diameter to remove all water and waste in proper manner.

Wet Vent System

- Vent piping shall extend through the roof flashing and terminate vertically at least 6 inches above the roof surface and at least 1 foot from any vertical surface, 10 feet from and 3 feet above a window, door or air intake, or 10 feet from a hot line.
- All vent piping is to be on rear side of the roof without visibility from front.
- All vent piping is to conform to the local plumbing and building code.

PLUMBING INSPECTION

Rough-In

- ☐ All supplies and drains specified are present and of proper material (PVC, CPVC, copper, cast iron, polybutylene).
- ☐ Sewer tap is done.
- ☐ No pipes are pierced by nails.
- ☐ Hot water fixture is at left of spigot.
- ☐ There is no evidence of any leaks. This is particularly critical at all joints, elbows and FHA straps.
- ☐ All plumbing lines are inside of stud walls. They must allow for a flush wall.

- ☐ FHA straps are used to protect pipes from nails where necessary.
- ☐ All cut-out framing done by plumber is repaired so as to meet local building code.
- ☐ Tub is properly centered in bathroom and secured in place.
- ☐ Tub levelers are all in contact with tub. Tub does not move or rock.
- ☐ Toilet drain is at least 12 inches to center from all adjacent walls to accommodate the toilet fixture.
- ☐ Toilet drain is at least 15 inches to center from tub to accommodate the toilet fixture.
- ☐ Exterior spigot stub-outs are high enough (minimum of 6 inches) so that they will not be covered over by backfill.
- ☐ Icemaker line for refrigerator is in place (¼-inch copper pipe).
- ☐ Roof stacks have been properly flashed with galvanized sheet metal.
- ☐ All wall-hung sinks have metal bridge support located with center at proper level.
- ☐ Water main shut-off valve works properly.
- ☐ Rough-in inspection is approved and signed by local building inspector.

Finish

- ☐ Tub faucets (hot and cold) operate properly. No drip. Drain operates well.
- ☐ Sink faucets (hot and cold) operate properly. No drip. Drain operates well.
- ☐ Toilets flush properly and fill to the proper line; action stops completely with no seepage.
- ☐ Kitchen sink faucets (hot and cold) operate properly. No drips. Drain operates well.
- ☐ There is no evidence of water hammer in entire system. Turn each faucet on and off very quickly and listen for a knock.
- ☐ All water supplies: hot on the left and cold on the right.
- ☐ Turn on all sinks and flush all toilets at the same time and check for significant reduction in water flow. Some is to be expected.
- ☐ There are cut-off valves on all sinks, toilets and water heaters.
- ☐ All roof and exterior wall penetrations tested waterproof.

PLUMBING MATERIAL ESTIMATE

DESCRIPTION	SPECIFICATION	QTY.	UNIT	COST	TAX	TOTAL COST	COST TYPE	VENDOR
Plumbing								
Flexible pipe — sink cutoff kit								
Flexible pipe — toilet cutoff kit								
Water pipe — copper ½ inch								
Elbows — copper ½ inch								
Ts — copper ½ inch								
Caps — copper ½ inch								
Plumbing solder								
Solder flux								
FHA straps								
Hanger straps								
Waste water pipe — PVC 4 inch								
Elbows — PVC 4 inch								
Ts — PVC 4 inch								
Caps — PVC 4 inch								
Y branch — PVC 4 inch								
Clean out plug — PVC 4 inch								
Vent pipe — PVC 2 inch								
Elbows — PVC 2 inch								
Ts — PVC 2 inch								
Caps — PVC 2 inch								
Y branch — PVC 2 inch								
Kitchen drainage — S trap — PVC 1½ inch								
Bathroom drainage — S trap — PVC 1¼ inch								
Toilet flange — PVC 4 inch								
PVC cement								
Beeswax seal — toilet								
Shower — plumbing and vent stack kit								
Pressure reduction valve								

CHAPTER SEVENTEEN

Windows and Doors

WINDOWS

New windows and doors can open up, lighten up and dramatize a home's interior. Most remodelers find new windows to be a tempting addition to the home because many older homes have small, infrequent windows. Modern living requires light, open spaces. Windows can open up old closed spaces without the need to add space. Any room redesign will probably include the movement and addition of new windows, doors and passageways. Examine the condition of the existing windows and decide if you want to replace or repair them. Many older window styles are not manufactured anymore. Replacing one may require replacing several more to keep the exterior styling consistent. However, there are many good reasons to replace old windows. Newer windows are larger, have much better insulating qualities, and are easier to use and clean. They are also very expensive.

Until recent years, windows were not generally treated with a preservative, so moisture may have gotten into some joints, resulting in decay. Also, older windows allowed more air infiltration than newer types that have double panes and insulating strips. The older wood windows can swell and stick, making them difficult to open. Replacing old windows is not difficult where the same size window can be used; however, where the window size is no longer manufactured, framing changes will be necessary. This may cause structural complications and require removal of siding and drywall. If you are looking for better insulating windows, an alternative to explore is the addition of storm windows. Even when custom made, the cost of storm windows is much lower than the cost of reframing and installing new windows.

If you decide to replace your windows, the sequence of window replacement will depend on the type of siding used. When new horizontal lap siding is being applied, the window is installed before the siding. The new siding is then installed flush to the new window trim. When installing new panel siding, the window is installed after the paneling is put in place. Installing new siding makes the job of installing new windows much easier. It allows you the freedom to pull off old siding and make the necessary framing changes.

Repair of Existing Windows

Where the wood in windows is showing some signs of deterioration, but the window is still in good operating condition, a water-repellent preservative or resin-based wood treatment may stop further decay. First, remove any existing paint. Then, brush on the preservative, let it dry and repaint the window. Paint cannot be used over some preservatives, so check before applying.

A double-hung sash may bind against the stops, jambs or parting strip. Before doing any repair, try waxing the parts that rub against each other. If this does not eliminate the problem, try to determine where the sash is binding. Excessive paint buildup is a common cause of sticking and can be corrected by removing paint from stops and parting strips. Nailed stops can be moved slightly away from the sash. If stops are fastened by screws, it will probably be easier to remove them and plane them lightly on the face contacting the sash. Loosening the contact between sash and stop too much will result in excessive air infiltration at the window. If the sash is binding against the jamb, remove the sash and plane the vertical edges slightly.

You may want to add full-width weatherstripping and spring balance units to provide an airtight window that will not bind. These are easily installed, requiring only removal of the parting strip and stops. Follow the manufacturer's instructions and replace the stops.

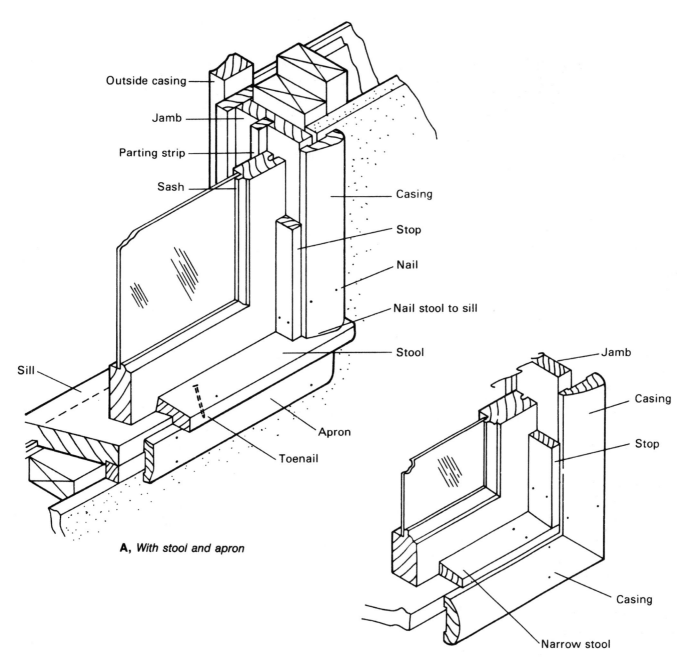

A, With stool and apron

Outside casing

Jamb

Parting strip

Sash

Casing

Stop

Nail

Nail stool to sill

Stool

Sill

Apron

Toenail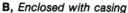

Jamb

Casing

Stop

Casing

Narrow stool

B, Enclosed with casing

Fig. 17-1. Installation of double-hung window frame.

Storm Windows

In cold climates, storm windows are necessary for comfort, for economy of heating and to avoid damage from excessive condensation on the inside face of the window. This is a thrifty alternative to new windows. If the old windows are not standard sizes, storm windows must be made by building a frame to fit the existing window and fitting glass to the frame. Storm windows are commercially available to fit all standard size windows in production today and many older sizes as well. The most practical type is the self-storing or combina-

tion storm and screen. These have minor adjustments for width and height, and can be custom fabricated for odd-size windows at moderate cost.

Replacement of Existing Windows

If windows require extensive repairs, you should probably replace them. New windows are usually purchased as a complete unit, including sash, frame and exterior trim. These units are easily installed in openings where a window of the same size and type is removed. Many older houses have tall, narrow windows of sizes that

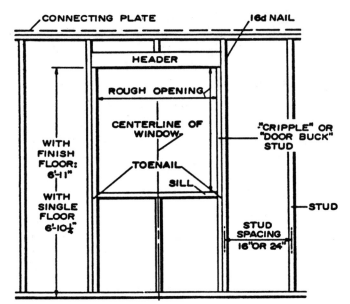

Fig. 17-2. Framing at window opening and height of window and door headers.

are no longer commercially available. In these cases, consider whether the house would be improved with larger windows. If you must reframe the window openings, why not use the opportunity to improve the design with new window sizes and shapes? Most window manufacturers list rough-opening sizes for each of their windows. Some general rules for rough-opening sizes are:

A. Double-hung window (single unit):
  Rough opening width = glass width plus 6 inches
  Rough opening height = total glass height plus 10 inches
B. Casement window (two sash):
  Rough opening width = total glass width plus 11¼ inches
  Rough opening height = total glass height plus 6⅜ inches

If you are considering extensive enlargement of the window space, you will need to change the load-bearing parts of the wall. This requires jacking up and supporting the existing wall while framing in the new window opening. The help of an experienced framer is strongly advised for this procedure.

Types of Windows

If you are replacing existing windows, you will find a variety of options available for replacements. The emphasis today is on energy efficiency and abundance of light. Since newer windows are much more energy efficient, homeowners can afford to install larger expanses

of windows without increasing the energy bill. Most windows sold today are some variation of double-pane windows. Most of these have an inert gas sealed between the panes to reduce heat transmission and to eliminate the possibility of condensation between the panes. Because of the double panes, most modern windows are made from a single pane of glass. Individual small panes are simulated in appearance with wooden inserts. One benefit of this approach is ease of cleaning. Just pop out the insert and clean the entire window at one time.

Many new windows also have special coatings and tints to reduce ultraviolet and infrared light. Ultraviolet light is the light that fades colors in fabric, photographs, and paints. Infrared light transmits heat energy. Most of these coatings are designed to block the heat from the sun while transmitting most of the visible light. These windows are more expensive but they can make up for their extra cost in energy savings.

Another popular window option is not a window at all but a wall. Light blocks are large blocks of glass 4 to 6 inches thick. They were very popular in the twenties and have recently had a resurgence of popularity. Most of the block styles allow diffuse light through, but are not transparent enough to see through. Therefore, they make excellent light sources with privacy for areas like the bathroom. Their insulating qualities are excellent for glass. Their structural strength makes them excellent separating walls between rooms while still letting light penetrate. The blocks are laid like a brick wall with mortar between the joints. Most building supply stores now stock them.

DOORS

Interior and exterior doors in older homes are almost exclusively made of solid wood in either smooth or paneled styles. Since about 1970, hollow-core luan doors have become popular. Due to the cost of hardwood, most modern doors are manufactured from other materials. Modern door types fall into three categories: hollow-core wood, solid-core wood or masonite, and insulated-core steel. If your house has solid wood doors, you may want to preserve them since they are a rarity today. Replacing the door frame or the latches can often solve many door problems. You can then use the original door in the new opening. Many door problems, such as sticking, are even easier to repair.

Doors in houses of all ages frequently cause problems

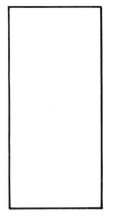

Flush

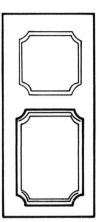

2-Panel

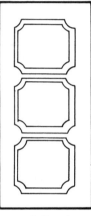

3-Panel

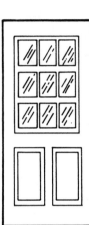

9-Light panel

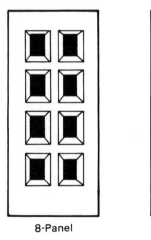

8-Panel

2-Light panel

Fig. 17-3. Exterior doors.

by sticking and by failing to latch. To remedy the sticking door, first determine where it is sticking. If the frame is not critically out of square, some minor adjustments may remedy the situation. The top of the door could be planed without removing the door. If the side of the door is sticking near the top or bottom, the excess width can also be planed without removing the door; however, the edge will have to be refinished or re-

painted. If the side of the door sticks near the latch or over the entire height of the door, remove the door and plane the hinge edge. Don't plane large amounts of wood from the latch side of the door. If you do, the hole for the latch and lock will be out of position. You will need to remove additional material under the hinge before the hinges are replaced. Where the door is binding on the hinge edge, the hinges may be routed too deeply. This can be corrected by removing the hinge and adding a filler under it to bring it out slightly.

If the latch does not close, remove the strike plate and shim it out slightly. Replace the strike plate by first placing a filler, such as a matchstick, in the screw hole and reinserting the screw so that the strike plate is relocated slightly away from the stop.

Exterior Doors

If exterior doors are badly weathered, you may decide to replace them rather than to attempt a repair. Doors can be purchased separately or with frames, including exterior side and head casing with jamb and sill. Exterior doors should be either panel or solid-core flush. Several styles are available, most of them featuring some type of glazing. Hollow-core flush doors should be limited to interior use, except in warm climates, because they warp excessively during the heating season when used as exterior doors. Modern steel doors work well as exterior doors and have a solid core of insulation for energy efficiency. The standard height for exterior doors is 6 feet 8 inches; standard thickness, 1¾ inches. The main door should be 3 feet wide. The service or rear door, at least 2 feet 6 inches, preferably 3 feet wide.

Interior Doors

Modern interior doors are usually hollow-core luan doors or solid hardboard. The hardboard doors come in both smooth and paneled types. Panel-type doors are available in a variety of patterns. Two popular patterns are the five-cross-panel and the colonial. If you are painting the doors, hardboard is an economical option with other benefits. Once painted, they look very similar to wood doors for much less money. They are also less susceptible to warping and swelling than traditional wood doors.

Standard door height is 6 feet 8 inches. However, a height of 6 feet 6 inches is sometimes used with low ceilings, such as in the upstairs of a story-and-a-half house or in a basement. Door widths vary, depending on use and personal taste; however, minimums may be

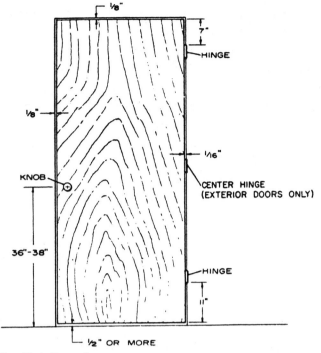

Fig. 17-4. Door clearances.

governed by building regulations. Usual widths are (a) bedrooms and other rooms, 2 feet 6 inches; (b) bathrooms, 2 feet 4 inches; (c) small closets and linen closets, 2 feet.

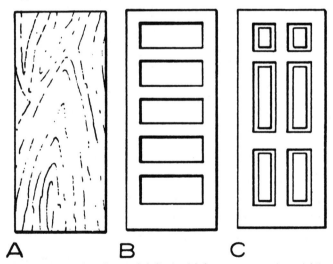

Fig. 17-5. Interior doors: (A) flush; (B) five-cross panel; and (C) colonial panel type.

WINDOW REPLACEMENT STEPS

1. Inspect windows for signs of decay or problems that are beyond repair. Factor this into your estimate. If you plan to enlarge the window opening, check around the window for additional structural framing or plumbing that might interfere with the enlargement.

2. Purchase windows. Many window types must be ordered from the factory and take time to be delivered. Make sure to order the windows far enough in advance to guarantee delivery before your project begins.

3. Perform the standard bidding process. If you are hiring a contractor, the carpenter or framer will probably do the window framing and installation.

4. Schedule framing and siding contractors so that siding can be finished as soon as windows are installed. Leaving the opening exposed without siding could allow moisture to enter the wall.

5. Remove the old window. After the existing window is removed, take off the interior wall covering to the rough opening width for the new window. If a larger window must be centered in the same location as the old one, half the necessary additional width must be cut from each side.

6. Place supports for the load-bearing wall if you are reframing the existing opening. For windows 3½ feet or less in width, no temporary support of the ceiling and roof should be required. Where windows more than 3½ feet wide are to be installed, provide some temporary support for the ceiling and roof before removing existing framing in bearing walls. Use floor jacks for this purpose.

7. Remove framing to the width of the new window and frame the window. The header must be supported at both ends by cripple studs. Headers are made up of two 2-inch-thick members, usually spaced with wood strips to produce the same width as the 2 × 4 stud space. For wider openings, independent design may be necessary. Do not oversize headers on the theory that, if a little is good, more is better. Cross-grain shrinkage causes distortion and should be kept to a minimum.

8. Cut the sheathing and siding to the size of the rough opening. If bevel siding is used, it must be cut to the size of the window trim so that it will butt against the window casing. Determine the place to cut the siding by inserting the preassembled window frame in the rough opening and marking the siding around the outside edge of the casing.

9. Caulk the rough opening before installing the window frame to ensure that water and wind do not come in around the finished window. When installing panel siding, place a ribbon of caulking sealant around the

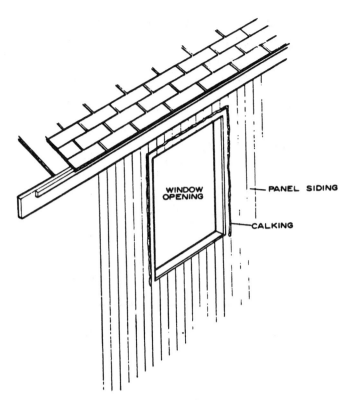

Fig. 17-6. Caulk around window before installing frame.

window frame. When installing horizontal siding over sheathing, loosen the siding around the opening and slide strips of 15-pound asphalt felt between the sheathing and siding to act as an additional moisture barrier.

10. Insert the frame in the rough opening, preferably with the sash in place to keep it square, and level the sill with a carpenter's level. If necessary, use shims under the sill on the inside. Make sure the side casing and jamb are level and square; then, nail the frame in place with 10d galvanized nails. Nail through the casing into the side studs and header, spacing the nails about 12 inches apart. When double-hung windows are used, slide the sash up and down while nailing the frame to be sure that the sash works freely. For installation over panel siding, place a ribbon of caulking sealer at the junction of the siding and the sill. Install a small molding such as quarter round over the caulking.

11. Frame in the old opening. If you are moving a window to a new location, the old opening must be framed in so it can be covered with new siding and drywall. Close the opening as follows: Add 2 × 4 vertical framing members spaced no more than 16 inches apart in the opening. Keep the framing aligned with existing studs under the window or in sequence with wall studs so that covering

materials can be nailed to them easily. Toenail new framing to the old window header and to the sill using three 8d or 10d nails at each joint. Install sheathing of the same thickness as the existing sheathing, add insulation, and apply a 6-mil poly vapor barrier on the inside face of the framing. Make sure the vapor barrier covers the rough framing of the existing window and overlaps any vapor barrier in the remainder of the wall. Insulation and vapor barriers are discussed more fully in chapter thirteen. Apply interior and exterior wall covering to match the existing coverings on the house.

12. Install siding and drywall.

13. Install trim around exterior and interior of window. Install screens.

14. Inspect windows by opening and closing each one. Make sure they operate without binding and latch properly.

15. Pay the carpenter.

DOOR REPLACEMENT STEPS

1. Inspect the door frame for signs of decay or problems that are beyond repair. If the frame is damaged but the door is acceptable, consider replacing the frame only.

2. Purchase doors or frames. Store doors on site so that they will be available when the project begins.

3. Perform the standard bidding process. If you are hiring a contractor, the carpenter or framer will probably do the door framing and installation.

4. Schedule framing and siding contractors so that siding can be finished after the doors are installed. Leaving the opening exposed without siding could allow moisture to enter the wall.

5. Support existing framing. If you are installing a new door opening, provide support for load-bearing walls the same way as for windows.

Exterior Doors

1. Frame in the new opening. Where rough framing is required, either for a new door location or because old framing is not square, provide header and cripple studs. Rough opening height should be the height of the door, plus 2¼ inches above the finished floor; the width should be the width of the door, plus 2½ inches. Use doubled 2 × 6s for headers and fasten them in place

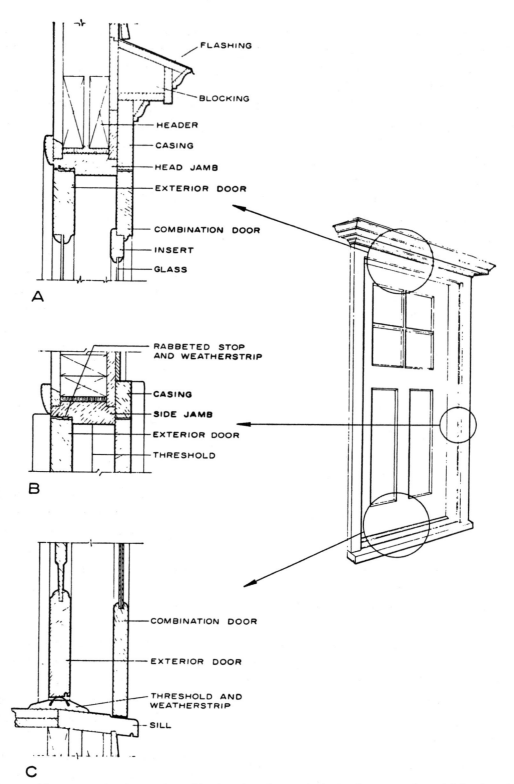

Fig. 17-7. Exterior door and frame. Exterior door and combination-door (screen and storm) cross sections: (A) head jamb; (B) side jamb; and (C) sill.

with two 16d nails through the stud into each member. If the stud space on each side of the door is not accessible, toenail the header to the studs. Nail extra studs, supporting the header on each side of the opening, to the full stud with 12d nails spaced about 16 inches apart and staggered.

2. Install the door frame. (See the figures for definitions of terms). After sheathing or panel siding is placed over the framing, leaving only the rough opening, the door frame can be installed. Apply a ribbon of caulking sealer on each side and above the opening where the casing will fit. Place the door frame in the opening and secure it by nailing through the side and head casing. Nail the hinge side first. In a new installation the floor joists and header must be trimmed to receive the sill before the frame can be installed. The top of the sill should be the same height as the finish floor so that the threshold can be installed over the joint. Shim the sill when necessary so that it will have full bearing on the floor framing. When joists are parallel to the sill, headers and a short support member are necessary at the edge of the sill. Use a quarter-round molding in combination with caulking under the door sill when a panel siding or other single exterior covering is used. Install the threshold over the junction with the finish floor by nailing it to the floor and sill with finishing nails.

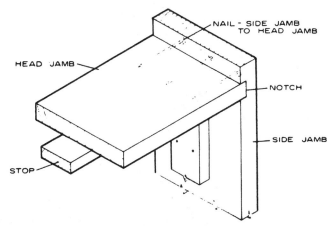

Fig. 17-8. Door jamb assembly.

3. Install the door. In-swinging exterior doors require 3½" × 3½" loose-pin hinges. Nonremovable pins are used on out-swinging doors for security. Use three hinges to minimize warping. Bevel the edges slightly toward the side that will fit against stops. Carefully measure the opening width and plane the edge for the proper side clearances. Next, square and trim the top of the door for proper fit; then, saw off the bottom for the proper floor clearance. All edges should then be sealed to minimize entrance of moisture.

4. Trim door to fit. Do any trimming to reduce the width of the door on the hinge edge. Hinges are routed or mortised into the edge of the door with about ³⁄₁₆-inch or ¼-inch back spacing.

Interior Doors

1. Frame the interior opening. If a new interior door is added or the framing is replaced, the opening should be rough framed identically to that of exterior doors. Rough framing width is 2½ inches plus the door width.

Rough framing height is 2 inches plus the door height above the finished floor. The head jamb and two side jambs are the same width as the total wall thickness when wood casing is used. When metal casing is used with drywall, the jamb width is the same as the stud depth. Jambs are often purchased in precut sets and can even be purchased complete with stops and with the door prehung in the frame.

2. Install the interior door frame. The prehung door is by far the simplest to install and is usually the most economical because of the labor savings. Even where the door and jambs are purchased separately, the installation is simplified by prehanging the door in the frame at the building site. The door then serves as a jig to set the frame in place and square up the frame. Before installing the door, temporarily put in place the narrow wood strips used as door stops. Stops are usually ⁷⁄₁₆-inch thick and may be 1½ to 2¼ inches wide. Install them with a mitered joint at the junction of the top and side jambs. Cut a 45-degree bevel on the stop 1 to 1½ inches above the finish floor. This bevel will eliminate a gap between the stop and the floor that would collect dirt. This is called a sanitary stop.

3. Install the interior door. Fit the door to the frame, using the clearances recommended by the manufacturer. Bevel edges slightly toward the side that will fit against the stops. Route or mortise the hinges into the edge of the door with about a ³⁄₁₆-inch or ¼-inch back spacing. Make adjustments, if necessary, to provide sufficient edge distance so that screws have good penetration in the wood. For interior doors, use two 3" × 3" loose-pin hinges. If a router is not available, mark the hinge outline and depth of cut. Remove the wood with a wood chisel. The surface of the hinge should be flush with the wood surface. After attaching the hinge to the door with screws, place the door in the opening, block it for proper clearances, and mark the location of door hinges on the jamb. Remove the door and route the jamb to the thickness of the hinge half. Install the hinge halves on the jamb, place the door in the opening and insert the pins.

4. The stops that were temporarily nailed in place can now be permanently installed. Nail the stop on the lock side first, setting it against the door face when the door is latched. Nail the stops with finishing nails or brads 1½ inches long and spaced in pairs about 16

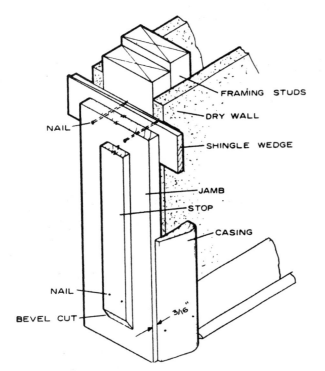

Fig. 17-9. Installation of door trim.

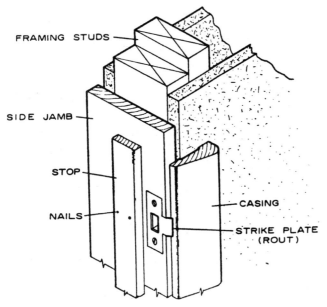

Fig. 17-10. Installation of door strike plate.

inches apart. The stop at the hinge side of the door should allow a clearance of ⅟₃₂ inch.

5. Install interior trim and casing. Casing is the trim around the door opening. Shapes are available in thicknesses from ½ to ¾ inch and widths varying from 2¼ to 3½ inches. A number of styles are available. Metal casing used at the edge of drywall eliminates the need for wood casing. Position the casing with about a ³⁄₁₆-inch edge dis-

tance from the face of the jamb. Nail it with 6d or 7d casing or finishing nails, depending on the thickness of the casing. Casing with one thin edge should be nailed with 1½-inch brads along the edge. Space nails in pairs about 16 inches apart. Casings with molded forms must have a mitered joint where the head and side casings join, but rectangular casings are butt-joined.

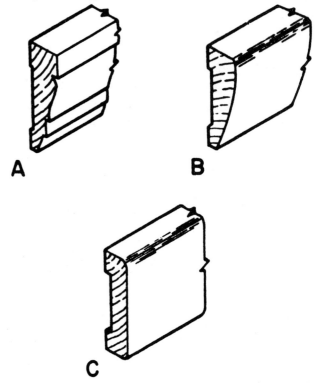

Fig. 17-11. Styles of door casings: (A) colonial; (B) ranch; and (C) plain.

Metal casing can be installed by either of two methods. In one method, the casing is nailed to the door buck around the opening; then the drywall is inserted into the groove and nailed to the studs in the usual fashion.

The other method consists of first fitting the casing over the edge of the drywall, positioning the sheet properly, and then nailing through the drywall and casing into the stud underneath. Use the same type of nails and spacing as for drywall alone.

6. Install the lock or latch set. Lock sets are classified in the following ways:

Entry lock sets (decorative, keyed locks)
Privacy lock sets (inside lock controls with a safety slot for opening from the outside)
Keyed lock sets
Latch sets (without locks)

The lock set is usually purchased with, and may even be installed with, the door. Prehung doors usually have

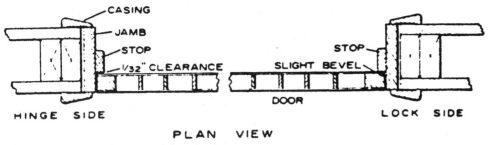

Fig. 17-12. Door stop clearances (plan view).

WINDOW INSPECTION

☐ Window frame is secure in place with leveling wedges or chips.

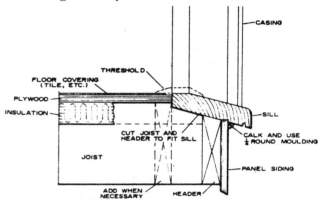

Fig. 17-14. Door installation at sill.

the opening for the latch set already drilled, especially on metal doors. If not, use the paper templates included with the lock set that provide for the exact location of the holes and follow the manufacturer's instructions for installation. After the latch is installed, mark the location of the latch on the jamb when the door is in a near-closed position. Mark the outline of the strike plate for this position and route the jamb so the strike plate will be flush with the face of the jamb.

7. Weatherstrip exterior doors. Check weatherstripping on old doors, and replace it where there is indication of wear. Also consider adding storm doors. They will not only save on heat, but also protect the surface of the exterior door from weather, reducing the likelihood of warping.

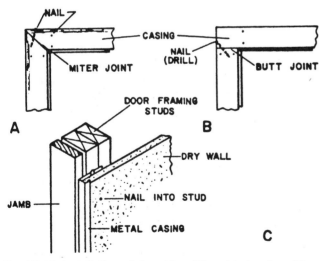

Fig. 17-13. Installation of door trim: (A) molded casing; (B) rectangular casing; and (C) metal casing.

8. Inspect the door to make sure it has an even gap all the way around the door frame. Check for dragging and a tight seal around weatherstripping.

9. Pay the carpenter.

☐ Windows are installed with less than ½-inch gap between wall and frame.
☐ Windows open and close smoothly and easily. Windows glide easily along tracks. Windows close evenly and completely.
☐ Window sash locks are installed and operating properly.
☐ There are no hammer dents in window or window casing.
☐ All window casing nails are set below surface and sealed with putty.
☐ Weatherstripping is in place if specified.
☐ Screens are installed if specified.
☐ All window pulls are in place and secure.
☐ There is no excessive damage to millwork.

DOORS INSPECTION

☐ Proper doors are installed (the correct style, size, type, etc.).
☐ Doors open and close smoothly and quietly. Hinges do not bind or squeak. Doors swing freely

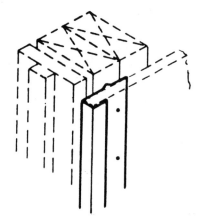

Fig. 17-15. Metal casing used with drywall.

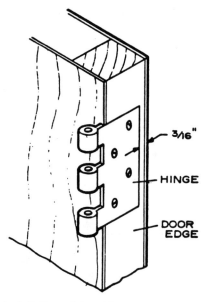

Fig. 17-16. Installation of door hinges.

with no noise or friction against adjoining surfaces. When opened at 30, 45 and 60 degree angles, doors remain where positioned. If not, remove center pin, bend it slightly with a hammer and replace it.

☐ Door knobs and latches align with latch insets. All dead bolt locks align properly. Privacy locks are installed on proper side of doors. Passage locks are on proper doors.

☐ All exterior doors lock and unlock properly. Locks function freely.

☐ All keys are available. All locks are keyed the same for ease of use.

☐ All doors open in proper direction. Door latch faces the proper direction.

☐ All doors are plumb against door jambs. (With door slightly open, check for alignment and evenness of opening.) There are two screws in each strike plate and a pin in each door hinge.

☐ All door casing nails are set below surface and filled with putty.

☐ Door knobs, door locks and dead bolts work properly without sticking.

☐ There are no hammer dents in door or door casing.

☐ Thresholds are in place and properly adjusted.

☐ Weatherstripping is in place if specified.

☐ Clearance from floor is proper (about ½ inch above carpet level). Consider height of carpet and pad, tile, wood floor, etc.

☐ Door stops are in the proper places.

WINDOWS AND DOORS MATERIAL ESTIMATE

DESCRIPTION	SPECIFICATION	QTY.	UNIT	COST	TAX	TOTAL COST	COST TYPE	VENDOR
Openings								
Studs — 2″ × 4″ × 8′ fir								
Headers — 2″ × 6″ × 8′ fir								
Headers — 2″ × 8″ × 8′ fir								
Drip cap galvanized								
15-pound roof felt — flashing								
Floor jacks — rental								
Carpenter — labor								
10d nails — framing								
8d nails — framing								
16d nails — framing								
12d nails — framing								
Windows								
Double-hung window 3′0″ × 4′6″								
Double-hung window 1′8″ × 3′10″								
Double-hung window 2′8″ × 4′6″								
Storm window 3′0″ × 4′6″								
Storm window 1′8″ × 3′10″								
Storm window 2′8″ × 4′6″								
Casing kit — colonial 3′0″ × 4′6″								
Casing kit — colonial 1′8″ × 3′10″								
Casing kit — colonial 2′8″ × 4′6″								
Wood shutters 4′6″								
Wood shutters 3′10″								
Glass block								
Glass block — spacers								
Glass block — mortar								
Exterior lock set								

WINDOWS AND DOORS MATERIAL ESTIMATE

DESCRIPTION	SPECIFICATION	QTY.	UNIT	COST	TAX	TOTAL COST	COST TYPE	VENDOR
Doors								
Exterior metal door with frame 3'0" × 6'8"								
Exterior metal door with frame 2'8" × 6'8"								
Casing — colonial								
Door stop molding								
Metal threshold								
Weatherstrip kit								
Door stop								
Interior door six-panel hardboard prehung — 2'6" × 6'8"								
Interior door six-panel hardboard prehung — 2'0" × 6'8"								
Interior door six-panel hardboard prehung — 2'4" × 6'8"								
Louver bifold closet 6'0" × 6'8"								
Interior latch set								
Interior latch set — privacy								

CHAPTER EIGHTEEN

Painting

No remodeling project would be complete without the venerable paint job. Painting has always been a tried and true do-it-yourself project. Most aspiring remodelers cut their teeth on a painting project. New paint brightens and freshens the look and feel of almost any home. It also hides the evidence of other remodeling changes.

Painting is a safe remodeling project for a beginner. It doesn't change anything structurally and mistakes can be remedied easily with another coat of paint. Most painting can be done without interrupting daily living for very long. This does not mean that painting is easy, however. Painting is very labor intensive and exacting. Since it is so labor intensive, you can save a lot of money by doing it yourself, if you don't mind the tedious nature of the job.

Painting and finishing of your house during remodeling will usually include stripping or repainting the existing surfaces and providing a finish over new siding, interior wall surfaces, floors and trim. Exterior paint finishes protect the appearance of the home and provide protection from weathering, moisture and insects. Interior finishes are primarily for appearance, wear resistance, and ease in cleaning the surface.

USING COLORS TO DECORATE

As any experienced remodeler can tell you, painting is one of the most cost effective remodeling projects of all. Because the human eye judges brightness and size partly by color, careful color coordination can completely change the ambience of a room. By using some of these visual effects of color you can remodel a room without even lifting a hammer.

Bright, saturated colors accent and appear to project forward. Pastel and muted colors appear to recede. Therefore, the human perceives bright colors as being closer than darker shades. You can use this technique in two-tone colors to add a three-dimensional effect to a room. By using a bright color on trim and a lighter pastel on the wall, you can give a house with a plain facade a much more dynamic look.

Lighter pastel colors can open up a room and have the added benefit of increasing the light level. Neutral colors and pastels are easier to coordinate with other colors. Many professional decorators place light neutral colors on walls and provide color accents with furniture, bric-a-brac, and curtains. Furniture and drapes are easier to move or replace than repainting a room. Neutral colors also don't go out of style as quickly as color accents.

Everyone's idea of color coordination is different. If you are unsure about the color scheme you want for your house, start collecting ideas by visiting hardware store displays, checking home decorating magazines, and driving around in the neighborhood. Look for ideas or color combinations that feel natural to you.

Most paint and hardware stores now carry sophisticated computer color-matching equipment that can match quite accurately the color of almost anything. One quick and easy decorating technique is to provide samples of your upholstery, wallpaper, or other room objects for color matching. The color-matching device has an electric eye that is aimed at the colored object and provides a color formula for mixing the paint. Even if you have no color sense at all, this subtle technique of repeating color accents throughout a room can be stunning.

Many older houses also provide the opportunity to accentuate natural wood tones throughout the home. Before lumber prices shot through the roof in recent years, most older homes were constructed with solid hardwoods for interior trim. It is not even unusual to find nineteenth century homes with solid mahogany framing. Many of these homes conceal hidden treasures of rich hardwoods and flooring. With appropriate stripping, staining and refinishing, natural wood finish trim can be spectacular. Before you get too excited about this possibility however, remove a sample piece of the trim and refinish it to get an idea of the finished appearance. You may decide that paint is more appropriate.

HIRING A PROFESSIONAL

Painting your home can be a very rewarding experience, but it is time-consuming and tedious. Before you decide to tackle the painting, ask yourself the following questions:

1. Do you have the time and patience for the job? If you are working full-time, your time is worth money. Is your time worth more than the painting contractor?

2. Do you have the skills to do the quality job you demand? Just because you know a good job when you see one doesn't mean you have the talent to do the job yourself.

3. Do you have the physical stamina? Painting itself is not hard, but setting up scaffolding, climbing ladders and scraping paint can be backbreaking work.

If you hire professional painters, make sure they carry worker's compensation and liability insurance. Since painting can be more of an "amateur" trade than most, anyone can call themselves a painter. They are less likely to carry the professional liability coverages that most other tradespeople carry. Ask for references from other jobs they have done and specify the masking and drop cloth requirements to protect your property.

TYPES OF PAINT

Paint formulations and technology have changed tremendously in the past few years. Before choosing the correct paint for your project you need to know the nature of the material underneath the paint, the composition of the existing paint finish, and the properties of the paint you plan to use. The many types of paint fall into three main categories:

1. Oil-based pigments use an oil like linseed oil as the carrier. This class of paint adheres well to most surfaces, provides a tough durable surface and creates a water-repellent surface. If your house is more than 20 years old, chances are that most of the paint layers are oil-based.

2. Latex paints use water as the carrier for the pig-

ment. These paints produce few or no fumes, dry fast, are easy to use, and produce a breathable finish that allows water vapor to escape. Latex is not quite as durable as oil-based paints, but recent improvements have narrowed the gap considerably.

3. Varnishes and other solvent based finishes use solvents such as mineral spirits, alcohol, and acetone as the carrier. These finishes provide a myriad of uses as penetrating finishes, floor finishes, epoxies, elastomer finishes, stains and other finishes.

All paints are made up of similar compounds that determine the quality of the paint. The carrier in paint is the liquid that suspends the pigments and additives and allows the material to penetrate the painted surface. As the carrier evaporates, the pigments harden into a solid surface that protects the surface against moisture and wear. Additional solvents also serve as carriers and are added to thin the paint to the proper consistency.

The pigments in the paint supply the holdout or covering ability of the paint. Pigments provide both opacity and tint to the paint. The most common pigments found in almost all paints today are the oxides: zinc oxide and titanium oxide. Lead oxide used to be quite popular before about 1970 until it was discovered to be a health hazard, especially to children. Removal of old paint that may contain lead oxide is a serious consideration when stripping old finishes. You need to take precautions to avoid inhaling the paint dust or fumes. The amount and quality of pigments in your paint will determine the total quality of the paint grade. Certain types of clay are used as budget pigments in less expensive paints to reduce the need for the oxide pigments.

Additives make up a diverse selection of compounds that serve many purposes in special paint formulations. Some examples are: rust inhibitors, drying agents, fungicides, bonding agents, antifreeze, emulsifiers and thickening agents. The specific use of the paint will determine which and how many ingredients are present.

Most paint is sold in at least three quality grades: premium, budget and professional. For maximum quality, durability, and coverage always choose the premium grades of paint. These may cost a little more, but they last much longer. Surprisingly, the professional grades of paint are actually the cheapest grades. These paints are sold in large quantities to contractors at low prices. Many contractors are mostly concerned with the price and coverage of the paint, not the durability. These grades usually contain more clays and chalk pigments, which cover very well but don't last as long as the oxide pigments. Don't assume that your "professional" contractor is using the best quality paint. Specify in your contract the grade of paint that you want.

Oil-Based Paint

Until recently, the most common paints were oil-based. These paints are still popular but have slowly been edged out in popularity by latex paints. Oil paints are still the most durable paints and are most appropriate for exterior finishes and trim. Oil paint bonds strongly to wood and metals and also bonds better on substandard finishes, such as chalky, dirty or oily surfaces. Because oil repels water, however, it does not adhere to damp surfaces at all. Oil paints *must* be applied to a dry surface. Cleanup also requires the use of smelly solvents such as mineral spirits. This makes oil paints less attractive for inside projects.

If you are unsure about the type of paint used on an older house, chances are it is oil-based. If you are about to paint over this surface and the existing paint is in good condition, consider an oil-based paint or primer as a safe finish to use. One strength of oil paint is also its greatest weakness—its waterproofness. Oil paint will protect surfaces from water damage and penetration better than latex. However, if your surface generates moisture that needs to escape, oil paint can trap the moisture and create paint blisters—evidence of water building up behind the paint. An example of this would be an older house with no interior vapor barrier. Moist air in the house would escape through the walls and become trapped by the paint. If you see evidence of blistering in oil paint, consider using a latex paint instead. It breathes and allows water vapor to escape. See chapter thirteen for more information about moisture problems.

Oil paints also provide greater holdout—the ability to keep stains and chemicals from the surface below from leaching through to the surface.

Oil-Based Stains

Oil-based stains are similar to the paints but contain much less pigment. Since they do not cover well, they are designed to be used on new unfinished wood as a protectant and waterproofer and allow the natural beauty of the wood to show through. They come in transparent, semitransparent and opaque stains. Penetrating stains are effective and economical finishes for all kinds of lumber and plywood surfaces. They are es-

pecially well suited for rough-sawn, weathered and textured wood and plywood. Knotty wood boards and other lower quality grades of wood that would be difficult to paint can be finished successfully with penetrating stains.

These stains penetrate into the wood without forming a continuous film on the surface. Because there is no film or coating, there can be no failure by cracking, peeling and blistering. Stain finishes are easily prepared for refinishing and are easily maintained.

Penetrating semitransparent stains form a flat and semitransparent finish, which allow only part of the wood-grain pattern to show through. A variety of colors is available, including shades of brown, green, red and gray. The only color that is not available is white, which can be provided only through the use of white paint. The opaque stains contain enough pigment to behave much like paint and can be used over previous stain colors.

Stains are quite inexpensive and easy to apply. To avoid the formation of lap marks, the entire length of a course of siding should be finished without stopping. Only one coat is recommended on smoothly planed surfaces; it will last 2 to 3 years. After refinishing, however, the second coat will last 6 to 7 years because the weathered surface has absorbed more of the stain than the smoothly planed surface.

A stained surface should be refinished only when the colors fade and the bare wood is beginning to show. A light steel-wooling or steel brushing with the grain, followed by a hosing with water to remove surface dirt and mildew, is all that is needed to prepare the surface. Restain after the surfaces have thoroughly dried.

Water-Repellent Finishes

These finishes contain little or no pigment and are designed only to penetrate and seal the wood grain. These are used mainly on patios and decks where foot traffic would damage a surface finish. A simple treatment of an exterior wood surface with a water-repellent finish greatly reduces the natural weathering process. Staining seals the wood and promotes uniform natural tan color in the early stages of weathering and a reduction of uneven graying that is produced by the growth of mildew on the surface.

Water-repellent finishes generally contain a preservative, a small amount of resin, and a very small amount of a water-repellent that is frequently wax-like in nature. The water-repellency greatly reduces warping, excessive shrinking and swelling, which can lead to splitting. It also retards the leaching of chemicals from the wood and the staining from water at the ends of boards.

This type of finish is quite inexpensive, easily applied and very easily refinished. Water-repellent finishes can be applied by brushing, dipping and spraying. Rough surfaces will absorb more solution than smoothly planed surfaces; the treatment will also be more durable. It is important to thoroughly treat all lap and butt joints and the ends of all boards. Two-coat application is possible on rough sawn or weathered surfaces, but both coats should be applied within a few hours of each other. When using a two-coat system, the first coat should never be allowed to dry before the second is applied. If it does, the surface will be sealed, preventing the second coat from penetrating.

Initial applications may be short lived (1 year), especially in humid climates and on species that are susceptible to mildew, such as sapwood and certain hardwoods. Under more favorable conditions, such as on rough cedar surfaces that will absorb large quantities of the solution, the finish will last more than 2 years.

Latex

Latex has become the paint of choice in recent years. It is durable, safe, and easy to clean up with water. It dries quickly and produces no fumes, making it ideal for interior application in living areas. It can also be used for exterior painting with some precautions.

Latex paints are called "breather" paints and are more porous than conventional oil paints. If latex paints are used on new wood without a good oil primer, or if any paint is applied too thinly on new wood (a skimpy two-coat paint job, for example), rain or even heavy dew can penetrate the coating and reach the wood. When the water dries from the wood, the wood chemicals leach to the surface of the paint. This happens most often with red cedar and redwood. Consider using an oil primer coat first and then finish with latex.

Latex also works well on stucco and masonry finishes. It is more resistant to the alkali by-products that can leach to the surface of masonry. Latex is thick and easily applied to stucco with a paint roller.

Varnishes

Clear finishes based on varnish, which forms a transparent coating or film on the surface, are used mainly for coating interior finishes such as floors and trim. The polyurethane type varnishes are very durable and resistant to water, alcohol and oil.

Regular varnishes should not be used on exterior wood exposed fully to the sun. These finishes deteriorate and often begin to disintegrate within 1 year. A special exterior varnish called spar varnish is appropriate for outside use. It contains UV blockers that filter out the ultraviolet rays from the sun that damage regular varnish (and give you a sunburn).

Special Purpose Paints

Several other types of paints are available for special painting needs. New water-based varnishes are available for interior finishing. These unique formulations combine the hardness and durability of polyurethane with the easy-to-clean properties of latex. They also create no fumes, which can make an interior paint job much more pleasant.

Porches and decks receive too much foot traffic to use standard exterior paints. Porch and deck paint dries to a much harder finish than standard paint. It comes in a limited number of colors and should be applied in two coats with no primer.

Steel or wrought iron fixtures are very prone to rusting. If painted with standard paint, any moisture that seeps through can cause a rust spot to develop. This rust spot will continue to grow and will eventually push the paint off the surface. Rust inhibitor paints and primers are available that contain the rust-inhibiting chemicals. They bond tightly to the metal and create a chemical bond that prevents rust from starting. Since they come in a limited number of colors, they are better used as primer coats instead of final finishes.

Concrete sealants are highly elastic paints designed to maintain a waterproof seal even if masonry cracks. They are so elastic that the surface will stretch and span any small cracks. They usually come in white only and are not very durable since the finish is soft. They will not hold back a large amount of moisture and can blister badly in extremely wet conditions. You can paint over them with latex, however, if you want a more versatile color selection.

Primers

Primers are designed to seal the surface so that subsequent layers of paint will be absorbed evenly. Primers are specially formulated to provide an optimum surface for final coats and come in most of the same formulations as finish coats. The difference is in the bonding and sealing agents. Primers are usually thinner so they can soak in and seal the surface better. They usually dry very fast. Oil-based primers can be used under latex paints and will function well as an intermediate layer between older questionable paints and newer latex or oil paints. A combination of oil primer and latex finish coat can provide the best of both worlds. The big disadvantage, however, is that two different cleanups are needed—one for the primer and one for the latex. Use primer coats under your final finish whenever possible. The final finish will usually be superior to just two coats of regular paint.

MATERIALS AND EQUIPMENT

Before starting your painting project, collect all the necessary equipment. Depending on whether you are painting indoors or outdoors, you may need some or all of the following equipment:

Brushes

You will need a variety of types and sizes of brushes—small brushes for trim and touch-up and 4-inch brushes for covering large areas. Natural bristle or china bristle brushes are the highest quality brushes for oil paints. Do not use these for latex, however; the water will cause the bristles to curl like bad hair on a humid day.

Synthetic bristle brushes made of nylon work well for both oil and latex paint. Look for the highest quality rating. The bristle ends should be frayed (similar to split ends) and the bristles soft but not limp. Flat wall brushes for painting large areas should be cut straight across. Smaller brushes for trim work should have the bristles cut at an angle. These are called sash brushes because the angled cut allows you to work paint into corners and maintain a straight paint line around trim. Don't try to save money on cheap brushes. They will always do a bad job. Properly maintained quality brushes will produce a superb finish for years.

Rollers

Paint rollers come in several varieties for different jobs. The rollers are made up of the roller handle, the roll itself, and some type of pan to hold the paint. Most handles come with a threaded hole that will accept an extension handle, allowing you to reach tall areas without a ladder. The most common roller size is 9 inches. The main difference between rollers is the size and composition of the roller covers. Rolls with a close nap look like velvet and apply the smoothest finish and should be used on the smoothest surfaces only. They don't hold much paint, however, so frequent trips to the paint are necessary. The largest nap looks like wool fleece and will hold a great deal of paint. Their thick nap allows the roller to deliver a lot of paint to rough surfaces such as stucco, masonry and rough siding. These woolly mammoth style rollers are great for outside jobs, but they create a lot of overspray. Make sure you have an ample covering of drop cloths. The most popular rollers fall somewhere between these two extremes.

Power rollers are available that force paint up a hose to the roller, eliminating the need to go back to the paint can. You can paint continuously. This makes the smaller nap rollers more practical, so your paint job will usually be smoother with less overspray. Power rollers are available at most hardware stores and are well worth the investment for large paint jobs.

A large flat pan is available to apply paint to the roller and allows you to roll out the excess paint on a ramp built into the pan. If you are starting a large paint job, you can forgo the pan and use a roller screen instead. This is a piece of wire mesh designed to fit into 5-gallon professional paint cans. You can dip your paint roller right into the 5-gallon can, which is wide enough to accept a standard roller. The wire screen allows you to roll out the excess paint from the roller. If you expect to use more than 3 to 4 gallons of paint for the job, these large paints cans are more economical and convenient.

Sprayers

Paint sprayers come in four types: the hand-held airless sprayer, the high-pressure compressed-air sprayer, the professional airless pump sprayer, and the new low-pressure air sprayers. The hand-held airless sprayers are the common sprayers many consumers buy for small paint jobs. They don't hold much paint, they are loud, and they emit paint in a diffuse cloud of spray that is difficult to direct to the painted surface. You are likely to get as much paint on yourself as the target area. These are not appropriate for large jobs.

Traditional air-compressor sprayers will work for larger jobs but they require that the paint be thinned out so that the paint will atomize properly. The sprayer has several adjustments to change the paint pattern, volume and pressure of the paint. Thick paint will splatter out of the nozzle in lumps. This type of spray gun works best for the thinner stains and varnishes and works less well for thicker latex and oil paints. It also requires an air compressor. Most paint stores rent these machines.

A new type of sprayer has taken the market by storm in recent years — the high-volume, low-pressure sprayer. These devices come with their own high-volume turbine compressors that look and act like vacuum cleaners in reverse. The high volume of compressed air drives the paint toward the target, so more paint reaches its destination with less overspray. The compressed air is hot and helps to speed adhesion and drying of the paint. The adjustments on the sprayer provide a variety of paint patterns and volume. This sprayer can produce a very professional job and can be adjusted to a fine spray pattern for working around trim areas. Like the traditional air gun, this type works best with thinner paints.

The airless diaphragm sprayers are the type you will most likely see professional painters using. They contain a high-volume airless compressor that pumps paint through a long hose to the spray nozzle. Most are designed to fit right on the edge of a 5-gallon paint can. They deliver a high-volume stream of paint with low overspray and can be used for inside and outside painting. It is amazing to watch a professional painter use one of these machines. They work well with the thicker latex paints and can paint an entire house in one day. You can rent these machines from paint stores as well.

Ladders and Scaffolds

Interior paint jobs usually require only stepladders. These come in several sizes and materials including wood, aluminum and fiberglass. The best quality ladders are usually fiberglass, but they are expensive. Always buy or rent the top quality grade. You put your life in danger with a flimsy ladder. The ladder should come with a foldout shelf for holding the paint can. The legs of taller ladders should have diagonal braces on the front for added stability. Most paint stores provide ladders for rental. Stepladders work best inside. The ground outside is usually too uneven.

Extension ladders are used outside or for high inside jobs. They come in a variety of lengths and the better ones have adjustable feet to help level the ladder on uneven ground. The tips of the ladder should have pads to protect the wall from scratches when resting the ladder against it. When choosing the length, always buy a ladder a little longer than the height of the paint job. Extension ladders are measured by the combined length of the two halves, even though the ladder will not extend to this full length. At least 2 feet of overlap is needed. When fully extended, most ladders are floppy and unwieldy. A slightly longer ladder will give you more of an overlap, which will provide additional stability.

If you paint outside, you will probably need scaffolding, which can be rented at the paint store or equipment rental store. Scaffolds are heavy and require two people to assemble and move them. A more economical approach is a ladder jack. These jacks attach to two extension ladders and allow a plank up to 16 feet to be placed between them. This allows the all important side-to-side movement necessary to paint horizontal lap siding.

Drop Cloths

Drop cloths should be placed on all furniture and floors in interior jobs and around bushes and sidewalks outdoors. The best drop cloths are old bed sheets or canvas sheets. They stay in place and are more durable than plastic. Use 6-mil poly sheeting to cover furniture or large areas where there is little foot traffic. Bushes near the house should be covered with canvas drop cloths so they can breathe. If they are very close to the house, you can tie the drop cloth around the plant and pull it away from the wall with a wooden stake driven into the ground.

Masking Tape

Masking tape comes in several widths and styles. If you plan to use a roller or sprayer, get the extra wide rolls that have adhesive along one edge. Note: Don't leave masking tape on trim longer than a few days. If you do, the tape will be almost impossible to remove. Labor-saving Hint: If you are installing new trim, doors, or windows, you can save a tremendous amount of labor by painting them before installation. This also allows you to paint the walls without worrying about getting paint on the trim. This can cut painting labor by 40 percent.

CHOOSING THE PAINTING METHOD

If you decide to paint the project yourself, you will need to determine the most effective painting method to use — brushing, rolling or spraying. Each has its advantages and disadvantages. Generally, cleanup and preparation time is inversely proportional to the speed of painting. Brushing is the slowest method but requires the least masking and preparation. Spraying is extremely fast but requires careful preparation to protect surrounding areas from overspray. Using a roller falls somewhere in between.

If your project is extensive, such as exterior painting, and everything needs to be painted, spraying is probably worth the extra preparation time. Once you prepare the site, you can often finish the job in one or two days. This helps to avoid interruptions for bad weather. Proper spraying requires a certain level of skill, however, so make sure you are up to the task.

Inside painting is best done by rolling or brushing unless you plan to paint the entire interior. Here, paint fumes and overspray can be dangerous and messy. Removing trim and doors and using a power roller can greatly increase the speed and ease of painting indoors.

ANALYZING AND PREPARING THE SURFACE

A new paint job will only be as good as the surface it is painted on. Make sure you prepare the painting surface properly so that the new paint will adhere properly. Examine the existing finish and look for underlying problems that might damage the new finish.

Repaint only when the old paint has worn thin and no longer protects the wood. Faded or dirty paint can often be freshened by washing. Where the wood surfaces are exposed, spot prime with primer before applying the finish coat. Repainting too often produces an excessively thick film that is more sensitive to the weather and is more likely to crack because it cannot expand and contract normally.

For the topcoat, try to use the same brand and type of paint originally applied. Changing paints can cause problems with adhesion. When repainting with latex paint over an oil-based paint, apply a nonporous, oil-base primer before applying the latex paint.

Mildew

When blotchy discolorations of mildew appear on the wood, remove blotches and rain spatters and lighten dark areas by steel brushing with the grain. Use a solution of one part chlorine bleach to three parts water and scrub the area thoroughly. This will clean the surface and kill the fungus. Consider using a paint with a fungicide additive to prevent recurrence of the mildew. This is especially critical with latex paints, since they are less resistant to mildew. Fungicide additives can be purchased at paint stores and added to standard paints.

Wood Stains

Water-soluble chemicals occur naturally in certain woods, such as western red cedar and redwood. Staining occurs when the chemicals are dissolved and leached from the wood by water. When the solution reaches the painted surface, the water evaporates, leaving the chemicals as a reddish brown stain. If wood stains have accumulated on the surface in protected areas, clean these areas by mild scrubbing with a detergent of trisodium phosphate solution. If this problem occurs, consider an oil-based paint, since it has greater holdout properties.

Siding nails can also create rust stains. Little can be done to stop this. Again, oil-based paints with greater holdout will cover these stains more effectively than latex. If the problem is bad, consider spot priming the nails with rust-resistant primer. Only aluminum or stainless steel nails will prevent discoloration on the siding. Galvanized nails will show light stains after several years. Steel nails without rust-resistant treatment should not be used.

Blistering and Peeling

Blistering occurs when too much water seeps through the wood, lifting the paint from the surface in small blisters. Moisture blisters normally appear first; peeling follows. Sometimes, however, paint peels without blistering. At other times, the blisters go unnoticed. Moisture blisters usually contain water when they form, or soon afterward, and eventually dry out. Small blisters may disappear completely upon drying. Large blisters may leave a rough spot on the surface. If the blistering is severe, the paint may peel.

Oil-based paints are more likely to blister in high-moisture conditions because the oil paint is impermeable to moisture. The water vapor is trapped and accumulates. Older and thicker coatings are too rigid to stretch and form blisters; instead they tend to crack and peel. When this occurs, the old paint must be completely removed.

House construction features that will minimize water damage of outside paint are (a) wide roof overhang, (b) wide flashing under shingles at roof edges, (c) effective vapor barriers inside the house, (d) adequate eaves, gutters and properly hung downspouts and (e) adequate ventilation of the house. If these features are lacking, persistent blistering and peeling may occur. Consider stripping the oil-based paint completely and repainting with a latex primer and paint. The latex will allow water vapor to escape more easily.

When peeling occurs between coats (which indicates a weak bond), complete paint removal is the only satisfactory procedure. To avoid intercoat peeling, clean the old painted surface well before repainting. Allow no more than 2 weeks between coats in two-coat repainting. When sheltered areas require repainting, wash the old painted surface with trisodium phosphate or detergent solution to remove surface contaminants that will interfere with adhesion of the new coat of paint. Following washing, rinse all sheltered areas with copious amounts of water; then, let them dry thoroughly before repainting. Roughen the surface of the paint with 60 grit sandpaper to improve the adhesion of the new paint.

Chalking

Chalking results when the binders in the paint degrade from exposure, sun or age. Cheaper paint with clay fillers are more likely to chalk excessively. Wash the surface thoroughly before applying a new coat of paint. Use a premium paint with quality binders to recoat the surface.

Rot

Two types of rot occur—dry rot and wet rot. Dry rot creates dry, crumbly wood that flakes easily. Wet rot occurs from moisture and fungus growth and creates a spongy surface that holds moisture. The fungus should be killed with a fungicide and the rotted wood removed. A new resin-based wood treatment is now available that works wonders on rotting problems. Historical renovators swear by this material for repair of difficult-to-replace wood trim. If you cannot easily replace the rotted wood, consider this alternative.

The wood treatment consists of a resin-based (epoxy) liquid that is thin and will readily soak into the wood. Make sure the wood is as dry as possible and soak the wood with the filler until no more liquid is absorbed. It will set up and create a new substance, more like plastic than wood, that will be as strong as wood and impervious to moisture. Then use a resin-based filler compound to fill any remaining gaps. When cured, it can be sanded and painted.

Cracks

Fill small cracks with caulk and allow to dry overnight. Cover with primer before painting. Large cracks should be stabilized first and then patched with resin-based compound or replaced completely.

Cleaning the Surface

If the existing paint is in good enough condition to paint over, then a thorough cleaning may be all that is needed. Scrubbing with a soft bristle brush and a solution of trisodium phosphate will prepare the surface. A wonderful laborsaving device for cleaning large areas is a high-pressure water sprayer. These can be rented and contain a high-pressure hydraulic pump that boosts the water pressure to 1500 psi. This high-speed jet of water will wash off dirt, mildew and loose paint flakes. Be careful not to aim the jet in one area too long or to aim it at an upward angle. Siding is designed to shed water coming from above, not below. Water can seep into the walls and damage insulation. Also make sure to let the walls dry completely before painting, especially if using oil paints.

Stripping

No one likes the backbreaking task of stripping old paint, but it is necessary for truly repairing bad paint jobs. There are several ways to accomplish this, depending on the surface and the severity of the paint problem.

Scraping and Sanding

Scrape the loose paint from the surface and then sand either by hand or with a belt sander. Sanding will smooth the edges between painted and unpainted areas and will rough up the surface so the paint will adhere better. Hand scrapers can be a putty knife, wire brush, a pull-type scraper, or a molding scraper for working in tight corners. Pull evenly across the surface taking care not to gouge the wood. Sanding can be done by hand, with a belt sander or with a rotary disk attached to a drill. Be very careful when scraping from a scaffold or ladder. Your back-and-forth motions can quickly tip over even a stable ladder.

Heat Stripping

Heat stripping is the most effective way to remove stubborn or thick layers of paint. A blowtorch or heat gun is usually the tool of choice. Heat guns are much safer than blowtorches and are preferred. They are similar to heavy-duty hair dryers that let out a blast of very hot air. Caution is required. These guns can start fires if held in one place or aimed at small gaps in the wall. Lay a drop cloth under the area being stripped and wear protective clothing. You don't want a hot sticky mass of old paint dropping on your arm or leg.

Chemical Stripping

Chemical strippers will peel off paint quite effectively but are very messy to work with. Make sure to wear protective clothing and goggles. Most strippers contain strong lye-type compounds that are irritating to the skin. After scraping off the old paint the surface must be neutralized by washing it with the manufacturer's recommended material, usually water or alcohol. An easier method for using chemical strippers is to apply a gel-type stripper and allow it to dry partially. Then rinse off the old paint with a water-pressure gun. This will also neutralize the stripper. The only disadvantage to this method is that it soaks the bare wood and raises the grain of the wood. If you use this method, expect to sand the surface lightly and allow it to dry completely before continuing.

Lead in Paint

If you intend to strip, scrape or sand an old finish you must be aware of the danger of lead contamination. Since most old paints contain lead oxides, stripping this material will throw dust particles of lead oxide into the air. If you are unsure of the paint content, have a sample of it tested by a hazardous materials laboratory for lead content. Check with your local building inspector for the name of a laboratory near you. If the paint contains lead, you *must* keep others away from the area and clean up thoroughly after finishing. You also *must* wear a Class 2 respirator, the type used for spray painting. A simple dust particle mask is not sufficient.

INTERIOR SURFACES

Interior surfaces are painted with a variety of finishes. Whether you choose to paint fixtures or go for a natural look will depend on the condition of the wood trim and walls.

Wood Floors

Hardwood floors of oak, birch, beech and maple are usually finished by applying two coats of wood seal or polyurethane, light sanding or steel-wooling between coats. This finish is easily maintained by rewaxing.

Wood Paneling and Trim

Wood trim and paneling are most commonly finished with a clear wood sealer or a stain-sealer combination.

Then, the top coat is applied after sanding, with at least one additional coat of sealer or varnish. The final coat of sealer or varnish can also be covered with a heavy coat of paste wax to produce a surface that is easily maintained by rewaxing. Good depth in a clear finish can be achieved by finishing first with one coat of high-gloss varnish followed with a final coat of semigloss varnish.

Wood trim of nonporous species such as pine can also be painted by first applying a coat of primer or undercoat, followed by a coat of latex, flat or semigloss oil-base paint. Semigloss and gloss paints are more resistant to soiling and are more easily cleaned by washing than the flat oil and latex paints. Trim of porous wood species, such as oak and mahogany, requires filling before painting.

Kitchen and Bathroom Walls

Kitchen and bathroom walls, normally of plaster or drywall construction, are usually finished with a coat of undercoat and two coats of semigloss enamel or latex. This type of finish wears well, is easy to clean, and is quite resistant to moisture.

Drywall and Plaster

Plaster and drywall surfaces, which cover most interior areas, are finished with two coats of either flat oil or latex paint. An initial treatment of primer will improve the coverage ability of the final coats, reducing the quantity of paint required for good coverage.

PAINTING STEPS

1. Choose paint body and trim colors. Minimize number of colors. Try not to rely only on paint samples since final colors may vary. Try a test mix on an entire wall if possible.

2. Inspect current paint finishes for potential problems of cracking, peeling, stains, etc. In the estimate, factor in the time and cost of repairs.

3. Test sample of previous paint for lead by sending to approved laboratory.

4. Estimate cost of painting if you are doing the work yourself. If you are hiring a contractor, this will help you to determine a fair range of prices for the job.

5. Perform the standard bidding process. If you are planning (or considering whether) to do the painting yourself, this will help you to determine how much you can save by doing the job yourself. If you are not up to doing the entire job, consider hiring the painter for the exterior work only and doing the interior work yourself.

6. Purchase all painting materials if you plan to paint yourself.

Exterior

1. Pick up rental equipment such as paint sprayer, scaffolding, ladders, power washer, etc.

2. Strip old paint from surface using scraping, stripping or sanding. Neutralize stripper with approved solutions.

3. Wash surfaces thoroughly. Remove chalking, mildew and stains with approved solutions. Allow surfaces to dry for 2 days before painting.

4. Cover and mask all areas and move outside furniture and automobiles to a safe location. Tie up plants in drop cloths and pull away from windows.

5. Patch knotholes, cracks, and rotten wood. Spot prime repaired areas.

6. Sand surfaces lightly for best quality results.

7. Prime and caulk all exterior surfaces: related trimwork, windows, doors, exterior corners and cornice.

8. Paint exterior siding, trim, shutters and wrought iron railing. Iron railing should be painted with a rust-retarding paint. Painting two-story fixtures can be simplified by coordinating with stucco, siding or masonry subs. They will have scaffolding on site that can be used for painting.

9. Paint all cornice work.

10. Paint gutters if needed. Note: If the gutter seams require soldering, don't paint them until the soldering is finished.

Interior

1. Move all furniture and plants to other rooms if possible. This will simplify painting and provide more room.

2. Remove any doors, windows and trim that need to be replaced. Paint replacements before installation to save time.

3. Cover and mask floors and furniture.

4. Patch any damaged walls, trim, etc. Spot prime repair areas if next coat is the finish coat.

5. Remove switch and outlet plates or mask them.

6. Isolate the painting area from rest of house if using solvent-based paint such as varnish, lacquer or oil paint. Use approved activated charcoal respirators when painting to avoid fumes.

7. Prepare painting surfaces. This involves performing the following tasks:

Dust off all drywall with a dry rag.

Apply trim caulk to joint between trim and wall. Smooth it with your finger. Wipe off excess. This is an important step that will help to yield professional quality results.

Repair any dents in drywall or moldings with spackle or wood filler.

Sand all repaired areas to a smooth finish.

Clean or strip old finishes. Old varnish should be cleaned with strong trisodium phosphate. Paint the surface soon after it has dried. Heavily alligatored varnish must be completely removed before cleaning.

8. Paint the prime coat on walls and trim. Before you even start, make sure you have excellent lighting available in every room to be painted. Even if you intend to wallpaper, paint a primer coat so that it will be easier to remove the wallpaper if you ever want to later. For a professional job, lightly sand the walls before the final coat after the primer has dried. Sand the trim also.

9. Paint or stipple ceilings. A paint roller with an extension arm makes this job easier. Wear goggles to keep paint splatters out of your eyes. If you have stippled ceilings, you won't be painting them.

10. Paint walls. Start with a small brush and paint around the ceiling, all windows and doors. Then cover the large areas with a roller, brush or sprayer. Do one wall at a time.

11. Paint or stain the trim. Start with the highest trim and work down. Allow the walls to dry first. It will be easier if you use a 1½-inch sash brush for doing windows and a 2-inch brush for all other trim. Stained trim should be coated with a varnish or other sealer.

12. Remove paint from windows with one-sided utility razor blades. Do this only when the paint has completely dried or the soft paint shavings will stick to the surface and make a mess.

13. Remove drop cloths and the remaining furniture from the room.

14. Clean and sand the floor.

15. Apply floor finish. Use wood seal or polyurethane. This is best done with a close nap roller. Allow varnish to dry thoroughly.

16. Sand or steel wool floor lightly between coats.

17. Apply second coat to floor.

18. Remove the remaining masking tape.

19. Touch up paint job.

Painting Completion

1. Clean up. Latex paints will come off with soap and warm water. Varnish and oil paints will require mineral spirits for removal. Avoid cleaning china bristle brushes with water. Dry out the brushes and store them wrapped in aluminum foil with the bristles in a smooth position. Place plastic wrap on the paint cans prior to attaching lids. Exhale into the cans just before closing. The resulting lack of oxygen will prevent paint skins from forming on the surface. Clean the paint rollers and pans so they can be used again.

2. Dispose of dirty solvents and paints properly.

3. Return rental equipment

4. Pay the painter (if applicable) and require a signed affidavit.

5. Inspect paint job for spots requiring touch-up. Make sure you are looking at the paint job either in good natural light or under a bright light. Wait until the paint has dried—many paints change color when dry.

6. Pay retainage after final inspection.

PAINTING SPECIFICATIONS

Exterior Painting

- Use only premium quality paints.
- Use 5-year warranty, exterior grade latex paint on exterior walls and shutters.
- Prime all exterior trim and shutters with an exterior grade primer.

- Caulk all trim area around windows, doors and corners with exterior grade caulk before final coat. Caulk color should match paint color.

Interior Painting

- Use only premium quality paints.
- Bid should include all material, labor and tools.
- Apply primer coat and one finish coat to all walls, including closet interiors.
- Touch sand walls after primer has dried.
- Use flat latex paint on drywall; use semigloss enamel on all trim work.
- Use ceiling white on all ceilings.
- Caulk and sand all trim joints before painting.
- Apply all paint evenly on all areas.
- Window panes are to be cleaned by painter.
- Painting contractor is to clean up after job.
- Excess paint is to be labeled and to remain on site when job is completed.

PAINTING INSPECTION

- ☐ Proper paint colors are used.
- ☐ Previous paint surface is cleaned and sanded properly. Seams between old paint and bare wood are sanded smooth.
- ☐ Paint is free of drips, cracks and crazing.
- ☐ All ceilings and walls appear uniform in color with no visible brush strokes.
- ☐ Trim is painted with a smooth appearance. Gloss or semigloss enamel is used as specified.
- ☐ All intersections (ceiling-wall, trim-wall, wall-floor) are sharp and clean. There is a clean, straight line between wall and trim colors.
- ☐ Window panes are free of paint inside and out.
- ☐ Extra touch-up paint was left at site.
- ☐ All exterior areas are painted smoothly and evenly.
- ☐ All painting areas are left clean and solvents disposed of properly.

PAINTING MATERIAL ESTIMATE

DESCRIPTION	SPECIFICATION	QTY.	UNIT	COST	TAX	TOTAL COST	COST TYPE	VENDOR
5-gallon cans wall paint — exterior								
5-gallon cans trim paint — exterior								
5-gallon cans wall paint — interior								
5-gallon cans ceiling paint — interior								
1 gallon cans trim paint — interior								
1 gallon cans polyurethane floor varnish								
Trisodium phosphate								
Medium- and fine-grained sandpaper								
Drop cloths — canvas								
Drop cloths — 6-mil poly								
Paint rags								
9-inch Paint roller								
9-inch paint roller cover								
Roller pan								
Extension roller handle								
Paint brushes — china bristle								
Paint brushes — polyester								
Paint thinner								
Can opener								
Paint stir sticks								
Paint tray								
Trim guard								
Rolls of 1-inch wide masking tape								
Tubes of trim caulk								
Caulk gun								
Single-edged razor blades								
Razor blade scraper								

PAINTING MATERIAL ESTIMATE

DESCRIPTION	SPECIFICATION	QTY.	UNIT	COST	TAX	TOTAL COST	COST TYPE	VENDOR
Dust mask								
Activated charcoal respirator								
Painting guide								
Putty knife								
Paint scraper								
6-foot stepladder								
12-foot extension ladder								
Extension ladders — rental								
Power roller — rental								
Paint sprayer — rental								
Scaffolding — rental								
Contract — painter								
Contract — old paint removal								

CHAPTER NINETEEN

Interior Finish

Interior finishing is the most crucial work you will do because it is the part of the remodeling job that will be noticed. Your home may need only minor repairs to bring the interior back to life. However, if your remodeling project includes the relocation of walls, doors or windows then you will have to install new interior finishing on at least part of the walls and ceilings. This chapter will cover three major areas:

1. *Wall coverings*. This may include wood paneling, plywood paneling, plaster and lath, or gypsum drywall.

2. *Ceilings*. Like the walls, most homes have ceilings of plaster or drywall. However, other ceiling finishes include elaborate tin ceilings, fiberboard ceilings, wood paneling, or suspended ceilings.

3. *Interior trim*. Most trim is wood-based and is painted or stained with a natural finish.

Floor finishing is covered in chapter twelve.

WALLS

In most homes, walls are usually finished with wood paneling, plaster and lath, or gypsum drywall. Lath and plaster walls were the most common in older homes. Plastered walls consist of wall lath—strips of wood with gaps in between—with a covering of wet plaster applied. Today, most interior walls are covered with plywood paneling, beveled paneling or most often, drywall.

Drywall is composed of gypsum sandwiched between two layers of heavy-gauge paper. It comes in $4' \times 8'$, $4' \times 10'$ and $4' \times 12'$ panels. Drywall can be applied vertically or horizontally. Panels that cover the entire length of a room can be applied horizontally, leaving only one joint at the midheight of the wall. Drywall comes in two common thicknesses: ⅜ inch and ⅝ inch. The thickness most often used is ⅝ inch because it does not warp as easily, especially where studs are 24 inches on center. Drywall sheets have the long edges tapered and the short edges full thickness. This allows room for the drywall mud and tape at the joints. Sheets should be installed so that the full edges butt against studs. After drywall is applied to studs, the joints between sheets of drywall are smoothed using special drywall tape and patching compound. Moisture affects drywall adversely, so store it in a dry place until used.

Repairing Walls

Minor cracks in plaster or drywall can be patched easily by filling the crack with a plaster-patching mix or spackling compound and sanding after the plaster dries. A fiberglass fabric applied over the crack helps to prevent additional cracking. A new type of lightweight spackling compound makes patching quick and easy. It is extremely light and usually covers well in one coat. Traditional patching compound shrinks when it dries and requires several applications. Lightweight spackling has another advantage—it can be painted over immediately after application. Spot patching works well when the cracks are limited in number; however, if traditional plaster is cracked extensively, or pulled loose from its backing, you should replace it with new sheets of drywall.

Larger holes in plaster are patched like cracks except that a backing for the hole must be created before filling the hole with plaster. The easiest way to do this is to cut out the hole to a square shape with beveled edges. Cut a replacement piece of drywall the same size as the hole with corresponding beveled edges, so that the patch can fill the hole without dropping through into the wall. Glue it in place and then cover with spackling compound, feathering out the edges gradually. Apply two to three coats on a larger hole and sand the patch smooth between coats. Damage to ceiling plaster or drywall can be patched the same way.

New Wall Covering

When you are covering a new wall or re-covering an old one, wood paneling or drywall is the most practical choice. Plywood paneling is extremely easy to install and makes a good do-it-yourself project. Beveled paneling requires the skills of a cabinetmaker and should be done by a professional. Applying drywall requires few special tools but requires some skill and patience. Experienced drywall subs can finish a room with drywall in the fraction of the time it takes a rookie. For this reason, you may find it cost effective to hire a drywall contractor.

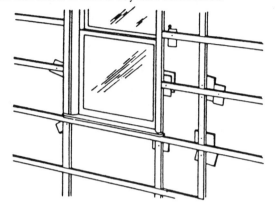

Fig. 19-1. Shingle shims behind furring to produce a smooth surface.

If the existing wall is cracked or damaged, drywall can be used to smooth out the unevenness and to cover imperfections. Wall covering is usually applied directly to the framing in new construction, or to furring strips over existing walls or wall finishes. If the existing wall finish is smooth, such as a concrete wall, drywall or paneling can sometimes be glued or nailed directly to the existing wall. In this direct application there is no thickness requirement for the new covering because it is continuously supported. When applying new wall coverings over studs or furring, use the table for proper thicknesses.

Minimum Thickness for Wall Coverings in Inches

Finish	Space Between Framing Studs	
	16 inches	24 inches
Drywall	3/8	1/2
Hardboard paneling*	1/4	1/4
Plywood paneling*	1/4	3/8
Wood paneling	3/8	1/2

*Note: The 1/4-inch plywood or hardboard may be slightly wavy unless applied over 3/8-inch drywall.

When applying new wall covering over existing walls, start by locating each stud. They are usually spaced 16 inches apart and at doors and windows. The easiest way to find them is to look for nail heads in the drywall or baseboard. These nails have been driven into studs. Where there is no evidence of nail heads, tap the wall finish with a hammer. At the stud, the sound will be solid, whereas the space between studs will sound hollow. Commercial stud finders are also available at hardware and building supply stores. These operate by using a magnet that points to nail heads. Mark the stud locations at the top and bottom of the wall so you can see the marks when installing furring strips or nailing to the wall material.

Furring Strips

Applying new wall covering to an existing wall, such as a basement wall, requires the use of furring strips. To apply furring, first check the walls for flatness by holding a straight 2×4 against the surface. Mark uneven spots. Check for true vertical alignment by holding a large carpenter's level against the wall. As furring strips are applied, use shingles as shims behind the furring where needed to produce a smooth vertical surface.

Apply standard 1×2-inch furring horizontally at 16- or 24-inch spacing, depending on the covering material to be used. Nail the furring at each stud. Remove existing base trim and window and door casings and apply furring around all openings. Also use vertical furring strips where vertical joints will occur in the drywall. After this preparation, any of the usual wall covering materials can be applied.

Drywall

For both horizontal and vertical applications, nail completely around the perimeter of the sheet and at each furring strip. For direct application to framing, nail at each stud. Use ring shank drywall nails or drywall screws. Space the nails 6 to 8 inches apart. Lightly dimple the nail location with the hammerhead, being careful not to break the surface of the paper. Drywall hammers make this job much easier because the hammer head surface is curved in the same shape as the dimple. A drywall hammer also has a drywall blade for punching holes in the drywall for openings. The minimum edge nailing distance is 3/8 inch.

The conventional method of preparing gypsum sheets for painting includes the use of a joint compound and perforated joint tape. After the gypsum board has been installed and each nail driven in a dimple fashion, the walls are ready for treatment. Joint cement (spackle compound), which comes in powder or ready-mixed form, should have a soft putty consistency so that it can be easily spread with a trowel or wide putty knife. The gypsum board edges are usually tapered so that, where two sheets are joined, there is a recessed strip to receive joint cement and tape. If a sheet has been cut, the edge will not be tapered. A square edge is taped in much the same manner as the beveled edge, except the joint cement will raise the surface slightly at the seam and edges have to be feathered out further for a smooth finish. Complete instructions are included with the taping material. A brief description of the procedure for taping is as follows:

1. Use a wide spackling knife (5 inches) and spread the cement over the tapered and other butt edges, starting at the top of the wall.
2. Press the tape into the recess with the knife until the joint cement is forced through the small perforations.
3. Cover the tape with additional cement to a level surface, feathering the outer edges. Allow to dry.
4. Sand lightly and apply a thin second coat, feather-

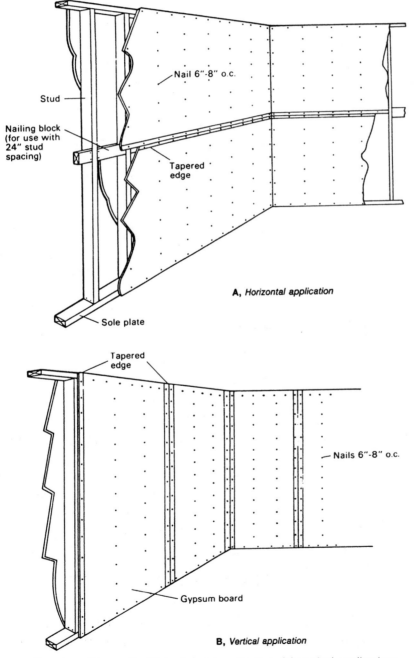

Fig. 19-2. Installing drywall on walls: (A) horizontal application; (B) vertical application.

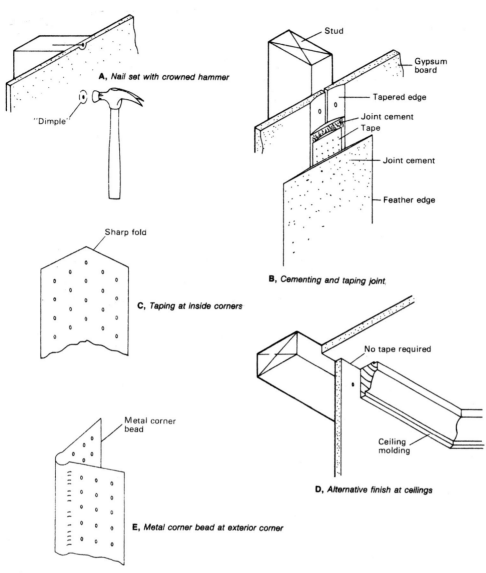

Fig. 19-3. Preparing drywall sheets for painting: (A) drive nails in "dimple" fashion; (B) detail of joint treatment; (C) corner tape; (D) ceiling molding; and (E) exterior corner treatment.

ing the edges again. A third coat may be required after the second coat has dried.

5. After the joint compound is dry, sand smooth.
6. For hiding nail indentations at members between edges, fill with joint cement. A second coat is usually required. Again, sand when dry.

Interior and exterior corners may be treated with perforated tape. Fold the tape down the center at a right angle. Now, (a) apply cement on each side of the corner, (b) press tape in place with the spackle or putty knife, and (c) finish with joint cement and sand when dry. Drywall corner beads of metal or plastic also can be added to provide strength on outside corners. Such metal corners are recommended. They are nailed to outside corners and are treated with joint cement. The

junction of the wall and ceiling can also be finished with a wood molding in any desired shape, which will eliminate the need for joint treatment. Use 8d finishing nails spaced 12 to 16 inches apart and nail into the top wall-plate.

Treatment around window and door openings depends on the type of casing used. When using a casing head and trim instead of a wood casing, install the jambs and beads during application of the gypsum wall finish. These details are covered in chapter seventeen.

Plywood and Hardboard

Plywood and hardboard are usually in 4 × 8-foot sheets designed for vertical application. However, 7-foot-long panels can sometimes be purchased for use in basements or other low-ceiling areas. Plywood can be purchased in many species and finishes, with wide variations in cost. Hardboard imprinted with a wood grain pattern is generally less expensive. The better hardboard paneling uses a photograph of wood to provide the wood grain effect, which produces a very realistic pattern. Both plywood and hardboard can be purchased with a hard, plastic finish that is easily wiped clean. Hardboard is also available with vinyl coatings in many patterns and colors.

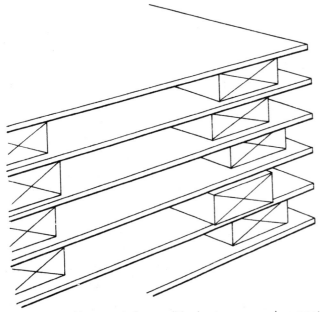

Fig. 19-4. Stacking panels for conditioning to room environment prior to use.

The plywood or hardboard interior finish material should be delivered to the site well before application to allow the panels to adjust to the conditions of moisture and temperature in the room. Stack the panels, separated by full-length furring strips, to allow air to get to all panel faces and backs. Panels should remain in the room at least a couple of days before application.

When you apply the panels to the walls, the starting point will depend partly on whether or not the wall corners are truly vertical. If the starting corner is straight, the first panel is merely butted to the corner and subsequent panels located so they intersect at studs. If the panel corner or other surface is not truly vertical, place the panel edge on a vertical line 2 inches away from the corner. Plumb that edge with a carpenter's level and use an art compass to scribe the outline of the cut by following the contour of the corner with one end of the compass and drawing the cut-line with the other end. Cut the panel and move it against the corner. Make sure the other end of the panel lines up with a stud or furring strip. After the first panel is placed, install successive panels by butting edges against the previous panel, being careful to maintain a true vertical line. Any misalignment is less noticeable, of course, if all walls are paneled. A similar procedure can be used for fitting panels against the ceiling.

Panels can be fastened with nails or adhesive. Adhesive is sometimes preferable because there are no nail heads to mar the finish. Most adhesives include instructions for application. Follow these instructions carefully. Use an adhesive that allows enough open assembly time to adjust the panel for a good fit. Where panels are nailed, use small finishing nails (brads). Use 1½-inch nails for ¼- or ⅜-inch thick materials and space 8 to 10 inches apart on edges and at intermediate supports. Most panels are grooved and nails can be driven in these grooves. Set nails with a nail set. Many prefinished materials are furnished with small nails having heads that match the color of the finish; thus, no setting is required.

Wood and Fiberboard Paneling

Wood and fiberboard paneling elements are tongue-and-grooved and are available in various widths. Wood is usually limited to no more than 8 inches in nominal width. Fiberboard paneling is often 12 or 16 inches wide. Paneling should also be stacked in the room to be paneled, as recommended for plywood and hardboard, to stabilize at the temperature and moisture conditions of the room. Paneling is usually applied vertically, but at times is applied horizontally for special effects.

Vertically applied paneling is nailed to horizontal furring strips or to nailing blocks between studs. Nail with 1½- to 2-inch finishing or casing nails. Blind nail through the tongue for 8-inch boards; face nail near the opposite edge. Where 12- or 16-inch wide fiberboard is used, two face nails may be required. Color-matched nails are sometimes supplied with the fiberboard. Staples may also be used in the tongue of fiberboard instead of nails. Where adhesive is used, the only nailing is the blind nail in the tongue.

CEILINGS

Ceilings can be finished with gypsum drywall or other sheet materials in much the same manner as interior walls. Because of the weight of the drywall, it is best to glue and screw the panels in place with drywall screws.

A variety of ceiling tiles can be used, including the

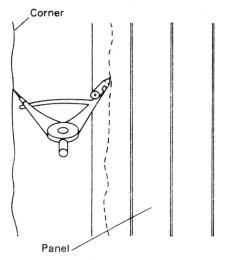

Fig. 19-5. Scribing of cut at panel edge to provide exact fit in a corner or at ceiling.

type for use with suspended metal or wood hangers. The suspended ceiling is particularly useful in renovations having high ceilings. It covers many imperfections and lowers the ceiling to a more practical height. The space above the new ceiling may be used for electrical wiring, plumbing or heating ducts added during remodeling. Since the suspended tiles can be easily removed, the mechanical equipment remains easily accessible.

Cracks in plaster ceilings can be repaired with plaster patching in the same manner as walls are patched; however, where cracks are extensive, a new ceiling is the only cure.

Gypsum Drywall

Drywall can be applied directly to ceiling joists by first removing existing ceiling material. It may also be applied directly over plaster or to furring strips nailed over the existing ceiling where plaster is uneven. Use $2'' \times 2''$ or $2'' \times 3''$ furring strips oriented perpendicular to the joists and spaced 16 inches on center for ⅜-inch gypsum board or 24 inches on center for ½-inch gypsum board. Nail the furring strips with two 10d nails at each joist.

Apply the gypsum boards with end joints staggered and centered on a joist or furring strip. Place the sheets so there is only light contact at joints. One or two drywall braces slightly longer than the ceiling height are quite useful in installing the gypsum sheets. (See Fig. 19-6) Nail the gypsum board to all supporting members with nails spaced 7 to 8 inches apart. Use drywall nails or preferably drywall screws for extra holding power. Nail heads should not penetrate the surface. Finish the joints and nail heads in the same manner described under interior wall finishing. If you are applying a textured ceiling finish or a blown-on finish, only two coats of joint compound are needed. The texture will serve to

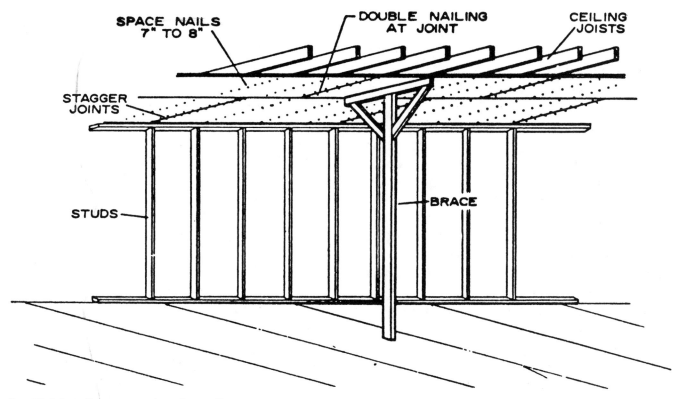

Fig. 19-6. Installing gypsum board on ceiling.

hide the joints. Ceiling finish should be applied before the wall finish is applied.

Ceiling Tile

Ceiling tile is available in a variety of materials and patterns, with a wide range in cost. It can be applied directly to a smooth backing, but the usual application is to furring strips.

If the existing ceiling has a flat surface, tile can be fastened with adhesive. Use an adhesive recommended by the tile manufacturer and follow directions carefully. A small spot of adhesive at each corner and center is usually sufficient. Edge-matched tile can also be stapled if the backing is wood.

A more common method of installing ceiling tile is fastening them to furring strips. Nominal $1'' \times 3''$ or $1'' \times 4''$ furring strips are used where ceiling joists are spaced no more than 24 inches apart. Nail strips with two 7d or 8d nails to each joist. Where trusses or ceiling joists are spaced up to 48 inches apart, use nominal $2'' \times 2''$ or $2'' \times 3''$ furring nailed to each joist with two 10d nails. The furring should be a low-density wood, such as the softer pines, if tile is to be stapled to the furring.

Locate the strips by first measuring the width of the room (parallel to joists). Place the first furring strip at the center of the room, establish the number of complete courses, and adjust edge spacing so that edge courses are equal in width. Plan spacing perpendicular to joists in the same manner so that the end courses will be equal.

Start at one side and continue across the room. For a close fit, do not cut the tile until the last row is being installed. Ceiling tile usually has a tongue on two adjacent edges and grooves on the other edges. In installing, keep the tongue edges on the open side so that they can be stapled to nailing strips. Use a small finishing nail or adhesive at the edge of the tile next to the wall. Use one staple at each furring strip on the leading edge and two staples along the side. A small finishing nail or adhesive is again required in the edge of the tile against the wall where each row is completed. In applying the tile, be careful not to soil the surface. It is usually factory-finished and requires no painting.

Suspended Ceiling

Suspended ceilings consist of a grid of small metal or wood hangers, supported by hanging them from the ceiling framing with wire or strap, and drop-in panels sized to fit the grid system. This type of ceiling can be adjusted to any desired height. Where the existing ceiling is normal height, the hangers can be supported only 2 or 3 inches below the ceiling and still cover any bulging plaster or other unevenness. Where existing ceilings are high, adjust the hangers to the desired ceiling height. Insulated ceiling tiles can be purchased to upgrade the insulation of the ceiling. Suspended ceilings are purchased as a system, assuring that the panels are compatible with the supporting grid. Detailed instructions for installation are usually supplied by the manufacturer.

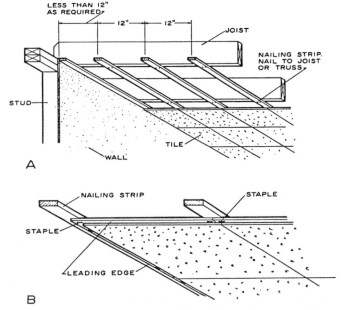

Fig. 19-7. Ceiling tile installation: (A) nailing strip location; (B) stapling.

INTERIOR TRIM

Interior trim consists of window and door casings and various moldings. Such trim in existing houses varies considerably, depending on age, style and quality of the house. The trim found in many older houses is probably no longer on the market, so matching it requires expensive custom fabrication. If the plan is to use existing trim, remove pieces carefully where windows, doors or partitions are changed. In so doing, be sure to mark each piece so that it can be reused where needed.

Decorative trim is one of the most visible items in your house and can make the difference between an ordinary interior and one that stands out. The workmanship of the trim installation will be very visible and hard to repair if not done properly. Good trim requires some of the most precise work to be found in a home. If you are not very experienced in this type of work, you may want to hire a trim carpenter. Interior trim carpenters usually will do the following:

1. Set interior/exterior doors and door sills.
2. Set windows and window sills.
3. Install base, crown, chair rail, picture and other molding.
4. Install paneling, raised paneling and wainscoting.
5. Install stairway trim.
6. Install fireplace and main entry door mantels.
7. Install closet shelves and hanger rods.
8. Install any other special trim.
9. Install door and window hardware, door stops, etc.

Trim subs charge for work in many ways:
- By the opening (for doors, windows and entryways).
- By the cut. The more cuts involved, the greater the cost.
- By the hour or day.
- By the job.

In choosing your trim material, you must first decide whether you plan to paint or stain the trim. You can use lesser grades of trim if they will be painted. Finger joint trim consisting of scraps glued together is fine if you plan to paint. If you plan to stain, you must use solid wood trim; but the fine appearance and low maintenance of stained trim may be worth the expense. Protect trim from abuse prior to installation to avoid dents, cracks, scratches and excessive waste. Lay trim on the floor in neat stacks. Don't purchase trim from different suppliers. The different pieces may not match.

When installing base molding, consider whether trim will go around wall registers or merely be interrupted by the register. The first example is more expensive, but yields a nicer appearance. If you use a tall base molding, you can build your registers and receptacles into the base molding.

Casing

Casing is the interior edge trim for door and window openings. New casing patterns vary in width from 2¼ to 3½ inches and in thickness from ½ to ¾ inch. Place the casing with about a ³⁄₁₆-inch edge distance from door and window jambs. Nail with 6d or 7d casing or finishing nails, depending on thickness of the casing. Space nails in pairs about 16 inches apart, nailing to both jambs and framing. Rectangular casings can be butt-joined at corners, but molded forms must have a mitered joint.

Baseboard

Baseboard, the finish between the finished wall and floor, is also available in several sizes and forms. It may be either one or two piece. The two-piece base consists of a baseboard topped with a small base cap that conforms to any irregularities in the wall finish. Except where carpet is installed, most baseboards are finished with a base shoe. The base shoe is nailed into the subfloor, conforming to irregularities in the finished floor.

Install square-edged baseboard with a butt joint at inside corners and a mitered joint at outside corners. Nail into each stud with two 8d finishing nails. Molded base, base cap and base shoe require a coped joint at inside corners and a mitered joint at outside corners. To cope a joint, use a coping saw (saw with small flexible blade) to saw the outline of the trim shape on the end of the piece to be butted into the corner. The shaped end will form an exact fit against the shape of the other trim piece.

Ceiling Moldings

Ceiling moldings are used at the junction of wall and ceiling. They may be strictly decorative or they may be used to hide a poorly fitted joint. They are particularly useful with wood paneling or other drywall that is difficult to fit and where plaster patching cannot be used to finish the joint. Attach the molding with finishing nails driven into the upper wall plates. Large moldings also should be nailed to the ceiling joists.

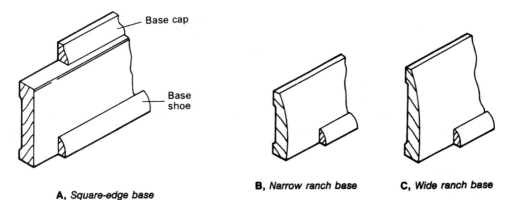

A, *Square-edge base*　　　　**B,** *Narrow ranch base*　　　**C,** *Wide ranch base*

Fig. 19-8. Baseboard: (A) square or traditional; (B) narrow ranch base; (C) wide ranch base.

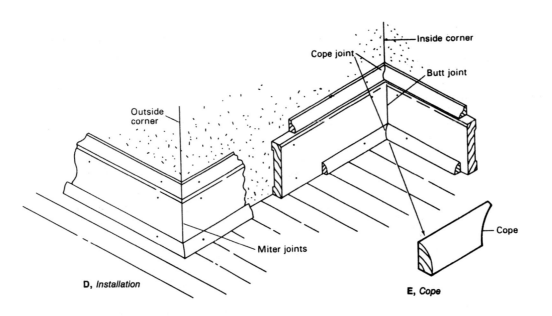

D, *Installation*　　　　　　　　　　　　　**E,** *Cope*

Fig. 19-9. Installation of base molding.

Miscellaneous Decorative Moldings

Decorative moldings can be used in a variety of ways. They can be applied to walls or doors to simulate relief paneling or carved doors. They can also add interest to existing cabinetwork. Check with a local building supplier for available types and ideas on how to use them.

DRYWALL STEPS

1. Inspect existing walls to determine if wall covering needs repairing or replacement.

2. Perform the drywall bidding process. You may wish to ask painters for names of good drywall subs; they know good finishing work since they paint over it for a living.

3. Order and receive drywall materials if not supplied by drywall sub.

4. Before drywall is installed, mark the location of all studs on the floor with a builder's pencil. This will make it easier for the trim sub to locate studs when nailing trim to the wall.

5. Seal off the rest of the house from the construction area with plastic sheeting. Create an overlapping joint at passageways that can be sealed shut. This is very important when installing drywall. The gypsum dust is very fine and will work its way into everything in the house.

6. Install furring strips if covering an existing wall such as the basement.

7. Hang drywall on ceiling. Use a drywall brace to hold material in place. Glue and screw the panels in place. Note: If you plan to use trim around the ceiling, you need to tape the ceiling corner joint only once to seal the seam. The trim will hide the seam. If you plan to use a textured finish on the ceiling, you need to apply only two finish coats of joint compound.

8. Hang drywall on all walls. Outside corners must be protected with metal edging. Inside corners must also be taped. If you are installing drywall over new framing, make sure to intersect existing walls at corners. New drywall and existing wall thicknesses may not match if intersection falls in the middle of the wall.

9. Install water-resistant drywall in bathrooms. Note: This type of drywall, called greenboard, is designed to be water resistant and makes an excellent backing for ceramic tile installation. A superior backing for ceramic tile is fiberglass mesh concrete panels. The joints do not need to be finished.

10. Finish the drywall. Drywall must be finished in a series of steps as outlined below:
    Spackle all nail dimples.
    Sand nail dimples smooth.
    Apply tape to smoothed nailed joints.
    Spackle tape joints (fill coat).
    Sand tape joints (as needed).
    Spackle tape joints (second coat).
    Sand tape joints (as needed).
    Spackle tape joints (finish coat).
    Sand tape joints (third time).

11. Inspect drywall. Refer to specifications and inspection guidelines. To do this properly, turn out all lights and look at the wall while shining a light on it from an angle. Slight shadows will appear if there are imperfections on the surface. Mark them lightly with a soft pencil for repair. Don't use a pen, as it will leave a mark that will show through the paint.

12. Touch up and repair imperfect drywall areas. There are always a few.

13. Pay the drywall sub, requiring a signed affidavit.

14. Pay drywall sub retainage. You may want to wait until the first coat of paint has been applied so that you can get a good look at the finished product.

TRIM STEPS

1. Determine trim requirements. Millwork samples can help. Mark all walls that get new or different trim pieces.

2. Select molding, window trim and door trim. Note: Windows and doors may come with trim kits that include precut pieces.

3. Conduct the standard bidding process.

4. Purchase all floor, window, and door trim.

5. Install window casing and aprons.

6. Install trim around cased openings.

7. Install any staircase molding—treads, risers, railings, newels, baluster, goosenecks, etc.

8. Install crown molding. This includes special-made inside and outside corners if specified. This molding is installed first so that the ladder legs will not scratch the base molding.

9. Install base and base cap molding. Where the final floor level will be higher than the subfloor (when hardwood is installed) the base should be installed a little higher.

10. Install chair rail molding.

11. Install picture molding.

12. Install, sand and stain paneling.

13. Clean all sliding door tracks.

14. Install shoe molding after flooring is installed. Painting the shoe molding before installation will reduce time and touch-up work.

15. Caulk all trim joints at corners and nail holes.

16. Inspect trim work. Refer to your specifications and the checklist that follows.

17. Correct any imperfect trim and stain work.

18. Pay trim sub and have him sign an affidavit.

DRYWALL SPECIFICATIONS

- Bid is to provide all material, labor and equipment to perform complete job per specifications. This includes
drywall, tape and drywall compound

metal corner bead
all nails
Sandpaper
ladders and scaffolding

- Apply ⅝-inch gypsum board (drywall), double nailed or glued and screwed at top. Four nails per stud.
- Tape all joints with three separate coats of joint compound, each sanded smooth.
- Reinforce all outside corners with metal corner bead.
- Reinforce all inside corners with joint tape.
- Make all necessary electrical outlet, switch and fixture cutouts.
- Make all necessary HVAC ductwork cutouts.
- Stipple all ceilings as specified.
- All ceiling sheets are to be glued and screwed in place.
- Apply wall adhesive to all studs prior to applying drywall.
- Use moisture-resistant gypsum along all wall areas around shower stalls and bathtubs.
- Drywall installation and thickness are to conform to fire code rating per local building code.
- Use drywall stilts at your own risk.

TRIM SPECIFICATIONS

- All materials except tools are to be furnished by contractor.
- Interior doors will be prehung.
- Finish nails are to be used exclusively and set below the surface, puttied and sanded over smooth.
- Bid is to include the following:
  A. Hang all interior doors. All doors are to be right- and left-handed as indicated on attached drawings.
  B. Install all door and window trim according to attached schedule.
  C. Install base molding and base cap molding as specified. Raise base molding in areas of hardwood flooring.
  D. Install apron and crown molding in living room, dining room and foyer area.
  E. Install two-piece chair rail molding in dining room as specified.
  F. Install 1-inch shoe molding in all rooms not carpeted.
  G. Install den bookshelves as indicated on attached drawings.
  H. Install staircase trim as indicated below:
  12 oak treads
  12 pine risers
  Solid oak railing with involute
  Gooseneck
  36 spindles
  I. Build fireplace mantel as indicated on attached drawings.
  J. Install door locks, door knobs, window hardware and dead bolts.
  K. All trim is to be paint grade unless otherwise stated.
  L. Install all closet trim, shelves and closet rods.

DRYWALL INSPECTION

Before Taping

- ☐ There is no more than a ⅜-inch gap between sheets.
- ☐ Nails are driven in pairs (2″ apart). Nail heads are dimpled below the surface of the drywall.
- ☐ Nails are not hit so hard as to break the surface paper. All joints shall be double-nailed or glued.
- ☐ No nail heads are exposed to interfere with drywall.
- ☐ There is no sheet warping, bowing or damage. Sheets are easier to replace before taping.
- ☐ Rough cuts around door and window openings are cut close so that trim will fit properly.
- ☐ Waterproof drywall, or wonderboard, is installed in shower stalls and around bathtubs. No taping is necessary here.
- ☐ Metal bead is installed flush on all outside corners.
- ☐ Three separate coats of mud are applied to all joints. Stippling will hide any imperfections. Each successive coat should leave a wider track and a smoother finish.

After Finishing

- ☐ Look down the length of installed drywall; there is no warping or bumps. If found, circle the area gently with a soft pencil (ink may show through when painted).
- ☐ All joints feathered smooth, with no noticeable bumps, either by sight or touch.

- All electrical wiring remains exposed, including bath and kitchen vent fans, garage door opener switches and doorbell in garage.
- Proper ceilings are smooth and stippled as specified.
- These are clean cuts around register openings, switches and outlets so that covers will cover exposed area.
- Nap of paper is not raised or roughened by excessive or improper sanding.
- All touch-up work is completed and satisfactory.
- There is no exposed corner bead.

Trim Inspection
- All crown molding is installed and finished as specified.
- All base molding is installed and finished as specified.
- All chair rail molding is installed and finished as specified.

NOTE: Some drywall imperfections will not appear until the first coat of paint has been applied. This is the first time you will see the wall as a single, uniform color. If you can, wait until this point to pay retainage.

- All wainscoting is installed and finished as specified.
- Trim joints are caulked, sanded smooth and undetectable, both by sight and feel.
- Trim intersects with walls, ceilings and floors evenly with no gaps or other irregularities.
- All trim is void of major material defects.
- All finishing nails are set below surface and sealed with wood putty.
- All paneling and shelving are installed and finished as specified.
- All closet shelving and coat racks are installed at proper height and level.

INTERIOR FINISH MATERIAL ESTIMATE

DESCRIPTION	SPECIFICATION	QTY.	UNIT	COST	TAX	TOTAL COST	COST TYPE	VENDOR
Drywall								
Gypsum Drywall ⅜-inch								
Gypsum greenboard ½-inch — water-resistant								
Perforated tape								
Joint compound								
Metal corner edging								
Sandpaper — nonclogging								
Nails — ring shank drywall								
Screws — drywall								
Construction adhesive								
Drywall stilts — rental								
Drywall lift — rental								
Drywall labor — contract								
Trim								
Base molding — colonial								
Base shoe molding								
Crown molding — ceiling								
Cove molding — ceiling								
Casing — colonial								
Aprons — window								
Chair rail								
Finishing nails								
Wood putty — color matched								
Caulk								
Suspended Ceiling								
2′ × 4′ ceiling tile ⅝-inch								
#12 wire — hangers								
Suspension channels 1½″ × ¾″								
Cross suspension channels								
Wall suspension channels								

INTERIOR FINISH MATERIAL ESTIMATE

DESCRIPTION	SPECIFICATION	QTY.	UNIT	COST	TAX	TOTAL COST	COST TYPE	VENDOR
Stairs								
Treads — oak								
Risers — oak								
Stringers — 2″ × 10″								
Balusters — oak								
Newels — oak								
Handrails — oak								

CHAPTER TWENTY

Roof System

Roof repair can vary from simple reroofing to more extensive repairs to correct sagging. Roof alterations may also encompass remodeling changes such as adding dormers, finishing attics and so on. Inspect the roof carefully to determine its current condition. Check the rafters to see if they are sagging. Examine the roof sheathing from the attic for cracks or signs of deterioration. Some sagging is acceptable but extensive sagging can spell disaster in bad weather and snow storms. The first steps in repairing a roof system are to level sagging ridge poles and to straighten sagging rafters. Then a new roof covering can be applied to the smooth, flat surface. If you are planning other construction that includes the roof, such as finishing the attic, do these projects first before adding new shingles. Extensive roof framing changes are complicated, dangerous, and require a structural knowledge of framing members. Applying new shingles is hot, dangerous and difficult work, but it can be done by a dedicated do-it-yourselfer. If you are planning an extensive roof renovation, consider working with a professional contractor. It is well worth it.

ROOF FRAMING

The sagging ridgepole can sometimes be leveled by jacking it at points between supports and installing props to hold it in a level position. When this is done, the jack must be located where the load can be traced down through the structure so that the ultimate bearing is directly on the foundation. Where there is no conveniently located bearing partition, install a beam under the ridge and transfer load to bearing points. After the ridgepole is jacked to a level position, cut a 2 × 4 just long enough to fit between the ceiling joist and ridgepole or beam and nail it at both ends. For a short ridgepole, one prop may be sufficient. Additional props

should be added as needed. In some repairs the addition of collar beams may be sufficient without requiring props. Where rafters are sagging, nail a new rafter to the side of the old one after forcing the new rafter ends into their proper position. Permanent set in the old rafters cannot be removed.

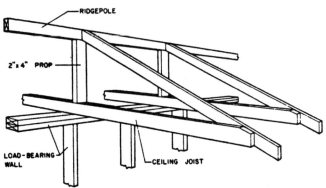

Fig. 20-1. Prop to hold sagging ridgepole in level position.

New construction in the attic can also serve to reinforce and straighten crooked or sagging framing members. The sagging framing will make the new construction more difficult, since there will be no straight lines.

SHEATHING

Sheathing may have sagged between rafters, resulting in a wavy roof surface. Where this condition exists, new sheathing is required. Often the sheathing can be nailed right over the old roofing. This avoids the problems of removing and disposing of the old roofing materials. Wood shingles that show any indication of decay should be completely removed before new sheathing is applied. Where wood shingles are excessively cupped or otherwise warped, they also should be removed. Wood shingle and slate roofs of older houses were often installed on furring strips instead of solid sheathing.

Sheathing nailed over existing sheathing must be secured with longer nails than would normally be used.

Nails should penetrate the framing 1¼ to 1½ inches. Nail edges of plywood sheathing at 6-inch spacing and to intermediate framing members at 12-inch spacing. Apply the plywood with the length perpendicular to the rafters. For built-up roofs, if the plywood does not have tongue-and-grooved edges, use clips at unsupported edges. Plywood clips are commercially available and should be installed in accordance with the manufacturer's instructions. For 16-inch rafter spacing, ⅜-inch plywood is the minimum thickness to be used; ½-inch plywood is preferable.

ADDING ROOF OVERHANG

The addition of a roof overhang where there is none will soon pay for itself in reduced maintenance on siding and exterior trim. Without the overhang, water washes down the face of the wall, creating moisture problems in the siding and trim and, consequently, more frequent painting is required. Additional roof overhang also does much to improve the appearance of the house.

Where new sheathing is being added, the sheathing can be extended beyond the edge of the existing roof to provide some overhang. This is a minimum solution and the extension should not be more than 12 inches where ½-inch plywood sheathing is used. Any greater extension would require some type of framing.

Framing usually can be extended at the eaves by adding to each rafter. First, remove the frieze board, or, in the case of a closed cornice, remove the fascia. Nail a 2 × 4 to the side of each rafter, letting it extend beyond the wall the amount of the desired overhang. The 2 × 4 should extend inside the wall a distance equal to the overhang. Framing for an overhang at the gable ends can be accomplished by adding a box frame. Extensions of the ridge beam and eaves fascia are required to support this boxed framing. An alternate extension is possible with a plank placed flat, cut into gable framing, extending back to the first rafter.

ROOF COVERINGS

Many types of roof coverings are available, and most can be used in rehabilitation in the same manner as for new construction. Sometimes there are local code requirements for fire safety.

Roofing is measured, estimated and bid based on squares (units of 100 square feet roof coverage). Common roofing compositions include asphalt, fiberglass

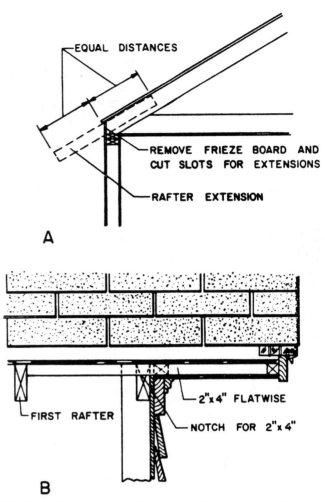

Fig. 20-2. Extension of roof overhang: (A) rafter extension at eaves; (B) extension at gable end.

and cedar shakes, although special roofs are also composed of tile, slate and other more expensive materials. Fiberglass is a popular choice due to its favorable combination of appearance, price and durability. Roofing warranties are most often a minimum of 20 years. This pertains to material only.

Cost usually influences your choice. In most houses the roof is a major design element and the covering material must fit the house design. Heavy materials such as tile or slate should not be used unless they replace the same material or unless the roof framing is strengthened to support the additional load. The most popular covering materials for pitched roofs are wood and fiberglass shingles. As previously discussed, these can be applied directly over old shingles or over sheathing; however, if two layers of shingles exist from previous reroofing, it is better to remove the old roofing before proceeding. Reroofing over one layer of existing shingles will still be covered under the manufacturer's warranty if the shingles are installed following the instructions included with the shingles.

Roll roofing is sometimes used for particularly low-cost applications or over porches with relatively low-pitched roofs. The most common covering for flat or low-pitched roofs is a built-up roof with a gravel topping. An underlayment of 15- or 30-pound roof felt should be used in moderate and low-sloped roofs covered with asphalt, fiberglass shingles, slate shingles or tile roofing. It is not commonly used under wood shingles or shakes.

A 45-pound or heavier smooth-surface roll roofing should be used as a flashing along the eave line in areas where moderate to severe snowfalls occur. The flashing should extend to a point 36 inches inside the warm wall. If two strips are required, use mastic to seal the joint. Also use mastic to seal end joints. This flashing gives protection from ice dams that form when melting snow runs down the roof and freezes at the colder cornice area. Ice gradually forms a dam that backs up water under the shingles. Wide flashing at the eaves will minimize the chances of this water entering the ceiling or the wall. Good attic ventilation and sufficient ceiling insulation are also important in eliminating ice dams. Roll roofing 36 inches wide is also required at all valleys.

When applying new shingles over old wood or asphalt shingles, remove 6-inch wide strips of old shingles along the eaves and gables, and apply nominal 1-inch boards at these locations. Thinner boards may be necessary where application is over old asphalt shingles. Remove the old covering from ridges or hips and replace it with bevel siding, butt edge up. Place a strip of lumber over each valley to separate old metal flashing from new. Double the first shingle course.

Wood Shingles. Wood shingles used for house roofs should be No. 1 grade, which are all heartwood, all edge grain and tapered. The most common species are western red cedar and redwood, which have heartwood with high decay resistance and low shrinkage. Widths of shingles vary, and the narrower shingles are most often found in the lower grades. Recommended exposures for common shingle sizes are shown below.

The general rules for applying wood shingles are:

1. Extend shingles 1½ to 2 inches beyond the eaves line and about ¾ inch beyond the rake (gable) edge.

2. Soak the wood shingles thoroughly before installing to reduce splitting.

3. Nail each shingle with two rust-resistant nails spaced about ¾ inch from the edge and 1½ inches above the butt line of the next course. Use 3d nails for 16- and 18-inch shingles and 4d nails for 24-inch shingles.

Where shingles are applied over old wood shingles, use longer nails to penetrate through the old roofing and into the sheathing. A threaded ring-shank nail is recommended where the plywood roof sheathing is less than ½ inch thick.

4. Allow a ⅛- to ¼-inch space between each shingle for expansion when wet. Lap vertical joints at least 1½ inches by the shingles in the course above. Space the joints in succeeding courses so that the joint in one course does not line up with the joint in the course above it.

5. Shingle away from valleys, selecting and precutting wide valley shingles. The valley should be 4 inches wide at the top and should increase in width at the rate of ⅛ inch per foot from the top. Use valley flashing with a standing seam. Do not nail through the metal.

Valley flashing should be a minimum of 24 inches wide for roof slopes under 4-in-12, 18 inches wide for roof slopes of 4-in-12 to 7-in-12, and 12 inches wide for roof slopes of 7-in-12 and over.

6. Place a metal edging along the gable end of the roof to aid in guiding the water away from the end walls.

Wood Shakes. Apply wood shakes in much the same manner as shingles, except longer nails must be used because the shakes are thicker. Shakes have a greater exposure than shingles because of their length. Exposure distances are 8 inches for 18-inch shakes, 10 inches for 24-inch shakes, and 13 inches for 32-inch shakes. Butts are often laid unevenly to create a rustic appearance. An 18-inch wide underlay of 30-pound asphalt felt should be used between each course to prevent wind-driven snow from entering between the rough faces of the shakes. Position the underlay above the butt edge of the shakes a distance equal to double the weather exposure. Where exposure distance is less than one-third the total length, underlay is not usually required.

Asphalt Shingles. The most common type of asphalt shingle is the square-butt strip shingle, which is 12″×36″, has three tabs, and is usually laid with 5 inches exposed to the weather. Bundles should be piled flat so that strips will not curl when the bundles are opened for use. Add an underlayment of 15-pound saturated felt before installing the shingles.

Begin application of the roofing by applying a wood-shingle course or metal edging along the eave line. Double the first course of asphalt shingles and extend the

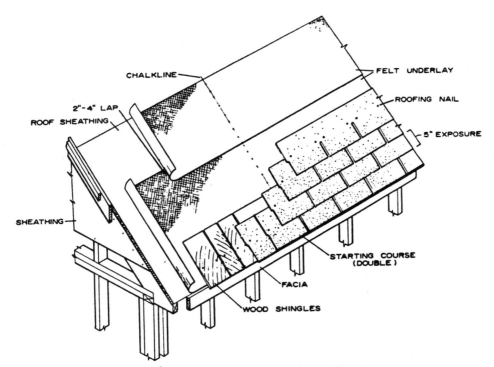

Fig. 20-3. Application of asphalt shingle roofing over plywood with strip shingles.

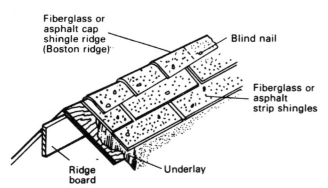

Fig. 20-4. Boston ridge using asphalt shingles.

course downward beyond the wood shingles (or edging) about ½ inch to prevent the water from backing up under the shingles. A ½-inch projection should also be used at the rake. Make several chalk lines on the underlayment parallel to the roof slope to serve as guides in aligning the shingles so that the tabs are in a straight line. Follow the manufacturer's directions in securing the shingles. Nailing each 12″ × 36″ strip with six 1-inch galvanized roofing nails is prudent in areas of high winds. Shingles with self-sealing tabs should be used in these areas. When a nail penetrates a crack or knothole, remove the nail, seal the hole, and replace the nail in sound wood. If the nail is not in sound wood, it will gradually work out and cause a bump in the shingle above it.

Built-Up Roof. Built-up roof coverings are limited to flat or low-pitched roofs and are installed by contractors who specialize in this work. The roof consists of three, four or five layers of roofers' felt, with each layer mopped down with tar or asphalt. The final surface is then coated with asphalt, which is usually covered with gravel embedded in asphalt or tar.

Other roof coverings. Other roof coverings, such as slate, concrete, tile and metal, require specialized applicators. Consequently, their application is not described in detail. They are generally more expensive and are much less widely used than wood or asphalt shingles and built-up roofs.

Shingles on the Ridge

The Boston ridge is the most common method of treating the roof ridge and is also applicable to hips. When installing asphalt shingles, cut the 12″ × 36″ strips into 12″ × 12″ sections. Bend them slightly and lay them over the ridge with a 5-inch overlap. Locate nails where they will be covered by the lap of the next section. A small spot of asphalt cement under each exposed edge will give a positive seal.

Wood-shingle roofs can also be finished with a Boston ridge. Flashing should first be placed over the ridge. Then 6-inch wide shingles are alternately lapped, fitted and blind-nailed. Exposed shingle edges are alternately lapped.

A metal ridge vent can also be used on asphalt-shingle or wood-shingle roofs. This ridge of copper, galva-

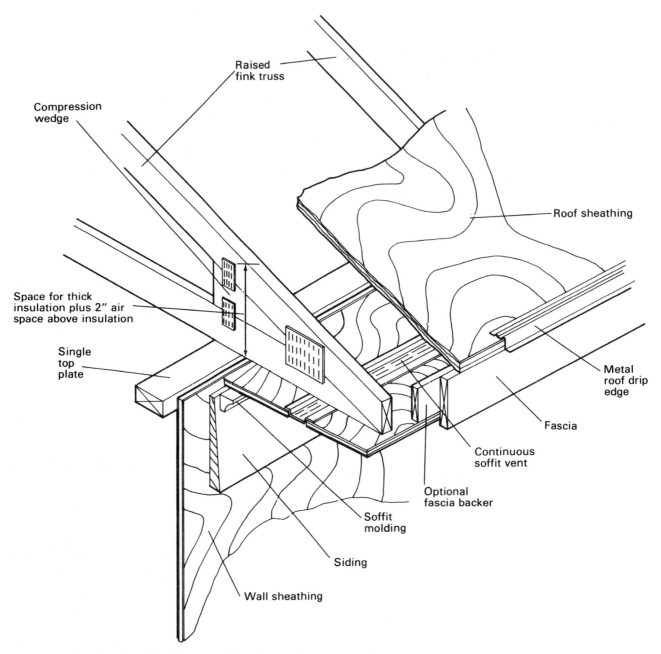

Fig. 20-5. Application of metal edging at gable end.

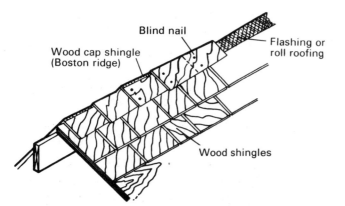

Fig. 20-6. Boston ridge using wood shingles.

nized iron or aluminum is formed to the roof slope and is used together with soffit vents for attic ventilation. If you finish the attic, you will use a different method of ventilation.

ROOFING CONTRACTORS

Roofing subs should quote a price with and without material. The steeper the roof pitch, the steeper the price per square installed. Prices start to get high after about a 10/12 pitch, which represents 10 feet of rise for every 12 feet of run (horizontal). Hence, 12/12 is a 45-

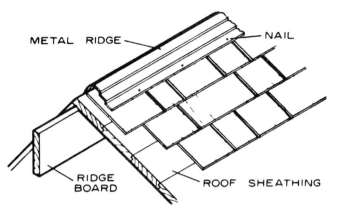

METAL RIDGE — NAIL

RIDGE BOARD — ROOF SHEATHING

Fig. 20-7. Metal ridge roll.

degree angle. Appeal is growing for steeper and steeper pitches. Make sure the roofing sub has plenty of worker's compensation insurance or deduct heavily from his fee if you have to add him to your policy. He's one fellow with a very high risk of injury. If you plan to supply the shingles, make sure they are at the site a day or so early.

> NOTE: Since asphalt and fiberglass shingles are by far the most common used, the steps on the following pages relate specifically to them. If you use roofing materials other than these two, refer to a handbook and detailed construction methods. Due to the high asphalt content in asphalt and fiberglass shingles, make sure to apply them in weather 50 degrees Fahrenheit or warmer, as they are highly susceptible to cracking in cold weather.

ROOFING STEPS

1. Inspect the roof for sagging ridge beam or sagging roof sheathing. If found, factor the cost of repair into the estimate.

2. Select shingle style, material and color.

3. Perform the standard bidding process for material and labor.

4. Order shingles and roofing felt (tar paper) if you have decided to use your roofer for labor only. Check to make sure that the roofer knows of the brand and how to install them.

5. Install 3-inch metal drip edge on eave nailed 10 inches on center. Roofing paper will go directly on top of this drip edge (optional).

6. Install roofing felt. This should be done immediately after the roofing deck has been installed and inspected. This step protects the entire structure from immediate water damage. If you are installing new shingles over existing shingles, felt will not be needed.

7. Install 3-inch metal drip edge on rake. This drip edge goes over the roofing paper. Also install aluminum flashing at walls and valleys if needed.

8. Install roofing shingles. Roofs over 30 feet wide should be shingled starting in the middle. Shorter roofs can be shingled starting at either rake. Starter strips, normally 9 inches wide, are either continuous rolls of shingle material that start at the eave or doubled shingle strips. Shingles are laid from the eave, overlapping courses up to the highest ridge.

9. Pay roofing subcontractor, requiring a signed affidavit. Deduct for worker's compensation if applicable.

10. Inspect roofing. Refer to contract specifications and inspection checklist for guidelines. You will have to get up on the roof to check most of this.

11. Pay roofing sub retainage.

ROOFING SPECIFICATIONS

- Bid is to perform complete roofing job per attached drawings and modifications.
- Bid is to include all materials and labor and 20-year warranty against leakage.
- Install two thermostatically controlled roof vents on rear of roof as indicated.
- Install continuous ridge vent per specifications.
- Roofing felt to be applied and stapled to deck as indicated below: No. 15 asphalt-saturated felt over entire plywood deck.
- All roofing felt is to have a vertical overlap of 6 inches.
- Install 3-inch galvanized eave and rake drip edges nailed 10 inches O.C.
- All work and materials are to meet or exceed requirements of the local building code and be installed per manufacturer's specifications.
- Roofer is to notify owner immediately of any condition that is or may be a violation of the building code.

- Nails are to be threaded and corrosion-resistant. Either aluminum or hot-dipped galvanized roofing nails are to be used depending upon shingle manufacturer recommendations.
- Nails are to be driven flush with shingles and installed per roofing specs.
- Soil stacks are to cover all vents. All vents are to be sealed to the shingle surface with plastic asphalt cement.
- Flashing is to be installed at chimney, all roof valleys, soil and vent stacks and skylights.

ROOFING INSPECTION

- ☐ Shingle lines are inspected for straightness with string drawn taught. Tips of shingles line up with string.
- ☐ There is even shingle pattern and uniform shingle color from both close up and afar (at least 80 feet away).
- ☐ Shingles extend over edge of roofing deck by at least 3 inches.
- ☐ All roofing nails are galvanized and nailed flush with all shingles (random inspection).
- ☐ No shingle cracks are visible through random inspection.
- ☐ Hips and valleys are smooth and uniform.
- ☐ Water cannot collect anywhere on the roof.
- ☐ Shingles fit tightly around all stack vents and skylights. Areas are well sealed with an asphalt roofing compound that blends with the shingles.
- ☐ Drip edges have been installed on eave and rakes.
- ☐ No nail heads are visible while standing up on the roof.
- ☐ All shingles lie flat (no buckling).
- ☐ There are no visible lumps in roofing due to poor decking or truss work.
- ☐ Edges of roof are trimmed smooth and evenly.
- ☐ All vents and roof flashing are painted proper color with exterior grade paint.
- ☐ All garbage on roof has been removed.
- ☐ All trash and roofing nails have been removed from the yard around the job site.

ROOFING MATERIAL ESTIMATE

DESCRIPTION	SPECIFICATION	QTY.	UNIT	COST	TAX	TOTAL COST	COST TYPE	VENDOR
Roof Framing								
Fir — rafters — 2″ × 6″ × 14′								
Fir — ridge board — 2″ × 8″ × 16′								
Fir — valley rafters — 2″ × 8″ × 18′								
Fir — gable studs 2″ × 4″ × 8′								
CDX plywood exterior sheathing — ½-inch								
Nails — galvanized ring shank sheathing								
Aluminum plywood clips								
Roofing								
235-pound asphalt shingles								
15-pound asphalt roofing felt								
Aluminum flashing — roll								
Galvanized drip edge								
Continuous ridge roof vent								
Soffit vents								
Galvanized roofing nails — ridged								
Ladder — rental								
Roofing labor — contract								

CHAPTER TWENTY-ONE

Siding

Siding determines the overall appearance and period styling of a house. Changing siding styles can completely change the look of the house. This is a major undertaking and usually requires removing the existing siding and starting over. One possible advantage of re-siding a house is the ability to fix electrical and insulation problems in the wall from the outside. Before taking this drastic approach examine the existing siding. Many things can be done to improve existing siding without replacing it. In some cases, new siding can be attached right over the existing siding.

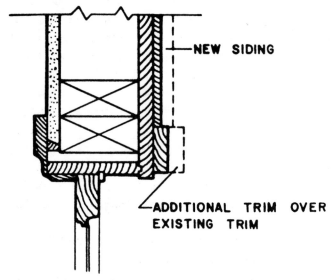

Fig. 21-1. Top view of window casing extended by adding trim over existing trim.

Solving wood siding problems often involves corrective measures in other parts of the home. Failure of the paint is frequently not the fault of the siding, but can be caused by moisture moving out through the walls or water washing down the face of the wall. Corrective measures for these problems are discussed in chapters thirteen and twenty. Siding may then need only refinishing as discussed in chapter eighteen.

Even some "permanent" sidings such as vinyl that

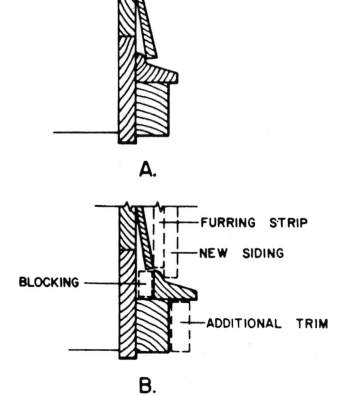

Fig. 21-2. Change in drip cap with new siding: (A) existing drip cap and trim; (B) drip cap blocked out to extend beyond new siding and added trim.

require no painting may cause other serious problems. Moisture can be trapped in the wall, creating a moisture problem. In this case, the siding you choose should allow water vapor to escape from inside the wall unless other corrective measures are taken. If new horizontal wood or nonwood siding is used, it is best to remove the old siding. Vertical board and panel-type siding may be successfully applied over the old.

The main difficulty in applying new siding over existing siding is in adjusting the window and door trim to compensate for the added wall thickness. The window sills on most houses extend far enough beyond the siding so that new siding should not affect them; however, the casing may be nearly flush with the siding and require some type of extension. One method of extending the casing is by adding an additional trim member over the existing casing. When this is done, a wider drip cap may also be required. The drip cap could be replaced, or it could be reused with blocking behind it to hold it out from the wall a distance equal to the new siding thickness.

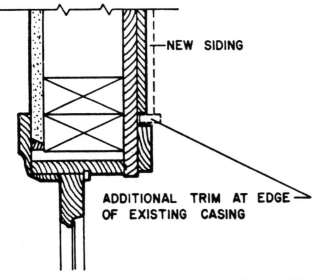

Fig. 21-3. Top view of window casing extended for new siding by adding trim at the edge of existing casing.

Another method of extending the casing is to add a trim member to the edge of the existing casing, perpendicular to the casing. A wider drip cap will also be required. Exterior door trim can be extended by the same technique used for the window trim. Any of the conventional siding materials can be used for re-siding, but some may be better suited to this application than others. Siding types include panel siding, horizontal wood siding, vertical wood siding, wood shingles, masonry veneer, aluminum and vinyl.

PANEL SIDING

Panel-type siding is probably the simplest to install and one of the most versatile. It can be applied over most surfaces, helping to smooth out unevenness in the existing walls. Panel siding is available in plywood, hardboard, particleboard and numerous nonwood materials. The most popular of these are probably plywood and hardboard. Always specify exterior type for both—the hardboard must be tempered. The grade of plywood depends on the quality of finished surface desired.

Plywood panel siding is available in a variety of tex-

tures and patterns. Sheets are 4 feet wide and are often available in lengths of 8, 9 and 10 feet. Rough-textured plywood is particularly suited to finishing with water-repellent preservative stains. Smooth-surfaced plywood can be stained, but it will not absorb as much stain as rough-textured plywood. The finish, therefore, will not be as long lasting. Paper-overlaid plywood is particularly good for a paint finish. The paper overlay not only provides a very smooth surface, but also minimizes expansion and contraction due to moisture changes. Most textures can be purchased with vertical grooves. The most popular spacing of grooves is 2, 4 and 8 inches. Battens are often used with plain panels. They are nailed over each joint between panels and can be nailed over each stud to produce a board-and-batten effect.

In new construction, plywood applied directly over framing should be at least $\frac{3}{8}$ inch thick for 16-inch stud spacing and $\frac{1}{2}$ inch thick for 24-inch stud spacing. Grooved plywood is normally $\frac{5}{8}$ inch thick with $\frac{3}{8}'' \times \frac{1}{4}''$ deep grooves.

For installation over existing siding or sheathing, thinner plywood can be used; however, most available sidings are in the thicknesses listed above. Nail the plywood around the perimeter and at each intermediate stud, using galvanized or other rust-resistant nails spaced 7 to 8 inches apart. Use longer nails than those used for applying the siding directly to the studs.

Some plywood siding has shiplap joints. These should be treated with a water-repellent preservative and the siding nailed at each side of the joint. Square-edge butt joints between plywood panels should be caulked with a sealant, with the plywood nailed at each side of the joint. Where battens are used over the joint and at intermediate studs, nail them with 8d galvanized nails spaced 12 inches apart. Longer nails may be required where thick existing siding or sheathing must be penetrated. Nominal $1'' \times 2''$ battens are commonly used.

If existing siding on gable ends is flush with the siding below the gable, some adjustment will be required in applying panel siding in order to have the new siding extend over the siding below. First, remove the existing siding if you plan to keep it and apply furring strips on the gable. The strips must be the same thickness as the new siding applied below. Nail a furring strip to each stud and apply the existing siding over the furring strips in the same manner as applying it directly to studs. If you are applying new siding over the gable, then it will be applied like the rest of the siding and will line up without any additional furring.

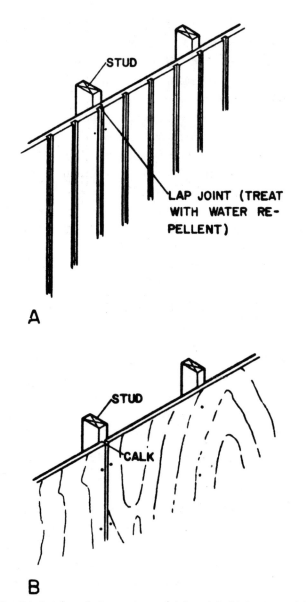

Fig. 21-4. Joint of plywood panel siding: (A) shiplap joint; (B) square-edge joint.

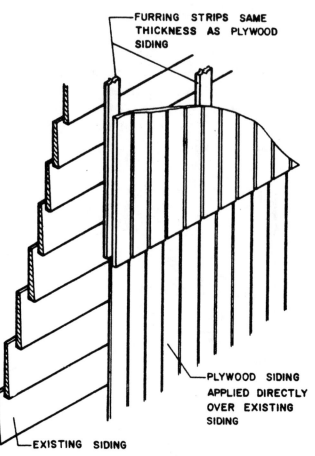

Fig. 21-5. Application of plywood siding at gable end.

Plywood siding can be purchased with factory-applied coatings that are almost maintenance free. Although the initial cost of these products is higher than uncoated plywood, savings in maintenance may compensate for this. Such coated siding is usually applied with special nails or other connectors in accordance with the manufacturer's instructions.

Hardboard siding is also available in panels 4 feet wide and up to 16 feet long. It is usually ¼ inch thick, but may be thicker when grooved. Hardboard, applied in the same manner as plywood, is usually factory-primed and finished coats of paint are applied after installation. Hardboard is a dense material that withstands moisture and warping. Because it has no actual grain, painting is more appropriate than staining.

Corners are finished by butting the panel siding against corner boards as shown. Use a 1⅛″ × 1⅛″ corner board at interior corners and 1⅛″ × 1½″ and 1⅛″ × 2½″ boards at outside corners. Apply caulking wherever siding butts against corner boards, window or door casings and trim boards at gable ends.

HORIZONTAL WOOD SIDING

Horizontal lap siding has been one of the most popular sidings for many years. It is available in 4- to 12-inch widths. The sawn face is exposed where a rough texture is desired and a stain finish can be applied. The smooth face can be exposed for either paint or stain. Siding boards should have a minimum 1-inch horizontal lap. The exposed face should be adjusted so that the butt edges line up with the bottom of the window sill and the top of the drip cap.

Lap siding is now available in many other materials besides wood. Hardboard siding is dense and sturdy and is very resistant to warping and splitting. For painted siding, this material is actually more durable than tradi-

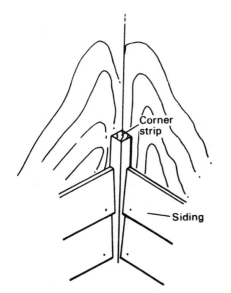

Fig. 21-6. Corner board for application of horizontal siding at interior corner.

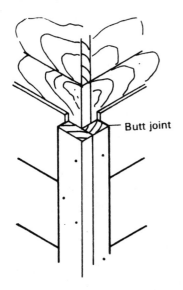

Fig. 21-7. Corner board for application of horizontal siding at exterior corner.

tional wood and usually less expensive. It usually comes preprimed, which can save an additional painting step. Do not use this material to spot-repair bad wood siding pieces. Its expansion and moisture properties are quite different from wood. Although it may look fine when first painted, after a few years the paint finish on the hardboard pieces will begin to age differently than on wood and the difference will become obvious. The general rule is, always use the same material as existing siding for spot repairs.

Another material available in lap siding is OSB board. This oriented strand board is made up of large wood chips glued together under pressure. It behaves simi-

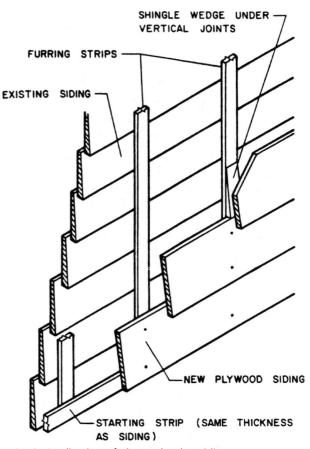

Fig. 21-8. Application of plywood as lap siding.

larly to hardboard siding but with additional strength.

Horizontal siding must be applied over a smooth surface. If the old siding is left on, it should either be covered with panel sheathing or have furring strips nailed over each stud. Nail siding at each stud with a galvanized siding nail or other corrosion-resistant nail. Use 6d nails for siding less than ½ inch thick and 8d nails for thicker siding. Locate the nail to clear the top edge of the siding course below. Butt joints should be made over a stud. Interior corners are finished by butting the siding against a corner board 1⅛ inches square or larger, depending on the thickness of the siding. Exterior corners can be mitered, butted against corner boards 1⅛ inches or thicker and 1½ inches and 2½ inches wide, or covered with metal corners.

Strips of plywood or hardboard can be applied horizontally. The strips are lapped just as bevel siding, but a starting strip is required at the base and a shingle wedge is required at each vertical joint. The starting strip should be the same thickness as the siding. Nail the siding at each vertical joint in the same manner as bevel siding. If manufacturer supplies special clips for applying the siding, follow the instructions.

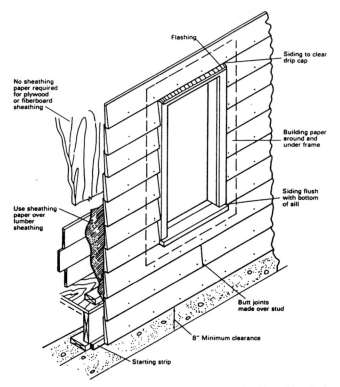

Fig. 21-9. Application of bevel siding to coincide with window sill and drip cap.

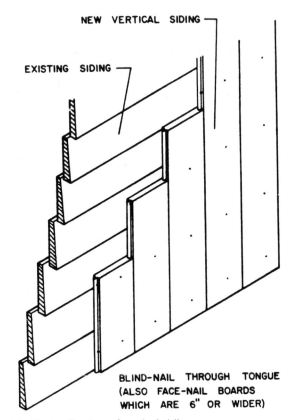

BLIND-NAIL THROUGH TONGUE (ALSO FACE-NAIL BOARDS WHICH ARE 6" OR WIDER)

Fig. 21-10. Application of vertical siding.

Siding can be painted or stained before it is installed. This is a project that you might consider doing yourself to save money. Siding must be sealed on both sides before attempting to install it. If the siding is painted or stained on one side only prior to installation, it will cup severely and be difficult to install.

VERTICAL WOOD SIDING

Vertical siding is available in a variety of patterns. Probably the most popular is matched (tongue-and-grooved) boards. Vertical siding can be nailed to 1-inch sheathing boards or to ⅝- and ¾-inch plywood. Furring strips must be used over thinner plywood because the plywood itself will not have sufficient nail-holding capacity. When the existing sheathing is thinner than ⅝ inch, apply 1" × 4" nailers horizontally, spaced 16 to 24 inches apart vertically. Then, nail the vertical siding to the nailers. Blind-nail through the tongue at each nailer with galvanized 7d finish nails. When boards are 6 inches or wider, use 8d nails and add a nail in the middle of the board. Vertical siding can be applied over existing siding by nailing through the siding into the sheathing.

Another popular vertical siding consists of various combinations of boards and battens. It also must be nailed to a thick sheathing or to horizontal nailers. The first board or batten should be nailed with one galvanized 8d nail at center or, for wide boards, two nailers spaced 1 inch on each side of center. Close spacing is important to prevent splitting if the boards shrink. The top board or batten is then nailed with 12d nails, being careful to miss the board underneath and nail only through the space between adjacent boards. Use only corrosion-resistant nails. Galvanized nails are not recommended for some materials, so be sure to follow the siding manufacturer's instructions.

WOOD SHINGLE AND SHAKE SIDING

Some architectural styles may be well suited to the use of shakes or shingles for siding. They give a rustic appearance and can be left unfinished, if desired, to weather naturally. They may be applied in single or double courses over wood or plywood sheathing. Where shingles are applied over existing siding that is uneven or over nonwood sheathing, use 1" × 3" or 1" × 4" wood nailing strips applied horizontally as a base for the shingles. Spacing of the nailing strips will depend on the

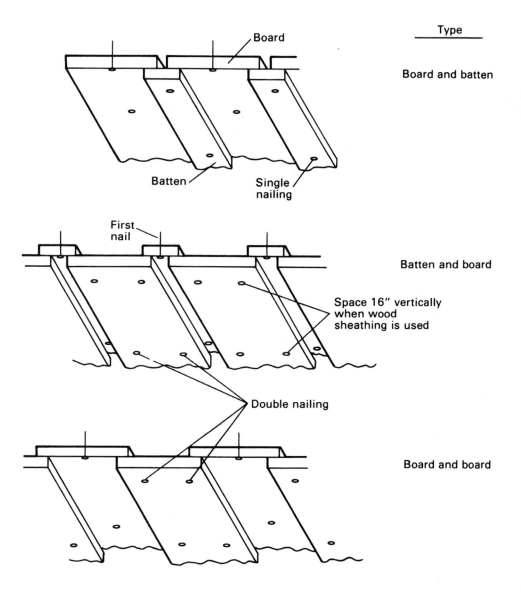

Board and batten

Board

Batten   Single
            nailing

First
nail

Batten and board

Space 16" vertically
when wood
sheathing is used

Double nailing

Board and board

Note: Nail for first board - 8d or 9d
      Nail for second board - 12d

Fig. 21-11. Application of vertical wood siding.

length and exposure of the shingles. Apply the shingles with about ⅛ inch to ¼ inch space between adjacent shingles to allow for expansion during rainy weather.

The single-course method consists of simply laying one course over the other similar to lap siding application. Second-grade shingles can be used because only half or less of the butt portion is exposed.

The double-course method of laying shingles consists of applying a bottom course and nailing a top course directly over it with a ¼- to ½-inch projection of the butt over the lower course shingle. Less lap is used between courses. The bottom course shingles can be of lower quality. The top course should be first grade because of the shingle length exposed.

Regardless of the method of applying the shingles, all joints must be broken so the vertical butt joints of the upper shingles are at least 1½ inches from the bottom shingle joint. Cedar shakes should be soaked in water for 24 hours before installation to prevent splitting.

Use rust-resistant nails for all shingle applications. Shingles up to 8 inches wide should be nailed with two nails. Wider shingles should be secured with three nails. Zinc-coated 3d or 4d shingle nails are commonly used in shingle coursing. Zinc-coated nails with small flat heads are commonly used for double coursing where nails are exposed. Use 5d nails for the top course and 3d or 4d for the bottom course. When plywood sheath-

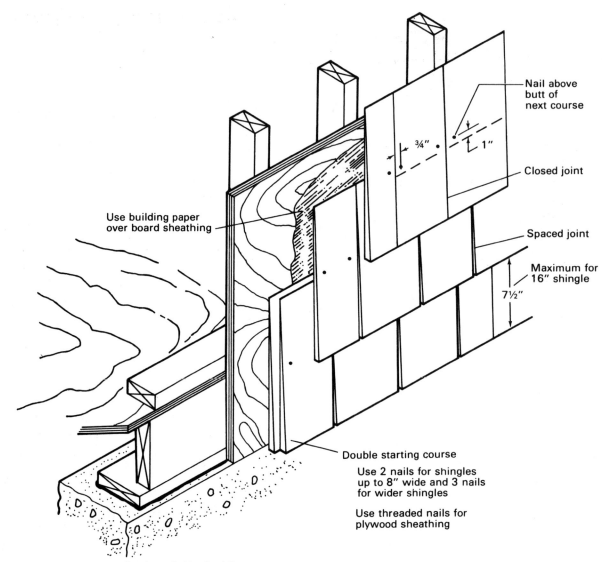

Use building paper over board sheathing

Nail above butt of next course

¾"

1"

Closed joint

Spaced joint

Maximum for 16" shingle

7½"

Double starting course

Use 2 nails for shingles up to 8" wide and 3 nails for wider shingles

Use threaded nails for plywood sheathing

Fig. 21-12. Single-course application of shingle siding.

ing less than ¾ inch thick is used, threaded nails are required to obtain sufficient holding power. The nail should be ¾ inch from the edge. They should be 1 inch above the horizontal butt line of the next higher course in the single-course application and 2 inches above the bottom of the shingle in the double-course application.

MASONRY VENEER

The mortar between brick or stone veneer may become loose and crumble or uneven settlement may cause cracks. In either case, new mortar should be applied both to keep out moisture and to improve appearance. Repair is accomplished in much the same manner as for masonry foundations, except that more attention to appearance is required. After removing all loose mortar and brushing the joint to remove dust and loose parti-

cles, dampen the surface. Then apply mortar and tamp it well into the joint for a good bond. Pointing of joints should conform to existing joints. Particular care should be exercised in keeping mortar off the face of the brick or stone unless the veneer is to be painted. Brick or stone veneer should be cleaned gently, using soft-bristled brushes and water under low pressure. When a chemical cleaner is required, the services of a professional masonry cleaner are recommended.

You may decide to install brick veneer over existing siding. This can change the look of the house completely. Be forewarned that this is a major operation and takes considerable planning. The additional thickness of the masonry will require adjustments to all doors, windows, gable siding and cornice. You will have to pour a concrete ledge at the foundation for the masonry to rest on. This requires digging down to the bottom of the foundation and pouring a new concrete ledge at the frostline which extends to the height at which you want to start the wall. The time and expense may not be worth the effort unless the improvement is dramatic.

STUCCO

Stucco is an excellent siding alternative if you want to change the complete look of the house and install new siding over existing siding. Stucco is usually applied over a coated expanded metal lath that is attached to framing or sheathing. Applying stucco to sheathing is recommended because the sheathing provides a stable surface between the stucco and framing that does not measurably expand and contract. The sheathing can be attached directly over the existing siding and the stucco applied.

NONWOOD SIDING

Nonwood sidings, such as aluminum, steel or vinyl, come in many styles and colors. They are often applied by contractors who specialize in one of these products. The manufacturer's literature usually gives complete instructions for application and maintenance. If you are doing it yourself, follow these instructions closely.

Many companies advertise these nonwood sidings as the ultimate solution to siding maintenance. Most of the time, the company will install the siding as part of the price. Vinyl siding in particular has become very popular because it looks good and is very easy to maintain. It also never needs painting. Be very cautious about using this material on an older home for the following reason. These materials don't breathe. Wrapping a house with vinyl can be like wrapping it in plastic. Any moisture trying to escape will become trapped in the old siding and insulation, reducing the insulation's effectiveness and causing possible moisture damage. On newer homes with effective vapor barriers inside, this should not be a problem, but many older homes were built without interior vapor barriers. Check the existing paint finish for blistering or peeling. This is a sure sign that large amounts of moisture escape the house through the walls. The more reputable vinyl companies use installation techniques to increase breathability, so question the company thoroughly and ask the advice of local builders or contractors before using vinyl.

SIDING AND CORNICE STEPS

1. Inspect existing siding and determine if re-siding is needed. Check for signs of excessive moisture such as paint blistering and peeling.

2. Select siding material, color, style and coverage.

3. Conduct the standard bidding process. Most often the siding, cornice, and window trim will be bid as a package deal. Masonry and stucco will be installed by a different contractor than siding or trim.

4. Order any windows and doors that will be installed. Before ordering, have the window supplier walk through the site to check openings. The supplier can help to provide more exact dimension information. All construction work on expansion and new doors and windows should be completed before re-siding begins.

5. Pour concrete brick ledge if installing brick veneer.

6. Remove old siding if necessary. This is a good time to install new flashing, insulation, electrical wiring, plumbing, phone lines, cable, security wiring, and insulated sheathing while you have access to the walls. This is much easier than working through drywall or plastered walls. If you don't mind the extra work, removing the siding rather than re-siding over it is preferred for the above reasons. It also allows you to examine the walls for other potential problems and eliminates the need to readjust window and corner trim for the additional siding thickness.

7. Install new windows and doors. If installing brick veneer, nail a 2×4 under exterior door thresholds for additional support until brick is installed. Inspect the positioning of windows and doors. They should be plumb and secure. Galvanized finish nails should be used, with the heads of the nails set below the surface of the trim.

8. Install insulated sheathing if desired. Remember that this will make the overall thickness of the siding even greater if you are re-siding over old siding.

9. Install furring strips if needed for re-siding over existing siding. Remove gable siding and add furring strips to bring gable flush with new siding. Install masonry wall ties to siding or sheathing if installing masonry. Mason will use them to tie brick wall structurally to existing wall.

10. Install siding, stucco, or brick.

11. Install second coat of stucco, if applicable. You need to wait a few days for the first coat to dry completely. Place a thick mat of straw at base of house to prevent mud from staining stucco. Second coat should contain stucco tint color.

12. Install siding trim around corners, windows and doors. Add additional trim to cornice and windows if needed to bring trim level with new siding.

13. Clean up excess bricks and dried mortar. Spread any extra sand in the driveway and sidewalk area.

14. Caulk all areas where siding butts against trim or another piece of siding.

15. Reinstall cornice. If you are installing masonry or stucco, the cornice (and maybe the fascia, frieze, soffit and eave vents) will be reinstalled by a different sub and will be completed after the new siding is installed.

16. Inspect siding and trim work.

17. Correct any problems noted.

18. Pay the sub for siding and cornice work. Make sure to retain a portion of payment for callbacks.

19. Correct any problems noted with the siding after it has had time to shrink.

20. Arrange for painter to paint and caulk trim.

21. Pay siding and trim retainage and have subs sign an affidavit.

SIDING AND CORNICE SPECIFICATIONS

Siding

- Exterior galvanized ring shank finish nails are to be used exclusively.
- All nails are to be flush or counter sunk.
- All laps of siding are to be parallel.
- Joints are to be staggered between courses.
- All work and materials are to conform to the local building code.
- All siding edges are to be terminated in a finished manner and caulked.
- All openings and trim are to be caulked and flashed.

- All metal or vinyl siding is to provide proper ventilation for water vapor.
- Furring strips are to be used with vertical siding to provide proper nailing surface.

Trim

- All soffit and fascia joints are to be trimmed smooth and fit tight.
- All fascia are to be straight and true.
- All trim is to be extended beyond new siding to retain original trim style.
- All flashing is to be extended beyond new siding.

Masonry

- All brick, sand and mortar mix are to be furnished by mason.
- All necessary scaffolding is to be supplied and erected by mason.
- All excess bricks are to remain stacked on site.
- Bricks are to be moistened before laying to provide superior bonding.
- Mortar joints are to be tooled concave.
- Steel lintels are to be installed above all door and window openings.
- Masonry walls are to be reasonably free of mortar stains as determined by owner
- Flashing is to be installed at the head and sill of all window openings.
- Bid is to include all necessary touch-up work.

Stucco

- Bid is to provide all material, labor and tools to install lath and stucco per contract.
- Stucco is to be finished smooth, sand texture. (Specify color.)
- All trim areas are to be 2 inches wide unless otherwise specified.
- Quoins are to have beveled edges, alternating 12 and 8 inches wide.
- Two coats of stucco are to be applied, with pigment in the second coat.
- Stucco work is to come with a 20-year warranty for material and labor against defects, chipping and cracks.
- Expansion joints are to be as indicated on blueprint or as agreed upon.

SIDING AND CORNICE MATERIAL ESTIMATE

DESCRIPTION	SPECIFICATION	QTY.	UNIT	COST	TAX	TOTAL COST	COST TYPE	VENDOR
Wood Siding								
Plywood sheathing— ½″ × 4′ × 8′								
Insulated sheathing—⅝-inch Styrofoam								
Kraft paper—rolls								
Siding—lap								
Siding—plywood sheet								
Siding—board and batten								
Battens—1″ × 2″ rough sawn								
Siding—cedar shakes								
Nails—ring shank splitless siding								
Nails—screw shank hardboard								
Furring strips—1″ × 4″								
Siding and trim labor—contract								
Stucco								
Insulated sheathing—⅝-inch Styrofoam								
Stucco lath								
Stucco								
Stucco labor—contract								
Trim labor—contract								
Masonry								
Brick								
Galvanized wall ties								
Masonry cement—bags								
Washed sand								
Masonry labor—contract								
Trim labor—contract								

Landscaping

When you consider how much resale value and curb appeal a good landscaping job can add to a home, it is surprising that so many owners scrimp on this important effort. Many owners just throw in a few bushes and then seed or sod. Hopefully you will be willing to spend just a bit more time and effort to do the job right. If you don't want to spend all the money at once, you can devise a two- or three-year implementation plan, beginning with the critical items such as ground coverage.

Sometimes a major improvement can be achieved just by trimming and pruning back older shrubs and trees. Many older homes are totally obscured by overgrown shrubs planted years ago. They will hide any hard-earned improvements you make to the rest of the house.

Important items to keep in mind are:

- Plan for curb appeal. Your lawn should be a showplace.
- Plan for low maintenance. If you don't want to trim hedges and rake leaves forever, be smart about the trees and bushes you add or keep.
- Work with the sun, not against it. Maximize sunlight into the home by careful planning of trees.
- Plan for proper drainage. This is *critical*. Water must drain away from dwelling and not collect in any low spots.
- Consider doing much of this work yourself.
- Consider assistance from a landscape architect.

Every lot has one best use and many poor ones. A good landscape architect can help you do more than select grass. Landscape architects can be helpful in determining:

- What trees to retain and what additional trees and/or bushes to plant for privacy and lowest maintenance.

- What soil additives are needed based on the present soil condition.
- Whether to prune or remove existing shrubs.
- Whether drainage is adequate and ground coverings are appropriate and how to correct the situation.

You can normally pay an independent landscape architect by the hour, but if you do a lot of work with him or her, work up a fixed price. Meet together at your lot with the lot survey. Walk the lot together, getting his or her initial impressions and ideas. From there, you may request a site plan. The site plan will normally be a large drawing showing exact home position, driveway layout, existing trees and bushes, sculptured islands and other topographical features.

LANDSCAPING STEPS

1. Evaluate your lot in terms of trees to keep, drainage, privacy, slopes, high and low spots, and exposure to morning and afternoon sun. A landscape architect can help you greatly with this step, and can also help you determine what plants should stay and what plants should go.

2. Conduct soil tests. Soil samples should be made for every several thousand feet of yard. Soil to be tested should be taken from 6 inches down. Soil testing will help to determine pH (level of acidity) and the lack of essential nutrients. Most counties have an extension service that will test the samples for you at little or no charge. Good general purpose soil conditioners are peat moss, manure and lime.

3. Develop a rough site plan. This is a bird's-eye view of what you want the finished site to look like, including exact position of home, driveway and all other paved surfaces such as walks and patios, major trees, islands, grass areas, flower beds, bushes, and even an underground watering system if you intend to add one. When determining grass areas, consider shade. Most grasses do not grow well or do not grow at all in shade. No amount of fertilizer or lawn care can compensate for a lack of sun. This is critical in older homes where years of tree growth has created a lot of natural shade.

4. Finalize a complete landscaping site plan. This can be produced by you or a professional landscape designer. The master plan will help visualize the landscaping and produce a order list of materials. Make several copies in blueprint form. You will need at least one for yourself and one for a landscaper if you hire one.

5. Deliver additional topsoil, if needed, to site. Make sure topsoil is clean and dry. Wet dirt will form lumps and clods as it dries.

6. Pay landscape architect if different from landscaping contractor.

7. Till the top 4 to 6 inches of soil, adding soil conditioners as needed. Cut down any unwanted trees and grind the stumps before sod is laid down. Rake surface smooth first one way and then another.

8. Apply soil treatments as needed. You may also wish to add a slow release, nonburning fertilizer (no stronger than 6-6-6) to help your young grass grow. Apply gypsum pellets to break down clay.

9. Install underground sprinkling system as needed. This normally consists of a network of ½-inch PVC pipe purchased from a garden supply store.

10. Plant flower bulbs. This is the easiest and best time to plant daffodils, crocus, hyacinths, gladioli, etc.

11. Apply seed or sod to exposed areas. If you choose seed, use a broadcast spreader or a special seed-dispensing device. Cover the seed with hay or straw to protect seeds from washing away with rain. If you sod, this will be a tougher job, but doing it yourself could really save some money. Sod always has at least three prices: direct from a sod farm, delivered by a sod broker, or delivered and installed by a sod broker. If you can, buy direct from a sod farm. Visit them if you have time to see before you buy. Have them drop the sod in shady areas all around the grounds to be covered to reduce carrying. Keep sod slightly moist until installed. Have a large crew to help you lay sod because it will live on pallets for only a few days.

12. Soak lawn with water if sod is applied. Sprinkle lightly for long periods of time if a seeded lawn is used. Roll lawn with a heavy metal cylinder. The lawn should be watered regularly for several weeks whenever the soil dries out. This will ensure that the grass has time to establish a complete root system.

13. Install bushes and trees. If you plan to install trees, please keep them at least 4 feet from the driveway area. Trees are notorious for breaking up a driveway when the roots begin to spread.

14. Prepare landscaped islands. Place pine bark, pine straw, mulch or gravel in designated areas. Over time, pine straw will kill some grasses, particularly Bermuda. Keep pine straw in islands only.

15. Inspect landscaping job. Refer to specifications and checklist.

16. Correct any problems noted.

17. Pay landscaping contractor for job, requiring a signed affidavit.

18. Pay landscaping contractor retainage after grass is fully established without bare areas.

LANDSCAPING SPECIFICATIONS

- Finely rake all area to be seeded or sodded.
- All grass is to be lightly fertilized with 6-6-6 and watered heavily immediately to prevent drying.
- Sod pieces are to butt each with no gaps, with joints staggered.
- Islands are to be naturally shaped by trimming sod.
- Sod is to be rolled after watering.
- Prepare three pine straw islands as described in attached site plan.
- Install trees and bushes according to attached planting schedule and site plan.
- Cover all seeded areas with straw to prevent run-off.
- Install splash blocks for downspouts.
- Burlap is to be removed from root balls prior to installation.
- Trees and shrubs are to be watered after installation.

LANDSCAPING INSPECTION

- ☐ All areas are sodded/seeded as specified.
- ☐ All trees and bushes are planted as specified.
- ☐ Sod and/or seed is alive and growing.
- ☐ Sod is smooth and even with no gaps.
- ☐ Straw covers are seeded evenly with no bare spots.
- ☐ All specified bushes and trees are alive and in upright position.
- ☐ Splash blocks are installed.
- ☐ Grass is cut if specified.
- ☐ There are no weeds in yard.
- ☐ There is no exposed dirt within 16 inches of siding or brick veneer.
- ☐ Pine bark or pine straw islands are installed as specified.

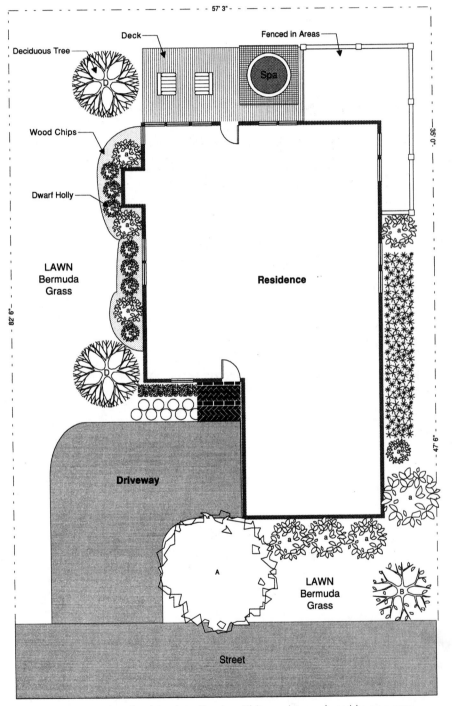

Fig. 22-1. A complete landscaping site plan. This can be produced by you or a professional landscape designer. The master plan will help visualize the landscaping and produce an order list of materials.

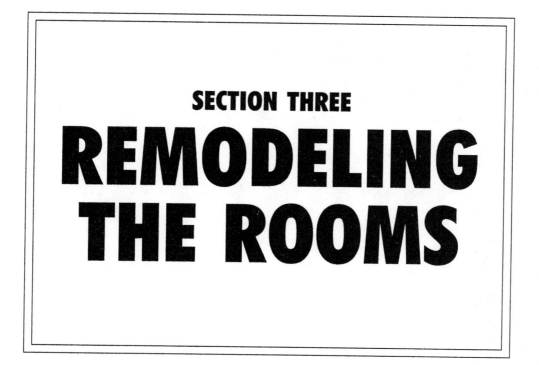

SECTION THREE
REMODELING THE ROOMS

CHAPTER TWENTY-THREE

Changing the Interior Layout

Modest changes in the interior layout of a house can be one of the easiest upgrades to a house. An efficient layout can have a tremendous effect on traffic flow, perceived space, storage efficiency and light levels. Moving or eliminating an interior wall is much more cost effective than constructing new space. The biggest challenge is to keep the interior changes from interfering with normal day-to-day living. These alterations will require changes to the floor, ceiling, trim, walls and structural supports of the house.

Here is a list of some possible changes:

1. Add a bathroom or make one bath into two.
2. Add a bay extension to enlarge an existing living area.
3. Remove hallways that restrict or close in a living area.
4. Remove a partition between a dining and living area.
5. Add or enlarge a closet.
6. Add or remove a fireplace.

RELOCATING PARTITIONS

One reason for moving partitions is to develop a more convenient room layout. It may mean eliminating a partition or moving a partition to another location. Walls should not be moved without researching their structural contribution to the house. Many interior walls are load-bearing—supporting the weight of the roof or the upper floor. If they are removed, other supports such as beams must be put in their place. Most load-bearing walls run perpendicular to the direction of floor or ceiling joists.

Removing a Partition

Removing a nonload-bearing partition is simple because none of the components of the house depend on it for structural support. The framing members of a nonload-bearing wall can be reused if carefully removed. If the wall covering is plaster or drywall, it cannot be salvaged, so remove it from the framing and dispose of it. The main problem presented by removing a wall partition is the unfinished strip left in the ceiling, wall and floor. These strips will have to be repaired or covered cosmetically.

The unfinished strip in the ceiling and wall can be finished by plastering to the same thickness as the existing plaster or by cutting strips of gypsum board to fit snugly into the unfinished strip and finishing the joints with joint compound and tape. Flooring can also be patched by inserting a wood strip of the same thickness and species as the existing floor. If existing flooring runs parallel to the wall, patching is fairly effective; however, where the flooring runs perpendicular to the wall, the patch will always be obvious unless a new floor covering is added. In making the patch, cut the flooring to fit as snugly as possible. Even where the new flooring is well fitted and of the same wood species, it may not be exactly the same color as the existing flooring.

Removing a load-bearing partition involves the same patching of walls, ceiling and floor as for the nonload-bearing partition. In addition, however, some other means of supporting the ceiling joists must be provided. If attic space above the partition is available, a supporting beam can be placed above the ceiling joists in the attic so that the joists can hang from the beam. The ends of the beam must be supported on an exterior wall, a bearing partition or a post that will transfer the load to the foundation. Wood hanger brackets are installed at the intersection of the beam with each joist. One method is illustrated. This type of support can be installed before the wall is removed, eliminating the need for temporary support.

An exposed beam can be installed after the partition

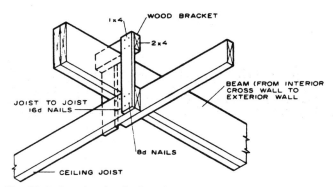

Fig. 23-1. Framing for flush ceiling with wood brackets.

is removed to support the ceiling from below. A series of supporting walls or jacks should be placed on each side of the partition while the transition between the partition and the beam is being made. The bottom of any beam installed should be at least 6 feet 8 inches above the floor.

There may be situations where an exposed beam is undesirable and no attic space is available, as in the ground floor of a two-story house. In this case the beam can be inserted in the ceiling with the existing joists tied into the sides of it with joist hangers. This will take much more effort to install but will hide the support completely. Temporary support for the joists is required while the beam is being installed. The joists must be cut to make room for the beam. Install joist hangers on the beam where each joist will frame into it. Put the beam in place and repair the damaged ceiling.

The size of the required beam will vary greatly, depending on beam span, span of joists framing into it, and material used for the beam. The determination of the proper size should be made by an engineer or professional contractor. Because of the complexity of this job, hire a professional to do the critical work. Mistakes made here can be very costly.

Adding a Partition

A partition can be added anywhere by framing it in just as in new construction. Framing is usually done with 2 × 4s, although 2 × 3 framing can be used for non-load-bearing partitions to save space. If the new partition is load-bearing, headers must be installed over door and window openings to transfer weight to the surrounding studs.

If the existing ceiling is very straight, the new partition can be assembled on the floor and tilted into place. In most cases, however, the ceiling will be uneven, making installation of a preassembled partition difficult or impossible. In this case, frame the wall in place, one

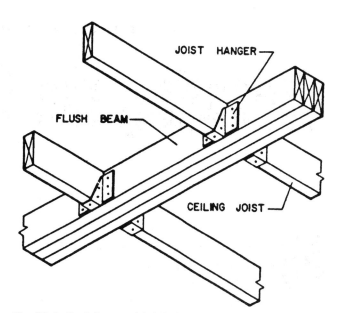

Fig. 23-2. Flush beam with joist hangers.

piece at a time. First, install the top plate. If ceiling joists are perpendicular to the partition, nail the top plate to each joist using 16d nails. If ceiling joists are parallel to the partition and the partition is not directly under a joist, install solid blocking between joists at no more than 2-foot spacing; then nail the top plate to the blocking. This will require removing any drywall from the ceiling between the joists. To assure a plumb partition, hold a plumb bob along the side of the top plate at several points and mark these points on the floor. Nail the bottom plate to the floor joists or to solid blocking between joists in the same manner as the top plate.

The next step is to install studs to fit firmly between the plates at a spacing of 16 or 24 inches. Check the required stud length at several points. There may be some variation. Toenail the studs to the plates, using 12 to 16d nails.

ADDING A CANTILEVER

Adding a cantilever (punch out) or bay extension can be an excellent way to gain much needed extra space for a room or bath enlargement. If the extension is less than 4 feet, then no foundation is necessary. The roof of the bay can be framed directly into the exterior wall.

The installation of the cantilever floor framing is tricky and should be done by a professional framer. It requires jacking up and supporting the existing floor joists while the extension's floor joists are added. If the joists of the cantilever run parallel to the existing floor

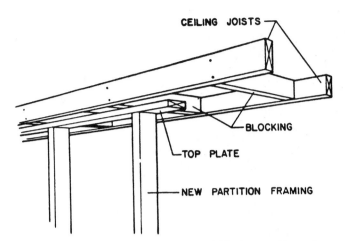

Fig. 23-3. Blocking between joists to which the top plate of a new partition is nailed.

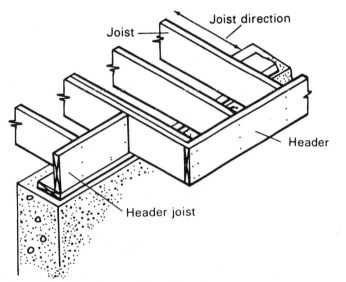

Fig. 23-4. Projection parallel to floor joists.

joists, this job will be a little easier. The extension joists can be nailed or bolted to the existing joists without the need for any cutting except the joist header. Extend the new joists at least 6 feet back under the house.

Installing extension joists that run perpendicular to the existing floor will require cutting several joists under the house and tying in the new joists with joist hangers. Joists must be supported properly before cutting them and the new joists will have to be snugly fit into place. Most cantilevers should be 2 feet or less. A longer extension will require cutting more existing joists and extending the cantilever joists farther back under the house. This is not work for the meek. If you insist on doing most work yourself, at least get a qualified specialist to do this work. You can then finish the remaining framing.

Bay Opening

When a bay extension is added to the exterior wall, the opening it creates must be handled exactly like a window or door opening; in other words, it must have a header to distribute the load from the roof around the opening to surrounding studs. If the bay is less than 6 feet in width, such as for a bathroom extension, standard window-type headers can be used. Wider openings will require more substantial beams. All openings should be at least 6 feet 8 inches tall. Once the opening is framed in, the remaining framing will be conventional exterior wall framing.

FRAMING FOR UTILITIES

The heating, plumbing and electrical systems should be updated by skilled, licensed contractors. Some structural alterations may also be required to adapt to the new utilities. Because heating ducts, plumbing stacks and drains, heat pipe, and electrical conduit must be run throughout the house, some framing members may need to be cut. Plumbers and HVAC subs should be cautioned against cutting load-bearing framing members. This can compromise the structural integrity of the house. If the structure is altered, make sure it is done at the direction of someone qualified. Framing members that are cut should be reinforced.

Cutting Floor Joists

Floor joists must often be cut to accommodate pipe for water-supply lines or electrical conduit. This is usually done by notching the top or bottom of the joist or by drilling holes through the joist. Notching of joists should not be done except in the last one-fourth of the joist span and to not more than one-sixth of the depth of the joist. Holes can be drilled through joists anywhere if the size of hole is limited to 2 inches in diameter and the edges of the hole are not less than 2½ inches from the top or bottom of the joist. If a joist must be cut and the above conditions cannot be met, add an additional joist next to the cut joist or reinforce the cut joist by nailing supporting framing on each side.

Utility Walls

Walls containing plumbing stack or vents may require special framing. For example, 4-inch soil stacks will not fit in a standard 2×4 stud wall. Where a thicker wall is needed, it is usually constructed with 2×6 top and bottom plates and 2×4 studs placed flat along the edge

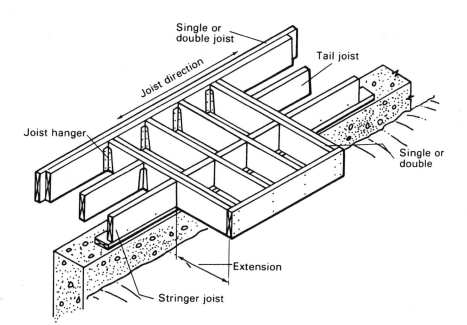

Fig. 23-5. Projection perpendicular to floor joists.

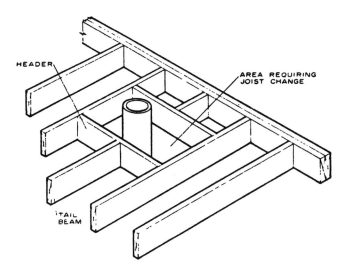

Fig. 23-6. Headers for joists to eliminate cutting.

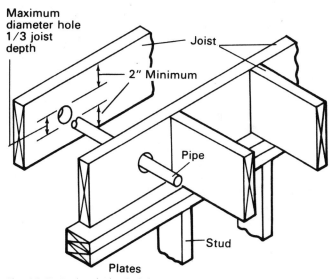

Fig. 23-7. Boring holes in joists.

of the plates. This leaves the center of the wall open for running both supply and drain pipes through the wall.

Although 3-inch vent stacks will fit into 2×4 stud walls, the hole for the vent requires cutting away most of the top plate, and may cause problems if the plumbing is not centered properly. Metal straps can be nailed to the plate on each side of the vent to reinforce it.

ALTERING EXISTING CLOSETS

Most upgrades of the layout will include improvements to closet areas. One thing that will improve closet access is a full front opening to replace a small door. Bifold doors are available in a great variety of widths and come in solid, louvered, and mirror finishes. Remove the wall finish and studs to the width required for a desired bifold door set. Frame in the opening like any other door or window opening. If the closet wall is load-bearing, use header sizes listed for window openings.

The header can be eliminated for a non-load-bearing wall, and a full ceiling-height bifold door can be used. This will allow easy access to the storage shelf. Frame the opening in the same manner as other door openings, with the rough framed opening 2½ inches wider than the door. Most closet doors usually come with installation instructions.

Closets can be improved by adding shelves and clothes rods. The usual closet has one rod with a single shelf over it. Where hanging space is limited, install a second clothes rod about half way between the existing

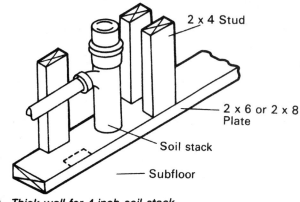

A, Thick wall for 4-inch soil stack

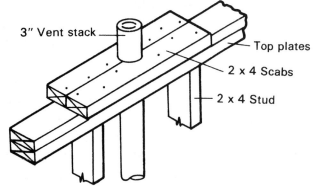

B, Reinforcing scabs for 3-inch vent stack in 2 by 4 wall

Fig. 23-8. Framing for vent stack: (A) 4-inch soil pipe; (B) 3-inch stack vent.

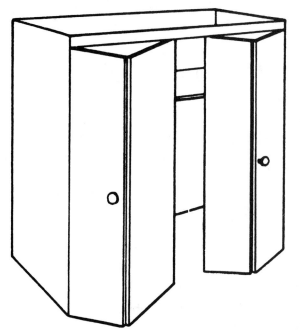

Fig. 23-9. Double-hinged door set for full-width opening closet.

rod and the floor. This type of space can be used for children's clothing or for shorter adult clothing. Many companies now market closet upgrade kits for this purpose.

To add either a shelf or a pole, support them by

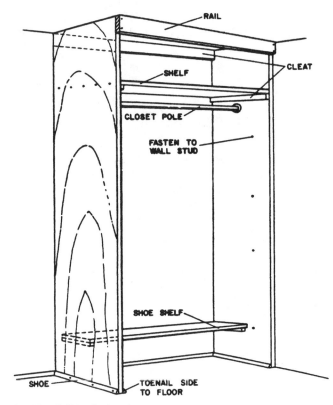

Fig. 23-10. Wardrobe closet.

$1'' \times 4''$ cleats nailed to the end walls of the closet. Nail these cleats with three 6d nails at each end of the cleat and at the intermediate stud. Shelf ends can rest directly on these cleats. Attach clothes rods to the cleats that support the shelf.

NEW CLOSETS

New closets can be constructed by adding a partition around the closet area, using $2'' \times 3''$ or $2'' \times 4''$ framing and drywall just like any other partition. Using $2'' \times 3''$ lumber and ⅜-inch drywall can help to squeeze a closet into a tight area. If the space is extremely tight, construct the closet without framing, which will save an additional 3 inches. Use ⅝-inch or ¾-inch plywood or particleboard mounted on cleats.

Use a $1'' \times 4''$ top rail and back cleat. Fasten the cleat to the wall and then fasten the plywood to the cleat. In a corner, fasten the sidewall to a wall stud. Toenail base shoe moldings to the floor to hold the bottom of the sidewalls in place, or cover the bottom of the closet with plywood to act as a brace. Add shelves and closet poles where desired. Similar units can be built with shelves for linens or other items. Add plywood or standard bifold doors as desired. Drywall can then be glued or screwed to the plywood and finished conventionally.

CHIMNEYS AND FIREPLACES

Defective chimneys are difficult to repair, so it may be best to replace them. Their location may also get in the way of plans you have to relocate walls. Gas and oil heaters usually require only a small metal chimney. Sometimes new chimneys can be placed in the stud space of an interior partition for low-capacity heaters; then the defective chimney can be eliminated. The chimney of an existing heating system should be replaced only by a licensed HVAC contractor. Most local building codes have stringent requirements about placement and clearances of chimneys. If you have upgraded your existing heating system, the chimney may not be required and can be removed.

Many old homes had several fireplaces, since they were the principal source of heat for the home. These old fireplaces may restrict your options when redesigning rooms. If the fireplaces are not operational, they can be removed. The additional space recovered can be used for other more valuable space needs, such as a new bathroom or to allow a wall to be removed. Removing an interior fireplace is a messy and difficult job and should be attempted only by professionals. But if the removal of the chimney helps rework the existing space without the need to build new construction, then the expense may be worth it.

Old fireplaces may not draft well and may allow smoke to enter the room. A metal extension across the top of the fireplace opening will sometimes improve the draft. This improvement can be tested by holding a board against the fireplace just above the opening and by observing the change in draft. Draft can sometimes be improved by extending the height of the flue or by adding a chimney cap for venturi action. Another possible solution where draft is inadequate is to install a fan in the chimney for forced exhaust. Older chimneys that you want to save can also be relined. This must be done by a professional.

If a new fireplace is desired, professional help is usually required; however, prefabricated metal fireplaces are available that require no special skills for installation. They are called zero clearance fireplaces because they can be installed in walls with no clearance needed between the fireplace and the walls. They can be placed on the conventional floor without a separate foundation, and no masonry work is required. Fireplace liners are also available that only require masonry added around them.

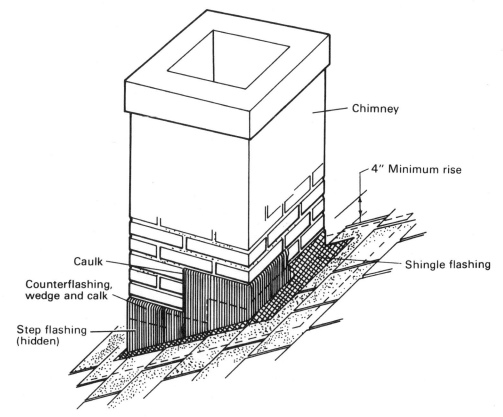

Fig. 23-11. Chimney flashing.

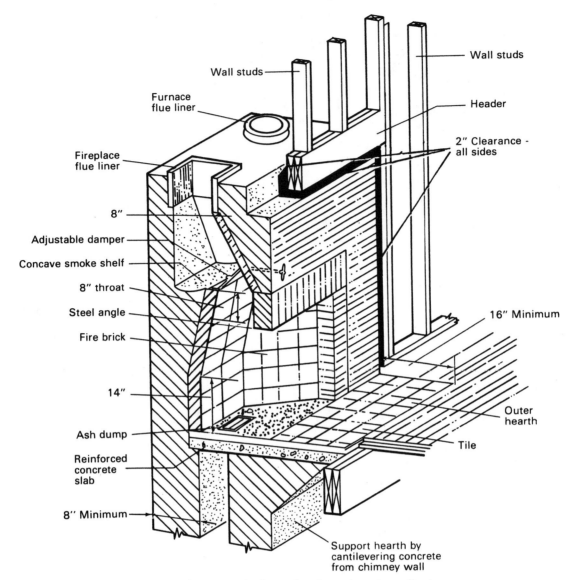

Fig. 23-12. Diagram of an entire chimney that serves the house heating unit and one fireplace.

Labels in figure:
- Wall studs
- Furnace flue liner
- Fireplace flue liner
- 8"
- Adjustable damper
- Concave smoke shelf
- 8" throat
- Steel angle
- Fire brick
- 14"
- Ash dump
- Reinforced concrete slab
- 8" Minimum
- Wall studs
- Header
- 2" Clearance - all sides
- 16" Minimum
- Outer hearth
- Tile
- Support hearth by cantilevering concrete from chimney wall

PARTITION REMOVAL STEPS

Planning

1. Examine the roof rafters or upper floor joists to determine if the wall to remove is load-bearing. Load-bearing walls usually run perpendicular to the ceiling joists and are located near the middle of the house. Truss roofs usually do not require load-bearing walls. They are recognizable by the webbing that bonds the truss together and distributes the load. If you are not sure, contact an engineer. Do not proceed without a full understanding of the support structure of your house. Follow the path of plumbing and wiring through the walls to see if it runs through the section of wall you plan to remove. If it does, consult an electrician or plumber and plan for the necessary rerouting.

2. Determine the best way of installing any necessary supporting beams. The supports can be placed under, in, or above the ceiling. Hire a contractor if a beam is necessary and ask for advice on the best choice of beam materials and installation methods. Beam types include custom steel beams in plates or I beams, glue-lam beams made of several pieces glued together, and laminated veneer beams.

3. Examine the other elements in the room to assess the steps required after partition removal. Remove the drywall where walls intersect adjoining walls to see how the walls are connected. If you plan to repair a hardwood floor after removing the wall, shop for planks that closely match the existing floor. Test stains and finishes

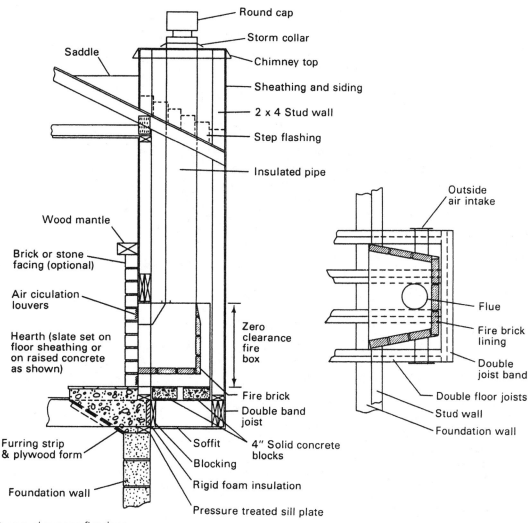

Fig. 23-13. A zero-clearance fireplace.

on sample pieces to find a good color match. Don't start the project until you find and purchase suitable replacement stock.

4. Perform the standard bidding process. Obtain a signed proposal from an experienced carpenter with standard provisions and specifications. An electrician or HVAC sub may be needed to reroute wiring or ducting.

5. Obtain building permit if needed.

6. Purchase all framing materials, flooring and structural beams. Make sure to allow ample delivery time for special order items like beams. Have all material delivered to the site before the carpenter arrives. Hardwood flooring should remain in the room in which it will be installed for several weeks in order for it to expand and contract based on local humidity conditions.

Partition Removal

1. Schedule framer for structural work.

2. Rent or purchase jacks and buy steel I beams for support of the ceiling, if needed. Temporary bracing walls will work just as well.

3. Seal off the rest of the house from the construction area with plastic sheeting. At passageways, create an overlapping joint that can be sealed shut. This is very important when removing and installing drywall. The gypsum dust is very fine and will work its way into everything in the house. Plan a passageway for bringing in lumber and supplies that will be protected from dirt and scratches.

4. Erect temporary supports if structural work is needed.

5. Remove carpet from floor if you are replacing it or roll it back out of the way until the construction is completed.

6. Remove trim from around the wall. Save any pieces you plan to reuse. Carefully remove any doors that you plan to install elsewhere.

7. Turn off any plumbing or electricity that may run through the wall to prevent accidental damage.

8. Remove drywall from wall and from ceiling areas where structural beams are to be installed. Locate the approximate position of each stud by tapping on the wall with a hammer. The studs will sound solid. Then knock a hole in the drywall or plaster between the two studs to look for wiring or plumbing. If you don't find any surprises, you can continue to remove the wall covering.

9. Install new support beam. Installation procedures will vary depending on the type and location of the beam. If the beam is installed above the floor joists, the work will be done from the attic without disturbing the drywall. The beam is laid across the joists and connected to them with joist hangers or metal straps. A beam below the joists must be supported on both ends by existing or new framing. Drywall between the joists and beam should be removed to ensure solid contact between the joists and beam. Installing a beam in the ceiling requires that existing joists be cut to make room for the beam. The beam is then moved into position and the joists attached with joist hangers. Make sure to be available to inspect the contractor's work during this critical phase. Make sure that proper temporary support is in place and that the beam is installed according to engineering specifications.

10. Remove existing wall framing. If a beam is installed in place of the wall, the wall removal will probably happen first, to make room for maneuvering the beam in place. Remove the partition studs by hammering out the bottom of each stud from the bottom plate. If the studs are removed carefully, they can be reused. Pry the top and bottom plates loose with a crow bar, taking care not to damage the surrounding finishes.

11. Patch the gap in the floor. Clean the gap of all debris and adhesive. For tile and carpet, cut strips of sheathing or underlayment the same thickness as the surrounding floor and install the strips with flooring nails. New tiles must then be cut and custom fit into

the gap. A strip of carpet can be glued in the gap but it will be almost impossible to match colors unless you are using existing carpet from another part of the house. If you don't want to replace the entire carpet but you have no matching carpet, try using a decorative strip of carpet of another color. You can run this new color around the entire perimeter of the room like a decorative border. This can add a nice accent to the room and disguise the fact that you are just filling in one strip of carpet. An experienced carpet installer can cut the carpet strips and glue them together with a special heat-sensitive carpet glue. For hardwood floor planks, fit in the new planks and rip the last piece to fit the last gap. This will also remove the tongue of the plank, which will allow it to fit into the slot flush. This last strip cannot be blind nailed, so use small finishing nails and countersink them. Fill in the hole with wood putty.

12. Install drywall patch strips in wall and ceiling gaps. Tape the joints and patch with three coats of joint compound.

13. Paint patched areas.

14. Reinstall trim.

15. Pay the contractor draw for removal of wall and have him sign an affidavit.

Partition Installation

1. Prepare the area around the new partition in the same manner as when removing a partition.

2. Measure the ceiling at several points along the path of the new partition. You may need to cut the studs to different lengths to conform to any differences in ceiling height.

3. Assemble the partition and lift it into place. The fit should be snug. If the ceiling has a rough texture or the ceiling height varies more than 1/4 inch, the partition should be assembled in place so the studs can be custom cut to fit. Start by nailing the top plate to the ceiling joists. If the wall is nonload-bearing, the ceiling finish does not need to be removed. Once the top plate is attached, run a plumb bob from the edge of the top plate to the floor and mark several points along the plate. The plumb bob ensures that the bottom plate will be positioned directly below the top plate, and that the resulting wall will be perfectly plumb. Snap a chalk line along the dots and nail the bottom plate in place. The bottom plate can be nailed directly to the subfloor or hardwood planking. For ceramic tile, drill holes in the tile with a masonry or tile bit and then nail or screw through the hole into the subfloor underneath. Install each stud in place and toenail it to the top and bottom plates. If the partition is load-bearing, any openings will require a header over the opening. Otherwise, frame in the top of the opening with cripples as shown in the illustration.

Try to position a new partition so that it lines up with the studs on intersecting walls. The partition can then be anchored to the wall by nailing through the existing drywall into the stud with 16d nails. If the wall intersects between studs, you will need to remove a portion of drywall from the intersecting wall so you can install at least one piece of horizontal bridging. Then nail to the top and bottom plates of the other wall and to the horizontal bridging. The hole cut to install the bridging can be patched while installing the wall covering on the new partition.

4. Install all rough-in plumbing and wiring in the partition. Any wiring will be spliced into the existing electrical circuits or a new circuit will be installed by the electrician.

5. Install wall covering. See chapter nineteen for more information. Tape the joints between the existing walls and ceiling and the new partition. If the ceiling has a textured surface, finishing the joint between the new partition and the ceiling will be difficult. Consider installing ceiling trim to hide the joint instead.

6. Finish the wall covering as described in chapter nineteen.

7. Install any doors or windows as described in the windows and doors chapter.

8. Reinstall trim and carpet. Install new carpet strips around the bottom of the new wall. The carpet will be cut to fit around the new wall and restretched to fit.

9. Paint walls and trim. Touch up any marks on the ceiling.

10. Install lighting and electrical fixtures. Refer to electrical wiring section.

11. Turn on water and electric utilities.

12. Pay all contractors and have them sign affidavits.

PARTITION MATERIAL ESTIMATE

DESCRIPTION	SPECIFICATION	QTY.	UNIT	COST	TAX	TOTAL COST	COST TYPE	VENDOR
Framing								
Subfloor patch ⅝-inch tongue-and-grooved								
Subfloor patch ¾-inch tongue-and-grooved								
Underlayment								
Beam — glue-lam								
Beam — steel flinch plate								
Beam — laminated veneer								
Plates — 2″ × 4″								
8-foot Studs — 2″ × 4″								
10-foot studs — 2″ × 4″								
Bracing								
Framing — Nails								
12d common								
10d common								
8d common								
3d finish								
4d finish								
6d finish								
Component costs								
Interior trim								
Windows								
Doors								
Flooring								
Lighting fixtures								
Paint								
Drywall								

PARTITION MATERIAL ESTIMATE

DESCRIPTION	SPECIFICATION	QTY.	UNIT	COST	TAX	TOTAL COST	COST TYPE	VENDOR
Labor								
Framing structural — contract								
Plumbing — contract								
Electrical — contract								
HVAC — contract								
Flooring patch — contract								

CHAPTER TWENTY-FOUR

Kitchen

The kitchen has historically been the focal point of most households. Many of our fondest childhood memories center on the aromas and tastes we experienced while socializing in the kitchen. Indeed, in many households, the kitchen has evolved into the social center for families and for entertaining. The old adage that the "kitchen sells the house" is more true today than ever. That is why almost all serious remodeling projects include a kitchen renovation.

PLAN THE RENOVATION

Before undertaking the remodeling of your kitchen, evaluate carefully how you and your family use that room. Besides the usual—cooking and cleaning—do you use that room to eat, to congregate around the table and converse, to chat on the phone, to study, to pay bills, to write? When you entertain, do you like to have your guests help with food preparation or at least visit with you in the kitchen while you add the finishing touches to the meal? Or, do you prefer that the kitchen be isolated so that food preparation can be done in private and so that guests cannot see the kitchen in a mess during food preparation? The factors to consider are its present floor plan, traffic patterns, available counter space, storage needs, appliances, surfaces of all areas (floor, walls, ceilings, counters), necessary lighting and your personal taste.

Traffic Patterns

A work triangle is the triangle created by connecting the three major kitchen appliances—the sink, the stove and the refrigerator. An efficient kitchen is one with a work triangle having sides of no more than 4 to 7 feet. The total distance around the triangle should not exceed 22 feet. By graphing your work triangle on your kitchen plan, many current inefficiencies will immediately become obvious. Draw arrows showing the usual traffic flow of family members and guests through the kitchen and out again. Often, you may find that your "unworkable" kitchen can be improved tremendously by reorganizing an inefficient work triangle, without needing major remodeling. If this is the case, you can achieve an efficient work area by simply relocating the major appliances rather than undergoing costly changes in cabinetry, appliances and other structures such as walls and doors.

The four generally recognized kitchen arrangements are the U, L, corridor and sidewall types. The arrangement you select will depend on the amount of space available, the shape of the space, and the location of the doors. If you are adding a new kitchen, select the layout you prefer and plan the addition in accordance with that. The smallest work triangles are the U and corridor layouts. The sidewall arrangement works well where space is quite limited and the L arrangement fits best in a relatively square kitchen that includes a dining table.

Counter Space and Storage

One major goal in any kitchen renovation is to increase the availability and quality of storage space. A modern kitchen should have at least 6 square feet of storage space in the wall cabinets for each resident. An additional 12 square feet should be added for miscellaneous storage and entertaining. Since the base cabinets usually occupy all the space under the wall cabinets, triple the above figures to arrive at total usable storage space.

Counter space should be sufficient and located in strategic locations. There should be at least 3 feet of counter space between the sink and the refrigerator for food preparation and to make room for a dishwasher under the counter (2 feet). A minimum of 2 feet of counter space should surround the stove top to make

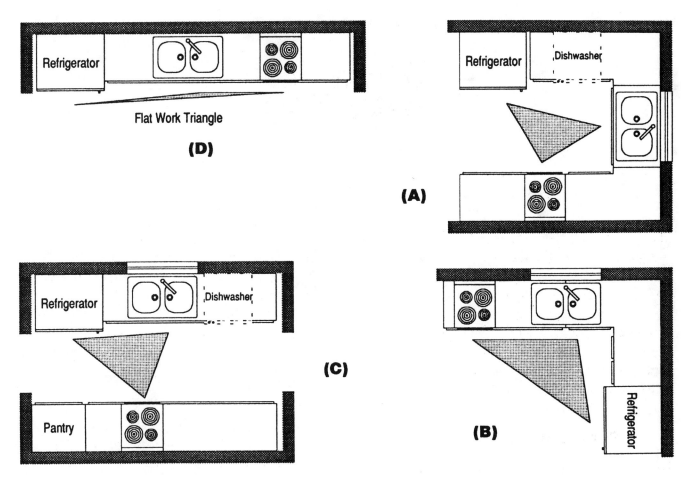

Fig. 24-1. Kitchen arrangements: (A) U-type; (B) L-type; (C) corridor; and (D) sidewall.

room for pots or food preparation. Try to leave about 2 feet of space next to the refrigerator on the side where the door opens as a transition space for food going in and coming out. Countertop dimensions are affected by the size of conventional base and wall cabinets. Most standard cabinets increase in size in 3-inch increments, so adjust your dimensions accordingly. Leave at least 3½ to 4 inches of aisle space between counters for traffic flow.

Doorways

Doorways should be located to direct traffic away from the work triangle. Doorways in corners should be avoided and door swings should not interfere with the use of appliances, cabinets or other doors. If swinging the door out would interfere with traffic in a hall or other activity area, consider using a sliding or folding door. Sliding doors and their installation are expensive, but in certain situations they may be worth it.

Lighting

The kitchen is a socializing center in most homes. The windows should be large enough to make the kitchen a light, cheerful place. The current trend toward indoor-outdoor living has fostered the patio kitchen, with large windows over a counter that extend to the outside and provide a pass-through or an outdoor eating counter. This is particularly useful in warmer climates, but it also has merit for summer living in any climate. Window lighting can be supplemented with careful placement of accent lights and track lighting, to concentrate the light in critical areas.

DRAW THE PRESENT FLOOR PLAN

After analyzing how you would like your kitchen to function, you are then ready to start a detailed analysis of your present kitchen and to draw the changes necessary to convert it into the kitchen of your dreams. The best way to perform this analysis is to draw a kitchen plan and elevation. Use ½-inch or ¼-inch scale, so that all details of the plan will be highly visible.

The first step in graphing the layout of your new kitchen is to graph the existing kitchen and attached rooms to scale. This will determine the limits of your new plan. Initially, you will sketch your new ideas on

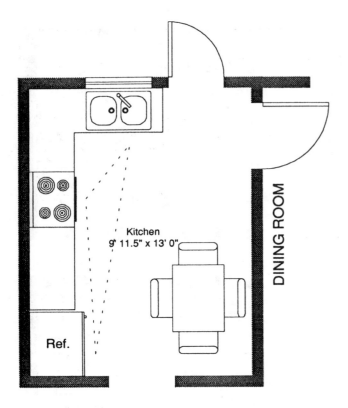

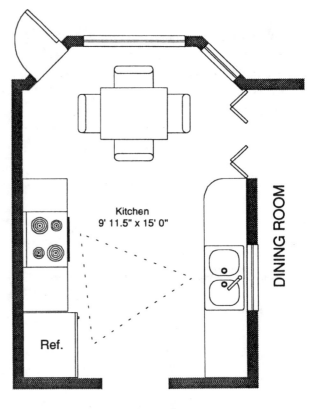

BEFORE   **AFTER**

Fig. 24-2. An example of a kitchen renovation using structural and position changes to enhance functionality. Note after remodeling that the space is opened up with much more light, traffic patterns are straightened out, and the work triangle is shortened. In addition, the kitchen is opened more to the dining area for entertaining through the bifold door and pass-through window over the sink.

top of the older plan. This helps you to visualize the changes needed and the difficulty of making those changes. Measure the inside width and length of the kitchen. Be sure to indicate the precise position and width of all doors and windows, placing them on your plan in their exact location. After graphing the entire inside perimeter of the kitchen, draw a second line the thickness of the stud wall, parallel to and outside the line you have just drawn. Shade the area between these lines. If you are remodeling an older home whose walls are 6 or more inches thick, indicate the dimension on your plan. This can be important if additional plumbing is necessary.

Mark the direction of swing of doors (and windows if casement type). Depending on the age of the house you are remodeling, the size of all openings — doors and windows — as well as the depth of the walls may vary greatly from present day norms. These variances should be indicated on your plan so that structural changes that may be necessary can be identified and so that when purchasing doors or windows the proper sizes can be ordered.

The next items that must be drawn in on your plan are the cabinets. First, draw in the base cabinets. To-

day's standard depth is 24 inches; however, older homes often have cabinets that are shallower by varying amounts. So, be sure that you measure all cabinets carefully. After you have drawn in your base cabinets, indicate your wall cabinets by a dotted line through the base cabinet drawing to represent how far the wall cabinets overhang onto the base cabinets. Like the base cabinets, the usual amount of overhang is 12 inches; however, older homes may vary. Do not assume the standard, but actually measure each cabinet.

Should you have a pantry or other storage area which accesses from the kitchen, draw it as you have the rest of the kitchen. If your laundry area opens into the kitchen, draw the washer and dryer and their enclosure. If your heating, air-conditioning and water heater units are in the kitchen area, draw them and their enclosures. If the kitchen contains an eating area, draw it in precisely, even if it is not a built-in unit. Draw in the size and shape of the table, followed by the number and size of the chairs. Place the eating area on the floor plan exactly as it is in your kitchen. With the chairs, indicate how far back they are pushed to get up and down from the table.

Now, draw in all appliances in the kitchen. On the outline of your base cabinets, draw in your sink opening and cooktop, indicating the exact size and placement of each burner, vent or barbecue grill, if your range includes these features. After you have drawn in all appliances, draw a dotted line to mark the position of each appliance's door in its fully opened position. Any resulting traffic jam created by overlapping doors becomes painfully obvious. Simply moving one appliance or another a few inches or feet can often solve the problem, without having to run new plumbing or wiring.

Finish the plan by drawing all plumbing and wiring. Mark with arrows which outlets control the electricity to what appliances and light fixtures. Older homes often have only 110 volt wiring, which must be updated. Adding a few new outlets will be easy if the cabinets have been removed. If you do not feel confident in assessing your present wiring and future needs, please consult a registered electrician. Failure to do so can result in anything from overload nuisances to fires.

Next, outline each counter area so you can assess your present work surfaces. Do you have enough room next to the cooking area for placement of heated cooking utensils? If so, is the surface heat resistant? If there enough room next to the sink for jobs like chopping and grinding that are better done near the sink for easy cleanup? Do you have an area suitable for rolling out dough and other baking functions? Do you have counter space next to the refrigerator so that grocery bags can be placed there for ease of unloading? After placing canisters, small appliances, and other decorative pieces on the counters, is there workable space remaining?

Elevation drawings are just as important to planning as floor plans. Stand back from the wall and draw exactly what you see to scale. You can use the floor plan drawing under the elevation drawing to help you draw each item in the proper place. Draw in each opening, window covering, cabinet, appliance, hanging light fixture, and any other item that can be seen, such as tables, chairs and hutches. You will use these drawings to assess symmetry, suitable color combinations, suitable wall covering patterns, window coverings and cabinetry.

DRAW THE NEW KITCHEN DESIGN

Now that you have fully graphed the existing kitchen, it is time to identify all the changes you want to make. To do this, take the basic floor plan you graphed and make copies of it. Experiment on the copies by moving

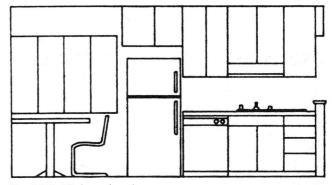

Fig. 24-3. Kitchen elevation.

appliances, changing cabinets, adding work surfaces, adding an island, changing or adding an eating nook. This is your time to dream. Make any changes you want. Make as many drawings as you like. Slowly, you will begin to see a pattern emerge of your predominant preferences in placement of appliances, work surfaces, storage needs and desired traffic patterns. This will help you refine your "needs" and "wouldn't it be nice" lists.

As you lay out the new design, pay attention to proper clearances and design options. The National Kitchen and Bath Association (NKBA) has developed a comprehensive set of kitchen guidelines and specifications for modern kitchens. These are included in the kitchen specifications at the end of this chapter as NKBA specifications. Refer to them while developing your new kitchen plan.

Once this is completed, it is time to evaluate your style preference. The best way to avoid costly mistakes and to evaluate the overall effect of your remodeling ideas is to draw and color them on copies of the wall elevations.

Colors fall into two main categories — warm and cool. Colors in the blue family are considered cool and tend to enlarge a room. Colors in the red/yellow/orange family are warm and tend to make a room smaller and cozier. It has always been a good rule of thumb to avoid dark colors in a very small room so that the room does not appear even smaller. Lighter hues tend to make a room appear larger. Experiment with dark and light hues of whatever color scheme you have chosen. On copies of the elevations, shade in the colors you have chosen. Try varying the tints used from wall to wall. Try painting two walls one color and the other two either a contrasting one or a different hue. Go through this same exercise with several different color schemes. You will quickly begin to see which combination you find aesthetically pleasing.

Look at the color scheme you have chosen and the overall feeling you are trying to create. Do you want a warm and cozy kitchen? Do you want a sterile, efficient appearance? Or, are you trying to use color to mask a ceiling that is too high, a room that is too small, or a room that is too large to appear cozy? It is well known that colors can be used to achieve just about any effect you wish. If you would like some additional professional guidance, there are interior designers who specialize just in kitchen design.

Do not forget the color of the appliances. If their color no longer fits your design scheme, but you do not wish to purchase new appliances, have a new enamel finish baked on at your nearest automobile paint shop. Most new appliances, however, have removable color panels to make decorative changes even easier.

After you have narrowed your ideas down to those you wish to implement, look at the complete plan and analyze your lighting needs. You may like the new track lighting fixtures or Tiffany hanging lamps; however, evaluate their light beams and the shadows they will cast on your work surfaces. Make sure that you have ample under-the-counter lighting to illuminate your work area without casting shadows. If you prefer a kitchen in which at least one light is left illuminated at night, dimmer switches can be installed for varied lighting effects.

Plan Ahead to Avoid Interruptions

Next to the bathroom and bedroom, the kitchen is the most critical room in the house. A long drawn out project can prevent meals from being prepared and wreak havoc on a well-organized household. Develop a contingency plan for cooking during the project and make sure all materials are on hand before the project begins.

Find a space to store any ordered materials on site so that they will be instantly available once the project begins. If possible, find an alternate place to set up a temporary kitchen or plan to eat out a lot. Make sure your subcontractors understand the importance of showing up on time by adding a performance clause to their contract.

Try to get as many peripheral projects such as rewiring, lighting, or additional plumbing finished before you are forced to tear down the cabinets. Once the cabinets are removed, you are out of commission until the entire job is completed.

SPECIFIC PROBLEMS

If your current kitchen is very old, chances are that its layout, appliances and cabinets are outdated and non-standard. Cabinets may be an odd size, the current layout may not reflect modern needs, and kitchen space is probably undersized. The following is a brief list of items to examine.

Electrical

If the kitchen was built before 1979, the current electrical system is probably inadequate. There are many more electrical appliances in the modern kitchen. Hire an electrician to inspect the electrical load capacity of the kitchen. An additional circuit may be needed. Electrical outlets on the counter should be replaced with ground fault interrupters (GFIs) for additional safety from shock. If the wiring in the rest of the house is old and frayed, the kitchen wiring is almost certainly worse. Pull out a cabinet near an outlet and inspect the wiring in the walls. If your kitchen remodeling project includes major structural changes, it will be much easier to update the wiring.

Flooring

Moisture in the kitchen (like the bathroom) increases the chance of warped, sagging or rotted flooring. If you plan to move cabinets from their present position, a new subfloor will almost certainly be needed. Replace any rotting lumber and cover with a new plywood or chipboard floor. If the floor is sound but uneven, a thin subfloor (to create a smooth surface) may be all that is needed. Use ¼-inch plywood for this purpose.

Modern Appliances

Older kitchens seldom had trash compactors, disposals, dishwashers, range tops or microwave ovens. The current layout may not make room for these new appliances. In this case, consider a major restructuring of the kitchen layout to make room for these items. Keep the availability of electrical and plumbing connections in mind when locating the new appliances.

CABINETS

If the cabinet space in your kitchen is adequate and well arranged, updating the cabinets may be the only change you need to make. New doors and drawer fronts can be added to the old cabinet framing. Even refinish-

Existing cabinets can be given a facelift by refinishing the existing doors or by installing new doors and hardware. Cabinet face kits are available that allow you to replace just the part of the cabinet you can see. Since most cabinet dimensions are standardized, these face kits will fit over most cabinets. Stripping and refinishing cabinets is time consuming but can achieve phenomenal results at low cost.

Repainting existing cabinets and adding new hardware may be all that's needed for a new look. Adding storage racks to the inside can alleviate cramped storage.

If the edges of your laminated countertop are chipping and delaminating, try removing the edges and replacing them with a wood border. This will fix the problem and provide a color accent as well.

Precast laminate tops are inexpensive and come with integrated backsplashes. Install a new countertop to freshen the kitchen appearance.

ing or painting the old cabinets and adding new hardware can sometimes do much to improve an old kitchen. If your kitchen has adequate cabinets, the improvement that will have the greatest impact is installing new countertops. Tops should be fabricated and installed by a good custom counter shop. Plastic laminate over particle board backing is commonly used.

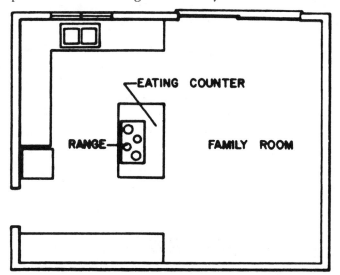

Fig. 24-4. Island counter dividing kitchen and family room.

If your kitchen is quite large, it may be convenient to use part as a family room. The combined kitchen-

family room concept can also be achieved by removing a partition to expand the kitchen or by adding on a large room. One method of arranging workspace conveniently in such a room is by using an island counter, which can also serve as an eating counter for informal dining.

Existing Cabinets

The existing kitchen cabinets in your house may be out of style and may be arranged quite inconveniently; however, new hardware and door fronts may do much for the appearance of old cabinets. For a natural finished wood, new doors and drawer fronts can be used on the old cabinet frame. Moldings can be added to achieve the desired character.

Repair of Existing Cabinets

Even if existing cabinets are adequate and well arranged, certain repairs may be in order. One problem may be latches that do not operate. These are easily replaced. One of the popular types is the magnetic catch. The magnetic part is attached to a shelf or the side of the cabinet and a complementary metal plate is attached to the inside face of the door. New door and drawer pulls to match any decor can also be easily added.

New door and drawer fronts can be added where more extensive face-lifting is desired. All framing can be completely concealed by using flush doors with concealed hinges. Doors are fitted edge-to-edge to give a continuous panel effect. Finger slots in the bottom edge of the door can be used for a simple modern design, or door pulls can be added for any desired character.

New Cabinets

Kitchen cabinets can be custom made or purchased in units as stock items. Stock cabinets can be purchased in widths varying in 3-inch increments between 12 and 48 inches. These units are fastened to the wall through cleats at the back of each cabinet. Wall-hung cabinets should be attached with long screws that penetrate into each wall stud.

Because of the cabinetry, the kitchen invariably turns out to be the most expensive room in the house. The same cabinets may be used in both the kitchen and baths. Money spent on high-quality cabinets can really add value to your home. Cabinetry can be prefabricated or custom built for your installation. Although custom cabinets are nice, the extra expense and time

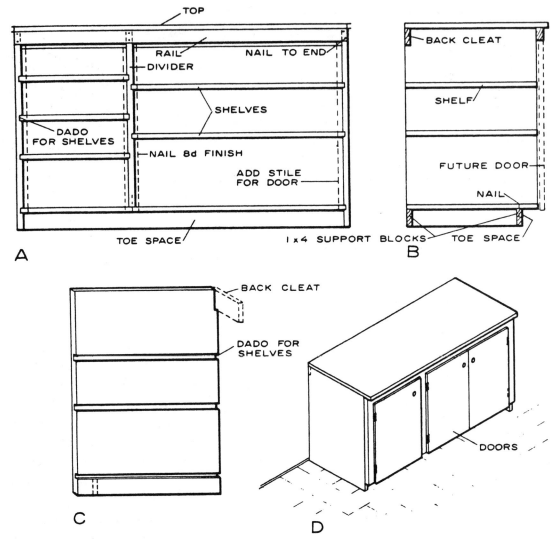

Fig. 24-5. Kitchen cabinet base unit: (A) front view; (B) section; (C) end from interior; and (D) overall view.

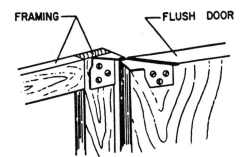

Fig. 24-6. Concealed hinge used with flush cabinet door.

involved is rarely worth it. Many high-quality prefab cabinets are available today.

When shopping for cabinets, pay attention to space-saving devices such as revolving corner units, drop down shelves and slide-out shelves. These options can significantly increase the usable space in your cabinets.

Visit a few kitchen cabinet stores or kitchen design stores to become acquainted with the many functional types of cabinets that are available. Look at sample kitchen layouts to get ideas. Select your material (wood, Formica, etc.), hinge and knob styles and finish. Also important, determine how much cabinet space you need. How the cabinet space is used is more important than the amount of space. Many American companies are turning out impressive reproductions of fine, expensive European models at a fraction of the price. The cabinetry should be an integral part of your kitchen design, complementing appliances, lighting and space. Remember, kitchens and baths sell houses.

COUNTERTOPS

Where cabinets are adequate, the best way to update a kitchen is to apply new countertops. Custom shops will measure, fabricate and install them.

Countertops typically should have a standard depth

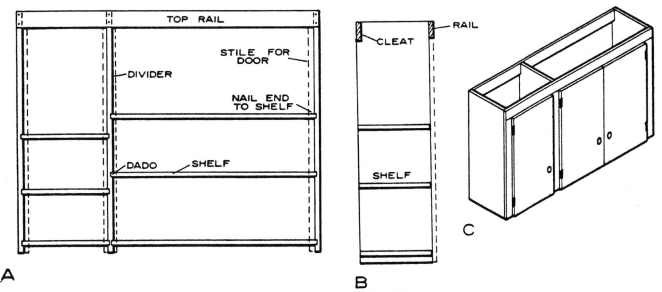

Fig. 24-7. Kitchen cabinet wall unit: (A) front view; (B) section; and (C) overall view.

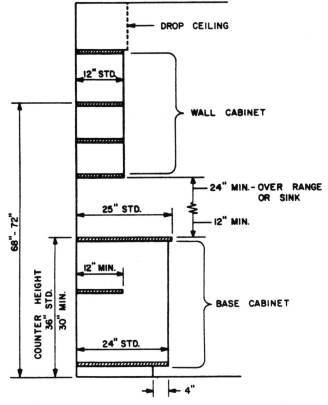

Fig. 24-8. Kitchen cabinet proportions.

of 24 inches and may have a 3- or 4-inch splashblock against the wall. Countertops are priced and installed by the foot, while special charges may be incurred to cut openings for stoves, sinks and fancy edgework. If you get a separate company to do the kitchen and vanity tops, which is most likely when cultured marble is used, installation is normally included in the price—but get

this confirmed. Advantages to cultured marble tops is the lack of a seam between the top and the sink, no sink bowl to purchase, and an easier job for the plumber.

Countertops are normally made of plastic laminate. But other materials have become popular including butcher block, tile, Corian and marble (natural or cultured). Formica is by far the most popular and least expensive. Some companies sell bathroom vanities and countertops with the sink built in.

Several sheet and roll materials that can be glued to clean, smooth backing are available. These include plastic laminate, laminated polyester, vinyl and linoleum. They are normally applied to ¾-inch exterior-type plywood and are flexible enough to be shaped to a coved backsplash. Other materials can be applied only flat, so the backsplash is covered separately and a metal strip is used to cover the joint between the backsplash and the countertop.

Marble is shop-fabricated, self-edged and requires no backing material. It must be precut to size in the shop because special tools are required. Marble is hard and costly, so it is usually limited to bath counters.

Ceramic tile can be set in a mortar bed or applied with adhesive. It is the only material that must be applied at the building site rather than in a shop or factory. It is available in a variety of sizes. The smaller 1-inch-square tiles are often preassembled on a mesh backing in 1-foot-square units. Tile countertops are quite attractive and were once very popular, but the joints are a maintenance problem.

PROFESSIONAL KITCHEN SERVICES

Whether you hire a remodeling contractor or contract your kitchen project yourself, you will need to deal with at least one of the following services:

Architect

If you are using an architect for a whole-house renovation, he will usually take care of the kitchen design as well, drawing the elevations and contacting the subs. However, many architects can be hired just to do the kitchen design. This can be expensive and usually isn't worth it unless your project is quite elaborate.

Kitchen Designer

This may be an interior designer, independent cabinet dealer, or an in-house designer at a material supply store. They usually charge a flat fee for designing the kitchen or, if they are selling you a cabinet set, they may include the design fee in the cost of the cabinets. Many suppliers now have in-house design facilities with computerized design services. These are used to promote the sales of their own cabinet lines. A kitchen designer can be very helpful for designing a stunning kitchen layout, but may not be knowledgeable about the technical issues of renovating the space. You will still need to hire installation or renovation contractors to complete the other kitchen remodeling chores.

Remodeling Contractor

If you have hired one, the remodeling contractor will usually take care of all the kitchen designs. Make sure the sub is capable of designing a quality kitchen or works with an experienced kitchen designer. This will be the most costly option for renovating the kitchen.

Cabinet Sub

If you decide to contract the job yourself, the cabinet subcontractor is the person you will contact. This sub will normally manufacture or supply all cabinets and install them along with the countertops. This includes making all the cuts for sinks, stoves, etc. Since many cabinet subs manufacture their own cabinets, you can request many custom options that are not available on premade units. Cabinet subs normally bid the job at one price for material and labor. Try to have any appliances that are to be installed on site when the cabinet sub installs the cabinets. He will install the appliances in place to insure that his cabinets fit properly.

KITCHEN CONVERSION STEPS

Planning

1. Confirm kitchen design. Make sure you have enough cabinets to store all pots, pans, utensils and food items.

2. Complete diagram of cabinet layout for kitchen and baths. This is a critical step to perform prior to electrical and plumbing installation. Show locations of all plumbing connections on diagram: icemaker, dishwasher and sink.

3. Select cabinetry/countertop styles/colors.

4. Perform standard bidding process. Obtain a signed proposal with standard provisions and specifications.

NOTE: Add information in bidding section about items to include in bid-list of tasks performed, start and end date, list and description of materials with delivery dates, liabilities, lien waivers, guarantees, schedule of payments, etc.

---

5. Obtain signed contract for installation and/or manufacture.

6. Obtain building permit if needed.

7. Purchase or have constructed all cabinetry and countertop surfaces. If your countertops come from a separate sub, coordinate the cabinetry and countertop sub. You can't install tops until cabinets are in. If you have new stud walls, wait for the drywall to be installed before having the cabinet sub measure dimensions. This gives more exact figures to work from and a place to mark on the wall.

Give your cabinet sub specs for all appliance dimensions and locations of all doors and windows. This will insure that the cabinets will install properly under the window sill. At a minimum, wait for framing to be finished. Walk through the structure with the cabinet sub. Countertops are typically 36 inches above the floor, kitchen desks 32 inches high with a minimum 24-inch knee space. When measuring, remember to account for ½-inch drywall on walls and widths of adjacent trim. Mark dimensions on the floor with builder's chalk or crayon.

8. Prepare storage area for delivery of cabinets, appliances, etc.

9. Check delivered items for correct model, color, size, etc. Check for any damaged material now before time to install. Discovering a damaged item at installation time can delay the project while you wait for a replacement.

10. Make arrangements for getting rid of trash after installation.

Removal of Old Items

1. Create temporary kitchen.

2. Block off other parts of house with plastic over openings and floor to contain dust and dirt.

3. Schedule plumbing, flooring and cabinet subs.

4. Turn off gas, water and electric power before starting removal of cabinets or appliances.

5. Remove countertops, cabinets, and finally wall units.

6. Remove paneling, trim, wallpaper and flooring. (See related chapters on removing old items.)

7. Remove lighting fixtures.

8. Fix holes in walls.

9. Paint or wallpaper walls, ceilings, etc. To save time and energy, paint and wallpaper after old cabinets are removed and before new cabinets are installed. After installation, walls can be touched up if marred or scratched. Caution: If you apply wallpaper now, be careful not to mar or scratch the surface while installing cabinets.

Installation

1. Install any new plumbing fixtures, disposal connections and icemaker connections.

2. Prepare floor surface for new floor. If installing a new floor over existing subfloor, make sure floor surface is level and even with no seams, bumps or soft spots. If the floor sags or is uneven, a new subfloor may be required. Cabinets will not install straight and level if the floor sags.

3. Install new subfloor

4. Install hardwood or tile floor. (See chapter twelve.) Note: Vinyl or linoleum floors are usually installed *after* cabinets are installed.

Cabinets

1. Mark the walls for installation of cabinets. Measure from the *top of the new floor* to the height of the cabinets, making sure to add in the height of the countertop and mark. Draw a line or pull a chalk line across the wall where the tops of the cabinets will line up. Measure down from the ceiling and draw the line for the bottom of the wall cabinets. Mark the locations of all wall studs and make corresponding marks on the wall cabinets. Drill pilot holes at these marks for the wall-unit anchor screws. *Tip*: Tack a straight board across this line to create a ledge for the wall units to rest on while attaching them to the wall. Use shims to level the wall and floor units when installing.

2. Stain and seal, paint or otherwise finish all cabinet woodwork. Stains will stain the grout and other nearby items, so cabinets should be stained before they are installed.

3. Precut holes in wall cabinets for range vent hoods and install any ducting in place before installing wall cabinets.

4. Install kitchen wall cabinets. If you install base cabinets first, they get in your way while installing wall units.

5. Install kitchen base cabinets. Also, make necessary cutouts for sinks and cooktops. Show the cabinet sub where cutouts are to be made. Don't make any cutouts until the units have arrived.

6. Install cabinet doors, drawers and hardware. Adjust cabinetry hardware: pulls, hinges, etc.

7. Install base for countertops.

8. Mark hole for sink in countertop. If sink has a lip, make sure the hole is *smaller* than the outside diameter of the sink lip.

> **NOTE:** If you are installing a tile countertop, the sink should be installed now, before the tile, so that the tile and grout can be installed flush to the sink edge. With all other countertops, a sink with a lip is installed *after* the countertop is in place.

9. Install countertops, backsplashs and aprons.

10. Install surface-mounted sink and sink fittings in countertop.

11. Install and hook up built-in appliances—disposal, stove top, built in microwave, trash compactor and stove vent hood.

12. Caulk all wall/cabinetry joints as needed.

Completion

1. Install vinyl floor (see chapter twelve). Allow one to two days drying time before moving appliances across vinyl floor.

2. Install and hook up remaining appliances—refrigerator, oven, icemaker and dishwasher.

3. Install lighting and electrical fixtures. (See chapter fourteen.)

4. Turn on water, electric and gas utilities.

5. Install floor trim or quarter-round trim.

6. Inspect all cabinetry and countertops.

7. Touch up and repair any scratches and other marks on cabinetry and countertops.

8. Pay cabinet sub, requiring a signed affidavit.

9. Pay other subs (flooring, tile, plumbing, electrical). Have them sign an affidavit.

KITCHEN SPECIFICATIONS

- Also refer to flooring specs and tile specs in chapter twelve, and electrical specs in chapter fourteen.

Cabinets

- Bid is to provide and complete cabinetry and countertop installation as indicated on attached drawings.
- All cabinets are to be installed by qualified contractors.
- All cabinets are to be installed plumb and square and as indicated on attached drawings.
- All hardware such as hinges, pulls, bracing and supports is to be included in bid.
- All necessary countertop cutouts and edging are to be included in bid.
- All exposed corners on countertops are to be rounded or covered.
- All tile countertops are to be glazed tile only.
- All grout seams are to be sealed.
- Install one double stainless steel sink (model/size).

- Special interior cabinet hardware includes:
  Lazy Susan
  Broom rack
  Pot racks
  Sliding lid racks

Countertops

- Bid is to manufacture and install the following cultured marble tops in ¾-inch solid color material. Sink bowls are to be an integral part of top.
- Vanity A is to be 24 inches deep, 55 inches wide, finished on left with backsplash; 19-inch oval sink cut with rounded edge with center of sink 22 inches from right side. Color is solid white. Spread faucet to be used.

NKBA Specifications

The following kitchen specifications represent the latest in kitchen standards and are provided by the National Kitchen and Bath Association.

- A clear walkway at least 32 inches wide must be provided at all entrances to the kitchen.
- No entry or appliance door may interfere with work center appliances and/or counter space.
- Work aisles must be at least 42 inches wide, and passageways must be at least 36 inches wide for a one-cook kitchen.
- In kitchens 150 square feet or less, at least 144 inches of wall cabinet frontage, with cabinets at least 12 inches deep and a minimum of 30 inches high (or equivalent), must be installed over countertops. In kitchens over 150 square feet, 186 inches of wall cabinets must be included. Diagonal or pie cut wall cabinets count as a total of 24 inches. Difficult-to-reach cabinets above the hood, oven or refrigerator do not count unless specialized storage devices are installed within the case to improve accessibility.
- At least 60 inches of wall cabinet frontage with cabinets that are at least 12 inches deep and a minimum of 30 inches high (or equivalent) must be included within 72 inches of the primary sink centerline.
- In kitchens 150 square feet or less, at least 156 inches of base cabinet frontage, with cabinets at least 21 inches deep (or equivalent) must be part of the plan. In kitchens over 150 square feet, 192 inches of base cabinets must be included. Pie cut/lazy Susan cabinets count as a total of 30 inches.

The first 24 inches of a blind corner box do not count.

- Kitchens 150 square feet or less, require at least 120 inches of drawer frontage or roll-out shelf frontage. Kitchens over 150 square feet require at least 165 inches of drawer/shelf frontage. (Measure cabinet width to determine frontage.)

- At least five storage items must be included in the kitchen to improve the accessibility and functionality of the plan. These items include, but are not limited to: wall cabinets with adjustable shelves, interior vertical dividers, pull-out drawers, swing-out pantries, or drawer/roll-out space greater than the minimum.

- At least one functional corner storage unit must be included. (Rule does not apply to a kitchen without corner cabinet arrangements.)

- Between 15 and 18 inches of clearance must exist between the countertop and the bottom of wall cabinets.

- In kitchens 150 square feet or less, at least 132 inches of usable countertop frontage is required. For kitchens larger than 150 square feet, the countertop requirement increases to 198 inches. Counter must be 16 inches deep to be counted; corner space does not count.

- No two primary work centers (the primary sink, refrigerator, preparation center, cook top/range center), can be separated by a full-height, full-depth tall tower, such as an oven cabinet, pantry cabinet or refrigerator.

- There must be at least 24 inches of counter space to one side of the sink and 18 inches on the other side. (Measure only countertop frontage; do not count corner space.) The 18- and 24-inch counter space sections may be a continuous surface, or the total of two angled countertop sections. If a second sink is part of the plan, at least 3 inches of counter space must be on one side and 18 inches on the other side.

- At least 3 inches of counter space must be allowed from the edge of the sink to the inside corner of the countertop if more than 21 inches of counter space is available on the return. Or, at least 18 inches of counter space from the edge of the sink to the inside corner of the countertop if the return counter space is blocked by a full-height, full-depth cabinet or any appliance that is deeper than the countertop.

- At least two waste receptacles must be included in the plan, one for garbage and one for recyclable or other recycling facilities.

- The dishwasher must be positioned within 36 inches of one sink. Sufficient space (21 inches of standing room) must be allowed between the dishwasher and adjacent counters, other appliances and cabinets.

- At least 36 inches of continuous countertop is required for the preparation center, and must be located close to a water source.

- The plan should allow at least 15 inches of counter space on the latch side of a refrigerator or on either side of a side-by-side refrigerator. Or, at least 15 inches of landing space that is no more than 48 inches across from the refrigerator. (Measure the 48-inch walkway from the countertop adjacent to the refrigerator to the island countertop directly opposite.)

- For an open-ended kitchen configuration, at least 9 inches of counter space is required on one side of the cooktop/range top and 15 inches on the other. For an enclosed configuration, at least 3 inches of clearance space must be planned at an end wall protected by flame-retardant surfacing material, and 15 inches must be allowed on the other side of the appliance.

- The cooking surface cannot be placed below an operable window unless the window is 3 inches or more behind the appliance, and/or more than 24 inches above it.

- There must be at least 15 inches of landing space next to or above the oven if the appliance door opens into a primary family traffic pattern. If the appliance does not open into traffic area, 15 inches of landing space that is no more than 48 inches across from the oven is acceptable.

- At least 15 inches of landing space must be planned above, below or adjacent to the microwave oven.

- The shelf on which the microwave is placed is to be between counter and eye level (36 to 54 inches off the floor).

- All cooking surface appliances are required to have a ventilation system, with a fan rated at 150 cfm minimum.

- At least 24 inches of clearance is needed between the cooking surface and a protected surface above. Or, at least 30 inches of clearance is needed between the cooking surface and an unprotected surface above.

■ The work triangle should total less than 26 feet. The triangle is defined as the shortest walking distance between the refrigerator, primary cooking surface, and primary food preparation sink. It is measured from the center front of each appliance. The work triangle may not intersect an island or peninsula cabinet by more than 12 inches. No single leg of the triangle should be shorter than 4 feet nor longer than 9 feet.

■ No major household traffic patterns should cross through the work triangle connecting the three primary centers (the primary sink, refrigerator, preparation center, cooktop/range center).

■ A minimum of 12″ × 24″ counter table space should be planned for each seated diner.

■ At least 36 inches of walkway space from a counter/table to any wall or obstacle behind it is required if the area is to be used to pass behind a seated diner. Or, at least 24 inches of space from the counter/table to any wall or obstacle behind it is needed if the area will not be used as a walk space.

■ At least 10 percent of the total square footage of the separate kitchen, or of a total living space that includes a kitchen, should be appropriated for windows/skylights.

■ Ground fault circuit interrupters must be specified on all receptacles that are within 6 feet of a

water source in the kitchen. A fire extinguisher should be located near tile cook top. Smoke alarms should be included near the kitchen.

CABINET INSPECTION

☐ All cabinet doors open and close properly with no binding or squeaking. Doors open completely and remain in place half opened.

☐ All pulls and other hardware are securely fastened. Check for excessive play in hinges.

☐ All specified shelving is in place and level.

☐ All exposed cabinetry has an even and smooth finish.

☐ There are no nicks, scratches, scars or other damage/irregularity on any cabinetry and countertops.

☐ Countertops are checked for level by placing water or marbles on surface. All joints are securely glued with no buckling or delamination.

☐ All drawers line up properly.

☐ All mitered and flush joints are tight.

☐ Cutouts for sinks and cooktops are done properly and units are fitted into place.

☐ All caulked seams are smooth and uniform.

☐ All plumbing fixtures are sealed with no leaks. Drains do not leak when a full sink is drained.

☐ There are no gaps between cabinets and appliances.

☐ There are no nicks or tears in vinyl flooring or wallpaper after installation of cabinets.

KITCHEN MATERIAL ESTIMATE

DESCRIPTION	SPECIFICATION	QTY.	UNIT	COST	TAX	TOTAL COST	COST TYPE	VENDOR
Cabinets								
Wall cabinets 12 inches deep								
Base cabinets 24 inches deep								
Blocking—2″ × 4″ for wall cabinets								
Island cabinet								
Pantry cabinet								
Corner lazy Susan								
Valance boards								
Mounting screws								
Cornice trim								
Floor								
Plywood underlayment—4′ × 8′ × ½″								
Flooring								
Floor felt—500 pound								
Flooring adhesive								
Flooring nails								
Quarter-round trim								
Finishing nails								
Tile								
Floor tile								
Grout compound								
Grout sealant								
Counter tile								
Tile adhesive								

KITCHEN MATERIAL ESTIMATE

DESCRIPTION	SPECIFICATION	QTY.	UNIT	COST	TAX	TOTAL COST	COST TYPE	VENDOR
Countertop								
Plywood subbase — 4′ × 8′ × ¾″								
Plastic laminate								
Laminate contact adhesive								
Wood counter trim								
Butcher block								
Lights and electrical								
Track lights								
Can lights								
Fluorescent fixture — ceiling								
Fluorescent fixture — sink								
Ground fault interrupters								
Fixtures								
Cooking range — built-in								
Range hood								
Stovetop								
Microwave								
Trash compactor								
Refrigerator								
Garbage disposal								
Dishwasher								
Plumbing								
Kitchen sink								
Faucet set								
Rough-in drain pipe								
Drain elbows								
Drain Ts								
Drain caps								
Rough-in water supply								
Water supply elbows								

KITCHEN MATERIAL ESTIMATE

DESCRIPTION	SPECIFICATION	QTY.	UNIT	COST	TAX	TOTAL COST	COST TYPE	VENDOR
Water supply Ts								
Water supply caps								
Icemaker fittings								
PVC cement								
Flux solder								
Finish								
Paint—primer—wall								
Paint—primer—trim								
Paint—primer—base coat								
Windows								
Sink								
Dining								
Labor								
Kitchen design								
Cabinet fabricate								
Cabinet install								
Electrical								
Plumbing								
Flooring								
Carpentry—miscellaneous								

CHAPTER TWENTY-FIVE

Bathrooms

The bathroom has changed from a purely functional design to a romantic escape where you can steam away the aches and pains of modern living in a sauna or enjoy the pristine view of a Japanese garden from a soaking tub. These expanded functions put a lot of demand on the limited space and access of older baths. Converting small, dark bathrooms into modern bathing areas without spending a fortune requires creative energy and extensive research.

Like the kitchen, a bathroom remodeling project can encompass many different projects: flooring, painting, plumbing, cabinetry, lighting, wallpaper and new plumbing fixtures. In an old home with one bathroom, you may try to find space for an additional bathroom. Proper planning is essential.

Remodeling the bathroom can significantly improve your home's value. Like the kitchen, the bathroom can be dated just by the style and technology of the fixtures. Modern bath appliances have changed considerably over the past few years, making older units obsolete in both appearance and function. Upgrading the house may consist simply of applying a new coat of paint; however, bath renovations usually require extensive changes. Bath areas also show wear faster because of their concentrated use and the effects of moisture on older materials.

PLANNING THE BATHROOM

Since remodeling the bathroom is so important, you should plan the renovation thoroughly. Work out all your plans on paper first, looking at space requirements, costs, and your other remodeling plans. This way, you can make maximum use of your remodeling budget and create a more functional design.

Shop thoroughly for materials and decorating ideas. Write off for remodeling ideas from bath accessory man-ufacturers. These brochures can be a gold mine of ideas, providing inventive and up-to-date creative suggestions.

Bath Designer

Many do-it-yourself stores now provide kitchen and bath design services that can help tremendously in planning an efficient bathroom remodeling project. Often, these services are provided free of charge.

You might consider using a kitchen and bath designer, such as an interior designer, an independent bath fixture dealer, or an in-house designer at a material supply store. They usually charge a flat fee or, if they are selling you bathroom fixtures, they may include the design fee in the cost of the fixtures. Many suppliers now have in-house design facilities with computerized design services. To find a reliable designer, check with local builders and suppliers. Another good source is the National Kitchen and Bath Association, an industry association that can provide a list of members in your area. Check the association listing section in the phone book for an address and phone number.

As mentioned in the kitchen section, designers can be very helpful creating an excellent layout, but may not be knowledgeable about the technical issues of bathroom renovation. You may still need to hire a plumbing contractor or remodeling contractor to complete removal and installation of new plumbing fixtures.

Remodeling Contractor

If you hire a remodeling contractor to complete your bathroom remodeling project, this will add considerably to the cost of the project. The contractor will be subbing out the plumbing work to a licensed plumber and will charge you a percentage for the plumbing work. Make sure to get several written estimates with firm starting and completion dates. Considering the importance of the bathroom, you can't afford to have delays that lengthen the period the bathroom is unusable. You may be shocked at the variance in bids, so make sure to include as many specifics about materials and workmanship in your bids as you can. Plumbing work generally includes a large markup. If you feel confident in contracting the job yourself, you can save a considerable amount of money.

Minor remodeling would consist of the following items:

- Fresh coat of paint
- New wallpaper
- New towel racks and fixtures

A more complete rehabilitation might include:
- New plumbing fixtures on sink and tub
- New sink and cabinet
- New tile floor, vinyl floor covering or carpet
- Converted shower enclosure
- New mirror or lights above the sink
- New or refinished tub
- A new bath layout, requiring repositioning of fixtures
- A new bathroom addition

MAJOR RENOVATIONS

Extensive structural changes to the bathroom, such as tearing out an old tub or expanding the bathroom size, will be time consuming and require limiting access to the bathroom. Most structural changes require rerouting the plumbing. This may be very difficult without tearing out additional walls to gain access to the plumbing. If your house is situated on a crawl space or basement foundation, locating plumbing will be much easier. If your house is located on a concrete slab, adding new baths or fixtures may require tearing up the slab. In homes with slab construction, try to tap off existing plumbing or consider constructing a new addition. Extensive structural changes will be more cost effective if you are planning to add an additional bath adjoining the existing bathroom area. The increased value of an additional bathroom can make this extensive work more worthwhile.

If you plan to relocate plumbing yourself, investigate the use of CPVC or polybutylene plastic pipe. CPVC is a stiff plastic pipe made of chlorinated polyvinyl chloride that is easier to install and less costly than copper pipe. Polybutylene is a new plastic compound that is easy to use, quick to install and very inexpensive. In many ways it outperforms its copper cousins. Its flexibility makes it easy to snake around framing with a minimum of joints. It is very resistant to freezing and water hammer (a thumping sound caused by the sudden shutting off of the water supply). Many do-it-yourself stores are switching from CPVC to polybutylene because of its many advantages, but you may still have to shop around to find it. Make sure your local building codes allow polybutylene.

If the tub or shower needs replacing or repositioning, take a look at the new ready-to-assemble kits. These kits consist of acrylic or fiberglass panels that can be assembled after fitting the parts through the door of the bathroom. You may find it next to impossible to fit a new one-piece molded shower into an existing space, since many shower stalls are bigger than standard door openings.

ADDING A BATHROOM

If you are remodeling an old house, it probably suffers from a shortage of bathrooms. Extra bathrooms and powder rooms can add considerable value to your house and can be fitted into surprisingly small spaces. Finding a convenient location for a bath addition in an existing house is difficult. Adding a room to the house is seldom a good solution because bathrooms need access from a bedroom hallway. A half-bath near the main entrance or in the work area is desirable.

Finding Space

If you need an additional bathroom, see if you can steal space from a bedroom, closet or other bath. Extra-small showers can be fitted into areas that were once closets. Extra deep tubs as short as 42 inches can be used in tight spaces. Small sinks can be purchased to fit into corners.

Even when the bath area is smaller than you like, you can make confined spaces seem larger with the use of decorative techniques. Use light colors for wallpaper and tile. Add a skylight or window garden to give the space a more open feel. Sometimes the best wall covering is not wallpaper, but mirrors. They expand the perspective and perceived space of the room, and also provide an easy-to-clean, durable surface.

If your challenge is to find room for an additional bath or two, the best sources, in order of preference, are listed in the following paragraphs:

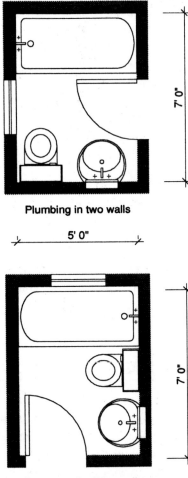

Plumbing in two walls

|← 5' 0" →|

Common plumbing wall

Fig. 25-1. Minimum size bathroom (5 feet by 7 feet).

1. *The "wet wall"* between the current bathroom and the new bathroom. This is the wall that houses all current plumbing. By using this wall, you can tie your new fixtures into the existing plumbing with a minimum of effort and cost.

2. *The current bathroom location.* If the present bathroom is large enough and has access to it from more than one side, split it into two bathrooms. Often the space will be just a bit too small for this option. If so, check the possibility of cantilevering the present bathroom over the outside wall. This can add up to 4 feet of length to the bath area without requiring alteration of the foundation. You can now use this expanded area to create two baths from one.

3. *An existing laundry room.* This area is perfect for a conversion because the plumbing is already present in the wall. With careful planning, you can combine the laundry room with a bathroom by enclosing the washer and dryer behind folding doors. If your new bath area is not large enough for the washer and dryer, investigate the new stackable washer and dryer combinations. These extra-small appliances will handle a standard laundry load, but they take up less than half the wall space of conventional units. Unfortunately, most laundry rooms are not located in the best place for a bathroom and most open into the kitchen. Fitting in a bathroom may require moving the door to provide better access to the bedrooms.

4. *Adjoining closet areas.* Closets that back up to existing bathroom areas can be merged into the new bath area to create a compartmented bathroom or a half bath. The closet location usually allows private access to the new bath from the bedroom—a valuable feature.

5. *Room additions.* This is the least desired location for new baths since it requires a major structural remodeling of the building structure. Bathroom structural additions seldom return their invested value because the cost of adding to an existing structure is so much greater than the increased value of the house. If you add space to the house for a new bath, consider adding other living spaces at the same time. You have already incurred the major costs of engineering, foundation work, alteration of the exterior walls and framing, so why not increase the value of your project by also adding a laundry room, bedroom extension or playroom? This makes the investment much more worthwhile.

One common mistake in adding a bath to older homes is to place it in any unused space without regard to the convenience of the location. Consequently, many bathrooms are placed in what was formerly a pantry, a large closet or under a stairway. This usually means the only access to the bathroom is through the kitchen or bedroom, or that the bathroom is totally removed from the bedroom area. If this mistake has been made in your home, it is important to add another bath in a good location.

In a house with large bedrooms, part of one bedroom can be taken for a bath. Such a bedroom should have at least one dimension of at least 16 feet. If the bedrooms are all small and needed, there may be no choice but to build an addition. It may be more advantageous to make a small bedroom into a bath (or two baths) and add another bedroom in another area of the house, such as the basement or attic. A possibility in the 1½-story house is to add a bath in the area under the shed dormer. Make sure that the wall containing the plumbing has a wall below it on the first floor where piping can run. The same is true of two-story homes.

The minimum size for a bathroom is 5 feet by 7 feet,

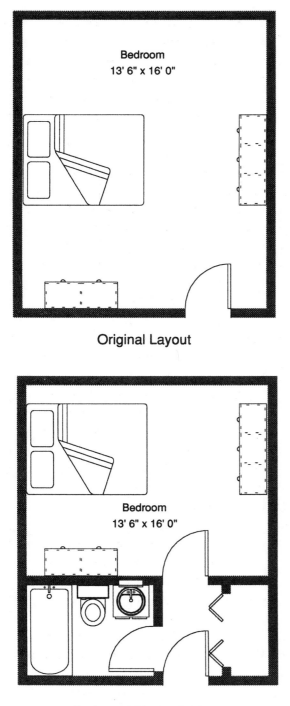

Original Layout

Bath and Closet Added

Fig. 25-2. Portion of a large bedroom used to add a bath.

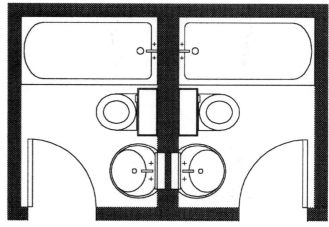

Fig. 25-3. Two bathrooms with economical back-to-back arrangements.

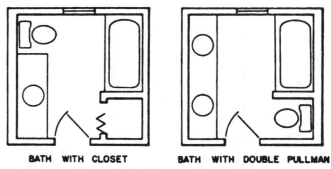

BATH WITH CLOSET　　**BATH WITH DOUBLE PULLMAN**

Fig. 25-4. Moderate-size bathrooms (8 feet by 8 feet).

although larger sizes are more desirable. Increasing the size slightly would make the bath less cramped and can provide space for a storage closet for towels, cleaning equipment or supplies. If you plan to add only one bath, consider making it an area with compartments for use by more than one person at a time. Two baths can be most economically built with fixtures placed back to back, but do not sacrifice a convenient location to ac-

complish this. Bathrooms built on both floors of a two-story house are most economically built with the second-floor bath directly over the first-floor bath.

Adding a Cantilever

Most spaces available for a bathroom addition, such as closets, laundry rooms and portions of bedrooms, always seem to be just a little too small. Sometimes, only a small increase in space would make the conversion practical. This is a perfect opportunity to add a cantilever or bay. Cantilevers (also known as punch outs) are inexpensive — they require no foundation if the extension is 4 feet or less. An existing bathroom can be extended to accommodate a new whirlpool bath with windows on three sides. A bedroom can be extended to allow a bathroom addition while keeping the bedroom space intact. The cantilever may add enough space to split an existing bathroom into two separate baths. Cantilevers are very versatile.

Adding a cantilever will require changes to the existing floor framing. Floor joists must be supported with jacks and cut to tie in the floor members of the cantilever. This is a job for pros, so hire an experienced framer for this part of the job. If the floor is not supported properly during the floor framing, the exterior wall can sag and cause extensive cracking and warping of interior finishes.

Compartmented Bath Areas

If your existing plan is just too small for a bathroom addition, you can increase the functionality of the existing bathrooms by breaking up the space into distinct areas. A compartmented bathroom is designed to permit several persons to use the space simultaneously. It uses more space than a standard bathroom and less space than two separate bathrooms. It has several unique properties which make it appropriate for many remodeling jobs.

1. Existing space is more easily adapted to the new bathroom plan since it can consist of several small spaces tied together into one functional area.

2. Fewer plumbing fixtures are needed for the number of people using the bathroom. This can save a lot of expense, since the fixtures are the most expensive parts of the bathroom.

3. Compartmenting reduces traffic jams by making the bath area available to more than one person at a time.

4. Each user's privacy is enhanced.

LIVING AROUND MAJOR REVISIONS

Major revisions can require a good deal of skill and time to accomplish. If this is your only bathroom, such overhauls can make the normal task of bathing a formidable challenge. Plan ahead so that fixtures are not all out of service at one time, or arrange with neighbors to use their facilities.

Minor Revisions

Sometimes a fresh coat of paint, new wallpaper or a decorative mirror can do wonders without the expense of a major remodeling project. New medicine cabinets can be installed in existing walls for additional storage. New wallpaper can brighten the bathroom and make it seem larger. You may be surprised at the change light pastels can have on the brightness of an existing bathroom. Select paint and wallpaper samples and check to see if they match current fixtures.

Many bathroom projects include replacing old or obsolete fixtures. Old sinks with double faucets can be replaced with a new vanity with an inset sink and one-touch faucets. This type of installation can be done easily in a weekend without the need for major plumb-

ing or structural changes. A little remodeling effort can go a long way.

DRAWING A BATH PLAN

Before beginning your bathroom project, plan your changes thoroughly on paper. From a drafting store, purchase an architectural template that includes most common bath fixtures. This will help you to plan your space efficiently. The drawings included in this chapter can help you lay out the floor plan. Make sure that your new layout will accommodate existing and new fixtures. Bathroom fixtures vary in size, so be sure to obtain the dimensions of the fixtures you plan to use prior to drawing your detailed plan. Measure and lay out the current bathroom plan and then trace the new plan on top of the existing one. Use scaled graph paper with the same scale as your bathroom template (usually ¼ inch to the foot).

As you lay out the new bathroom design, pay attention to proper clearances and accessories required by modern baths. Lifestyle changes have changed consumer expectations. Many old bathrooms do not meet these new bathroom standards. This is partly because no official guidelines existed for standardizing bathroom dimensions and minimum requirements. This prompted the National Kitchen & Bath Association to develop a comprehensive set of bathroom planning guidelines. These are included in the bathroom specifications section.

FLOOR

If you plan to install a new floor, first check the condition of the subfloor. Do this before the project is started. Whether the subfloor needs replacing should be determined before new plumbing fixtures are installed, since all or part of the floor must be removed. A common problem in many older bathrooms is decayed flooring around the toilet. This results from condensation or leaks that let water accumulate around the toilet base. A badly decayed floor will feel "springy" or "mushy" when stepped on. If the floor is decayed, you will need to remove the cabinets, fixtures and floor near the problem and put in new subfloor.

PLUMBING

One consideration in locating a bath economically is to keep all piping runs as short as possible. Also, all fixtures

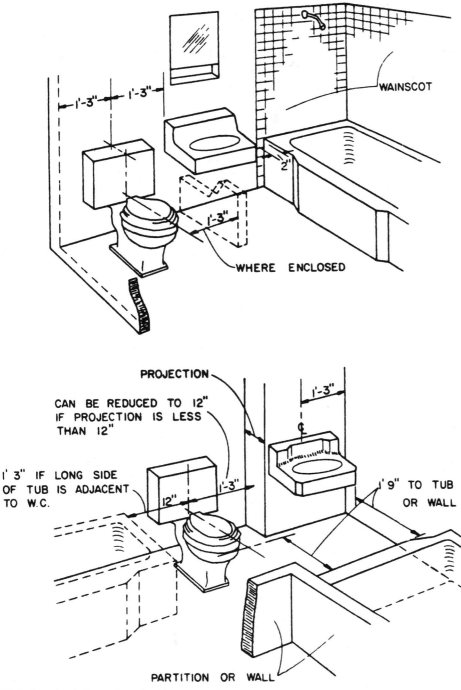

Fig. 25-5. Standard dimensions for fixture spacing.

on one plumbing wall can use a common vent. If you are adding a new bathroom, try to arrange the layout of the new bath so it can use the same plumbing wall as the existing bathroom. This will reduce the time and expense of running new plumbing lines and vent stacks. The vent stack can be very costly, since it must be run through existing walls all the way through to the roof.

If your bathroom renovation includes changing the existing layout, try to leave the toilet connection in the existing location. Plan the other fixtures around the toilet fixture. The toilet fixture is the most difficult one to move and is usually located adjacent to the vent stack. Other fixtures can be moved and vented more easily. A plumbing contractor can help you determine the best location for fixtures.

Almost any addition or movement of plumbing fixtures will require cutting new holes in the existing framing. If the framing is load-bearing, you must be careful

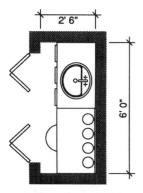

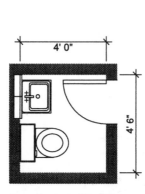

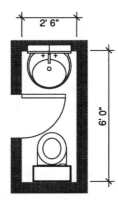

Small Bathrooms

These are examples of small bathrooms that use space to maximum advantage. Complete bathrooms can be built in a surprisingly small area.

Combination sink and makeup table installed in an existing closet.

Example of a half-bath that will fit in a small area such as a closet or laundry room.

Will fit under a stairway or in a coat closet.

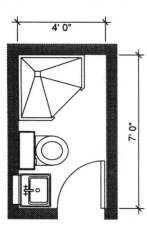

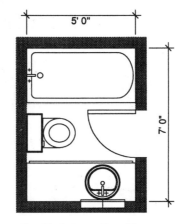

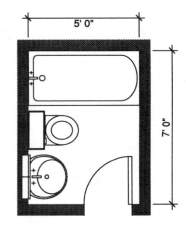

Smallest bath space possible with shower. Will fit in a closet or wall extension.

Small bathroom with a side entrance that allows a full length countertop for extra storage.

Typical small bathroom with a front entrance. Sink space is limited.

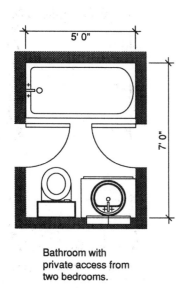

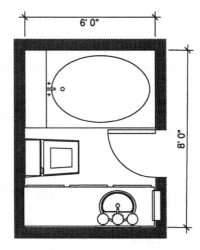

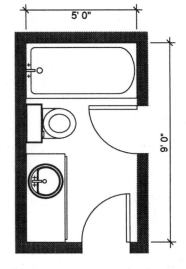

Bathroom with private access from two bedrooms.

Even a small bath space can accomodate luxury bath fixtures with proper planning.

A bathroom with public access and private access from the master bedroom.

Fig. 25-6. Small bathroom floor plans.

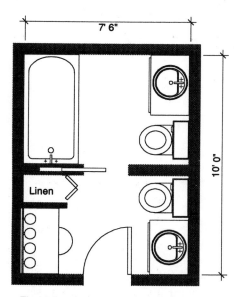

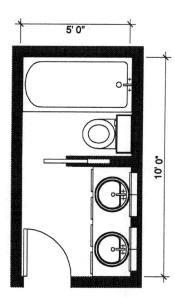

Compartmented Bathrooms

Compartmented baths allow additional privacy and functionality, allowing more than one person to use the bath at one time.

The sliding pocket door, two sinks, and makeup area provide a multi function bath to meet the needs of the entire family.

A sliding pocket door provides complete privacy, allowing two people to maximize use of the bath.

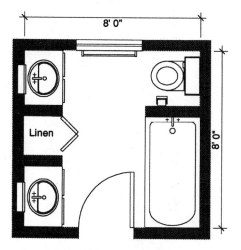

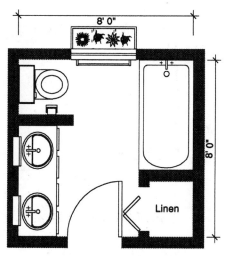

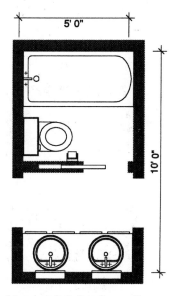

A bath with two separate sink areas for more working room.

A bath with ample counter space with his and hers lavatories.

A two zone bath for privacy with access from two separate bedrooms.

Fig. 25-7. Compartmented bathrooms.

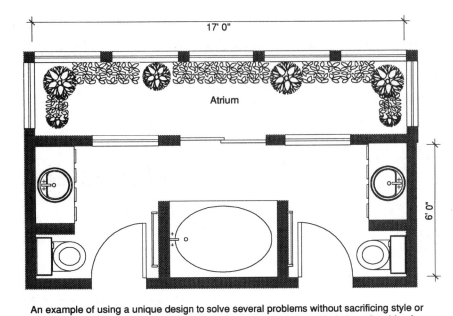

Luxury Bathrooms

If you have sufficient space, available, you can upgrade existing bathrooms to modern standards.

An example of using a unique design to solve several problems without sacrificing style or functionality. The long narrow design allows the bathroom to be added along the side of the master bedroom or as a "punch out". The atrium provides total privacy from neighboring houses while allowing light into the bathroom.

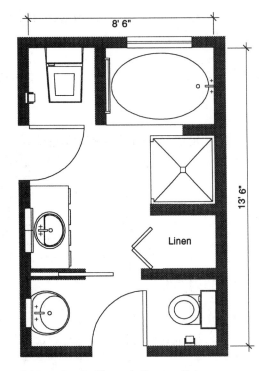

A compartmented luxury bathroom with two separate zones. The front zone is accessible as a half bath or second sink. The sliding pocket door allows privacy while still retaining access to both areas from the hallway or the master bedroom.

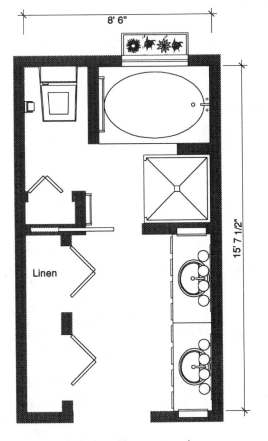

A luxury bathroom with two zones, shower and bath, and lots of storage space. The toilet is isolated for privacy.

Fig. 25-8. Luxury bathrooms.

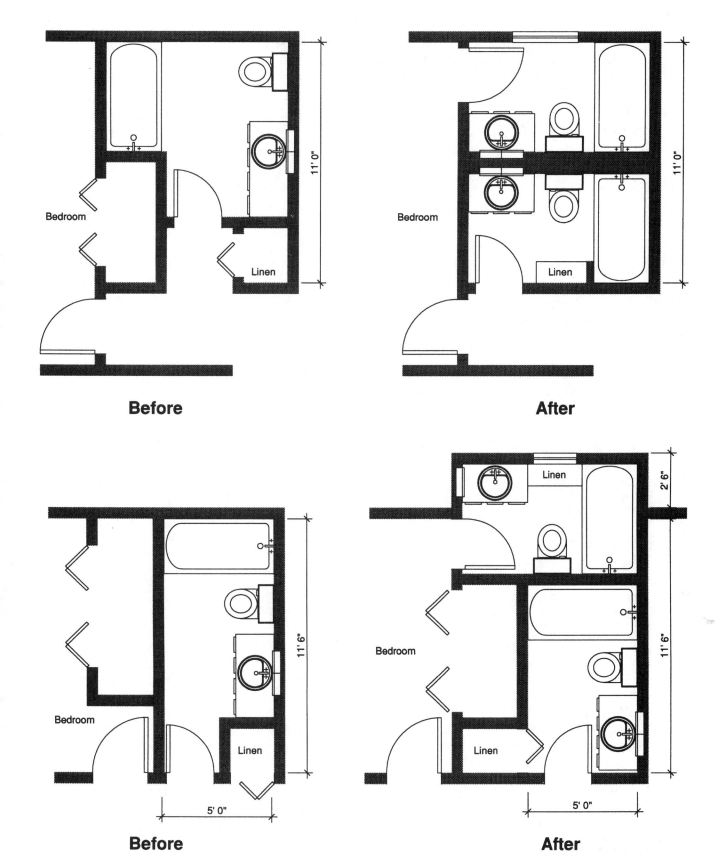

Before

After

11' 0"

11' 0"

Bedroom

Bedroom

Linen

Linen

Before

After

2' 6"

11' 6"

11' 6"

Bedroom

Bedroom

Bedroom

Linen

Linen

Linen

5' 0"

5' 0"

Fig. 25-9. Two possible approaches to add another bathroom. Note how a room extension provides just enough additional space to fit in a bathroom off the master bedroom.

If your bathtub does not have a shower fixture, you can install one in the wall behind the tub if you have access to the wall from the other side. Cut a hole in the wall for access and connect a T plumbing connector to the original faucet and run the shower pipe up the wall. Install tile or acrylic sheeting to the walls around the tub to protect against overspray.

Ceramic tile that is damaged or has an out-of-date color scheme can sometimes be repaired without complete replacement. Remove the damaged tiles and replace them with new tiles of a different color. Remove tiles so that the new tiles form a decorative pattern within the existing tiles. This avoids the impossible task of color matching old and new tiles. Use the replacement tiles as accents or borders.

Use new wallpaper to bring old and new color schemes together in a pleasing combination.

Many do-it-yourself stores now market several prepackaged shower systems. These usually consist of a new acrylic tub with preshaped wall panels that can be glued over existing walls.

Installing new tile has become much easier. Tile can be purchased in large panels held together with fiberglass netting, reducing the tedious spacing of each tile. Complete pregrouted panels are also available. Glue each panel in place and grout the seams in between for a professional job in a fraction of the time.

Adding extra large mirrors to the walls can create the illusion of a much larger bathroom while covering old finishes with a durable new wall covering.

to preserve the structural properties of the partition. Use metal strapping to bridge the gap between a partition's top or bottom plate. Holes cut in floor or ceiling joists should be smaller than 4 inches or the joist should be reinforced. Do not anchor plumbing pipes to framing with a strap or bracket. The pipe needs to move freely in the wall to manage the expansion and contraction caused by hot and cold water running through it. If the pipe is pressed tightly against a framing member, you may hear mysterious pops and cracks in the wall whenever someone turns on the water.

Fixtures

Examine the condition of all fixtures in the bathroom. If they work properly, you may not wish to change them; however, fixtures are an important part of the bathroom decor. Make sure the present fixtures blend in with your new decorating ideas. Although some old plumbing fixtures can be preserved for atmosphere, such as the old-fashioned cast iron bathtubs, most fixtures seldom meet the needs of present-day homeowners. Many old sink fixtures have separate hot and cold faucets, unacceptable in modern bathrooms.

Match new styles and colors to existing fixtures for a consistent style. If you plan to retain many old fixtures, choose colors and accessories that will accent them. Use brass fixtures or natural wood to emphasize Victorian styling. If you plan to modernize all fixtures, you will have greater artistic freedom in choosing colors and styles.

Shop around for specials on fixtures. Many stores run specials on old models, odd lots or discontinued lines. Shopping specials can save you a considerable amount of money and possibly allow you to upgrade to higher quality fixtures.

Tub refinishing has become a new industry that involves re-coating the existing tub with a new durable finish that rivals the original porcelain finish. It works wonders on old antique tubs that have mineral stains or chips from age and costs less than a new tub.

CABINETS

Vanities are installed the same way as kitchen cabinets. They are usually installed by the same contractor. If you are renovating the kitchen, try to coordinate with the cabinet contractor so both sets of cabinets can be manufactured simultaneously.

BATHROOM CONVERSION STEPS

Planning

1. Confirm bathroom design. Check dimensions of any new fixtures to make sure they will fit in the allotted space and will fit through available openings.

2. Complete diagram of plumbing fixture layout. This is a critical step to perform prior to electrical and plumbing installation. Show locations of all plumbing connections on diagram: shower, toilet and sink.

3. Select cabinetry, countertop, plumbing fixture, flooring, and wallpaper styles/colors.

4. Determine type and quantity of plumbing fixtures (styles and colors). This includes:

Sinks (free-standing or cabinet).

Bathtubs. Consider one-piece fiberglass units with built-in walls requiring no tile. If you go this route get a heavy-gauge unit.

Shower stall and fixtures.

Toilets and toilet seats.

Water heater. If adding a new bathroom, check to see if the existing water heater will provide sufficient hot water. If not, consider upgrading to a higher capacity water heater.

Septic tank, if needed.

5. Conduct the standard bidding process. Shop prices carefully; subs who bid on your job may vary greatly on their bid price, depending on what materials they use and their method of calculating their fee. This is where you will decide what kind of plumbing pipe to use. Obtain a signed proposal with standard provisions and specifications.

Note: Add info in bidding section about items to include in bid-list of tasks performed, start and end date, list and description of materials with delivery dates, liabilities, lien waivers, guarantees, schedule of payments, etc.

---

6. Obtain signed contract for installation.

7. Obtain building permit if needed.

8. Walk through site with plumber to discuss placement of plumbing and any special fixtures.

9. Order special plumbing fixtures. This needs to be done well in advance because supply houses seldom stock large quantities of special fixtures.

10. Apply for water connection and sewer tap, if needed. This will be necessary only if you are adding a new bathroom to the existing structure. If you are connected to an existing septic tank, contact a local septic tank installer to check the existing capacity of the tank to make sure it will handle the additional load of a new bathroom.

11. Purchase or have constructed all cabinetry and countertop surfaces.

12. Prepare storage area for delivery of cabinets, new plumbing fixtures, etc.

13. Check delivered items for correct model, color, size, etc. Check for any damaged material now before time to install. Discovering a damaged item at installation time can delay the project while you wait for a replacement.

14. Make arrangements for getting rid of trash after installation.

Removal of Old Items

1. Plan for temporary bathroom facilities. If you have another bathroom, delay any renovations on it until the existing bathroom project is finished. Although this may seem wasteful at first, you will soon find just how indispensable a bathroom is. If you are renovating the only bathroom, plan to stay at a motel or a friend's house during the critical phases of remodeling.

2. Block off other parts of the house with plastic over openings and floor to contain dust and dirt.

3. Schedule plumbing, flooring, cabinet and glazing subs.

4. Turn off water and electric power before starting removal of cabinets or plumbing fixtures.

5. Remove plumbing fixtures that are to be replaced and any countertops or cabinets.

6. Remove paneling, trim, wallpaper and flooring, if necessary.

7. Remove lighting fixtures.

8. Rough-in any framing. Make sure to use 2 × 6 walls wherever plumbing must be installed. This provides more room for plumbing and drain pipe clearance.

Rough-In Plumbing

1. Mark location of all plumbing fixtures including sinks, tubs, showers, toilets and water heater. Make sure the plumber knows whether you have a regular vanity or pedestal sink. The plumbing for a pedestal sink must come up from the floor instead of the wall. Mark the end of the tub where the drain will be located. Mark areas in wall and ceiling where pipes must not be located, such as locations for recessed lights or medicine cabinets.

2. Install rough-in plumbing. This involves the laying of hot (left) and cold (right) water lines, sewer and vent pipe. Pipe running along studs should run within holes drilled (not notched) in the studs. All pipe supports should be in place. Your plumber should use FHA straps to protect pipe from being pierced by drywall subs where ever cutouts are made. FHA straps are metal plates designed to protect the pipe from puncturing by nails.

3. Connect to sewer line or septic tank. Mark locations of other pipes (water or gas) so diggers will avoid puncturing them.

4. Schedule plumbing inspector, if needed.

5. Conduct rough-in plumbing inspection. This is a *very* important step. No plumbing should be covered until your county inspector has issued an inspection certificate. Plan to go through the inspection with the inspector so you will understand any problems and get a good interpretation of your sub's workmanship.

6. Correct problems found during the inspection.

7. Pay plumbing sub for rough-in, requiring a signed receipt or equivalent.

Finish Plumbing

1. Install finish plumbing. This involves installation of all fixtures selected earlier. Sinks, faucets, toilets and shower heads are installed.

2. Tap into water supply. Open the water valve *gradually* to prevent damage to the pipes. You will have to open all the faucets to allow air to bleed out of the system. The water will probably look dirty for a few minutes, but don't be alarmed. The system needs to be flushed of excess debris and solvents.

3. Conduct finish plumbing inspection. Call your inspector several days prior to the inspection. Make every effort to perform this step with your local inspector to see what the inspector is looking for so you will know exactly what to have your sub correct if anything is in error.

4. Correct any problems found during the final inspection.

5. Pay plumbing sub for finish, requiring a signed affidavit.

6. Pay plumber retainage.

Flooring Installation

1. Prepare the floor surface for new floor. If installing a new floor over existing subfloor, make sure floor surface is level and even with no seams, bumps or soft spots. If floor sags or is uneven, a new subfloor may be required. Make sure any soft or rotten timbers have been completely replaced.

2. Install new subfloor.

3. Install tile floor. (Refer to chapter twelve for more information.) Note: Vinyl or linoleum floors are usually installed after cabinets are installed.

Counters

1. Fix holes in walls.

2. Mark the walls for installation of cabinets.

3. Stain and seal, paint or otherwise finish all cabinet woodwork. Stains will stain the grout and other nearby items, so cabinets should be stained before they are installed.

4. Install base cabinet. Also, make necessary cutouts for sinks and cooktops. Show the cabinet sub where cutouts are to be made.

5. Install cabinet doors, drawers, and hardware. Adjust cabinetry hardware: pulls, hinges, etc.

6. Install base for countertops.

7. Mark hole for sink in countertop. If sink has a lip, make sure the hole is *smaller* than the outside diameter of the sink lip.

> **Note:** If you are installing a tile countertop, the sink should be installed now, before the tile, so that the tile and grout can be installed flush to the sink edge. With all other countertops, a sink with a lip is installed *after* the countertop is in place.

8. Install countertops, backsplashes and aprons.

9. Install surface mounted sink and sink fittings in countertop.

10. Install and hook up remaining plumbing fixtures — toilet, sink and shower fixtures, towel holders, toothbrush holders, medicine cabinets, etc.

11. Caulk all cabinetry joints as needed.

Completion

1. Install vinyl floor (Refer to chapter twelve for more information).

2. Install lighting and electrical fixtures. (Refer to chapter fourteen.)

3. Install floor trim or quarter-round trim.

4. Touch up and repair any scratches and other marks.

5. Pay cabinet sub, requiring a signed affidavit.

6. Pay other subs (flooring, tile, plumbing, electrical), requiring a signed affidavit.

BATHROOM SPECIFICATIONS

- Bid is to perform complete plumbing job for bathroom as described on attached drawings.
- Bid is to include all material and labor, including all fixtures listed on the attached drawings.
- All materials and workmanship shall meet or exceed all requirements of the local plumbing code.

NKBA SPECIFICATIONS

The following bathroom specs represent the latest in bathroom standards and are provided by the National Kitchen and Bath Association.

- A clear walkway of at least 32 inches must be provided at all entrances to the bathroom.
- No doors may interfere with fixtures.
- Mechanical ventilation system must be included in the plan.
- Ground fault circuit interrupters must be specified on all receptacles. Place no switches within 60 inches of any water source. All light fixtures above tub/shower units are moisture-proof special-purpose fixtures.
- If floor space exists between two fixtures, at least 6 inches of space should be provided for cleaning.
- At least 21 inches of clear walkway space exists in front of lavatory.
- The minimum clearance from the lavatory centerline to any sidewall is 12 inches.
- The minimum clearance between two bowls in the lavatory center is 30 inches, centerline to centerline.

- The minimum clearance from the center of the toilet to any obstruction, fixture or equipment on either side of toilet is 15 inches.
- At least 21 inches of clear walkway space exists in front of toilet.
- Toilet paper holder is installed within reach of person seated on the toilet. Ideal location is slightly in front of the edge of toilet bowl, the center of which is 26 inches above the finished floor.
- The minimum clearance from the center of the bidet to any obstruction, fixture or equipment on either side of the bidet is 15 inches.
- At least 21 inches of clear walkway space exists in front of bidet.
- Storage for soap and towels is installed within reach of person seated on the bidet.
- No more than one step leads to the tub. Step must be at least 10 inches deep, and must not exceed 7¼ inches in height.
- Bathtub faucets are accessible from outside the tub.
- Whirlpool motor access, if necessary, is included in plan.
- At least one grab bar is installed to facilitate bathtub or shower entry.
- Minimum useable shower interior dimension is 32" × 32".
- Bench or footrest is installed within shower enclosure.
- Minimum clear walkway of 21 inches exists in front of tub/shower.
- Shower door swings into bathroom.
- All shower heads are protected by pressure balance/temperature regulator or temperature-limiting device.
- All flooring is of slip-resistant material.
- Adequate storage must be provided in plan, including: counter/shelf space around lavatory, adequate grooming equipment storage, convenient shampoo/soap storage in shower/tub area, and hanging space for bathroom linens.
- Adequate heating system must be provided.
- General and task lighting must be provided.

BATHROOM MATERIAL ESTIMATE

DESCRIPTION	SPECIFICATION	QTY.	UNIT	COST	TAX	TOTAL COST	COST TYPE	VENDOR
Plumbing Fixtures								
Lavatory sink — set-in type								
Pedestal sink								
Cultured marble vanity top								
Sink faucet set								
Bathtub								
Jacuzzi oval bathtub								
Bathtub faucet/shower set								
Shower stall								
Shower stall faucet/shower set								
Bidet								
Toilet								
Other Fixtures								
Shower curtain rod								
Toilet tissue dispenser								
Towel rods								
Medicine cabinet with mirror								
Mirror installation								
Shower door								
Soap dish								
Plumbing Supplies								
(See chapter sixteen)								
Cabinets								
Vanity base cabinets 24 inches deep								
Mounting screws								
Vanity top								
Medicine cabinet								

BATHROOM MATERIAL ESTIMATE

DESCRIPTION	SPECIFICATION	QTY.	UNIT	COST	TAX	TOTAL COST	COST TYPE	VENDOR
Floor								
Plywood underlayment— 4′ × 8′ × ½″								
Flooring								
Floor felt—500 pound								
Flooring adhesive								
Flooring nails								
Quarter-round trim								
Finishing nails								
Tile								
Floor tile								
Wall tile								
Tile—trim								
Grout compound								
Grout sealant								
Tile adhesive								
Soap holder—tile								
Lights and electrical								
Track lights								
Can lights								
Fluorescent fixture—ceiling								
Lighting fixtures—sink								
Ground fault interrupters								
Ceiling vent fan								
Heat lamp								
Framing								
See chapter nineteen								

BATHROOM MATERIAL ESTIMATE

DESCRIPTION	SPECIFICATION	QTY.	UNIT	COST	TAX	TOTAL COST	COST TYPE	VENDOR
Finish								
Paint — primer — wall								
Paint — primer — trim								
Paint — primer — base coat								
Wallpaper								
Wallpaper glue								
Windows								
Frosted glass								
Glass block								
Glass block grout								
Labor								
Bathroom design								
Cabinet fabrication								
Cabinet install								
Electrical								
Plumbing								
Flooring								
Tile installation								
Carpentry — miscellaneous								

Attic

If your house has a relatively steep roof slope, it may have some very usable attic space that can be a prime candidate for use as an additional bedroom, den, study, hobby room or an apartment for a relative. It is inexpensive to convert to living space because it already has a floor system, roof, and access to heating, plumbing and electrical systems.

First determine the practicality of converting the space. To become a usable living area, the attic must meet the following requirements: It must have the proper height, a non-truss roof framing system, and access through a stairway.

If the attic is the third floor of the house, check local codes. Some codes do not permit use of the third floor for living areas; others require a fire escape.

HEIGHT REQUIREMENTS

Attic rooms require a minimum ceiling height of 7 feet 6 inches over at least one-half the width of the room and a minimum ceiling height of 5 feet at the outer edges of the room. The space near the lower ceiling height can be used for built-in furniture, beds, or storage space. If the ceiling does not have this height, it can't be finished as living space. If there is sufficient headroom only in a narrow strip at the center of the attic, you can consider building a large shed dormer to increase the usable side-to-side space. Dormers, though not always needed for increasing usable space, may be desired to add windows and ventilation to the room.

Many older homes were built with steeply pitched roofs that make excellent candidates for conversion. This is especially true in the north where snow loads make steeply pitched roofs necessary. Homes built in the fifties and sixties, however, were usually built with much flatter roof pitches to lower construction cost. Take a tape measure into the attic and mark off the

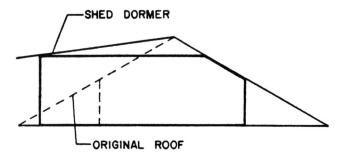

Fig. 26-1. Shed dormer for additional attic space.

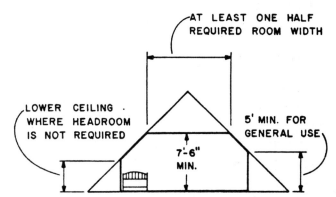

Fig. 26-2. Headroom requirements for attic rooms.

area that has a roof height of at least 7 feet 6 inches and then mark the area that is at least 5 feet high. Transfer these measurements to a piece of graph paper. This will be the working area of your finishing project.

ROOF FRAMING

Almost all attics have cross bracing of some sort to help support the roof framing. If this consists of collar beams and diagonal braces nailed to the rafters, these can be replaced by the walls of the room, which will still provide adequate support. Many modern homes have switched to truss roofs, which are usually fabricated at a factory. The bracing is engineered to minimize framing material and consists of several webs of diagonal bracing that tie the ceiling joists and rafters together. Truss roofs are not practical candidates for finishing. The position of each web is too critical to the integrity of the roof and cannot be removed or altered. If you are not sure about your attic, hire a qualified framing engineer to examine the structure and give recommendations.

ATTIC ACCESS

An item sometimes overlooked in expanding into the attic area is the stairway. A typical straight-run stairway requires a space at least 30 inches wide and at least 10 feet long, plus a landing at both top and bottom. There must also be a minimum overhead clearance of 6 feet 8 inches at any point on the stairs. To finish the attic, you must find room for this access. The usual folding stair access will not be sufficient. Look for part of a room or a closet downstairs that could be converted into stairs. Remember when looking for space that the stairs should terminate in the highest part of the attic. This rules out stairs along the edge of the house unless they start at the edge and end up toward the center. Stairs as short as 9 feet can be constructed by turning the steps at the two landings 90 degrees by using diagonal steps called winders. A good location for these stairs would be a hall closet. Or, you can turn the steps in a U shape to fit a space 6 feet wide and 5 feet long—in what used to be a walk-in closet or pantry.

If space is limited, spiral stairs may be the solution. Some spiral stairs can be installed in a space as small as 4 feet in diameter. Although spiral staircases work in a pinch, they are very steep, making them unsuitable for the elderly. Also, you won't be able to move furniture through the opening, so decide how you will move furniture in and out of the attic space. This may be the determining factor when deciding how to use that area. A solution might be a double-wide window or balcony.

PLAN YOUR PROJECT AROUND OBSTACLES

Start your project by laying out the floor plan and deciding what additions and walls you want to add. Making an attic usable may be a simple matter of installing finish ceiling, wall and floor coverings; however, it will often require adding a shed or gable dormer for more space or for natural light and ventilation. The location of dormers, windows, plumbing and chimneys will influence the floor plan you develop. Try to fit these items into the plan to make maximum use of the space.

The design and drawing of an attic plan can be very tricky. You must visualize the project in three dimen-

sions. You will have the angles of the stairway entering the space, gable dormer angles, and the angle of the roof itself. Using an experienced architect or drafter at this point can be a great investment. Their experience in dealing with three-dimensional spaces can help to produce a quality plan that will be well worth the investment. A formal blueprint can also simplify the construction process, for you or a contractor.

Chimney

If a chimney passes through the attic, it must either be hidden or worked into the decor. Never frame into the chimney. The building code requires framing to be at least 2 inches from the chimney. Where framing is placed completely around the chimney, fill the space between the chimney and framing with noncombustible insulation. The best approach is to frame the chimney into wall partitions. Add a bookcase to one side or build a closet next to the chimney the same depth as the chimney box-in. Do *not* attempt to tie in to the chimney flue for gas heaters. You must install a new flue for proper ventilation.

Vent Stacks

All the existing plumbing vent stacks pass through the attic on their way to the roof. Try to build the stacks into partition walls, preferably the plumbing walls of any bathroom or kitchen. This will make attachment of any plumbing easier. Note: Plumbing code requires that all vent stacks intersect the main vent stack *above* any other sewer lines. If you add a bathroom in the attic, your sewer lines will probably be above the vent intersections of plumbing on lower floors. This would invalidate the vent hookups of previous plumbing. You then must connect the new sewer lines below the intersections of the other vent stacks. Plumbing lines can be run up to the attic from the partition walls of downstairs bathrooms. Do this before covering floor joists.

Partition Walls

Try to plan the placement of walls to take advantage of existing structural components. When you frame in a partition wall it must be nailed to something. When laying out your floor plan, try to line up the partition walls with existing roof rafters so you can nail the wall directly to the rafter. Line the partition to the rafters, not the joists, for the following reasons. First, nonload-bearing walls do not need to rest directly on floor joists if the subfloor is ⅝ inch thick or thicker. You can just

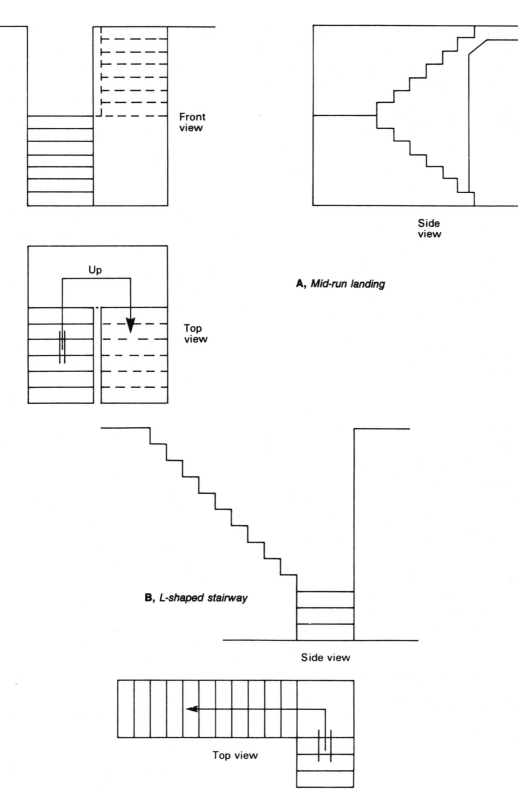

Front view

Side view

A, *Mid-run landing*

Up

Top view

B, *L-shaped stairway*

Side view

Top view

Fig. 26-3. Space saving stair designs.

nail the partition directly to the subfloor. Second, if you want the wall to intersect vent stacks, the stacks will usually fall to one side of the floor joist. The rafters also fall to one side of the floor joist. If you are lucky, the vent and the rafter will line up. This is where you will want to place the wall if possible.

Windows

Attics are usually hot places and need adequate ventilation and light. Plan to add windows to gable ends, in dormers or by installing skylights. Plan the location of these windows to maximize the design. For instance, if you are installing a dormer, try to place a window seat, bed or bathroom sink under the gable window where the wall will continue vertically for the entire ceiling height. If you must use a spiral staircase to access the attic, the window may be the only practical way to move large furniture into the attic. If this is the case, consider building a small balcony on the end of one gable and install a sliding glass door. At least you will now have the option of moving in large furniture over the balcony. Also plan now for a method of getting the framing and drywall supplies into the attic. The most practical way may be through freshly cut openings in the gable for your windows. Most drywall trucks are equipped with cranes for lifting drywall through upper windows.

Dormers

Shed dormers can be made any width and are sometimes made to extend across the entire length of the roof. They are less attractive than gable dormers and are usually placed at the back of the house. They can almost double the usable space in the attic by extending the ceiling height all the way to the outer wall. Where light and ventilation, rather than additional space, are the main requirements, gable dormers are often used. They are more attractive in exterior appearance than shed dormers, so they can be used on the front of the house for great visual effect. Due to the roof slope, they are usually limited to a small size. Plan placement of dormers so they fall symmetrically in the roof line.

FRAMING THE ATTIC

Floor Framing

Most ceiling joists in attics are framed with 2×6 joists. These may not be adequate to support a full floor load. It may be best to get professional advice on this unless tables are available that show allowable joist and rafter spans. If the joists are inadequate, the best solution is usually to double the existing joists. Use the same size lumber as the existing joists and nail them directly to the other joists with 10d or larger nails.

Electrical wiring and plumbing can be run through the joists before the subfloor is installed. Drill small holes in the center of the joists to run these lines. Do not notch the joists. Be careful when working around the joists that you don't knock a hole through the drywall of the downstairs ceiling.

One of the trickiest construction details will be framing in the stairway opening. You probably can't use the existing opening for the disappearing stairs since they usually open into hallways downstairs. So you will have to frame in this opening after creating the new stair opening. Toenail blocking across the old opening with the same size lumber as the floor joists and line the blocking up with existing joists, if possible, to simplify nailing subfloor.

Before cutting the joists for the new opening, it is wise to remove the drywall first. Outline the opening on the ceiling (of the floor below) and cut out the drywall with a keyhole saw. This will give you access to the joists from the top and bottom. The opening will require double joists around the perimeter. If your opening runs parallel to the joists, try to use the existing joists as one side of the opening; it probably has doubled joists already. If your opening is perpendicular to the joists, frame in the opening as shown in Fig. 26-4. Before you cut any joists, make sure they are supported. One way to do this is to screw or nail a 1×4 across the joists to be cut and at least two joists on either side. Use two or three double-headed nails (so you can remove them) or screws per joist. This will hold the joists in place until the opening headers are attached. Joist hangers work well for attaching headers. Once the opening is framed, the 1×4 can be removed or unscrewed. This work is some of the trickiest in the attic project. A mistake here can cause quite a few headaches. Hire a carpenter for this work unless you are very confident in your framing ability.

Stairs

Most carpenters really earn their keep when it comes to stairs. They are very tricky to construct properly. Once you have priced the cost of extra 1×12 stringers, you may not be so confident in your ability to get it right the first time. Hire a carpenter for this work. Ask to see some other stairs that the sub has built. Use this sub to frame in the opening in the attic as well. The carpenter will want to anyway, since the stairs will be attached to the opening. Ask that temporary treads be applied to the stairs so you won't damage the good ones during the rest of the project.

Subfloor

The subfloor should cover the entire attic floor even if you are installing knee walls, so that the space behind the knee wall can be used for storage. You probably already have material stored in the attic and you will need a place to put it after the renovation is complete.

When applying it, glue the subfloor to the joists with

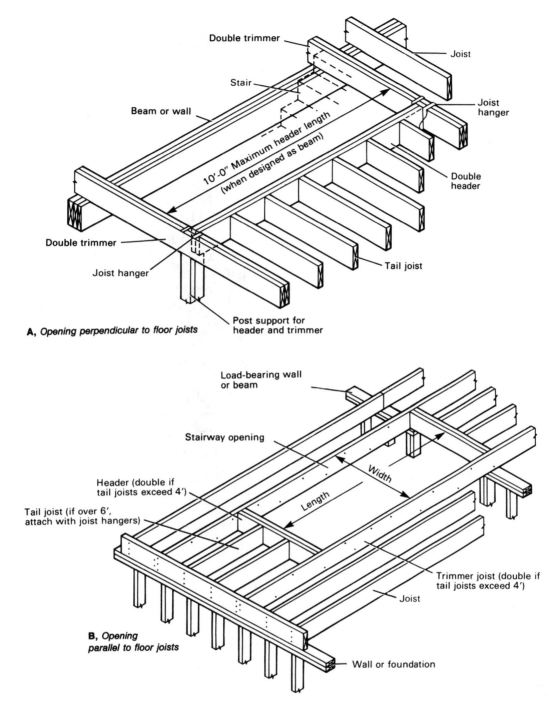

Double trimmer

Joist

Stair

Beam or wall

Joist hanger

10'-0" Maximum header length (when designed as beam)

Double header

Double trimmer

Double header

Joist hanger

Tail joist

Post support for header and trimmer

A, *Opening perpendicular to floor joists*

Load-bearing wall or beam

Stairway opening

Width

Header (double if tail joists exceed 4')

Length

Tail joist (if over 6', attach with joist hangers)

Trimmer joist (double if tail joists exceed 4')

Joist

B, *Opening parallel to floor joists*

Wall or foundation

Fig. 26-4. Floor framing for stairwell opening.

construction adhesive. This will create an integral structure that spreads the load across joists, making a much stronger floor. Use at least ⅝-inch or ¾-inch tongue-and-grooved CDX plywood or OSB panels and 6d ring shank nails or screws.

Shed Dormer

Adding a shed dormer will require the removal of the existing roof rafters to make room for the shed framing. Remove them carefully. You can probably reuse the raf-

ters to frame the dormer. Make sure to temporarily brace the remaining rafters until the new framing is completed. The sides of the shed dormer should coincide with existing rafters. The low-slope roof of the dormer should have rafters framed directly into the ridgepole of the original roof. See Fig. 26-5. Ceiling joists should bear on the outer wall of the dormer, with the opposite ends of the joists nailed to the main roof rafters. The slope of the dormer roof should be enough to allow good drainage during rain. This will give you a flat or slightly sloped ceiling in the dormer area, making partition framing simpler.

Make sure to have tarps or 6-mil poly available during the framing of the dormer to protect against a sudden rainstorm. Once you start the framing, try to complete it as fast as possible. Use this opportunity to get other materials into the attic, such as drywall. Set the bracing in place before cutting the opening in the roof. Mark the opening on the roof and remove the shingles. Now would be a good time to install new roofing shingles on the entire roof. If that is not an option, use the new shingles on the roof of the dormer section—they will be virtually hidden from view—and use the removed shingles to patch around the edge of the dormer. Once the shingles are removed, cut through the sheathing with a power saw set to the depth of the sheathing. Recover the dormer roof as you would any roof. See the chapter twenty for more details.

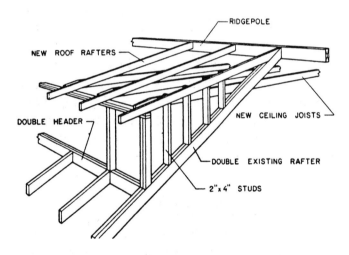

Fig. 26-5. Framing for shed dormer.

The vertical walls of the shed dormer should be covered with siding, preferably with the same material as the gable ends or the house siding. Treat these vertical walls in much the same way as any other exterior wall. Frame in headers over window openings as you would on the exterior walls. Assemble the wall panels in the attic and lift them into position. The sidewalls will be level along the top plate and angled along the bottom plate. The studs must be cut at an angle at the bottom plate, just the reverse procedure used when creating the angled partition walls described earlier in this chapter under the heading Partition Walls. Apply siding, sheathing, wall insulation, etc. Make sure to apply aluminum flashing along the seam between the walls and the roof line. Seal the flashing with asphalt roofing sealant.

Gable Dormer

Gable dormers are more complicated to build than shed dormers. Many more complex angles must be calculated and cut. To simplify the task, consider using one of the new prefab dormers sold by many material suppliers. They can greatly simplify the construction. They are available in most common roof pitches and are designed to fit between conventionally spaced rafters. As mentioned before, a skilled carpenter can be worth the extra expense on an attic framing project.

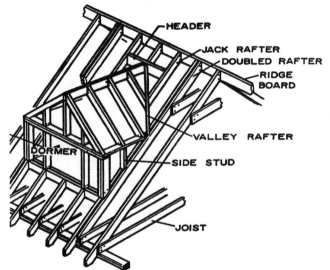

Fig. 26-6. Framing for gable dormer.

The roof of the gable dormer usually has the same pitch as the main roof of the house. The dormer should be located so that both sides intersect an existing rafter. Rafters are then doubled to provide support for the side studs and short valley rafters. Tie the valley rafter to the roof framing by a header. Frame the window and apply interior and exterior covering materials.

Like the shed dormer, proper flashing at the intersection of dormer walls and roof is critical. When roofing felt is used under the shingles, it should be turned up the wall at least 2 inches. Shingle flashing should be used at this junction. This flashing consists of aluminum, tin or galvanized metal shingles bent at a 90-degree angle to extend a minimum of 4 inches up the side of the wall over the sheathing. Use one piece of flashing at each shingle course, lapping successive pieces in the same manner as shingles. Apply siding over the flashing, allowing about a 2-inch space between the bottom edge of the siding and the roof. Cut ends of siding should be treated with water-repellent preservative.

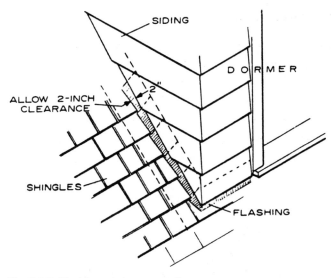

Fig. 26-7. Flashing at dormer walls.

Knee Walls

Once any dormers are in place, clean up the attic and start on the interior partitions. The side walls of the attic rooms are provided by nailing 2 × 4 inch or 2 × 3 inch stud walls vertically to each rafter at a point where the stud wall will be at least 5 feet tall. These are called knee walls. In a pinch, you can get away with 4-foot walls but the usefulness of the extra space will be limited. The wall will have a bottom and top plate like other partition walls, except that the top plate will be angled to line up with the angled rafters. See Fig. 26-8. Nail blocking between rafters at the top of the knee wall to provide a nailing surface for the ceiling finish.

PARTITION WALLS

Partition walls that run parallel to the ridge line will be installed identically to other rooms in the house except that the wall height might be different. Partition walls running perpendicular to the ridge line will have to be angled to match the shape of the rafters and will have to be nailed to the rafter or bridging. Go ahead and finish installing the floor, kneewalls, insulation, ceiling and drywall before adding partition walls. These other components will install much faster without the partition walls getting in the way. You can then install the partitions right over the subfloor and drywall. If your partition lines up with an existing rafter, you can nail directly to it. If the partition falls between rafters, you must install bridging between the rafters *before* the drywall goes on. See Fig. 26-8. Nailing to the floor is no problem. Most modern codes do not require nonload-

bearing walls to be located over joists if the subfloor is ⅝ inch thick or thicker.

To construct your partition at the same angle as the roof, you will need to cut the tops of the studs at the same pitch as the roof and then attach the top plate to them as in Fig. 26-8. Cut the tops of the studs first and nail them to the top plate, then cut the bottoms of the studs to the correct length. Nail the angled top plate to the rafter or bridging and the bottom plate directly to the subfloor.

CEILING

Nail collar beams between opposite rafters to serve as the ceiling framing. These should be at least 7½ feet above the floor. Nail blocking between collar beams and between rafters at their junction to provide a nailing surface for the finish wall and ceiling materials.

An alternate method of installing the ceiling is to eliminate the collar beams and to apply the ceiling finish directly to the rafters. This results in a cathedral ceiling. Even if you want a cathedral ceiling, it is best to create a level ceiling with collar beams at some height so there is still a small air space at the ridge top. This will help in attic ventilation and will leave space for an attic ventilating fan and wiring for light fixtures. The collar beams also provide extra stability.

INSULATION

It is crucial to install the best possible insulation, vapor barriers and ventilation when finishing attic space. Attics are particularly hot in the summer. Insulate your attic space well. Install vapor barriers around all walls and the ceiling of the finished space and ventilate the attic space above and on each side of the finished space. Provide good cross ventilation through the finished area.

The insulation will create a protective shell that extends from the floor, through the knee walls, rafters and ceiling joists to create a continuous insulation barrier. When you install insulation in the rafters you must leave a ventilation space of at least 1 inch between the insulation and the roof sheathing. This is easy for 2 × 6 rafters — install regular 4-inch wall batt insulation. The resulting 2-inch gap will allow air to enter soffit vents and rise through the gap to a ridge vent at the rooftop. If you don't have these vents in your roof, now is the time to add them. The ventilation will also help cool the

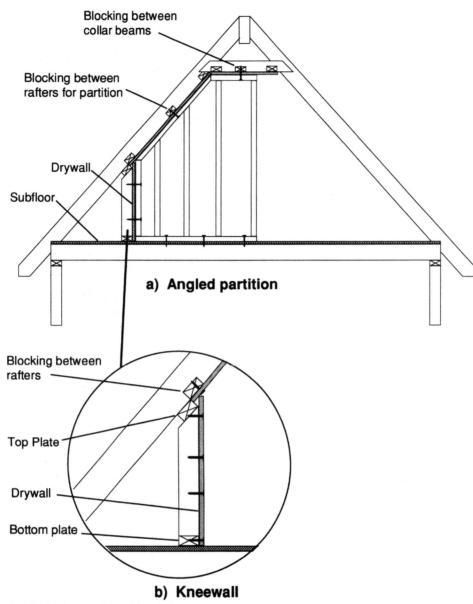

a) Angled partition

Blocking between collar beams

Blocking between rafters for partition

Drywall

Subfloor

Blocking between rafters

Top Plate

Drywall

Bottom plate

b) Kneewall

Fig. 26-8. Framing details for kneewalls and insulation.

attic. If you have an air space above the ceiling, consider installing one or two roof-mounted ventilating fans instead of ridge vents to increase airflow.

The only problem with this method is that 4 inches of insulation may not be enough. One alternative is to nail 2 × 2 strips to the front of each rafter so that 6-inch insulation can be used. An easier method is to apply 1-inch foil-backed urethane sheathing to the rafters before applying the drywall. Sheathing adds about the same R-value as 2 inches of batt insulation and provides two other benefits. The foil backing serves as the vapor barrier and as a radiant barrier. Research shows that reflective coatings can greatly reduce heat buildup by stopping the radiant heat energy from passing from the roof shingles into the living space. Insulate above the

collar beams as you would above a standard ceiling.

SKYLIGHTS AND WINDOWS

Most attics will need a lot of light and ventilation. Gable and dormer windows should be sufficient. Don't skimp here. The low ceiling in the attic will seem somewhat claustrophobic. A lot of glass will help counteract that feeling. Use double-wide windows in the gables. An arch above the window is a nice stylistic touch. If you are short on dormers, consider installing skylights. They provide excellent light and ventilation.

A skylight can be the lazy man's dormer. It costs less, is much easier to install, and requires much less alteration of the existing roof than a dormer. If the cur-

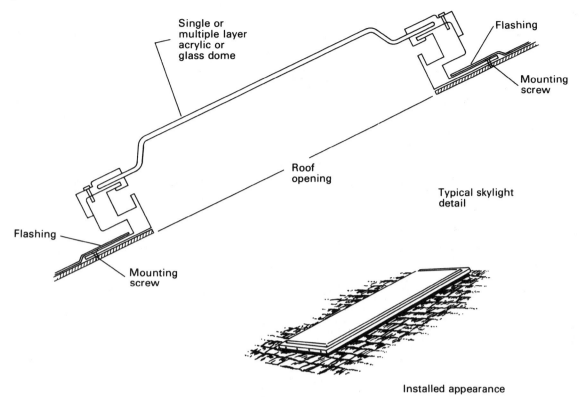

Single or multiple layer acrylic or glass dome

Flashing

Mounting screw

Roof opening

Typical skylight detail

Flashing

Mounting screw

Installed appearance

Fig. 26-9. Surface-mounted skylight.

rent shingles are in good shape, a skylight won't disturb anything. A gable or shed dormer will almost guarantee a new roofing job.

Skylights come in an incredible variety of sizes, types and styles. They can be opened automatically or hand-cranked open. They come with built-in louvered shades for light control. You can even purchase fully automated models that will open and close according to temperature or light. Since skylights are not vertical, but angled toward the sun, heat buildup can be a problem. The newest models come equipped with integral Venetian blinds and double-insulated tinted glass. Energy efficient tinting can significantly reduce the amount of radiant heat transferred while still letting most of the light through.

The easiest skylight installation is one where the skylight fits between the rafters—16 inches or 24 inches O.C. This makes a good do-it-yourself project. No structural changes are necessary.

Each skylight is installed differently, so follow manufacturer's instructions carefully. Wider skylights require cutting a rafter or two and installing headers.

The placement of the skylight is also very important. If you want privacy, use a translucent skylight and place it high. The higher the placement, the more light will be delivered to the living space. If you have a good view

that shouldn't be wasted, then place the skylight at eye level. For window-type installations, use a tall skylight. Since it is installed at an angle, the viewing area will be smaller unless a larger skylight is used to compensate.

ATTIC CONVERSION STEPS

Planning

1. Confirm attic design. Check the locations of stairways or other access. Measure height of attic to confirm viability of attic as a conversion project.

2. Hire an architect or designer to help in laying out the attic design. This can be very helpful. If possible, have the designer draft the actual conversion blueprint.

3. Complete diagram of attic layout. Mark exact dimensions of stairs and dormers. Position is critical.

4. Select windows, skylights, cabinetry, countertops, plumbing fixtures, and appliance styles and colors.

5. Perform the standard bidding process. Obtain a signed proposal from an experienced carpenter with standard provisions and specifications.

6. Obtain signed contract for construction.

7. Obtain building permit if needed.

8. Purchase all windows, skylights, cabinetry, countertops, plumbing fixtures, shingles, framing supplies and prefab units. Have all the material delivered to the site before construction begins. Once the project begins, the framing must proceed quickly. Large shower fixtures, skylights, etc. must be moved upstairs while access is available. Once the project is dried in, many large items will be impossible to move in. Purchase tarps and plastic to cover roof if adding a dormer.

NOTE: Add info in bidding section about items to include in bid-list of tasks performed, start and end date, list and description of materials with delivery dates, liabilities, lien waivers, guarantees, schedule of payments, etc.

Framing

1. Prepare storage area for delivery of construction materials.

2. Check delivered items for correct model, color, size, etc. Check for any damaged material now before it is time to install it. Discovering a damaged item at installation time can delay the project while you wait for a replacement.

3. Make arrangements for getting rid of trash after construction. Call your local city or county government for disposal regulations.

4. Schedule plumbing, electrical and framing subs.

5. Block off other parts of the house with plastic over openings and floor to contain dust and dirt. Provide a means of access through the house and outside the house for contractors.

6. Create a ramp for disposing of material from attic. This usually consists of a wooden trough that allows for collecting garbage with a dumpster at the bottom. Contractors will usually provide this.

7. Cut and frame opening for stairs in attic.

8. Frame in stairway. Cover the stringers with temporary treads until construction traffic is over.

9. Remove any existing subfloor in attic. Stack the material to one side if it can be reused.

10. Turn off gas, water and electric power to attic before starting rough-in.

11. Install all plumbing and wiring rough-in between floor joists. Provide access to rough-in connections after subfloor is installed.

12. Install subfloor. Glue and screw subfloor for maximum strength. Run floor all the way to the soffit to make room for additional attic storage.

13. Cut and frame opening for dormers in roof. Brace the remaining rafters before cutting. Remove sheathing and set aside reusable pieces. Frame in walls and window openings.

14. Cut openings for gable windows and reframe openings with headers. See chapter seventeen for more details.

15. Cover dormer roof with sheathing.

16. Install flashing around intersection of dormer wall and roof. Install valley flashing along valley between roof and dormer roof. Install drip cap and flashing around window openings.

17. Apply wall sheathing and siding to dormer walls.

18. Cut and frame openings for skylights, roof ventilation fans or ridge vents and install them. Add soffit vents now, if needed, so you can visually check them for unrestricted ventilation.

19. Install exterior windows.

20. Frame in kneewalls. Add bridging and blocking above the kneewall to provide a nailing surface for drywall. If you prefer, you can also frame in the partition walls at this time, but many attic conversions contain a lot of angled walls. It is usually easier to add the partitions after the drywall is installed on exterior walls.

21. Nail collar beams in place at the ceiling height.

22. Add bridging between rafters and collar beams for any partition walls that do not intersect a rafter.

23. Run additional rough-in plumbing, electrical, and HVAC ducts. Leave access to rough-in material that will need to be extended into partition walls. If you plan to install the interior partitions after installing the drywall on the exterior walls (the easiest method), you will need to know where to cut holes for access to the rough-in wiring and plumbing that will be behind the drywall. Coil up the extra wiring needed for the partition and mark its location on a piece of graph paper, so you can find it. Leave the plumbing just short of the drywall and add the additional sections after you create access holes in the drywall.

24. Inspect rough-in plumbing, electrical, and HVAC. If this requires a visit by a building inspector, discuss the partition framing with the inspector. The inspector may prefer to visit when the rough-in is completed on interior partitions, but check first. If you wait for the inspection until the interior partitions are framed, the inspector may complain about not being able to see the rough-in work behind the previously installed drywall.

25. Install insulation in kneewalls, dormer walls and ceilings, rafters, and collar beams. Add vapor barrier if insulation doesn't have one. The other option is to cover the walls with foil-backed insulated sheathing in place of the vapor barrier.

26. Install drywall on exterior walls, rafters and ceilings. You will not finish the joints until the interior drywall is installed. See chapter nineteen.

27. Frame in and install all remaining interior partition walls.

28. Pay the carpenter or framer draw. Quite often you will use the same carpenter to complete framing, setting of windows and doors, and final trim work. If so, the sub will want payment for work completed so far. Make the payment equal to or less than the value of the work done so far. Always give the carpenter a reason to come back.

29. Complete rough-in plumbing, electrical and HVAC.

30. Inspect rough-in plumbing, electrical and HVAC.

31. Apply the remaining drywall.

32. Finish drywall with joint tape and compound. This will require three coats.

33. Install any custom shelving or cabinetry.

34. Paint walls and ceiling.

35. Install any bath or kitchen plumbing and cabinet fixtures. (See chapters sixteen, twenty-four and twenty-five.)

> **NOTE:** To save time and energy, paint the walls before installing trim. This avoids the tedious masking step. Also, since this is new construction, drop cloths are not needed to protect the existing floors. Walls and ceilings can be painted very quickly with a paint sprayer or power roller. Paint the primer coat on trim before installing. See chapter eighteen for more details.

36. Set interior doors and trim.

37. Finish painting trim.

38. Install hardwood, tile and carpet. (Refer to chapter twelve.)

39. Install lighting and electrical fixtures. (Refer to chapter fourteen.)

40. Turn on water, electric and gas utilities.

41. Install floor trim or quarter-round trim.

42. Pay electrician, plumber, painter, HVAC and cabinet sub, requiring each to sign an affidavit.

43. Pay carpenter/framer, requiring a signed affidavit.

ATTIC MATERIAL ESTIMATE

DESCRIPTION	SPECIFICATION	QTY.	UNIT	COST	TAX	TOTAL COST	COST TYPE	VENDOR
Framing—Subfloor								
Floor joist—2×6								
Bridging								
Glue								
Subfloor—⅝" tongue-and-grooved								
Subfloor ¾" tongue-and-grooved								
Joist hangers								
Lag bolts								
Underlayment								
Framing—Walls								
Plates—2×4								
8-foot studs—2×4								
10-foot studs—2×4								
2×6 headers								
2×8 headers								
2×10 headers								
Interior beams								
Bracing								
1×4								
Framing—Ceiling/Roof								
Ceiling joist								
Rafters								
Barge rafters								
Beams								
Ridge beam								
Wind beam								
Roof bracing material								
Ceiling bracing								

ATTIC MATERIAL ESTIMATE

DESCRIPTION	SPECIFICATION	QTY.	UNIT	COST	TAX	TOTAL COST	COST TYPE	VENDOR
Framing — Stairs								
Stringers — 2 × 12								
Framing 2 × 4								
Cap								
Rail								
Baluster								
Post								
Riser								
Tread								
Bracing								
Framing — Nails								
12d common								
10d common								
8d common								
10d duplex head								
16d galvanized casing								
8d galvanized casing								
8d ring shank galvanized								
3d finish								
4d finish								
6d finish								
8d finish								
Dormer								
Prefab dormer								
Siding								
Cornice material								
Fascia material								
Wall sheathing								

ATTIC MATERIAL ESTIMATE

DESCRIPTION	SPECIFICATION	QTY.	UNIT	COST	TAX	TOTAL COST	COST TYPE	VENDOR
Roofing								
Asphalt shingles								
Roof sheathing								
Flashing — roof to wall								
Flashing — ridge								
Ventilators								
Soffit vents								
Ridge vent								
Roof felt, 15 pound								
Plyclips								
Nails — 8-inch galvanized roofing								
Nails — 1½-inch galvanized roofing								
Insulation								
Insulated sheathing								
Walls								
Ceiling								
Floor								
Vapor barrier								
Interior Trim								
Bath								
Kitchen								
Windows								
Doors								
Skylights								
Flooring								
Lighting fixtures								
Paint								
Drywall								
Roofing								

ATTIC MATERIAL ESTIMATE

DESCRIPTION	SPECIFICATION	QTY.	UNIT	COST	TAX	TOTAL COST	COST TYPE	VENDOR
Labor								
Attic design — contract								
Plumbing — contract								
Electrical — contract								
HVAC — contract								
Framing/carpentry — contract								
Roofing — contract								

CHAPTER TWENTY-SEVEN

Basement

An unfinished basement can be an easy or extremely difficult remodeling project, depending on the conditions. Only certain basements are appropriate for finishing into living areas. Building codes put restrictions on the placement and makeup of habitable areas. Your basement must meet these conditions if you hope to convert it into livable space. A habitable room is defined as a space used for living, sleeping, eating or cooking. Rooms not defined formally as habitable rooms include bathrooms, toilet compartments, closets, halls, storage rooms, laundry rooms, utility rooms and basement recreation rooms. Your plans for the basement space will determine the restrictions you will have to work with. Year-round habitable rooms require that the *average* finished-grade elevation at exterior walls cannot be more than 48 inches above the finished floor. That means that bedrooms or kitchens must have less than 4 feet of the exterior basement wall covered by dirt in the areas where you plan to build these rooms. Average ceiling height for habitable rooms must be no less than 7 feet 6 inches. Local codes may vary, so check for your area's exact limitations. Other basement rooms not defined as habitable need a minimum ceiling height of 6 feet 9 inches. These limitations have a useful function. They prevent living areas from being built where ground conditions make the area dangerous or unlivable because of moisture.

Basements are built for different reasons in different parts of the country, so some are more appropriate for conversion than others. In northern climates, basements are built to extend the foundation down below the frost line. They are often completely buried on all four sides if built on level ground. If built before 1960, they probably have a dirt floor and little or no waterproofing treatment. They will be very difficult to convert because of structural and moisture problems.

In the south, most basements are built solely for extra space or to place a house on a sloped lot. These basements are often only half buried, and many have drive-in garages. Basements are very inexpensive storage areas. These partial or walk-out basements are much easier to turn into livable spaces.

Consider these issues when planning the type of space you want to create in the basement. The demands for a storage area or small recreation area are much different than for an extra bedroom or den. Above all, make sure your basement meets the following requirements:

1. It must be dry.
2. It must have convenient access.
3. It must have adequate headroom.

MOISTURE CONTROL

Dampness in the basement can be partially overcome by installing vapor barriers and insulation on the floor and walls if they were not installed at the time of original construction. Dampness can be caused by many factors, some curable and some not. Simple condensation is caused by warm moist air coming in contact with the cool basement wall, which is usually cooler than the air. This problem will virtually disappear once you install adequate insulation on the walls and floor. Some moisture can be caused by infiltration — moisture transpiring through the wall from the outside. Water infiltration can be spotted by white crystalline markings on the basement wall. These are caused by salts in the concrete that are dissolved by the moisture and carried to the surface. This problem is harder to fix. If the problem is minor, sealing the wall with waterproof elastomeric paint may fix it (see chapter eighteen). If water is visible on the wall or is trickling down the wall, sealing the surface will only hide the problem. The water will build up in the basement wall, where it can cause structural problems later. To permanently fix major water seepage you will have to seal the basement from the outside. A less expensive alternative is to add a sump house or drain in the basement to pump the excess water out of the basement. But face it, if you have this much water in the basement, creating a pleasant living space will be very difficult without major repairs. Try using the space as a work room or storage only.

Proper waterproofing of the basement requires that the outside wall be sealed (parged) with an asphalt or rubber sealant and proper drainage installed. This will require excavating the entire perimeter of the basement back from the wall for at least 24 inches so the parging can be applied. This is no small project. Make sure your basement is worth upgrading before planning this fix and hire a professional. Improper sealing will permanently ruin your renovation later on.

If you excavate the wall, place plastic drainage pipe at the base of the footings around the entire perimeter of the house and cover it with 4 inches or more of gravel. Connect the end of the drainage pipe to a sewer or drainage area so that excess moisture will be drained away from the basement walls. Then apply the parging. If you are going to the trouble to excavate the basement, then you might consider adding an exterior door or additional windows. This is major structural work. When do you need it? Fire codes require an exit directly to the outside for any habitable space. If you plan a bedroom in the basement an exterior door or window will be necessary.

Fig. 27-1. Large basement window areaway with sloped sides.

BASEMENT OPENINGS

One of the main disadvantages of basement rooms is the lack of natural light and of a view. If the house is on a sloping lot or graded to permit large basement windows above grade, it is much more usable than in the house where the basement has only a few inches of the top of the wall above grade. Even the completely sunken basement, however, can have natural light if large areaways are built for windows and the walls of the areaways are sloped so that sunlight can reach the

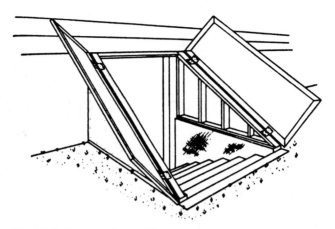

Fig. 27-2. Areaway type of basement entrance.

windows easily. If you have existing areaways, you may want to extend them to form a small sunken garden so the view will be more pleasant. Make sure to provide adequate drainage. At least one window large enough to serve as a fire exit will be needed and is often required by code.

The usefulness of the basement can also be increased by adding a direct outside entrance. This adds to fire safety by providing an additional fire exit. Direct outside access is very useful if the basement is used as a shop or for storing lawn and garden equipment. If an outside stairway is desired, a 4- by 11-foot area must be excavated to provide for the opening and stairs. A drain must be installed in front of the basement door so rain does not build up at the door step. Cutting openings in an existing basement wall, especially poured concrete, is difficult and critical work. Steel lintels must be inserted over the block openings and the floor above the opening should be supported by floor jacks during the conversion. Hire a well-qualified professional if you plan to attempt this project.

Premanufactured basement entrances are available with doors covering the entire opening. These look like the old outside basement doors so prevalent in the twenties and thirties. These entrances were used to load coal into the basement for fueling the old coal-fired furnaces. If your home is old, it might already have one of these. The modern equivalents are easy to install and provide rain-proof double doors on the outside that can be locked from the inside. You will also need to install a door in the basement wall.

BATHROOMS

Bathrooms pose a special problem when installed in basements. The existing sewer pipe seldom extends

Fig. 27-3. Sunken garden forming large basement window areaway.

to the floor of the basement. You may be required to purchase a flush-up toilet designed for this very problem. The other restriction is the concrete slab. You won't be able to run plumbing under the floor as usual. There are a couple of approaches that can be used to overcome this problem. Neither one is easy, so make sure you really need a bathroom in the basement before tackling this problem. The first approach is to cut a hole in the slab and run plumbing under the slab and through the foundation. It may then be possible to tie into the sewer line if that line is lower than the basement floor. The hole in the slab would then be patched with concrete.

Another approach may be easier if the sewer pipe exits the basement at floor level. You can build up the floor of the bathroom about 6 inches and install the plumbing underneath this frame, effectively creating a false floor. If the drainage pipe is not low enough, drill through the basement wall right above the slab and run the sewer pipe out to connect to the sewer.

> **Note:** Be very careful if you drill through basement walls. If your basement is not waterproofed and draining well, punching a hole at the bottom of the wall can be like taking your finger out of the dike. This makes a perfect place for leaks to occur. Make sure to seal around the hole with urethane foam or equivalent.

merely painting the existing concrete walls and floors. Keep in mind that basement areas, even with no major moisture problems, tend to be damp. Dehumidification is a good idea. Basements may also be cooler so the rooms may require more heat. If the furnace for the rest of the house is located in the basement, additional ducts can be easily added to channel warmth to the new living area. An electric baseboard heater is another practical alternative. The insulation of the walls, floor and ceiling will reduce heating needs considerably.

FINISHING THE BASEMENT

Basements can be finished to any desired style or degree, depending on the investment made and the use of the space. This may vary from insulated walls with quality paneling, wood floors and acoustical ceiling, to

STAIRS

Unlike the attic, the basement will have some type of stairway providing access. It is usually impractical to move the stairs, so plan your renovation around them. You will want to upgrade their appearance. This will be much simpler than building new stairs. The stair stringers are already in place but probably have utilitarian treads attached with no risers. Plan to remove these and replace them with hardwood treads and risers. If the treads rest on nailing strips, remove them and replace them with triangular nailing boards that provide nailing areas for treads and risers. Build the stairway into any new partitions to achieve the built-in look.

WALLS

If the basement walls were waterproofed properly on the outside, there should be no problem in applying most kinds of wall finish. If there is any possibility of water entry, however, you should apply an elastomeric waterproof coating to the inner surface. Many coatings of this type are available commercially; however, they cannot be applied over a painted surface. If a more finished appearance is not essential, walls can simply be painted for a bright, clean appearance. If you want a better interior finish with insulation, you will need to apply it over furring strips or rigid insulation.

Furring strips, 2 × 2 inches or larger, are nailed to the wall using concrete nails. Strips should be pressure treated for decay resistance, especially if the walls are not waterproofed. Anchor a 2 × 2-inch bottom plate to the floor at the junction of the wall and floor. Fasten a 2 × 2-inch or larger top plate to the bottom of the joists above, to nailing blocks or to the wall. Then fasten 2 × 2-inch or larger furring strips at 16- or 24-inch intervals. Apply the furring strips vertically between top and bottom plates just like studs in partition walls. If you are applying drywall horizontally, you might want to attach more furring strips at the joint between the top and bottom sheets of drywall.

Before going any farther with the finish wall, install all the required electrical conduit and outlet boxes between the furring strips. Place blanket-type insulation with a vapor barrier on the inside face in each space between furring strips. The wall is then ready to receive the interior finish. The drywall can be applied as described in the chapter nineteen.

As an option, you can apply the wall finish material over rigid foam insulation, which is applied directly to the basement walls with latex-based adhesive. Do not use construction adhesive because it will dissolve the foam instead of bonding to it. No furring strips are needed. For this method, walls must be smooth and level without protrusions so that the sheets of foam

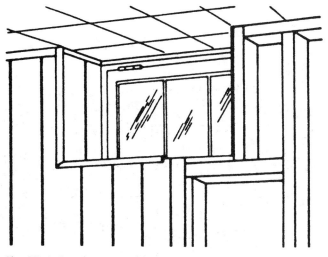

Fig. 27-4. Framing around basement window of a wall finish application.

insulation can be secured to the walls smoothly.

Once the adhesive on the insulation has dried, use drywall adhesive to secure the wall finish to the insulation. Follow the manufacturer's recommendations on adhesives and methods of installation for both the foam insulation and the drywall. Select a foam insulation with good vapor resistance to eliminate the need for a separate vapor barrier.

Interior basement partitions are framed just like any other wall. The only difference is in securing the bottom plate to the slab with concrete nails or other types of concrete anchors. Bridging must be installed between ceiling joists if the wall doesn't line up directly with a joist.

Try to conceal unsightly items such as steel beams, columns and exposed piping inside the interior partitions. These items can be covered by building a simple box around them and paneling over the box. Ducts and piping can also be boxed in with framing and covered with drywall. If the basement has a beam supporting the floor, it will usually be located in the middle of the room. Try to frame it into the interior partition.

FLOORS

If the concrete floor is dry most of the year, it suggests that a vapor barrier was probably applied under the slab at the time it was constructed. In such a basement, resilient tile or indoor-outdoor carpeting can be applied directly to the smooth slab. Any protrusions from the slab should be chipped off and smoothed. If the slab is uneven, use an underlayment over sleepers as the floor surface. Resilient tile is a low-cost option for the base-

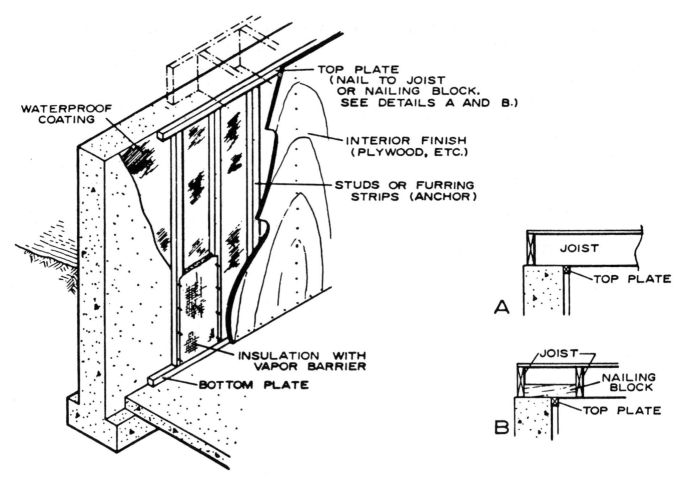

WATERPROOF
COATING

TOP PLATE
(NAIL TO JOIST
OR NAILING BLOCK.
SEE DETAILS A AND B.)

INTERIOR FINISH
(PLYWOOD, ETC.)

STUDS OR FURRING
STRIPS (ANCHOR)

JOIST

TOP PLATE

A

JOIST

NAILING
BLOCK

TOP PLATE

B

INSULATION WITH
VAPOR BARRIER

BOTTOM PLATE

Fig. 27-5. Basement wall finish over framing.

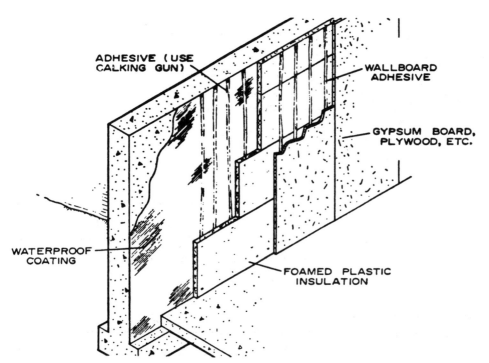

ADHESIVE (USE
CALKING GUN)

WALLBOARD
ADHESIVE

GYPSUM BOARD,
PLYWOOD, ETC.

WATERPROOF
COATING

FOAMED PLASTIC
INSULATION

Fig. 27-6. Basement wall finish over rigid insulation.

ment, but it won't provide much cushion or insulation. This is fine for a recreation room, however. Do not use the self-stick type of resilient tile; the latent moisture and coolness of the slab will prevent a good bond. Use tile meant for attachment with a floor adhesive. This will also serve as a vapor barrier. Install the tile as described in chapter twelve following the manufacturer's recommendations on adhesives and installation.

A very low-cost floor can be achieved by merely applying a deck paint. It should be a latex paint to avoid chipping or peeling. Although painting may not give the finished appearance provided by a floor covering, it does brighten the basement and produce a smooth surface that is easily cleaned. Painting the basement floor is particularly suited to shops, utility rooms and playrooms.

ring strips. They provide a springy floor surface and make applying a vapor barrier extremely easy. Use furring for carpet or hardwood floors for the best possible effect. Follow this procedure:

1. Mop or spread a coating of tar or asphalt mastic on the concrete, followed by an asphalt felt paper.
2. Lay pressure-treated 2 × 4s in a coating of tar or asphalt, spacing the rows about 12 inches apart, starting at one wall and ending at the opposite wall.
3. Place batts of insulation or rigid foam between the furring strips for additional insulation.
4. Install wood-strip flooring across the 2 × 4s or apply a subfloor of ½-inch or ⅝-inch plywood to provide a base for resilient tile or carpet.

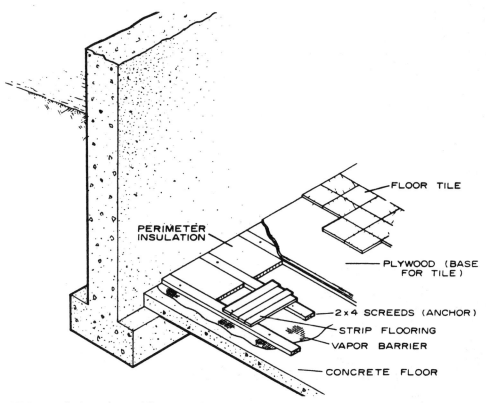

Fig. 27-7. Installation of wood floors in a basement.

If the concrete floor is very uneven or cracked, a vapor barrier can be laid over the existing floor and a 2- to 3-inch topping of lightweight concrete fill can be added to level the floor. Don't use this method if the floor was slanted toward a drain—it is there for a reason.

Carpeting can be just cut to size and laid flat, with only double-faced tape at the edges and seams if the floor is exceptionally dry. Use a high-quality pad under the carpet.

The best basement floors will result from using fur-

A variation of this preparation for flooring consists of laying a good-quality vapor barrier directly over the slab and anchoring the furring strips to the slab with concrete nails. Insulation and strip flooring is then applied as just described.

CEILINGS

If all the plumbing, ducting and beams can be framed in, the ceiling finish can be applied using the same materials and techniques described in the section on ceilings in chapter nineteen. In many basements however, obstructions usually make this difficult. In this case, a suspended ceiling system will be best. It can be placed below piping and electrical conduit, and panels are easily removed for repair or changes. Suspended ceilings can be installed with a minimum 7 feet of ceiling height from floor to ceiling. Box in all obstructions that fall below the height of the suspended ceiling and cover them with drywall or plywood. Make sure to leave a 2-inch clearance between the frame and any ducting. Then attach the ceiling tracks directly to the boxed-in area and install tiles as usual. High windows flush with the ceiling will cause a similar problem. Frame in a valance around the window so that you can attach the suspended ceiling tracks to it. Then cut out tiles to fit around the valance and drop them in. See chapter nineteen for more details on suspended ceilings.

Before installing any ceiling, insulate cold-water pipes. When the basement has a high relative humidity, water condenses on the cold pipes and this condensation drips down on the ceiling under the pipes. Molded insulation made specifically for wrapping around pipe is commercially available.

BASEMENT CONVERSION STEPS

Planning

1. Examine the basement for evidence of leaking or moisture problems. Look for cracks, standing water or mineral deposits on basement walls. Measure the height of the basement to confirm viability as a conversion project. Check for adequate drainage.

2. Complete diagram of basement layout. Mark exact locations of stairs and walls. Position walls to cover ducts, pipes and beams.

3. Select plumbing fixtures, lighting fixtures, flooring and ceiling styles.

4. Perform the standard bidding process. Obtain a signed proposal from an experienced carpenter with standard provisions and specifications.

5. Obtain signed contract for construction.

6. Obtain building permit if needed.

7. Schedule waterproofing contractor and framer. The waterproofing should be completed before framing begins.

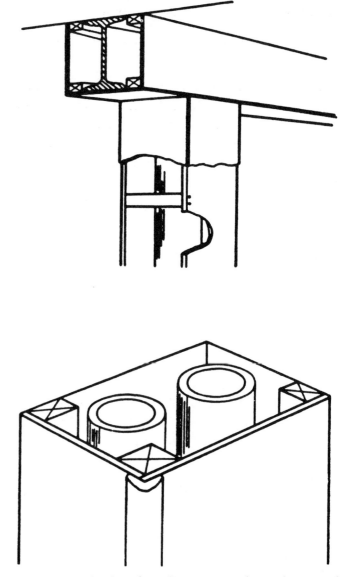

Fig. 27-8. Application of paneling to cover columns, beams and pipes.

8. Purchase all plumbing fixtures, lighting fixtures and flooring. Request that the supplier store the material until you are ready for it. You will probably not have adequate storage space because the basement will have to be cleared out to apply the floor. Special plumbing fixtures such as flush-up toilets will probably have to be special-ordered. Allow plenty of time for delivery.

Exterior Waterproofing

1. Mark the location of all utilities including phone, cable, gas, plumbing, electrical and sewer lines if outside excavation is planned. Follow these utilities to their outside entrance and mark the surrounding areas with stakes and orange surveying ribbon. Check your plat drawing for any utility easements that may pass through your yard. If you are not sure of the location, call the utility company and ask them to help.

2. Rent a sump pump to drain water from the bottom of the trench.

3. Excavate outside of basement walls. Schedule an excavator with a backhoe to do the job. Make sure to be on site during this process. The grader must be very careful not to damage the basement wall or to cut underground utility lines. Excavating around these areas must be done by hand.

4. Install any new sewer lines or plumbing while the walls are exposed.

5. Install any new exterior doors or windows. Hire a professional for this job. The floor joists above the opening to be cut should be supported with floor jacks. Cut the opening with a masonry saw by cutting both on the inside and outside of the wall. Install a steel lintel across the top of the opening and reinstall any concrete blocks removed above the lintel. Frame the opening with pressure-treated wood and secure it to the opening with concrete anchor screws. Set the door or window into the opening. Note: Use vinyl-clad windows in the opening if possible. This will reduce future problems with wood decay.

6. Install premanufactured entryway.

7. Clean the exterior of the basement walls thoroughly with muriatic acid or a power washer and let the concrete dry for a couple of days before applying parging.

8. Apply parging to material. Parging is mortar that is applied to the concrete block before applying the sealant. Apply two coats, allowing the first coat to dry for 2 days before applying the second coat. A cove joint is created at the intersection of the blocks and foundation. Parging is not necessary on poured concrete walls.

9. Apply waterproof sealant. Asphalt sealant is the least expensive material and does a reasonable job. Apply an extra thick layer at the joint between the wall and footing. Attach a sheet of 6-mil poly to the warm asphalt for additional protection. Extend the plastic over the footing so it will be covered with the drainage gravel. If you are concerned about settling or cracking, or if your moisture problems are severe, consider using one of the more advanced rubber-based sealants. They are very expensive but they can stretch to span cracks and are guaranteed for 10 years. Finish all the exterior

waterproofing completely before starting construction on the inside.

10. Lay gravel and drainage tile at the base of the foundation. Apply 4 inches of gravel first and then lay the drainage tile in place, making sure that the pipe slants toward the drainage point about 1 inch for every 20 feet of distance. Cover the tile with additional gravel to ensure adequate drainage.

11. Cover the waterproofing with rigid insulation or drainage netting to protect the coating while backfilling the wall. This step is additional insurance against future leaking and increases the insulation of the basement. Drainage netting is a special 1-inch thick porous blanket that helps channel excess moisture down to the drainage tile and also protects the coating.

12. Backfill the basement walls. Make sure the backhoe operator takes care not to damage the waterproofing.

13. Allow basement interior to dry out for at least a week after sealing exterior walls. Use a dehumidifier if possible.

Basement Finishing

1. Check delivered items for correct model, color, size, etc. Check for any damaged material now before it is time to install. Discovering a damaged item at installation time can delay the project while you wait for a replacement.

2. Make arrangements for getting rid of trash after finishing. Call your local city or county government for disposal regulations.

3. Schedule plumbing, electrical and framing subs.

4. Renovate stairway. Frame in the stringers and replace tread supports with triangular supports to allow installation of risers. Leave the existing treads in place until construction traffic is over; then install finish treads and risers.

5. Seal basement interior walls and floor. If you are installing furring strips and a plastic vapor barrier, this is optional. If you have minor moisture problems, you will want to seal the walls and floor anyway to prevent water from seeping through the walls and accumulating behind the plastic vapor barrier.

6. Install resilient floor tile, if applicable. It is easier to install resilient tile before any interior partitions are framed. Also, by using floor adhesive, you will get an unbroken vapor barrier.

7. Apply floor runners and vapor barrier on floor if applicable. Nail or glue the runners to the floor and cover with 6-mil poly. Try to position a runner below any planned partition wall to provide a nailing surface.

8. Install hardwood floor or subfloor, if carpet is chosen. See chapter twelve for more details.

9. Attach furring strips to wall. If you plan to glue siding to the wall, the plumbing and wiring will have to run on the outside of the wall or be placed in the framed partition walls.

10. Install bridging between ceiling joists for any partition that does not intersect a joist.

11. Frame in interior partition walls. Anchor them to the concrete floor with concrete nails or to the floor runners.

12. Turn off gas, water and electric power to basement before starting to rough-in utilities.

13. Install all of the plumbing, electrical and HVAC rough-in.

14. Inspect rough-in plumbing, electrical and HVAC. This may require a visit by one or more inspectors. Have the contractors contact their respective inspectors. Plan a specific day for inspections so you can be there.

15. Box in all remaining ducts, pipes and beams. Leave a 2-inch space around heating ducts. Build valances around exterior windows if you plan to use a suspended ceiling.

16. Install insulation on walls and ceilings. If a suspended ceiling is used, consider purchasing insulated ceiling tiles. These will eliminate the need to insulate and will reduce noise transmission.

17. Install drywall on exterior walls, ceiling (if applicable) and partition walls. See chapter nineteen for more details.

18. Finish drywall with joint tape and compound. This will require three coats.

19. Complete rough-in plumbing, electrical and HVAC.

20. Inspect rough-in plumbing, electrical and HVAC.

21. Install any custom shelving or cabinetry.

22. Paint walls and ceiling (if applicable).

23. Install any bath plumbing and cabinet fixtures. See chapter sixteen for more details.

> **NOTE:** To save time and energy, paint the walls before installing a suspended ceiling or adding trim. This avoids the tedious masking step. Since the floor was installed first, drop cloths may be needed. Walls and ceilings can be painted very quickly with a paint sprayer or power roller. Paint the primer coat on trim before installing. See chapter eighteen for more details.

24. Set interior doors and install trim.

25. Finish trimwork on stairs and install the finish treads and risers.

26. Paint the trim.

27. Install carpet, if applicable. (See chapter sixteen.)

28. Install suspended ceiling. This is not messy, so it can be done before or after carpet installation.

29. Install lighting and electrical fixtures. (Refer to chapter fourteen)

30. Turn on water, electric and gas utilities.

31. Pay all subs, requiring each to sign an affidavit.

WATERPROOFING SPECIFICATIONS

- Bid is to include all material and labor required to excavate and waterproof dwelling based on specifications.
- Excavation is to be done by hand around marked utilities to prevent damage.
- Exterior basement walls are to be cleaned thoroughly with muriatic acid before applying parging.
- Two ¼-inch coats of portland cement are to be applied smoothly and evenly to block foundation. First coat is to be applied to moistened masonry blocks and roughened before drying. Second coat is to be kept moist for 48 hours to set (block wall only).

- Portland cement is to be applied smoothly to intersection of footing and wall.
- Sharp points in portland cement coating are to be removed prior to application of tar coating, as they will puncture 6-mil poly.
- Asphalt coat is to be applied hot, covering entire subgrade area. Coat to be a minimum of $\frac{1}{64}$ inch.
- A 4-inch diameter perforated PVC drain pipe is to be installed around the entire foundation perimeter. Tile sections are to be separated $\frac{1}{4}$ inch with tar paper to cover all joints. Drain tile should have a minimum slope of 1 inch in 20 feet. There should be drain holes every 6 inches in pipe.
- Drain pipe is to be connected to sewer line, sump well or to drainage area as specified.

EXTERIOR OPENINGS SPECIFICATIONS

- Floor joists above proposed opening are to be fully supported by floor jacks during removal.
- Approved steel lintel is to be installed above opening. All blocks above lentil are to be reinserted and mortared to match surrounding blocks.
- Pressure-treated lumber is to be used for all framed openings.
- Blocks below opening are to be sealed with concrete and troweled smooth. Concrete sill is to be fabricated below window openings.
- Concrete steps are to have slope of at least $\frac{1}{8}$ inch for drainage. Concrete is to be roughened for traction.

- Below ground steps are to have 2-inch drain at bottom attached to approved drainage. Concrete is to slope toward drain.

WATERPROOFING INSPECTION

- ☐ Portland cement is relatively smooth and even with no sharp edges protruding.
- ☐ Portland cement completely covers intersection of wall and footings.
- ☐ Asphalt coating completely covers entire subgrade area, including intersection of wall and footings.
- ☐ Black 6-mil poly completely covers entire tar coating and adheres firmly to it. Look for any tears or punctures in poly that need to be patched before backfill. If more than one sheet is used, top sheet overlaps bottom by at least 6 inches. Remove large rocks and roots from backfill area so that poly will not be torn during backfill process later.
- ☐ Tarred area does not go above grade level or where stucco is to be placed.
- ☐ Poly is secured to stay in place during backfill.
- ☐ Backfill is applied and tamped in place. Grade of backfill drains away from house with allowance for settling.
- ☐ There is no water in basement.
- ☐ There are no wet spots on interior basement walls.

BASEMENT MATERIAL ESTIMATE

DESCRIPTION	SPECIFICATION	QTY.	UNIT	COST	TAX	TOTAL COST	COST TYPE	VENDOR
Framing								
Runners 1" × 4"								
Runners 2" × 4"								
Runner glue								
Subfloor ⅝-inch tongue-and-grooved								
Subfloor ¾-inch tongue-and-grooved								
Underlayment								
Furring — 1 × 4								
Valance — 1 × 6								
Plates — 2 × 4								
8-foot studs — 2 × 4								
10-foot studs — 2 × 4								
Bracing								
Framing — Stairs								
Stringers — 2 × 12								
Framing — 2 × 4								
Cap								
Rail								
Baluster								
Post								
Riser								
Tread								
Bracing								
Framing — Nails								
12d common								
10d common								
8d common								
Concrete nails								

BASEMENT MATERIAL ESTIMATE

DESCRIPTION	SPECIFICATION	QTY.	UNIT	COST	TAX	TOTAL COST	COST TYPE	VENDOR
8d galvanized casing								
3d finish								
4d finish								
6d finish								
Insulation								
Rigid foam insulation								
Walls								
Ceiling								
Vapor barrier — 6-mil poly								
Interior trim								
Bath								
Kitchen								
Windows								
Doors								
Flooring								
Lighting fixtures								
Paint								
Drywall								
Labor								
Basement design — contract								
Plumbing — contract								
Electrical — contract								
HVAC — contract								
Framing/carpentry — contract								
Waterproofing — contract								

CHAPTER TWENTY-EIGHT

Garage

The easiest space in a house to convert into living space is the garage. It already has a roof, floor and walls. No major structural changes are needed. If the garage is well built, the only work required is finishing. This is much less costly than adding onto the house.

The main consideration is whether the additional finished space is needed more than the garage is needed. Since the garage is often adjacent to the kitchen, it is an ideal candidate for conversion to a large family room. It could also be used for additional bedrooms, possibly another bathroom. When you expand into the garage, however, you must find replacement storage for the possessions you store there. Most garages fill up pretty quickly, especially with yard and shop tools. You will want to move these to a place that is easily accessible from the yard. This leaves two options—a basement with exterior access or a new utility building. If you don't have a basement, the utility building can be built onto the back of the house or constructed as a stand-alone building. Since it needs no heat or electricity for storage, the utility shed is very inexpensive to construct.

If you park the car in the garage, you will have to find an alternate location. You may be able to extend the driveway around the end of the house and build a carport or parking area in the back. Check your local building codes.

The existing driveway poses another problem. If you close in the garage opening and disguise it, the driveway will look weird running straight up to the house. Consider cutting the driveway short with a masonry saw and tearing out a 4-foot strip of concrete. This will make room for a row of shrubbery to disguise your handiwork. A less expensive alternative is to place a long wooden planter across the driveway to hold the shrubs. This will break up the area between the drive and the house.

There is one other approach—the partial garage conversion. If you have a double garage, why not convert half of it and leave the other side as a garage? This provides storage and convenience. You may still want to cut a piece of the driveway out in front of the closed-in area to plant shrubs. This will further visually separate the new area from the remaining garage.

Disguising the evidence of the old garage front will be challenging. Windows installed in the framed-in opening will not only let in light but will help break up the wall. Usually the existing siding runs right up to the edge of the garage door. If the garage is offset from the main house (not flush with the front), you may be able to replace the siding on the entire garage front wall and then repaint. If the siding is brick, blending in the framed-in opening will be more difficult. You can knock out the half bricks around the opening and cover the hole with new brick, but the old and new brick will seldom match. In this case, a bay window makes the perfect stylistic addition, since it can fill virtually the entire opening.

FINISHING THE GARAGE

The walls and ceiling of the garage can be finished in any conventional manner. The floor will probably require a vapor barrier, insulation and a new subfloor. Garage floors are slabs on grade and are usually 1 or 2 feet lower than the floor of the finished house. Building a subfloor will bring the floor levels much closer together and provide a space for new plumbing and heating. See chapter twelve for more details.

Garage Floors

Most garage floors are positioned lower than the house for several reasons. It prevents water from running into the house from the garage area. Houses must be placed on a crawl space or basement. Garage slabs must be

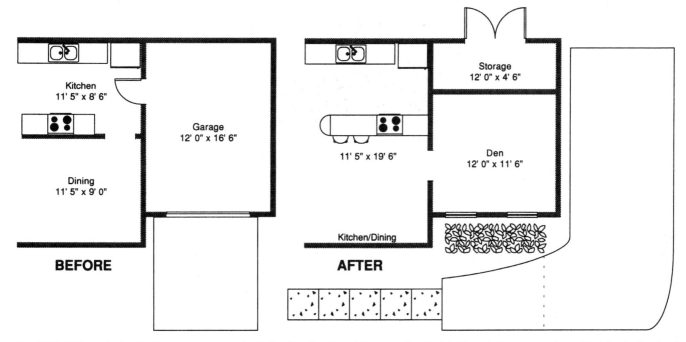

Fig. 28-1. When closing in the garage, use plants to disguise the old garage front. Additional storage can be added to the back of the garage conversion.

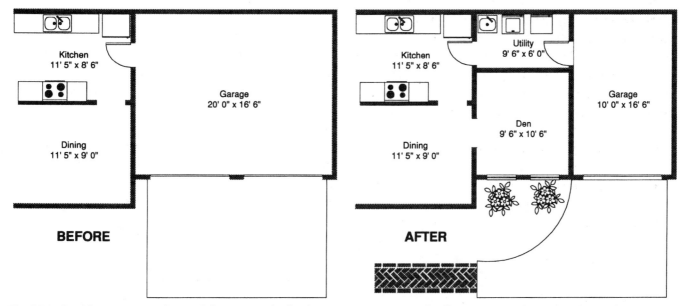

Fig. 28-2. Double garages can be partially converted, allowing use as a garage and utility room. Cut driveway in front of converted area to disguise old garage front.

poured on solid ground because of the weight of automobiles. Where the ceiling of the finished garage is at the same elevation as the house ceiling, the lower floor will create a ceiling height of 9 to 10 feet. New floor framing can be installed to place the new floor at the same level as the house floor. This provides a more springy floor and leaves a cavity for running plumbing and electrical.

The least expensive option is to apply the new finish floor directly over the existing concrete slab if no plumbing is needed. But this provides a cold, hard sur-

face. The garage floor is designed to slope toward the opening, so your floor will not be level. With carpet, this may not be noticeable. The lack of a vapor barrier is a bigger problem however. Building code requires a plastic vapor barrier underneath slabs in living areas, but not under garage floors. Builders seldom place vapor barriers under the garage slab. Make sure to seal the slab or install 6-mil poly before laying down carpet and pad. Unnaturally tall steps that jut out into the room will be needed to get from house level to garage level.

Whenever possible, build up the floor closer to the

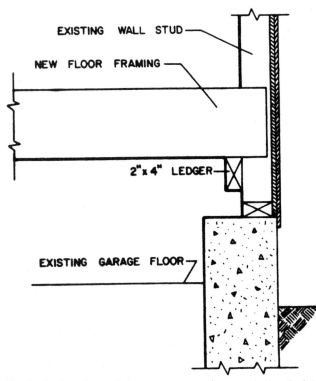

Fig. 28-3. Framing to bring new garage floor to the level of the house floor.

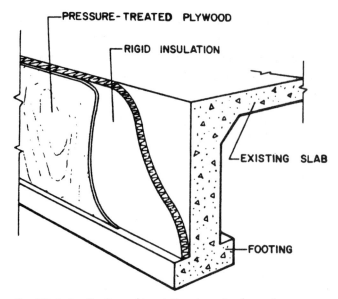

Fig. 28-4. Application of insulation to outer face of garage foundation wall.

height of the house. This can be achieved by applying flooring over sleepers or, where headroom is sufficient, over new floor framing above the slab. The framing may rest on the foundation wall or may be supported on ledger strip nailed to the wall studs. Consult joist tables to determine the correct size for the required span. Spans can be very short since joist support can be placed anywhere on the slab. Make sure to apply a vapor barrier below the floor and install a couple of vents just like you would under a conventional crawl space. The floor is installed as a conventional floor, as described in chapter twelve and insulated in the same manner as a crawl space house, as described in chapter thirteen.

When the garage roof is lower than the house roof, the floor must be placed directly on the concrete slab or on 1 × 4 runners. The finish floor can then be installed using the same materials and techniques as for a basement slab. If the garage floor is near ground level, insulation is required. If the finished floor is on runners over the concrete, place the insulation between the runners.

Garage Walls

The garage walls are not usually insulated, so blanket insulation with a vapor barrier on the inside face should be installed in the space between studs. If the walls are already covered with drywall, it may be possible to blow

in insulation through holes cut in the drywall. Since you won't be able to apply a vapor barrier, paint the walls with vapor barrier primer. Many garages are covered with pegboard, which will have to be removed. Remove it carefully. You may be able to reuse it in a storage building. Then, install insulation and apply any type of wall covering as described in chapter nineteen.

Partitions

Closing in the garage opening will first require a foundation across the opening the same height as the garage foundation. Garage foundations are typically constructed with concrete block or poured concrete. The slab is then poured inside, using the foundation walls as the form. The slab is probably slanted out toward the driveway for drainage right at the point where you need to lay new blocks. If the angle is not too bad, you can level the blocks with mortar or nail forms across the opening and pour a concrete wall. If you pour a concrete wall across a concrete block foundation, chisel grooves in the adjoining concrete blocks to serve as keys to hold the poured concrete in place.

Most headers over garage openings sag slightly, which means that studs cut for the middle of the opening must be shorter than studs near the edges of the opening. Jacking up the header and trying to force it level is probably not worth the trouble unless the sagging is severe. Trying to take the permanent set out of the header can cause cracking or gaps in surrounding walls. Just cut the studs a little shorter and tap them in snugly. Place an extra stud or two in the center for extra support. You can build the entire partition on the floor with a top plate and lift it into position, but because of the sagging beam, the partition will be difficult to set in place. You will find it easier to position each stud in place individually. Since the partition has a large header above it, it doesn't require a top plate or headers above window openings.

Frame any additional doors and windows as you would any other opening, keeping in mind that headers are not required on the garage opening. If you are installing a partition wall in the garage — to separate a utility room from a den, for instance — follow standard procedures for framing in partitions. The only difference is that the partition may be taller than 8 feet if the garage floor is not high enough. Make sure to order 10-foot studs in this case.

Garage Ceiling

Most garage ceilings are left open or covered with drywall. If it's covered with drywall, the finish probably was never applied. If so, the fastest way to finish the ceiling is to apply tap to the joints and then apply a textured ceiling compound. Use blown-in insulation for the garage attic.

GARAGE CONVERSION STEPS

Planning

1. Examine the garage for evidence of leaking or moisture problems. Check the walls and ceiling for insulation. Study the lot plan for the house and check building setback lines. Factor this information into the garage design decisions.

2. Complete diagram of garage layout. Mark exact locations of windows and walls. Measure height of floor in comparison to the rest of the house. Plan to have the finish garage floor level with or 8 inches below the house floor level. An 8-inch difference will accommodate one full step.

3. Select plumbing fixtures, lighting fixtures and floor type. Decide on a flush floor or built-up floor.

4. Perform the standard bidding process. Obtain a signed proposal from an experienced carpenter with standard provisions and specifications.

5. Obtain signed contract for construction.

6. Obtain building permit if needed.

7. Schedule framer and concrete contractor. Concrete contractor may be used for cutting and removing concrete, pouring additional driveways, or pouring a concrete foundation across the garage opening.

8. Purchase all plumbing fixtures, lighting fixtures and flooring. Request that the supplier store the material until you are ready for it. You will probably not have adequate storage space because the garage will have to be cleared out to apply the floor.

Floor

1. Remove concrete from the front of the garage. First, cut a line with a masonry saw at the garage opening and at the point where you want the driveway to end. Cut the line as deep as possible. This may take more than one pass. Gently break the seam at the cut with a sledge hammer. Remove the broken concrete and haul it away.

2. Measure and mark the new height of floor framing. If installing new joists, snap a chalk line at the new height. Mark the existing blocks on either side of the garage opening with the joist height to aid in setting a new foundation in the opening.

3. Remove garage door. Be very careful removing the door from the track. Once the counterweight has been removed, the door is very heavy.

4. Install new foundation across the garage opening with concrete block or with poured concrete. For poured concrete, attach a form on each side of the opening with plywood or lumber the right height for the final foundation. Once the forms are fabricated, use bar clamps to secure them to the opening.

5. Pour concrete for new foundation in opening. Use 3000 psi concrete or use bags of ready-made concrete on site. Level the concrete at the top with a 2 × 4 and screed smooth. Let the concrete set up for 3 to 4 days before continuing with the framing.

6. Install new floor joists. If the floor height is sufficient, attach ledger strips to the existing garage walls for the joists to rest on. A better, but more expensive method is to nail a header joist on the wall at the same height as the floor and attach the joists with joist hangers. If the floor joists are small and located just above the floor, lay pressure-treated runners on the concrete and cover them with 6-mil poly as a vapor barrier. Rest the joists on the runners and level them with shims nailed to the runners. Leveling the joists this way will take some time since the garage floor is probably not level.

7. Install all rough-in plumbing and wiring between floor joists. Provide access to rough-in connections after subfloor is installed.

8. Insulate floor if desired. If you are installing a joist floor, use batt insulation between the joists. Hold the batts in place with wood or wire slats pushed between the joists. Do not use blown-in insulation. The dampness of the garage floor requires that air circulate under any insulation to avoid moisture buildup. If you are using a subfloor on runners, place rigid insulation between the runners. See chapter thirteen.

9. Install subfloor. Glue and screw the subfloor to the joists for maximum strength. See chapter twelve.

10. Install hardwood floor or resilient tile if you have no floor joist system. This is easier to accomplish if done before any interior partition walls are installed.

Interior

1. Frame in the garage door opening. This can be done before installing the floor if you want to close the garage in from the elements; however, you can temporarily cover the opening with plastic until the floor is installed. You will then have greater access to the garage area for moving in lumber and supplies. Position the wall in the opening so that the studs are flush with the studs in the outside wall of the garage. This will ensure that the new exterior surface will be flush with the existing surface when sheathing and siding are attached.

2. Install exterior windows. See chapter seventeen.

3. Add new siding over the garage partition. If the garage is offset from the rest of the house, remove the existing siding just on the garage front and replace with all new siding. This will produce a much more uniform siding surface.

4. Install new siding trim.

5. Frame in and install all remaining interior partition walls.

6. Complete rough-in plumbing, electrical and HVAC.

7. Inspect rough-in plumbing, electrical and HVAC.

8. Install insulation in exterior walls. Add a vapor barrier if the insulation doesn't have one.

9. Install drywall on walls and ceiling.

10. Finish drywall with joint tape and compound. This will require three coats. See chapter nineteen.

11. Install any custom shelving or cabinetry.

12. Paint walls and ceiling.

13. Caulk all joints on exterior siding, openings, and trim.

NOTE: To save time and energy, paint the walls before installing trim. This avoids the tedious masking step. Walls and ceilings can be painted very quickly with a paint sprayer or power roller. Paint the primer coat on trim before installing. See chapter nineteen for more details.

---

14. Paint newly installed exterior siding. You can probably bargain for a better price if you have the painter complete the exterior at the same time as the interior painting.

15. Install any bath or kitchen plumbing and cabinet fixtures. See chapter twenty-four and twenty-five for more details.

16. Set interior doors and trim.

17. Finish painting trim.

18. Install hardwood, tile and carpet. See chapter twelve.

19. Install lighting and electrical fixtures. (See chapter fourteen.)

20. Turn on water, electric and gas utilities.

21. Install floor trim or quarter-round trim.

22. Pay electrician, plumber, painter, HVAC and cabinet sub, requiring each to sign an affidavit.

23. Pay carpenter/framer, requiring a signed affidavit.

GARAGE MATERIAL ESTIMATE

DESCRIPTION	SPECIFICATION	QTY.	UNIT	COST	TAX	TOTAL COST	COST TYPE	VENDOR
Framing								
Runners 1 × 4								
Runners 2 × 4								
Construction adhesive								
Subfloor ⅝-inch tongue-and-grooved								
Subfloor ¾-inch tongue-and-grooved								
Underlayment								
Plates — 2 × 4								
8-foot studs — 2 × 4								
10-foot studs — 2 × 4								
Bracing								
Framing nails								
12d common								
10d common								
8d common								
Concrete nails								
8d galvanized casing								
3d finish								
4d finish								
6d finish								
Insulation								
Rigid foam insulation								
Walls — batt								
Ceiling — blown in								
Vapor barrier — 6-mil poly								

GARAGE MATERIAL ESTIMATE

DESCRIPTION	SPECIFICATION	QTY.	UNIT	COST	TAX	TOTAL COST	COST TYPE	VENDOR
Interior trim								
Bath								
Windows								
Doors								
Flooring								
Lighting fixtures								
Paint								
Drywall								
Labor								
Garage design—contract								
Plumbing—contract								
Electrical—contract								
HVAC—contract								
Framing/carpentry—contract								
Concrete work—contract								

CHAPTER TWENTY-NINE

Porches, Sunrooms and Decks

I f expansion room is unavailable in the house, expand outward into new construction or close in existing structures such as porches. If the porch has a sound foundation below the floor, consider converting it into a sunroom. New energy-efficient glass can turn sunrooms into complete living areas. If a porch is unavailable for conversion, consider a prefabricated sunroom that can be easily installed. These manufactured units can be installed on a minimal foundation. Decks can also extend the perceived space of the house by providing alternate areas for relaxing and socializing. Decks are very inexpensive space additions.

RENOVATING THE PORCH

The first task in planning a porch renovation is to choose the most practical type of renovation. The typical porch foundation consists of posts sitting on concrete piers. This type of foundation will not support the added weight of walls and roof. However, this type of porch can be screened in or repaired with good results because little additional weight is added. If the existing foundation is sound, it may be feasible to replace just the worn out components, such as steps, floor, posts or roof. If the floor of the porch is a brick or concrete slab, the existing foundation is probably sufficient to support new construction, since the slab required a reinforced footing to keep it from cracking. Porches with conventional foundations supporting an extension of the existing roof are also good candidates for a room expansion or sunroom addition. If the porch foundation is settled or cracking, complete removal and replacement is rec-

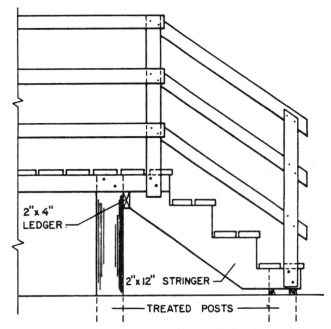

Fig. 29-1. Step stringer supported by porch framing and posts.

ommended. Building in a sunroom addition on an existing porch will require custom framing and construction. If the foundation is sound but the porch components are in disrepair, you might consider removing the porch and using the foundation as a base for a new sunroom.

Porch Steps

Check the condition of the steps. The bottom step and stringer of wood steps should not be in contact with soil. If the wooden steps are flush with the ground, the wood is probably decayed and will require replacement of the decayed components. A concrete step can be cast on the ground to support the new steps or a treated wood post can be imbedded in the ground. Apply a water-repellent preservative to all wood used in the steps.

Where completely new steps are required, use a 2 × 12 stringer with the lower end of each stringer bolted to a treated wood or concrete post. The upper end can be attached to the porch framing. Concrete or masonry piers provide the most permanent and maintenance-free support. The important thing is that the stringer be kept from contact with the soil. Use a galvanized bracket or bolt to suspend the stringer slightly above the ground so water can drain away.

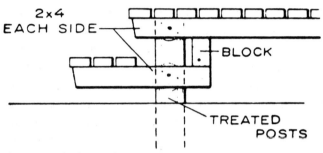

Fig. 29-2. Single porch step supported on a treated post.

Porch Floor

If the existing foundation of the porch is in good condition, inspect the floor framing as you would the floor of the house. Look for sagging or decayed joists and reinforce or replace them if necessary. Use the procedures explained in chapter twelve. If floor framing is decayed, it should be completely replaced with a pressure-treated lumber. Framing members should be at least 18 inches above the ground, and good ventilation should be provided under the porch. Framing should be installed to give the finished floor an outward slope of at least ⅛ inch per foot. If you are unsure about the condition of the foundation, it is much safer to tear it out and install a new one. Building on a questionable foundation will only bring problems later.

The most common porch flooring is 1 × 4-inch wood planking, tongue-and-grooved. It is blind-nailed at each joist in the same manner as regular flooring. The tongue-and-grooved feature ties all the floor planks together and adds to the rigidity of the floor. Use pressure-treated lumber if the porch is going to be open to the elements (not closed in) and apply a good stain or deck paint as quickly as possible after installation. If you plan to enclose the porch, leave the existing floor in place and install a new subfloor with a vapor barrier.

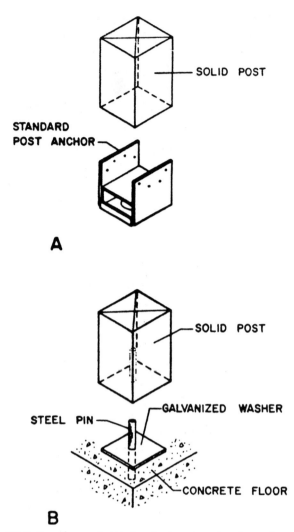

Fig. 29-3. Base for post: (A) standard post anchor for resistance to uplift; (B) galvanized washer and pin where resistance to uplift is not critical.

Porch Posts

Where a post rests directly on the porch floor, the base of the post will probably be decayed. The best solution may be to replace the post. If the existing porch posts are ornamental, they can sometimes be preserved by using a resin-based compound designed to soak into decayed wood. See chapter eighteen for more details. Remove the badly decayed wood and soak the remaining wood with the preservative compound. Then patch the holes with epoxy wood patch. Another technique for saving old posts is to cut off the decayed portion near the base and save the good portion. A base slightly larger than the post can replace the decayed portion.

When you install or repair posts, provide some way to support the post slightly above the porch floor to ventilate the base of the post to avoid further decay. One way to accomplish this is by using a small ⅜-inch or ½-inch diameter pin and a large galvanized washer. Drill a hole for the pin in the end of the post and a matching hole in the floor. Apply a mastic caulk to the area and position with the pin inserted and the washer between the post and the floor. This will allow moisture to evaporate from the end of the post and prevent decay. The gap between the post and the floor will be barely noticeable. This pinned method should be used only on small porches that do not have the potential for wind uplifting. In windy areas, use a galvanized post bracket designed to anchor the post to the floor.

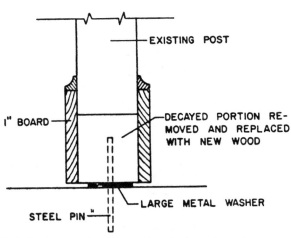

Fig. 29-4. Replacement of decayed end of porch post.

Porch Roof

A porch roof will exhibit the same problems, and can be repaired in much the same manner as the house roof. Quite often the porch roof will be an extension of the existing roof. Common roof problems include sagging rafters and decayed shingles. These problems can be repaired properly only if the standard roof is repaired simultaneously. See chapter twenty for more information. Some minor sagging of the porch roof can be caused by settling of a substandard foundation or decaying of the supporting posts. These type of problems can be fixed by supporting the roof with jacks and repairing the underlying problems.

Other porch roofs frequently extend out from the existing roof at a very low slope. They are often covered with roll roofing made up of an underlayment of asphalt-saturated felt and mineral-surfaced half-lap roll roofing. These old-style roofs are not very popular today. The repair process is tricky and should be done by a qualified roofing contractor.

Porch Ceiling

The ceiling of a porch usually consists of plywood sheathing or wood planks, applied in the same manner as the flooring. If you are planning to close in the porch, the ceiling will be protected from the elements. In this case, the best ceiling finish will usually consist of refinishing the existing wood planks or installing a new ceiling of drywall. If the existing ceiling is plywood and in good condition, a textured ceiling finish can be applied.

SUNROOMS

Sunrooms can be added to the house as a completely new structure or as a conversion from existing porches or decks. Sunroom additions are very popular in new houses and renovations because such additions add new space and additional light to existing homes. Most old homes have less window space than modern ones and a sunroom can quickly make up that deficit. If you are planning to use an existing porch for the sunroom, it is imperative that the existing structure is solid enough to support the additional weight. Glass is very heavy and will put a strain on any foundation that is substandard, so make sure you are confident about this before continuing. Start by repairing any existing problems, except for the porch posts. These will be removed and replaced with conventional exterior partitions with openings framed in for the glass.

The least expensive installation will consist of fixed panes of glass, but lack of ventilation can cause the room to heat up unbearably in the summer. Sliding glass doors or screened windows will provide additional ventilation, but will also drive up the cost. Try to settle on a combination of fixed panes and screened openings that are strategically placed to provide cross ventilation. Ceiling fans will also help keep the air moving. Since heat buildup is a strong consideration, consider using energy-efficient double-pane glass. This is commonly called Low-E glass because of its "low energy" requirement. This glass is usually tinted to keep out excessive heat in the summer and the double panes help hold heat in during the winter.

Solar heating in the winter is usually sufficient to heat a sunroom without additional heating systems. If the sunspace is open to the rest of the house the heat can also be distributed to reduce conventional heating needs. The summer is another story, however. In southern climates heat buildup can be considerable. Provide for adequate cross ventilation. Also, consider installing several deciduous trees around the sunroom for extra shade. They will drop their leaves in the winter and allow the solar energy in just when it is needed.

Many contractors specialize in installing new and retrofit sunrooms. They have all the specialized tools and knowledge to complete the job effectively. This job is best left to the professionals. Since most of the cost of a sunroom lies in the materials, little will be saved by attempting the installation yourself.

DECKS

An outdoor deck is a standard do-it-yourself project for beginning and advanced remodelers. It provides maximum value for the amount invested and requires a moderate level of expertise to construct. Many building supply stores provide a computerized deck design program to help in determining your design and material costs. If you purchase the materials there, the service is usually free.

The most common decks are low- or high-level decks that are attached to the back of the house. Detached low-level decks are also popular on one-story houses and around pool or patio areas.

Most decks are constructed from planking nailed down with a space between each board for ventilation and drainage. Less common but useful occasionally are solid decks. These decks are made of caulked planking or exterior plywood with a waterproof coating. This kind of deck can serve double duty as both an upper level deck and a roof for a carport or playroom. Sealed decks are hard to build properly and seal thoroughly, so plan carefully before constructing one of these types.

Decks constructed close to the ground are easy to lay out, requiring a minimum foundation — sometimes just concrete blocks set in the ground on solid dirt. This type of deck can be attached to the house at the foundation with nails or lag bolts.

Choosing Deck Materials

All deck materials are readily available at most building supply stores at reasonable cost. Just make sure that you buy material designed to hold up to the rigors of outside use and abuse, such as wind, rain, sunlight, snow and pests. In the past, redwood was a popular deck material. It was very attractive and stood up well to wind and weather. Unfortunately, redwood has become extremely expensive, which may lower your enthusiasm about using this traditional material. Cypress is another

very attractive but expensive material suitable for decks. Consider these materials if you are looking for a distinctive cost-is-no-object project.

Plywood is a common covering material for solid decks, because it is easy to seal and make totally waterproof. A word of caution: Make sure that you use only exterior grade plywood. Exterior grade plywoods use special glues that are resistant to moisture. Plywood decks are notoriously difficult to drain properly, and will quickly succumb to rotting, splitting and termites if constructed out of inferior grade materials or without proper drainage. For a premium quality sealed deck, use marine-grade high-density-overlay plywood with a skid-resistant surface specified.

Currently, the most common deck material is pressure-treated lumber. The wood has been impregnated under pressure with a copper arsenite solution that sinks into the wood, providing a pest and rot proof material that is more than skin deep. The copper solution provides an attractive color and surface and is the ultimate in simplicity for construction. Properly treated lumber can even be buried in moist soil for 20 years or more with little danger of rotting or pests. Choose pieces of lumber that are free from cracks, knots and warping.

Deck Lumber Sizes

The most common lumber sizes for decks are the commonly used framing sizes — 2×4, 2×6 and 2×8. These sizes are so commonly used in house construction that they are very cost effective. The 2-inch thickness of the lumber allows for greater spans between supporting joists than standard 1-inch flooring material. Use 2×4s for the floor decking whenever possible. Any stock wider than 4 inches (such as 2×6) is more susceptible to warping and splitting, and more expensive.

Deck Construction Hints

Proper drainage on a deck is all-important, so avoid construction techniques that allow water to build up and sit on parts of the deck. If the seam between the deck and the house is exposed to weather, cover it with flashing to prevent water from settling in the crack and rotting the siding of the house. On planked decks make sure to leave a drainage gap of at least 1/8 inch between each board. The easiest way to accomplish this is to use a 12d or 16d nail as a spacer when nailing down the boards. The surface of the deck should be slanted slightly away from the house to speed up drainage.

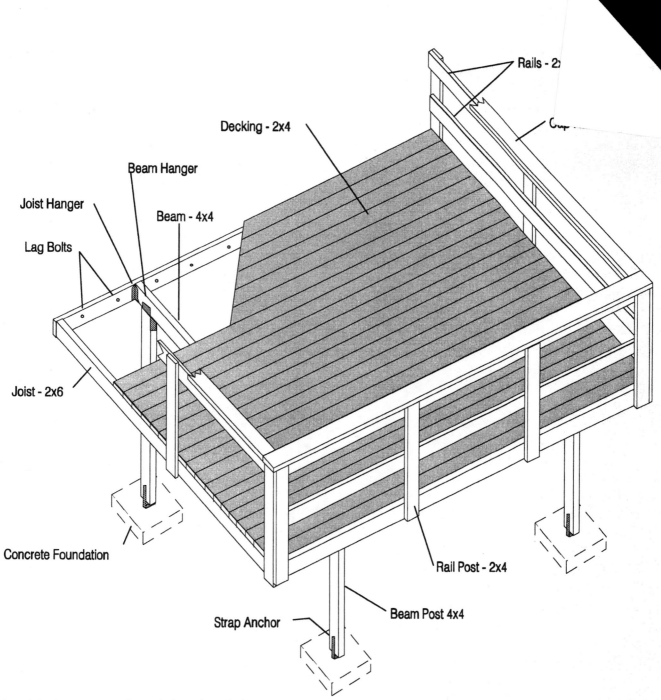

Fig. 29-5. Components of a typical outdoor deck.

Labels on figure: Rails - 2x; Decking - 2x4; Beam Hanger; Joist Hanger; Beam - 4x4; Lag Bolts; Joist - 2x6; Concrete Foundation; Rail Post - 2x4; Beam Post 4x4; Strap Anchor

Galvanized joist hangers will greatly speed up the construction project and are much easier to use than toe-nailing the lumber into adjacent members. This is especially true when attaching the joists to a beam that is bolted to the house. Make sure the joist hangers are exterior grade galvanized to prevent rusting. You should use hot dipped galvanized nails or screws if you want to prevent ugly rust spots around the nail heads. Smooth shank nails often lose their holding power when exposed to wetting and drying cycles. To prevent slippage, use a ring shank or spirally grooved nail.

Deck Foundation

In northern climes, you may need to pour a post foundation. This consists of a deep hole dug below the frost line, usually with a post hole digger, that is filled with concrete. The deck beam is then placed on top of the concrete column. In older construction, the beam is sometimes cast into the concrete. Avoid this technique if possible. The beam is exposed to a lot of moisture and will be difficult to replace if decayed.

The beams underneath the deck should rest securely

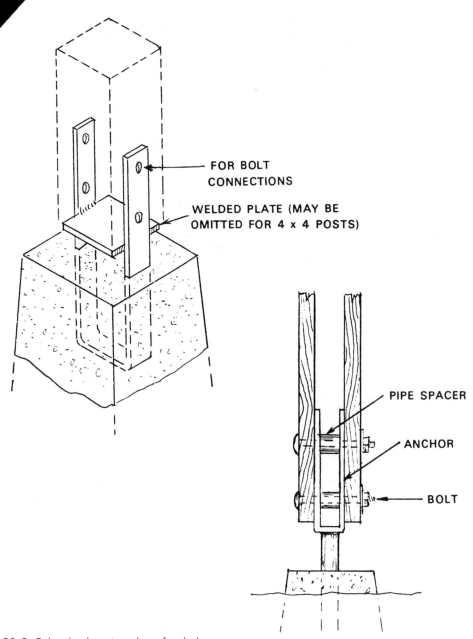

FOR BOLT
CONNECTIONS

WELDED PLATE (MAY BE
OMITTED FOR 4 x 4 POSTS)

PIPE SPACER

ANCHOR

BOLT

Fig. 29-6. Galvanized post anchors for decks.

on concrete foundation piers that have been poured. The piers should extend down to solid ground below the frost line for your area. Securely fasten the post to the foundation so that the post cannot slide laterally off the foundation. Galvanized strap anchors provide a convenient way to secure the deck beam to the foundation. This anchor will keep the beam from shifting or sliding and will keep the end of the beam from contacting the moist ground or foundation. This will keep the end of the beam from rotting. If the deck is close to the ground, you may have trouble with grass and weeds growing up between the boards, with no way to cut or trim them. You can prevent this by covering the ground with a layer of sand or fine gravel.

Safety

Even though constructing a deck is a simple and straightforward project, don't forget that it will become a structural part of your house. Make sure to follow proper construction techniques to insure that your deck structure is securely attached to the house and that proper bracing is applied to the deck posts when needed. If your deck rises more than 3 feet off the ground, you may need to reinforce the construction more carefully. As a rule, any deck more than 6 feet tall that is not securely fastened to the house should have diagonal braces attached between the deck posts.

If possible, fasten the deck securely to the house

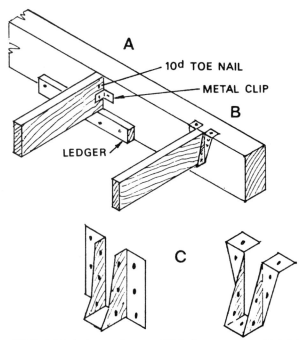

Fig. 29-7. Joists between beams: (A) ledger support; (B) joist hanger support; and (C) joist hangers.

with lag bolts screwed into the foundation or floor frame. Nails are not adequate. Use a lag bolt long enough to penetrate the deck header, house siding, and three-fourths the thickness of the house's framing.

Deck Finishing

Deck surfaces are difficult to paint or stain because of the amount of abuse and foot traffic the surfaces will endure. Common paints and stains wear off the surface, leaving unattractive paths at points of heavy foot traffic. The best coating for a deck consists of transparent or semitransparent water-resistant compounds. This seals the surface and reduces warping, splitting and fading without changing the natural color of the wood.

Pressure-treated wood has been saturated with a decay-resistant compound and may be very moist. Make sure the wood is completely dry before applying penetrating water-resistant compounds so that they can soak into the wood. This can take 6 to 8 weeks or longer in cold weather. If you can purchase the wood ahead of time, find a dry area to stack the lumber, using spacers to allow ventilation. If the lumber has dried for at least 4 weeks, you can coat the underside of the lumber with penetrating finish, since this side will be difficult to reach after installation. Leave the other side uncoated so the lumber can continue to dry after installation. Apply the final coat to the exposed lumber after it has completely dried. See chapter eighteen.

PORCH CONVERSION STEPS

1. Inspect foundation, floor framing and porch floor for rotting, termites, warping and inadequate support.

2. Conduct the standard bidding process for any structural repairs to the porch foundation. This may require tearing out the existing porch, building supports for the roof, removing the old foundation and installing a new foundation. Make sure the roof is adequately supported while the new foundation is installed

3. Purchase and store new framing members and support members, if any.

4. Rent or purchase floor jacks and steel I beams for support of roof. Jack up the structure slowly to prevent further warping or cracking. Attach temporary roof supports at each corner, angling them like a teepee so they will not obstruct the installation of the new foundation.

5. Pour new foundation. Allow 2 to 5 days for curing. Make sure to locate foundation below the frostline for your area. Since the new foundation is not tied into the regular foundation, it must be stable and protected from settling.

6. Replace porch floor joists and subfloor. See chapter twelve for more details.

7. Pay concrete/foundation sub, requiring a signed affidavit.

Closing in the Porch

1. Schedule framer to install walls.

2. Remove existing steps from porch unless the closed-in porch will have an access door to the outside.

3. Remove existing exterior siding from porch area. This siding will be replaced with the interior finish of the enclosure, usually drywall. Also, remove the trim around the roof soffit and exterior siding.

4. Build partition walls. Set walls in place and gently remove the roof supports.

5. Install exterior sheathing and siding. See chapter twenty-one for more information. Replace the original soffit and siding trim. Since the new siding will not match the original, plan to repaint the siding when the project is complete.

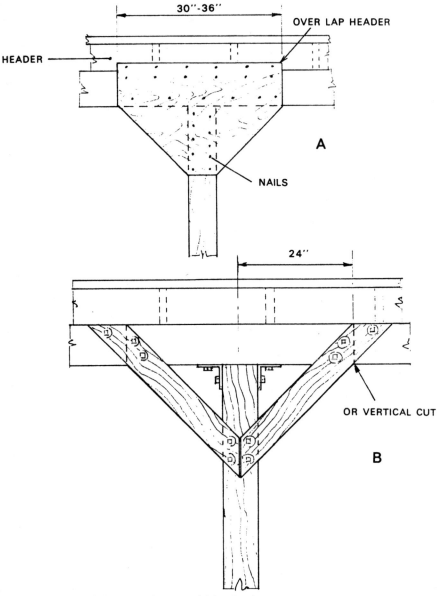

Fig. 29-8. Partial braces: (A) plywood gusset; (B) lumber brace.

6. Install windows, fixed glass and doors.

7. Install rough-in electrical. Run wiring for new overhead light fixtures and ceiling fans.

8. Inspect rough-in plumbing, electrical and HVAC.

9. Install interior insulation and vapor barrier.

10. Install drywall on walls and ceiling. If you are installing drywall on the existing ceiling surface, you can use construction adhesive and drywall screws for a secure application.

11. Finish drywall with joint tape and compound. This will require three coats. See chapter nineteen for more details.

12. Paint walls and ceiling.

13. Install flooring. Ceramic tile makes an excellent surface for a sunroom. The tile will absorb solar energy

> **NOTE:** To save time and energy, paint the walls before installing trim and flooring. This avoids the tedious masking step. Walls and ceilings can be painted very quickly with a paint sprayer or power roller. Paint the primer coat on trim before installing. See chapter eighteen for more details.

during the day and reradiate it at night. Hardwood flooring and carpet can also be used.

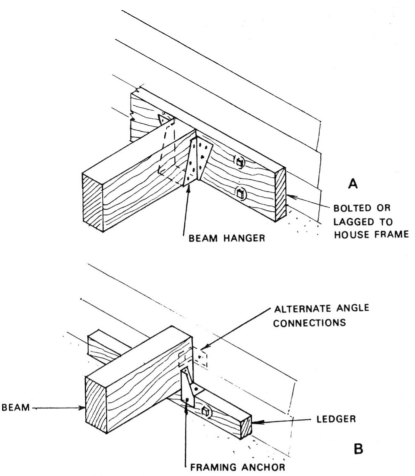

BOLTED OR
LAGGED TO
HOUSE FRAME

A

BEAM HANGER

ALTERNATE ANGLE
CONNECTIONS

BEAM

LEDGER

FRAMING ANCHOR

B

Fig. 29-9. Beam to house: (A) beam hanger; (B) ledger support.

14. Caulk all joints on exterior siding, openings and trim.

15. Paint newly installed exterior siding. You can probably bargain for a better price if you have the painter complete the exterior at the same time as the interior painting.

16. Install interior trim.

17. Finish painting trim.

18. Install lighting, electrical fixtures and ceiling fans. See chapter fourteen.

19. Turn on electric utilities.

20. Install floor trim or quarter-round trim.

21. Pay carpenter/framer, requiring a signed affidavit.

DECK CONSTRUCTION STEPS

1. Examine the building site carefully, taking into consideration the height of the deck in relation to the house and surrounding lot. Decks high above the ground will require larger supporting posts and perhaps cross bracing. Take this into consideration when ordering material.

2. Draw a complete plan for the deck.

3. Purchase materials for deck, including nails, hangers, lumber and concrete for footings. Lay out the lumber so it can balance its moisture content with the local humidity. Store ready-mix concrete inside or under a protective plastic cover to keep it from getting wet.

4. Remove any existing deck or porch that is not to be assimilated into the new design.

5. Lay out the deck design with string and stakes to locate the position of posts and concrete piers. Measure the diagonal distances from corner to corner of the layout to square up the design. The diagonal distances should be the same from corner to corner.

6. Dig footings and pour concrete piers. Place the tops of the piers slightly above the height of the sur-

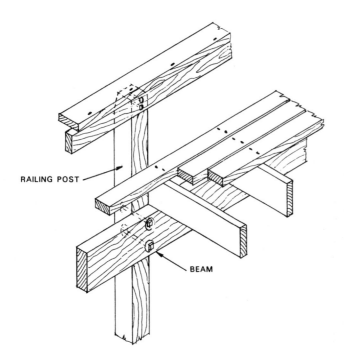

Fig. 29-10. Cross bracing and decking applied to deck.

rounding terrain to prevent water from collecting around the piers. The hole itself can function as the form for the pier. Use 1 × 4s at the top of the hole as forms to extend the concrete pier above ground level and to provide a smoother surface on the exposed part of the pier. Insert any imbedded-type post anchors into the concrete while it is still wet.

7. Pull a leveling line from corner to corner at the finish height of the deck and mark each corner post. The leveling line can be made with string and a string level or by using a garden hose. When using the garden hose, brace the posts in place and strap the ends of the garden hose to the posts. Fill the hose with water and adjust each end of the hose until each end is full of water all the way to the top. Keep adding water until this is accomplished. Since water always seeks its own level, this method produces very accurate results. Then mark the posts at each end of the hose. When marking the posts, make sure to allow for the height of the anchor plate that will attach the post to the concrete pier.

8. Install posts on pier anchors and make sure that they align with each other and are plumb. Use a carpenter's level to adjust the posts. Attach temporary braces to the posts to hold them in position.

9. Attach deck beams to the posts with lag bolts or galvanized beam hangers. This operation will take at least two people to position and attach the beams.

Make sure the structure remains square as you attach each corner of the deck together.

10. Install flashing on the tops of the beams where the beam and post are joined. This will keep rain from soaking the end grain of the post.

11. Mount the joist header to the house by running lag or stove bolts through the header, siding and the header of the house. Make sure to install a drip cap or flashing on top of the header to prevent standing water from accumulating between the header and the siding. The header should be placed so that the deck will slope away from the house slightly for better drainage.

12. Place the remaining headers on top of the beams and tie them together with bolts or angle irons.

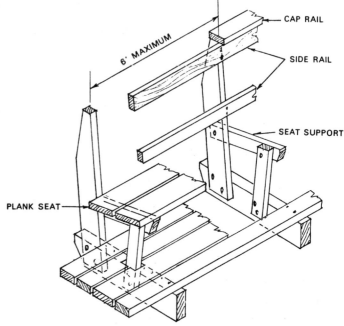

Fig. 29-11. Deck bench.

13. Install joists between the resulting frame with joist hangers or by resting them on ledgers nailed to the joist headers.

14. Mount cross bracing between the posts if the height of the deck is greater than 5 feet. This will strengthen the deck against side-to-side movement. Use 2 × 4s for the bracing and attach them to the posts and joist header with galvanized stove bolts.

15. Apply the deck boards to the joists with galvanized deck nails or screws. The best nails for the job are ring shank or spiral groove. Decking screws have become very popular recently for several reasons. They

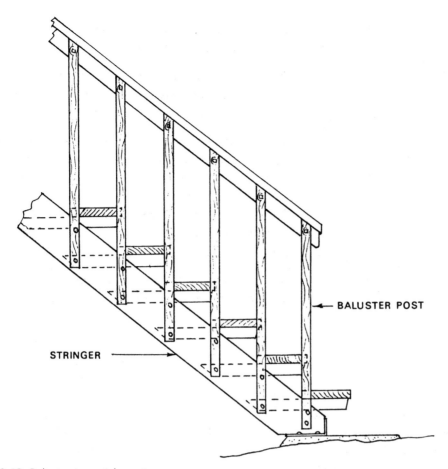

Fig. 29-12. Baluster-type stair posts.

BALUSTER POST

STRINGER

have greater gripping power and can pull a warped board into alignment during installation. They have the added benefit of being removed easily. If one of the deck boards warps or splits, simply unscrew and replace it with a new board. As the deck boards dry out, you can easily go back and re-tighten the deck screws to maintain a snug fit.

Leave a gap between each board for better drainage. The easiest way to do this is to use a 12d or 16d nail as a spacer. If the moisture content of the wood is high, leave a smaller gap—it will enlarge as the board dries and shrinks. Don't worry about cutting the exact length of each deck board. Leave a little extra hanging over the header joist.

16. Saw the deck boards flush with the header joist with a power saw after all boards are installed. This is much quicker, especially if you installed the deck boards diagonally. Pull a chalk line parallel to the header joist and follow the line with the power saw. This will give you a straight and accurate line.

17. Attach stairway stringers to header joist with galvanized strapping and mount the other ends of the stringers to the concrete piers with post anchors.

18. Install the treads between the stringers.

19. Install post rails around the perimeter of the deck and down the stair stringers. Attach the cap rails to the top of the posts.

20. Treat the deck with two coats of water-resistant wood preservative. Apply the second coat after the first coat has soaked in but before it has dried. This will ensure that the second coat can soak into the wood completely.

DECK MATERIAL ESTIMATE

DESCRIPTION	SPECIFICATION	QTY.	UNIT	COST	TAX	TOTAL COST	COST TYPE	VENDOR
Fasteners								
Bolts, lag — ⅜″ × 3″ long								
Galvanized joist hangers — 18 gauge								
Galvanized beam hangers — 18 gauge								
Galvanized strap anchors								
Nails — No. 10 galvanized deck								
Screws — galvanized deck								
Pressure-treated lumber								
Beam — 4 × 4								
Header joists — 2 × 8								
Joists — 2 × 6								
Deck board — 2 × 4								
Cap rail — 2 × 6								
Rail posts — 2 × 4								
Rails — 2 × 4								
Miscellaneous								
Waterproofing sealant								
Concrete for piers — ready mix								

PORCH MATERIAL ESTIMATE

DESCRIPTION	SPECIFICATION	QTY.	UNIT	COST	TAX	TOTAL COST	COST TYPE	VENDOR
Framing								
Subfloor ⅝-inch tongue-and-grooved								
Subfloor ¾-inch tongue-and-grooved								
Underlayment								
Plates—2×4								
8-foot studs—2×4								
10-foot studs—2×4								
Bracing								
Framing—Nails								
12d common								
10d common								
8d common								
Concrete nails								
8d galvanized casing								
3d finish								
4d finish								
6d finish								
Insulation								
Walls								
Ceiling								
Vapor barrier—6-mil poly								

PORCH MATERIAL ESTIMATE

DESCRIPTION	SPECIFICATION	QTY.	UNIT	COST	TAX	TOTAL COST	COST TYPE	VENDOR
Component Costs								
Interior trim								
Fixed glass								
Windows								
Doors								
Flooring								
Lighting fixtures								
Paint								
Drywall								
Labor								
Sunroom installation — contract								
Foundation — contract								
Electrical — contract								
Framing/carpentry — contract								

Acid. Cleaning agent used to clean brick.

Acrylic resin. A thermoplastic resin used in latex coatings. *See also* Latex paint.

Aggregate. Irregular-shaped gravel suspended in cement.

Air chamber. Pipe appendage with trapped air added to a line to serve as a shock absorber to retard or eliminate air hammer.

Air-dried. Dried by exposure to air, usually in a yard, without artificial heat.

Alkyd resin. One of a large group of synthetic resins used in making latex paints.

Amperage. The amount of current flow in a wire. Similar to the amount of water flowing in a pipe.

Apron. Trim used at base of windows. Also used as base to build out crown molding.

Asphalt. Base ingredient of asphalt shingles and roofing paper (felt composition saturated in asphalt base).

Attic ventilators. In houses, screened openings provided to ventilate an attic space. *See also* Louver.

Backfill. Process of placing soil up against foundation after all necessary foundation treatments have been performed. In many instances, the foundation wall must have temporary interior bracing or house must be framed in to support the weight of dirt until it has had time to settle.

Backflow. The flow of water or other fluids or materials into the distributing source of potable water from any source other than intended.

Backsplash. A small strip (normally 3 or 4 inches high) placed against the wall and resting on the back of a countertop, normally used to protect the wall from water and stains.

Baluster. Small vertical member in a railing, between a top rail and a stair tread or bottom rail. Vertical trim used in quantity to support staircase railings not supported by a wall.

Band. Decorative trim around windows and doors and horizontal relief; normally 2×4 or 2×6.

Base cabinet. A cabinet resting on the floor at waist level, supporting a countertop or an appliance.

Base coat. First coat of paint put on drywall, normally a very light color. Should also be put on prior to wallpaper so that the paper can be removed easily.

Base molding. Molding used to trim the upper edge of interior baseboards.

Base or baseboard. A board placed against the wall around a room next to the floor to finish properly the area between the floor and wall.

Base shoe. Molding used next to the floor on interior baseboards. Sometimes called a carpet strip.

Batten. Narrow strips of wood used to cover joints or as decorative vertical members over plywood or wide boards.

Batter board. A pair of horizontal boards nailed to vertical posts set at the corners of an excavation area used to indicate the desired level of excavation. Also used for fastening taut strings to indicate outlines of the foundation walls.

Bay window. Any window that projects out from the walls of the structure.

Bead. Any corner or edge that must be finished off with stucco.

Beam. A structural framing member of wood or metal used to support a load placed at right angles to the beam—usually floor joists.

Bearing partition. A partition that supports any vertical load in addition to its own weight.

Bend. Any change in direction of a line.

Blind-nailing. Nailing in such a way that the nail heads are not visible on the face of the work—usually at the tongue or matched boards.

Board foot. A unit of measurement equal to a piece of wood 1 inch thick and 1 foot square. Thickness × length × width equals board feet.

Boston ridge. A method of applying asphalt or wood shingles at the ridge or at the hips of a roof as a finish.

Brace. A diagonal piece of framing lumber applied to wall or floor to stiffen the structure. Often used on walls as temporary bracing until framing has been completed.

Brick veneer. A facing of brick that covers and is fastened to the sheathing of a framed wall.

Bridging. Diagonal metal or wood cross braces installed between joists to prevent twisting and to spread the load to adjoining joists.

BTU. British thermal unit. A standard unit of hot or cold air output.

Builder's level. A surveying tool consisting of an optical siting scope and a measuring stick. It is used to check the level of batter boards and foundation.

Building drain. The common artery of the drainage system that receives the discharge from other drainage pipes inside the building and conveys it to the sewer system outside the building.

Building sewer. That part of the drainage system extending from the building drain to a public or private sewer system.

Building supply. The pipe carrying potable water from the water meter or other water source to points of distribution throughout the building and lot.

Built-up roof. A roofing composed of three to five layers of asphalt felt laminated with coat tar, pitch or asphalt. The top is finished with crushed slag or gravel. Generally used on flat or low-pitched roofs.

Bulkhead. Vertical drop in footing when changing from one depth to another.

Bull. A covering for a wide soil stack so that rain will not enter.

Can. Recessed lighting fixture.

Cant strip. A piece of lumber triangular in cross section, used at the junction of a flat deck and a wall to avoid a sharp bend and possible cracking of the covering that is applied over it.

Cap molding. Trim applied to the top of base molding.

Cap. Hardware used to terminate any line.

Casement frames and sash. Frames of wood or metal enclosing part or all of the sash, which may be opened by means of hinges affixed to the vertical edges.

Casement window. A window that swings out to the side on hinges.

Casing nails. Used to apply finish trim and millwork. Nail head is small and is set below the surface of the wood to hide it.

Casing. Molding of various widths and thicknesses used to trim door and window openings at the jambs.

Caulk. To make a seam watertight by filling it with a waterproofing compound.

Center set. Standard holes for a standard faucet set.

Chair rail. Molding applied to the walls, normally at hip level.

Checking. Fissures that appear with age in many exterior paints. They are superficial at first, but in time they may penetrate entirely through the coating.

Circuit breaker. A device to ensure that electric current overloads do not occur by breaking the circuit when a dangerous overload or short circuit occurs.

Clean-out. A sealed opening in a pipe which can be screwed off to unclog the line if necessary.

Clear. Fine-textured millwork with no knots or other major imperfections.

Collar beam. Nominal 1- or 2-inch-thick members connecting opposite roof rafters. They serve to stiffen the roof structure.

Compressor. Component of the central air-conditioning system that sits outside of dwelling.

Condensation. In a building, beads or drops of water (and frequently frost in extremely cold weather) that accumulate on the inside of the exterior covering of a building when warm, moisture-laden air from the interior reaches a point where the temperature no longer permits the air to sustain the moisture it holds. Use of louvers or attic ventilators will reduce moisture condensation in attics. A vapor barrier under the gypsum lath or dry wall on exposed walls will reduce condensation in them.

Conduit. Metal pipe used to run wiring through when extra protection of wiring is needed or wiring is to be exposed.

Construction, frame. A type of construction in which the structural parts are wood or depend upon a wood frame for support. In codes, if masonry veneer is applied to the exterior walls, the classification of this type of construction is usually unchanged.

Coped joint. *See* Scribing.

Corbel. Extending a course or courses of bricks beyond the face of a wall. No course should extend more than 2 inches beyond the course below it. Total corbeling projection should not exceed wall thickness.

Corian. An artificial material simulating marble manufactured by Corning.

Corner bead. A strip of formed sheet metal, sometimes combined with a strip of metal lath, placed on corners before plastering to reinforce them. Also, a strip of wood finish three-quarters-round or angular placed over a plastered corner for protection.

Corner boards. Used as trim for the external corners of a house or other frame structure against which the ends of the siding are finished.

Corner braces. Diagonal braces at the corners of frame structure to stiffen and strengthen the wall.

Cornice. Overhang of a pitched roof at the eave line, usually consisting of a fascia board, a soffit for a closed cornice and appropriate moldings. The cornice may be flush with the siding or may overhang the siding by as much as 2 feet.

Cornice return. That portion of the cornice that returns on the gable end of a house.

Counterflashing. A flashing usually used on chimneys at the roof line to cover shingle flashing and to prevent moisture entry.

Countersink. To set the head of a nail or screw at or below the surface.

Course. (a) A horizontal row of shingles. (b) A horizontally laid set of bricks. A 32-course wall with ⅜-inch mortar joints stands 7 feet tall.

Cove molding. A molding with a concave face used as trim or to finish interior corners.

Coverage. The maximum number of shingles that overlap in any one spot. This determines the degree of weather performance a roof has.

CPVC. Chlorinated polyvinyl chloride. A flexible form of water pipe suitable for hot and cold water. No soldering involved.

Crawl space. A shallow space below a living area where no basement is used, normally enclosed by the foundation wall.

Creosote. A distillate of coal tar produced by high temperature carbonization of bituminous coal; it consists principally of liquid and solid aromatic hydrocarbons used as a wood preservative.

Cricket. A sloped area at the intersection of a vertical surface and the roof, such as a chimney. Used to channel off water that might otherwise get trapped behind the vertical structure.

Cripple. A short stud used as bracing under windows and other structural framing. A stud that does not extend full height.

Crown molding. The trim piece that tops off the trim on a vertical structure. Usually refers to the more ornamental pieces of cornice trim. Can also refer to the ornamental trim applied between the fascia and the roof.

Crusher run. Crushed stone with sharp edges, normally up to 2 or 3 inches in size. Used for driveway and foundation support as a base. Very stable surface, as opposed to gravel, which is not very stable.

Cube. A standard ordering unit for masonry block units (6′ × 6′ × 8′).

d. *See* Penny.

Dado. A rectangular groove across the width of a board or plank. In interior decoration, a special type of wall treatment.

Damper. A metal flap controlling the flow of conditioned air through ductwork.

Dead load. Load imposed by the weight of the materials that make up the structure. The total weight of walls, floors and roof bearing on the structure.

Decay. Disintegration of wood or other substance through the action of fungi.

Deck paint. An enamel with a high degree of resistance to mechanical wear, designed for use on such surfaces as porch floors.

Density. The mass of a substance in unit volume. When expressed in the metric system, it is numerically equal to the specific gravity of the same substance.

Dentil molding. A special type of crown molding with an even pattern of teeth.

Dewpoint. Temperature at which a vapor begins to deposit as a liquid. Applies especially to water in the atmosphere.

Dimension. *See* Lumber, dimension.

Direct nailing. To nail perpendicular to the initial surface or to the junction of the pieces joined. Also known as *face nailing*.

Door jamb, interior. The surrounding case into which and out of which a door closes and opens. It consists of two upright pieces, called side jambs, and a horizontal head jamb.

Dormer. An opening in a sloping roof, the framing of which projects out to form a vertical wall suitable for windows or other openings.

Downspout. A pipe, usually of metal, for carrying rainwater from roof gutters.

Drag time. Time required to haul heavy excavation equipment to and from the site.

Dressed and matched (tongue-and-grooved). Boards or planks machined in such a manner that there is a groove on one edge and a corresponding tongue on the other.

Dressed size. Dimensions of lumber after planing smooth.

Dried in. Term describing the framed structure after the roof deck and protective tar paper have been installed.

Drip cap. A molding placed on the exterior top side of a door or window frame to cause water to drip beyond the outside of the frame.

Drip edge. Metal flashing normally 3 inches wide that goes on the eave and rakes to provide a precise point for water to drip from so the cornice does not rot.

Drywall. Interior covering material, usually gypsum board with a paper finish, which is applied in large sheets or panels. The joints are then finished with a

joint compound. Has replaced plaster as the most common interior wall finish.

Ducts. Round or rectangular metal pipes for distributing warm air from the heating unit to rooms, or air from a conditioning device or as cold air returns.

Eaves. The portion of the roof that extends beyond the outside walls of the house. They provide visual separation of the roof and wall and protect siding and windows from rain.

EER (Energy Efficiency Rating). A national rating required to be displayed on appliances measuring their efficient use of electrical power.

Elastomeric. Having elastic, rubberlike properties.

Elbow. (a) A section of line that is used to change directions. Normally at right angles. (b) Ductwork joint used to turn supply or return at any angle. (c) Trough corner extending outward from roof.

Enamel. Oil base paint used in high-soil areas such as trim and doors.

Exhaust. Air saturated with carbon dioxide, the by-product of natural gas combustion in a forced-air gas system. This exhaust is usually vented directly out the top of the roof and is dangerous to breathe.

Expansion joint. A joint or gap between concrete structures to allow for expansion and contraction of the structures without cracking.

Exposure. The vertical length of exposed shingle (portion not lapped by the shingle above).

Face nailing. Nailing applied perpendicular to the members. Also known as *direct nailing*.

Fascia. A flat board, band or face, used sometimes by itself but usually in combination with moldings, often located at the outer face of the cornice.

Feathering. Successive coats of drywall compound applied to joints. Each successive pass should widen the compound joint.

Felt. Typical shingle underlayment. Also known as roofing felt or tar paper. *See also* Asphalt.

Ferrule. Aluminum sleeve used in attaching trough to gutter spike.

Fill dirt. Loose dirt. Normally dirt brought in from another location to fill a void. Sturdier than topsoil used under slabs, drives, and sidewalks.

Filler. Putty or other pasty material used to fill nail holes prior to painting or staining.

Filler (wood). A heavily pigmented preparation used for filling and leveling off the pores in open-pored woods.

Finger joint. Trim composed of many small scrap pieces by a joint resembling two sets of interlocking fingers. This trim is often used to reduce costs where such trim will be painted.

Finish grade. Final process of leveling and smoothing topsoil into final position prior to landscaping.

Fire stop. A solid, tight closure of a concealed space, placed to prevent the spread of fire and smoke through such a space. In a frame wall, this will usually consist of 2×4 cross blocking between studs.

Furring. Long strips of wood attached to walls or ceilings to allow attachment of drywall or ceiling tiles. Furring out refers to adding furring strips to a wall to bring it out further into a room. Furring down refers to using furring strips to lower a ceiling.

Fishplate. A wood or plywood piece used to fasten the ends of two members together at a butt joint with nails or bolts. Sometimes used at the junction of opposite rafters near the ridge line.

Fixture. Any end point in a plumbing system used as a source of potable water. Fixtures normally include sinks, tubs, showers, spigots, sprinkler systems, washer connections and other related items.

Flashing. Galvanized sheet metal used as a lining around joints between shingles and chimneys, exhaust and ventilation vents and other protrusions in the roof deck. Flashing helps prevent water from seeping under the shingles.

Flat paint. An interior paint that contains a high proportion of pigment and dries to a flat or lusterless finish.

Float. To spread drywall compound smooth.

Floating. A process used after screeding to provide a smoother surface. The process normally involves embedding larger aggregate below the surface by vibrating, removing imperfections and high and low spots, and compacting the surface concrete.

Flue lining. Fire clay or terra-cotta pipe, round or square, usually made in all ordinary flue sizes and in 2-foot lengths, used for the inner lining of chimneys with the brick or masonry work around the outside. Flue lining in chimney runs from about a foot below the flue connection to the top of the chimney.

Flue. The space or passage in a chimney through which smoke, gas or fumes ascend. Each passage is called a flue, which together with any others and the surrounding masonry make up the chimney.

Fly rafters. End rafters of the gable overhang supported by roof sheathing and lookouts.

Footing ditch. Trough area dug to accommodate concrete or footing forms.

Footing. A masonry section, usually concrete, in a rectangular form wider than the bottom of the foundation wall or pier it supports. Lowest perimeter portion of a structure resting on firm soil or rock that supports the weight of the structure.

Foundation. The supporting portion of a structure below the first-floor construction, or below grade, including the footings.

Framing, balloon. A system of framing a building in which all vertical structural elements of the bearing walls and partitions consist of single pieces extending from the top of the foundation sill plate to the roof plate to which all floor joists are fastened.

Framing, platform. A system of framing a building in which floor joists of each story rest on top plates of the story below or on the foundation sill for the first story, and the bearing walls and partitions rest on the subfloor of each story.

Freon. A special liquid used by an air-conditioning compressor to move heat in or out of the dwelling. This fluid circulates in a closed system. This fluid is also used in refrigerators and freezers.

Frieze. A vertical piece of wood used with or without molding to top off the intersection of the siding and the cornice. Frieze boards may be anywhere from 4 to 12 inches wide.

Frostline. The depth of frost penetration in soil. This depth varies in different parts of the country. Footings should be placed below this depth to prevent movement.

Fungi, wood. Microscopic plants that live in damp wood and cause mold, stain and decay.

Fungicide. A chemical that is poisonous to fungi.

Furring. Strips of wood or metal applied to a wall or other surface to even it and normally to serve as a fastening base for finish material.

Gable. The vertical part of the exterior wall that extends from the eaves upward to the peak or ridge of the roof.

Gem box. A metal box installed in electrical rough-in that holds outlets, receptacles and other electrical units.

GFI (Ground Fault Interrupter). An extra-sensitive circuit breaker usually installed in outlets in bathrooms and exterior locations to provide additional protection against shock. Required now by most building codes.

Girder. A large or principal beam of wood or steel used to support concentrated loads at isolated points along its length.

Gloss (paint or enamel). A paint or enamel that contains a relatively low proportion of pigment and dries to a sheen or luster.

Gooseneck. A section of staircase trim that has a curve in it.

Grading. Process of shaping the surface of a lot to give it the desired contours. *See also* Finish grade.

Grain, edge (vertical). Edge-grain lumber has been sawed parallel to the pitch of the log and approximately at right angles to the growth rings; i.e., the rings form an angle of 45 degrees or more with the surface of the piece. *See also* Grain, quartersawn.

Grain, flat. Flat-grain lumber has been sawed parallel to the pitch of the log and approximately tangent to the growth rings; i.e., the rings form an angle of less than 45 degrees with the surface of the piece.

Grain. The direction of the fibers in the wood.

Grounds. Guides used around openings and at the floor line to strike off plaster. They can consist of narrow strips of wood or of wide subjambs at interior doorways. They provide a level plaster line for installation of casing and other trim.

Grout. Mortar made of such consistency (by adding water) that it will just flow into the joints and cavities of the masonry work and fill them solid.

Grouted. Filled with a mortar thin enough to fill the spaces in the concrete or ground around the object being set.

Gusset. A plywood or similar type member used to provide a connection at intersection of wood members. Most commonly used at joints of wood trusses. They are fastened by nails, screws, bolts or adhesives.

Gutter or eave trough. A shallow channel or conduit of metal or wood set below and along the eaves of a house to catch and carry off rainwater from the roof.

Gypsum board. Same as drywall.

Gypsum plaster. Gypsum formulated to be used with the addition of sand and water for base-coat plaster.

Hang. To hang drywall is to nail it in place.

Head lap. Length (inches) of the amount of overlap between shingles (measured vertically).

Header. (a) A beam placed perpendicular to joists and to which joists are nailed in framing for chimney, stairway or other openings. (b) A wood lintel. (c) One or two pieces of lumber installed over doors and windows to support the load above the opening.

Heartwood. Older wood from the central portion of the tree. As this wood dies, it undergoes chemical changes that often impart a resistance to decay and a darkening in color.

Hip. The external angle formed by the meeting of two sloping sides of a roof.

Hip roof. A roof that rises by inclined planes from all four sides of a building.

Hot wire. A wire carrying electric current.

Humidifier. A device designed to increase the humidity within a room or a house by means of the discharge of water vapor. It may consist of individual room-size units or larger units attached to the heating plant to condition the entire house.

HVAC. A common abbreviation for heating, ventilation and air-conditioning.

Hydration. The chemical process wherein portland cement becomes a bonding agent as water is slowly removed from the mixture. The rate of hydration determines the strength of the bond and hence the strength of the concrete. Hydration stops when all the water has been removed. Once hydration stops, it cannot be restarted.

Inside miter. Trough corner extending toward roof.

Insulation board, rigid. A structural building board made of coarse wood or cane fiber in ½- or 25/32-inch thicknesses. It can be obtained in various size sheets, in various densities and with several treatments.

Insulation, thermal. Any material high in resistance to heat transmission that, when placed in the walls, ceiling or floors of a structure, will reduce the rate of heat flow.

Jack post. A hollow metal post with a jack screw in one end so that it can be adjusted to the desired height.

Jack rafter. A rafter that spans the distance from the wall plate to a hip, or from a valley to a ridge.

Jamb. The side and head lining of a doorway, window or other opening.

Joint cement. A powder that is usually mixed with water and used for joint treatment in gypsum-wallboard finish. Often called *spackle*.

Joint. (a) Mortar in between bricks or blocks. (b) The space between the adjacent surfaces of two members of components joined and held together by nails, glue, cement, mortar or other means.

Joist. One of a series of parallel beams, usually 2 inches in thickness, used to support floor and ceiling loads and supported in turn by larger beams, girders or bearing walls.

Kerf. The area of a board removed by the saw when cutting. Vertical notch or cut made in a batter board where a string is fastened tightly.

Key. Fancy decorative lintel above window made of brick, normally placed on various angles for a flared effect. Also known as a *keystone*.

Kiln-dried. Dried in a kiln with the use of artificial heat.

Knot. In lumber, the portion of a branch or limb of a tree that appears on the edge or face of the piece.

Lag screws. Large screws with heads designed to be turned with a wrench.

Laminate. Any thin material, such as plastic or fine wood, glued to the exterior of the cabinet.

Laminated beam. A very strong beam created from several smaller pieces of wood that have been glued together under heat and pressure.

Latex paint. Water soluble paint. Normally recommended because of ease of use for interior work.

Lath. A building material of wood, metal, gypsum or insulating board that is fastened to the frame of a building to act as a plaster base. A grid of some sort (normally metal or fiberglass) applied to exterior sheathing as a base for stucco.

Ledger strip. A strip of lumber nailed along the bottom of the side of a girder on which joists rest.

Let-in brace. Nominal 1-inch-thick boards applied into notched studs diagonally.

Line. Any section of plumbing whether it is copper, PVC, CPVC or cast iron.

Lineal foot. A measure of lumber based on the actual length of the piece.

Lintel. A horizontal structural member that supports the load over an opening such as a door or window. A section of precast concrete placed over doors and windows to support the weight of the bricks above the opening.

Liquified gas. A carrier of wood preservatives, this is a hydrocarbon that is a gas at atmospheric pressure but one that can be liquefied at moderate pressures (similar to propane).

Live load. Load superimposed on the structure by occupancy, furniture, snow, etc.

Load-bearing wall. Any wall that supports the weight of other structural members.

Lookout. The horizontal board (usually a 2 × 4 or 1 × 4) that connects the ends of the rafters to the siding. This board becomes the base for nailing on the soffit covering.

Louver. An opening with a series of horizontal slats so arranged as to permit ventilation, but to exclude rain, sunlight or vision. *See also* Attic ventilators.

Lumber. Lumber is the product of the sawmill and planing mill not further manufactured other than by sawing, re-sawing and passing lengthwise through a standard planing machine, crosscutting to length and marching.

Lumber, board. Yard lumber less than 2 inches thick and 2 or more inches wide.

Lumber, dimension. Yard lumber from 2 inches to, but not including, 5 inches thick and 2 or more inches wide. Includes joists, rafter, studs, plank and small timbers.

Lumber, dressed size. The dimension of lumber after shrinking from green dimension and after machining to size or pattern.

Lumber, matched. Lumber that is dressed and shaped on one edge in a grooved pattern and on the other in a tongued pattern.

Lumber, shiplap. Lumber that is edge-dressed to make a close rabbeted or lapped joint.

Lumber, yard. Lumber of those grades, sizes and patterns that are generally intended for ordinary construction, such as framework and rough coverage of houses.

Lumber timbers. Yard lumber 5 or more inches in least dimension. Includes beams, stringer, posts, caps, sills, girders and purlins.

Mantel. The shelf above a fireplace. Also refers to the decorative trim around a fireplace opening.

Masonry. Stone, brick, concrete, hollow-tile, concrete block, gypsum block or other similar building units or materials or a combination of the same, bonded together with mortar to form a wall, pier, buttress or similar mass.

Mastic. A pasty material used as a cement (as for setting tile) or a protective coating (as for thermal insulation or waterproofing).

Metal lath. Sheets of metal that are slit and drawn out to form openings. Used as a plaster base for walls and ceilings and as reinforcing over other forms of plaster base.

Millwork. Generally all building materials made of finished wood and manufactured in millwork plants and planing mills are included under the term. Millwork includes such items as inside and outside doors, window and door frames, blinds, porch-work, mantels, panel-work, stairways, moldings and interior trim.

Miter box. Special guide and saw used to cut trim lumber at precise angles.

Miter joint. A diagonal joint, normally 45 degrees, formed at the intersection of two pieces of molding.

Moisture content of wood. Weight of the water contained in the wood, usually expressed as a percentage of the weight of oven dry wood.

Molding. Decorative strips of wood or other material applied to wall joints and surfaces as a decorative accent. Molding does not have any structural value.

Mud. Slang for spackle or drywall compound. Used to seal joints and hide nail-head dimples.

Mullion. A vertical bar or divider in the frame between windows, doors or other openings.

Muntin. A small member that divides the glass or openings of sash or doors.

Natural finish. A transparent finish that does not seriously alter the original color or grain of the natural wood.

Neoprene. A synthetic rubber characterized by superior resistance to oils, gasoline and sunlight.

Nominal size. Original size of lumber when cut.

Nonleachable. Not dissolved and removed by the action of rain or other water.

Nonbearing wall. A wall supporting no load other than its own weight.

Nosing. The projecting edge of a molding or drip. Usually applied to the projecting molding on the edge of a stair tread.

O.C. (on center). The measurement of spacing for studs, rafters, joists and the like in a building from the center of one member to the center of the next. Normally refers to wall or joist framing of 12, 16 or 18 inches O.C.

Outrigger. An extension of a rafter beyond the wall line. Usually a smaller member nailed to a larger rafter to form a cornice or roof overhang.

Paint grade. Millwork of quality intended for a painted finish. Not as fine as stain grade.

Panel. In house construction, a thin flat piece of wood, plywood or similar material, framed by stiles and rails as in a door, or fitted into grooves of thicker material with molded edges for decorative wall treatment.

Paper, building. A general term, without reference to properties or uses, for papers, felts and similar sheet materials used in buildings.

Paper, sheathing. A building material, generally paper or felt, used in wall and roof construction as a protection against the passage of air and sometimes moisture.

Parging. Thin coatings (¼ inch) of mortar applied to the exterior face of concrete block where block wall and footing meet; serves as a waterproofing mechanism.

Parting stop or strip. A small wood piece used in the side and head jambs of double-hung windows to separate upper and lower sashes.

Partition. An interior wall in a framed structure dividing two spaces. A wall that subdivides spaces within any story of a building.

Penny. As applied to nails, it originally indicated the price per hundred. The term now serves as a measure of nail length and is abbreviated by the abbreviation d, as in 16d nails.

Pentachlorophenol (penta). A chlorinated phenol, usually in petroleum oil, used as a wood preservative.

Perm. A measure of water vapor movement through a material (grains per square foot per hour per inch of mercury difference in vapor pressure).

Pier. A column of masonry, usually rectangular in horizontal cross section, used to support other structural members.

Pigment. A powdered solid in suitable degree of subdivision for use in paint or enamel.

Pitch. The incline slope of a roof or the ratio of the total rise to the total width of a house; i.e., an 8-foot rise and 24-foot width is a one-third pitch roof. Roof slope is expressed in the inches of rise per foot of run. Example: A 10/12 pitch indicates that the roof rises 10 feet for every 12 feet of run.

Pith. The small, soft core at the original center of a tree around which wood formation takes place.

Plaster grounds. Strips of wood used as guides or strike-off edges around window and door openings and at base of walls.

Plastic. Term interchangeable with *wet* as in *plastic cement*.

Plate. A horizontal member used to anchor studs to the floor or ceiling. Examples: *Sill plate*: A horizontal member anchoring floor joints to a masonry wall. *Sole plate*: Bottom horizontal member of a frame wall. *Top plate*: Top horizontal member of a frame wall supporting ceiling joists, rafters or other members.

Plenum. Chamber immediately outside of the HVAC unit where conditioned air feeds into all of the supplies.

Plough. To cut a lengthwise groove in a board or plank.

Plugged exterior. A grade of plywood used for subfloor underlayment. The knotholes in the face plies are plugged and the surface is touch-sanded.

Plumb. The condition when something is exactly vertical to the ground, such as the wall of a house.

Plumb bob. A weight attached to a string used to indicate a plumb (vertical) condition.

Ply. A term to denote the number of thicknesses or layers of roofing felt, veneer in plywood, or layers in built-up materials, in any finished piece of such material.

Plywood. A piece of wood made of three or more layers of veneer joined with glue, and usually laid with the grain of adjoining plies at right angles.

oly (polyethylene). A heavy-gauge plastic sheet used for vapor barriers and material protection. The accepted construction thickness is 6 mil but plastic sheeting comes in many thicknesses.

Potable water. Water satisfactory for human consumption and domestic use, meeting the local health authority requirements.

Preservative. Any substance that, when the wood has been properly coated or impregnated with it, will for a reasonable length of time prevent the action of wood-destroying fungi, borers of various kinds and similar destructive agents.

Primer or prime coat. The first coat in a paint job that consists of two or more coats. The primer may have special properties that provide an improved base for the finish coat.

Purlin. A horizontal board that supports a roof rafter or stud to prevent bowing of the member by weight.

Putty. A type of cement usually made of whiting and boiled linseed oil, beaten or kneaded to the consistency of dough, and used in sealing glass in sash, filling small holes and crevices in wood and for similar purposes.

PVC (polyvinyl chloride). A form of plastic line used primarily for sewer and cold water supply.

Quarter round. A small strip of molding whose cross-section is similar to a quarter of a circle. Used with or without base molding. May be applied elsewhere.

Quoin. Fancy edging on outside corners made of brick veneer or stucco.

Rabbet. A rectangular longitudinal groove cut in the corner edge of a board or plank.

Racking resistance. A resistance to forces in the plane of a structure that tend to force it out of shape.

Radiant heating. A method of heating, usually consisting of (a) a forced hot water system with pipes placed in the floor, wall or ceiling or (b) electrically heated panels.

Rafter. One of a series of structural members of a roof designed to support the roof sheathing and shingles. The rafters of a flat roof are sometimes called roof joists.

Rafter, hip. A rafter that forms the intersection of an external roof angle.

Rafter, valley. A rafter that forms the intersection of an internal roof angle. The valley rafter is normally made of double 2-inch-thick members.

Rail. Cross members of panel doors or of a sash. Also the upper and lower members of a balustrade or staircase extending from one vertical support, such as a post, to another.

Rake. Trim members that run parallel to the roof slope and form the finish between the wall and the end of a roof that extends past the gable.

Rebar. Metal rods used to improve the strength of concrete structures.

Reflective insulation. Sheet material with one or both surfaces of comparatively low heat emissivity, such as aluminum foil. When used in building construction, the surfaces face air spaces, reducing the radiation across the air space.

Register. Metal facing plate on a wall, ceiling or floor where supply air is released into room or where air enters returns. Registers can be used to direct the flow of air.

Reinforcing. Steel rods or metal fabric placed in concrete slabs, beams or columns to increase their strength.

Relative humidity. The amount of water vapor in the atmosphere, expressed as a percentage of the maximum quantity that could be present at a given temperature.

Return. Ductwork leading back to the HVAC unit to be reconditioned.

Ribbon (girt). Normally a 1 × 4 board let into the studs horizontally to support ceiling or second-floor joists.

Ridge board. The board placed on edge at the ridge of the roof into which the upper ends of the rafters are fastened.

Ridge vent. Opening at the point where roof decking normally intersects along the highest point on a roof where air is allowed to flow from the attic. A small cap covers this opening to prevent rain from entering. When these are long, they are normally known as continuous ridge vents.

Ridge. Intersection of any two roofing planes where water drains away from the intersection. Special shingles are applied to ridges.

Ripping. Cutting lumber parallel to the grain.

Rise. In stairs, the vertical height of a step or flight of stairs.

Riser. Each of the vertical boards closing the spaces between the treads of stairways.

Roll roofing. Roofing material, composed of fiber and saturated with asphalt, that is supplied in 36-inch wide rolls with 108 square feet of material. Weights are generally 45 to 90 pounds per roll.

Roof sheathing. The boards or sheet material fastened to the roof rafters on which the shingle or other roof covering is laid.

Rough grade. First grading effort used to level terrain to approximate shape for drainage and landscaping.

Rout. The removal of material, by cutting, milling or gouging, to form a groove.

Row lock. Intersecting bricks that overlap on outside corners.

Run. In stairs, the net width of a step or the horizontal distance covered by a flight of stairs.

Saddle. Two sloping surfaces meeting in a horizontal ridge, used between the back side of a chimney, or other vertical surface, and a sloping roof.

Sagging. Slow dripping of excessively heavy coats of paint.

Sapwood. The outer zone of wood, next to the bark. In the living tree it contains some living cells (the heartwood contains none), as well as dead and dying cells. In most species it is lighter colored than the heartwood. In all species, it is lacking in decay resistance.

Sash. A single light frame containing one or more lights of glass.

Saturated felt. A felt that is impregnated with tar or asphalt.

Scratch coat. The first coat of plaster, which is scratched to form a bond for the second coat.

Screed. A small strip of wood, usually the thickness of the plaster coat, used as a guide for plastering.

Screeding. The process of running a straightedge over the top of forms to produce a smooth surface on wet (plastic) cement. The screeding proceeds in one direction, normally in a sawing motion.

Screen. Metallic or vinyl grid used to keep troughs free of leaves and other debris. Some screens are hinged.

Scribing. Fitting woodwork to an irregular surface. In moldings, cutting the end of one piece to fit the molded face of the other at an interior angle to replace a miter joint.

Sealer. A finishing material, either clear or pigmented, that is usually applied directly over uncoated wood for the purpose of sealing the surface.

Self-rimming. Term used to describe a type of sink that has a heavy rim around the edge that automatically seals the sink against the Formica top.

Semigloss. A paint or enamel that has a luster but does not look glossy.

Septic tank. A receptacle used for storage of water, retained solids and digesting organic matter through bacteria and discharging liquids into the soil (subsurface, disposal fields or seepage pits), as permitted by local health authorities.

Service panel. Junction where main electrical service to the home is split among the many circuits internal to the home. Circuit breakers should exist on each internal circuit.

Settling. Movement of unstable dirt over time. Fill dirt normally settles downward as it is compacted by its own weight or a structure above it.

Shake. A thick, hand-split shingle, resawed to form two shakes, usually edge-grained.

Sheathing paper. *See* Paper, sheathing.

Sheathing. The structural covering, usually wood boards or plywood, used over studs or rafters of a structure. Structural building board is normally used only as wall sheathing.

Sheet metal work. All components of a house employing sheet metal, such as flashing, gutters and downspouts.

Shellac. A transparent coating made by dissolving in alcohol lac, a resinous secretion of the lac bug (a scale insect that thrives in tropical countries, especially India).

Shingle butt. The lower, exposed side of a shingle.

Shingle. Uniform unit used in the coverage of a roofing deck. Shingles are manufactured from many materials including asphalt, fiberglass, wood shakes, tile and slate. Sizes normally vary from 12″ × 36″ to 12¼″ × 36¼″ with many sizes in between.

Shingles, siding. Various kinds of shingles, such as wood shingles or shakes and nonwood shingles, that are used over sheathing for exterior sidewall covering of a structure.

Shiplap. *See* Lumber, shiplap.

Shutter. Usually lightweight louvered or flush wood or nonwood frames in the form of doors located at each side of a window. Some are made to close over the window for protection; others are fastened to the wall as a decorative device.

Side lap. Length (inches) of the amount of overlap between two horizontally adjoining shingles.

Siding, bevel (lap siding). Wedge-shaped boards used as horizontal siding in a lapped pattern. This siding varies in butt thickness from ½- to ¾-inch and in widths up to 12 inches. It is normally used over some type of sheathing.

Siding, Dolly Varden. Beveled wood siding that is rabbeted on the bottom edge.

Siding, drop. Usually ¾-inch thick and 6 to 8 inches wide with tongue-and-grooved or shiplap edges. Often used as siding without sheathing in secondary buildings.

Siding. The finish covering of the outside wall of a frame building, whether made of horizontal weatherboards, vertical boards with battens, shingles or other material.

Silicone. A polymerized organic siloxane that is available as a resin, coating, sealant, with excellent waterproofing characteristics.

Sill caulk. Mastic placed between top of foundation wall and sill studs to make an airtight seal.

Sill. The lowest member of the frame of a structure, resting on the foundation and supporting the floor joists or the uprights of the wall. The member framing the lower side of an opening, as a door sill, window sill, etc.

Silt fence. A barrier constructed of burlap, plastic or bales of hay used to prevent the washing away of mud and silt from a cleared lot onto the street or adjacent lots.

Sleeper. Usually, a wood member embedded in concrete, as in a floor, that serves to support and to fasten subfloor or flooring.

Soffit. The underside of the cornice or any part of the roof that overhangs the siding.

Soil cover (ground cover). A light covering of plastic film, roll roofing or similar material used over the soil in crawl spaces of buildings to minimize moisture permeation of the area.

Soil stack. A vent opening out to the roof, which allows the plumbing system to equalize with external air pressure and allows the sewer system to "breathe." Prevents water in the sink traps from siphoning out of the trap, which would allow sewer gases to enter the house.

Sole or sole plate. *See* Plate.

Solid bridging. A solid member placed between adjacent floor joists near the center of the span to prevent joists from twisting.

Solids. Solid bricks used for fireplace hearths, stoops, patios or driveways.

Spackle. Soft putty-like compound used for drywall patching and touch-up that does not shrink as much as regular joint compound. Allows painting immediately after application.

Span. The distance between structural supports such as walls, columns, piers, beams, girders and trusses. The longest unsupported distance along a joist.

Splash block. A small masonry block laid with the top close to the ground surface to receive drainage from downspouts and carry it away from the building.

Spread set. Faucet set that requires three holes to be cut wider than normal.

Square. A unit of measure—100 square feet—usually applied to roofing material. Sidewall coverings are sometimes packed to cover 100 square feet and are sold on that basis.

Stack. Also known as vent stack or soil stack. A ventilation pipe coming out of the roofing deck.

Stain grade. Millwork of finest quality intended for a stain finish. Capable of receiving and absorbing stain easily.

Stain, shingle. A form of oil paint, very thin in consistency, intended for coloring wood with rough surfaces, such as shingles, without forming a coating of significant thickness or gloss.

Stair carriage. Supporting member for stair treads. Usually a 2-inch plank notched to receive the treads; sometimes called a *rough horse*.

Stair landing. *See* Landing.

Stair rise. *See* Rise.

Staking. To lay out the position of a home, the batter boards, excavation lines and depth(s).

Starter strip. A continuous strip of asphalt roofing used as the first course, applied to hang over the eave.

Stiffness. Resistance to deformation by loads that cause bending stresses.

Stile. An upright framing member in a panel door.

Stipple. Rough and textured coatings applied to ceilings. They do not have to be taped and sanded as many times as the walls.

Stool. A flat molding fitted over the window sill between jambs and contacting the bottom rail of the lower sash.

Stoop arms. Section of foundation wall extending out perpendicular to exterior wall used to support a masonry or stone stoop.

Stoop iron. Corrugated iron sheeting used as a base for the tip of a brick or stone stoop. This is to eliminate the need for completely filling the stoop area with fill dirt (which may settle) or concrete.

Stop valve. A shut-off valve allowing water to be cut off at a particular point in the system.

Storm sash or storm window. An extra window, usually placed on the outside of an existing one as additional protection against cold weather.

Story. That part of a building between any floor and the floor or roof next above.

Strike plate. A metal plate mortised into or fastened to the face of a door-frame side jamb to receive the latch or bolt when the door is closed.

String, stringer. A timber or other support for cross members in floors or ceilings. In stairs, the support on which the stair treads rest; also stringboard.

Strip flooring. Wood flooring consisting of narrow, matched strips.

Stucco. Most commonly refers to an outside plaster made with portland cement as its base.

Stud. One of a series of slender wood or metal vertical structural members placed as supporting elements in walls and partitions. Standard 2×4 lumber normally cut to 8- or 10-foot nominal lengths used for framing walls. (Plural: *studs* or *studding*).

Subfloor. Boards or plywood laid on joists over which a finish floor is to be laid.

Superstructure. The structural part of the deck above the posts or supports.

Supply. Ductwork leading from the HVAC unit to the registers.

Suspended ceiling. A ceiling system supported by hanging it from the overhead structural framing.

TAG. Tongue-and-grooved joining of edges.

Tape. Paper used to cover the joints between sheets of gypsum. Tape joints are then sealed with mud (spackle).

Termite shield. A shield, normally of galvanized sheet metal, placed between footing and foundation wall to prevent the passage of termites.

Thinwall. Thin flexible conduit used between outlet boxes.

Three-way switch. Switch allowing control of a lighting fixture from two locations, such as both ends of a hallway.

Threshold. A strip of wood or metal with beveled edges used over the finish floor and the sill or exterior doors.

Toe nailing. Nailing at an angle (normally 45 degrees) to bind two or more members. Normally used in nailing studs to plates.

Ton. An industry measure to express a quantity of cold air produced by an air-conditioning system.

Tongue-and-grooved. Boards that join on edge with a groove on one unit and a corresponding tongue on the other to interlock. Certain plywoods and hardwood flooring are tongue-and-grooved. *See also* Dressed and matched.

Topsoil. A 2- or 3-inch layer of rich, loose soil. This must be removed from areas to be cleared or excavated and replaced in other areas later. Not for load-bearing areas.

Touch sanding. Very light sanding of prime paint coat.

Transit. Similar to a builder's level except that the instrument can be adjusted vertically. Used for testing walls for plumb and laying out batter board, and establishing degree of a slope.

Trap. A device providing a liquid seal that prevents the backflow of air without materially affecting the flow of sewage or waste water. *S* shaped drain traps are required in most building codes.

Tray ceiling. Raised area in a ceiling. Looks like a small vaulted ceiling.

Tray molding. Special type of crown molding where a large portion of the molding is applied to the ceiling as opposed to the wall.

Tread. The horizontal board in a stairway on which the foot is placed.

Trig. A string support for guidelines to prevent sagging and wind disturbances on long expanses of wall.

Trim. The finish materials in a building, such as moldings, applied around openings (window trim, door trim) or at the floor and ceiling of rooms (baseboard, cornice and other moldings).

Trimmer. A beam or joist to which a header is nailed in framing for a chimney, stairway or other opening.

Troweling. A process used after floating to provide an even smoother surface.

Truss. A frame or jointed structure designed to act as a beam of long span, while each member is usually subjected to longitudinal stress only, either tension or compression.

Turpentine. A volatile oil used as a thinner in paints and as a solvent in varnishes. Chemically, it is a mixture of terpenes.

Undercoat. A coating applied prior to the finishing or top coats of a paint job.

Underlayment. A material placed under finish coverings, such as flooring or shingles, to provide a smooth, even surface for applying the finish.

Underlayment Exterior. *See* Plugged exterior.

Valley. Intersection of any two roofing planes where water drains at the intersection.

Vapor barrier. Material used to retard the movement of water vapor into walls and prevent condensation in them. It is installed on the warm side of exposed walls or as a part of batt or blanket insulation.

Varnish. A thickened preparation of drying oil or drying oil and resin suitable for spreading on surfaces to form continuous, transparent coatings.

Vehicle. The liquid portion of a finishing material; it consists of the binder (nonvolatile) and volatile thinners.

Veneer. Thin sheets of wood made by rotary cutting or slicing of a log.

Vent system. A pipe or network of pipes providing a flow of air to or from a drainage system to protect trap seals from siphoning or back pressure.

Vent. A pipe or duct that allows flow of air as an inlet or outlet.

Voltage. The force of electrical potential. Similar to the pressure of water in a pipe.

Wainscoting. Paneling and trim applied from the floor to a height of about 3 feet. Used in dining areas to protect against marks from dining chairs.

Water line. Decorative relief line around foundation approximately 3 feet from the ground.

Water-repellent preservative. Penetrates into wood and imparts water repellency and a moderate preservative protection. It is used for millwork, such as sash and frames, and is usually applied by dipping.

Wattage. The product of the amperage times the voltage. The higher the wattage, the more electricity used per hour.

Weatherstrip. Narrow or jamb-width sections of thin metal or other material to prevent infiltration of air and moisture around windows and doors.

Weep hole. Small gap in brick wall, normally on garage, that allows water to drain.

Wire mesh. A heavy-gauge steel mesh sold in rolls for providing reinforcing in concrete slabs.

Wood mold. A process that molds bricks, producing fancy shapes.

ASSOCIATIONS

American Architectural Manufacturers Association
1540 E. Dundee Road, Suite 310
Palatine, IL 60067
708-202-1350

American Concrete Institute (ACI)
P.O. Box 19150
Detroit, MI 48219
313-532-2600

American Institute of Architects
1735 New York Avenue NW
Washington, DC 20006
202-626-7300

American Insurance Association (AIA)
85 John Street
New York, NY 10020
212-669-0400

American Lighting Association
435 N. Michigan Avenue
Chicago, IL 60611
312-644-0828

American National Standards Institute (ANSI)
1430 Broadway
New York, NY 10018

American Plywood Association (APA)
7011 S. 19th Street West
Tacoma, WA 98466
206-565-6600

American Society of Interior Designers
608 Massachusetts Avenue NE
Washington, DC 20002
202-546-3480

Better Heating & Cooling Council
P.O. Box 218
Berkeley Heights, NJ 07922
908-464-8200

Gypsum Association (GA)
5700 Old Orchard Road, 1st Floor
Skokie, IL 60077
708-966-0008

National Association of Home Builders (NAHB)
1201 15th Street NW
Washington, DC 20005
202-822-0200

National Association of the Remodeling Industry
4301 N. Fairfax Drive
Suite 310
Arlington, VA 22203
703-276-7600

National Fire Protection Association (NFPA)
470 Atlantic Avenue NW
Washington, DC 20036
703-516-4346

American Forest and Paper Association
1111 19th Street NW, 7th Floor
Washington, DC 20036
202-463-2700

National Kitchen & Bath Association
687 Willow Grove Street
Hackettstown, NJ 07840
908-852-0033

Society of Plastics Industry, Inc. (SPI)
1275 K Street NW, Suite 400
Washington, DC 20005
202-371-5200

Southern Forest Products Association (SFPA)
P.O. Box 641700
Kenner, LA 70064-1700
504-443-4464

Southern Gas Association (SGA)
3030 LBJ Freeway, Suite 1300, LB 60
Dallas, TX 75234
214-620-8505

Tile Council of America (TCA)
P.O. Box 326
Princeton, NJ 08542
609-921-7050

Underwriters' Laboratories, Inc. (ULI)
333 Pfingsten Road
Northbrook, IL 60062
708-272-8800

SUPPLIERS/SUB-CONTRACTORS REFERENCE SHEET

NAME	PHONE	TYPE PRODUCT
ADDRESS	CALL WHEN	DATE
	PRODUCTS	
	WORKER'S COMP?	BONDED?

REFERENCE NAME	PHONE	COMMENTS

PRICES/COMMENTS

NAME	PHONE	TYPE PRODUCT
ADDRESS	CALL WHEN	DATE
	PRODUCTS	
	WORKER'S COMP?	BONDED?

REFERENCE NAME	PHONE	COMMENTS

PRICES/COMMENTS

MATERIAL ESTIMATE

DESCRIPTION	QTY.	UNIT	COST	TAX	TOTAL COST	COST TYPE	VENDOR
					TOTAL		

ITEM ESTIMATE WORKSHEET

VENDOR NAME	DESCRIPTION	MEASURING		CONVERSION FACTOR	ORDERING		PRICE EACH	COST	TAX	TOTAL COST	COST TYPE
		QTY.	UNIT		QTY.	UNIT					

EXPENSE CATEGORY	MATERIAL COST	LABOR COST	SUBCONTRACTOR COST	TOTAL COST

COST ESTIMATE SUMMARY

DESCRIPTION	MATERIAL	LABOR	SUB-CONTR.	TOTAL
EXCAVATION				
PEST CONTROL				
CONCRETE				
WATERPROOFING				
FRAMING				
ROOFING				
PLUMBING				
HVAC				
ELECTRIC				
MASONRY				
SIDING & CORNICE				
INSULATION				
DRYWALL				
TRIM				
PAINTING				
CABINETRY				
TILE				
CARPET				
OTHER FLOORING				
GLAZING				
GUTTERS				
LANDSCAPING				
SUB-TOTAL				
APPLIANCES				
LUMBER				
OTHER MATERIALS				
TOOLS/RENTAL				
LOAN/LEGAL				
INSURANCE				
PERMITS/LICENSE				
SUB-TOTAL				
			GRAND TOTAL	

COST ESTIMATE CHECKLIST

CODE NO.	DESCRIPTION	QTY.	MATERIAL		LABOR		SUB-CONTR.		TOTAL
			UNIT PRICE	TOTAL MATL.	UNIT PRICE	TOTAL LABOR	UNIT PRICE	TOTAL SUB	
SUB-TOTALS									
GRAND TOTALS									

SUB-CONTRACTOR BID CONTROL LOG

SUB/LABOR	NAME	BID	GOOD UNTIL	NAME	BID	GOOD UNTIL	NAME	BID	GOOD UNTIL	BEST BID	NAME
EXCAVATION											
CONCRETE											
PEST CONTROL											
FRAMING											
ROOFING											
PLUMBING											
HVAC											
ELECTRICAL											
MASONRY											
SIDING											
INSULATION											
DRYWALL											
TRIM											
PAINTING											
CABINETRY											
FLOORING											
TILE											
GLASS											
LANDSCAPING											
GUTTERS											
ASPHALT											

PURCHASE ORDER CONTROL LOG

PO NO.	DATE ORDERED	DESCRIPTION	VENDOR NAME	DATE DELIVERED	DISCOUNT		PAYMENTS				TOTAL PAID
					RATE	DUE	CHK#.	AMT.	CHK#.	AMT.	

PURCHASE ORDER

P/O NO.	**PAGE NO.**
DATE OF ORDER	JOB NO.
SALESMAN	REQ. NO.
DELIVER TO	

TO:

REQUESTED BY	DELIVER BY	SHIP VIA	TERMS

B/O	QTY. ORDERED	QTY. RECEIVED	DESCRIPTION	UNIT PRICE	TOTAL

PLEASE SEND A COPY OF THIS PO WITH DELIVERED MATE-
RIAL. CALL IF UNABLE TO MAKE DELIVERY DEADLINE.

PURCHASE ORDER cont.

P/O NO.	PAGE NO.

B/O	QTY. ORDERED	QTY. RECEIVED	DESCRIPTION	UNIT PRICE	TOTAL

PLEASE SEND A COPY OF THIS PO WITH DELIVERED MATE-
RIAL. CALL IF UNABLE TO MAKE DELIVERY DEADLINE.

CHANGE ORDER

TO (CONTRACTOR):

CHANGE ORDER NO.	
DATE OF CHANGE ORDER	JOB NO.
JOB PHONE	CONTRACT DATE
JOB LOCATION	

You are directed to make the following changes in this Contract:

Contract time will be ☐ increased ☐ decreased by:		Original Contract Price	
Days		Previously Authorized Change Orders	
New Completion Date		New Contract Price	
ACCEPTED — The above prices and specifications are satisfactory and are hereby accepted. All work to be done under same terms and conditions as original contract unless otherwise stipulated.		This Change Order	
		New Authorized Contract Price	
AUTHORIZED BY	SUB-CONTRACTOR		
SIGNATURE DATE	SIGNATURE DATE		

SUB-CONTRACTOR'S AGREEMENT

Sub. Name _____

Address _____

_____

_____

Phone _____

Have Worker's Comp? ☐Yes ☐No

Worker's Comp. No. _____

Expiration Date _____

Tax Id No. _____

Date _____

Job No. _____

Job Address _____

_____

_____

Plan No. _____

Bid Amount _____

Bid Good Until _____

Payment to be made as follows:

_____

_____

_____

_____

Deduct _____ % for worker's compensation.
Deduct _____ % for retainage.

All material is guaranteed to be as specified. All work to be completed in a timely manner, according to standard practices. Any alteration or deviation from specifications below involving extra costs will be executed only upon written order (refer to Change Order Form).

SPECIFICATIONS: (Attach extra sheets if necessary)

_____

_____

_____

_____

_____

_____

_____

_____

_____

Agreement

_____

Sub-contractor   (date)

PAYMENTS

DATE	CHECK NO.	AMOUNT PAID	AMOUNT DUE

SUB-CONTRACTOR'S AFFIDAVIT

STATE OF: _____

COUNTY OF: _____

Personally appeared before the undersigned attesting officer,

_____,
who being duly sworn, on oath says that he was the contractor in charge of improving the property
owned by _____,
located at _____.

Contractor says that all work, labor, services and materials used in such improvements were furnished
and performed at the contractor's instance; that said contractor has been paid or partially paid the full
contract price for such improvements; that all work done or material furnished in making the
improvements have been paid for at the agreed price, or reasonable value, and there are no unpaid
bills for labor and services performed or materials furnished; and that no person has any claim or lien
by reason of said improvements.

_____

(Seal)

Sworn to and subscribed before me,
this _____ day of _____, 19_____.

_____
Notary Public

INDEX